*Religion in the Américas*

RELIGIONS OF THE AMERICAS SERIES

Davíd Carrasco and Tracey E. Hucks, Series Editors

This series—which focuses attention on passages, rims, and borders—is dedicated to a study of the religions of the Americas since the commencement of the Atlantic world with the voyages of Columbus and the Great Encuentro that followed. The Americas, from this perspective, constitute multiple "contact zones"—that is, places where disparate cultures confront, clash, and exchange meanings, goods, and services. The series is devoted to understanding the dynamic histories, religious practices, and cultural patterns generated by these contact zones throughout North America, Mesoamerica, and South America.

Also available in the Religions of the Americas Series:

*With This Root about My Person: Charles H. Long and New Directions in the Study of Religion* edited by Jennifer Reid and Davíd Carrasco

*Shrines and Miraculous Images: Religious Life in Mexico Before the Reforma* by William B. Taylor

*Marvels and Miracles in Late Colonial Mexico: Three Texts in Context* by William B. Taylor

*Imagining Histories of Colonial Latin America: Synoptic Methods and Practices* edited by Karen Melvin and Sylvia Sellers-García

*Yoruba Traditions and African American Religious Nationalism* by Tracey Elaine Hucks

*Strange Jeremiahs: Civil Religion and the Literary Imaginations of Jonathan Edwards, Herman Melville, and W. E. B. Du Bois* by Carole Lynn Stewart

*Louis Riel and the Creation of Modern Canada: Mythic Discourse and the Postcolonial State* by Jennifer Reid

*Sacred Spaces and Religious Traditions in Oriente Cuba* by Jualynne E. Dodson

# Religion
## IN THE
# Américas

*Trans-hemispheric and Transcultural Approaches*

EDITED BY     Christopher D. Tirres

AND     Jessica L. Delgado

UNIVERSITY OF NEW MEXICO PRESS
ALBUQUERQUE

© 2025 by the University of New Mexico Press
All rights reserved. Published 2025
Printed in the United States of America

**Library of Congress Cataloging-in-Publication Data**

Names: Tirres, Christopher D., editor. | Delgado, Jessica L., 1972– editor.

Title: Religion in the Américas: trans-hemispheric and transcultural approaches / edited by Christopher D. Tirres and Jessica L. Delgado.

Other titles: Religions of the Americas series.

Description: Albuquerque: University of New Mexico, 2025. | Series: Religions of the Americas series | Includes bibliographical references and index.

Identifiers: LCCN 2024032517 (print) | LCCN 2024032518 (ebook) | ISBN 9780826367778 (cloth) | ISBN 9780826367785 (paperback) | ISBN 9780826367792 (epub) | ISBN 9780826367808 (pdf)

Subjects: LCSH: Anthropology of religion—Latin America—Cross-cultural studies. | Decolonization—Latin America. | Latin America—Religious life and customs.

Classification: LCC GN470.7 .R456 2025 (print) | LCC GN470.7 (ebook) | DDC 306.609—dc23/eng/20240716

LC record available at https://lccn.loc.gov/2024032517

LC ebook record available at https://lccn.loc.gov/2024032518

Founded in 1889, the University of New Mexico sits on the traditional homelands of the Pueblo of Sandia. The original peoples of New Mexico—Pueblo, Navajo, and Apache—since time immemorial have deep connections to the land and have made significant contributions to the broader community statewide. We honor the land itself and those who remain stewards of this land throughout the generations and also acknowledge our committed relationship to Indigenous peoples. We gratefully recognize our history.

Cover illustration: Close-up of a section from Martin Waldseemüller's 1507 world map, which was the first map to depict a separate Western hemisphere with the Pacific as a separate ocean. Geography and Map Division, Library of Congress.
Designed by Isaac Morris
Composed in Arno Pro, Athelas

This book is dedicated to:

Luis D. León (1965–2018), a pioneering Latine scholar of religion who was an impetus for many of the discussions that gave rise to this book and who, in his own creative and mischievous ways, embodied the wailing spirit of La Llorona,

and

Roger Rodriguez Delgado, Jr. (1946–2022), whose protective spirit guided us in this book's final stages.

# Contents

Acknowledgments     ix

Introduction. Religion in the Américas     1
*Christopher D. Tirres and Jessica L. Delgado*

### PART I. Fluidity in the Afro-Latine Diaspora

Chapter 1. Our Ladies of the 305     23
*Michelle Gonzalez Maldonado*

Chapter 2. Quimbanda and Ritual Polyphony in Minas Gerais, Brazil     39
*Cristina Borges, Alexandre F. S. Kaitel, Guaraci M. Dos Santos, and Steven Engler*

Chapter 3. Playful Masculinity: Labor, Relaxation, and Gender Formation in Loíza's Las Fiestas de Santiago Apóstol     65
*Alejandro S. Escalante*

### PART II. Aesthetics in Las Américas

Chapter 4. ¡*Mira, pa ya en el cielo!*: The Amazing Decolonial and Theological Adventures of *La Borinqueña*     83
*Joel Morales Cruz*

Chapter 5. Rockin' the Habit: Colliding Cultural Identities and a Peruvian Nuns' Rock Band     105
*Ann Hidalgo*

Chapter 6. The Afro Cuban Sense of Magic in Osha-Ifá: Its Representation in National Literature and the Visual Arts     124
*Axel Presas*

## PART III. Critical Feminist Epistemologies and Activism

Chapter 7. Sacred Motherhood in the Sanctuary Movement: Marian Imagery and the Family Fight for Immigrant Justice    143
*Lloyd D. Barba and Tatyana Castillo-Ramos*

Chapter 8. Subversive Indigenous Feminist Epistemologies: A Methodological Reflection on *El Mercado/Qhathu*    166
*Cecilia Titizano*

Chapter 9. Anzaldúa²: Beyond (in) Anzaldúa    187
*Laura E. Pérez*

## PART IV. Complicating Institutional Religion

Chapter 10. Liberation Theology and Its Limits in the Peruvian Andes    215
*Matthew Casey-Pariseault*

Chapter 11. The *Madres de Plaza de Mayo* in a Chapel of Mendoza: A Church that is Victimizer and Victim, Catholic and Subversive    234
*Ernesto Fiocchetto*

Chapter 12. From Gang Leaders to Church Leaders: Masculine Ideals among Peruvian Criminals Converting to Pentecostalism    253
*Véronique Lecaros*

## PART V. Spiritual Invasions and Contagions

Chapter 13. Immunity, Vaccines, and Other Holy Things    275
*Paul Ramírez*

Chapter 14. Contagious Women and Spiritual Status in Colonial Latin America: A Theoretical Proposal    300
*Jessica L. Delgado*

Chapter 15. Spectral Comrades and Comandantes: Latinx Hauntology and the Day of the Dead in Orange County, California    321
*Daisy Vargas and Jennifer Scheper Hughes*

Contributors    355

*Acknowledgments*

This book emerges out of many conversations that were initially fostered through the Religion in the Latina/o Americas Unit of the American Academy of Religion. As such, the editors of this volume would first like to extend thanks to all past and present steering committee members for their willingness to transgress traditional disciplinary boundaries in order to open up new pathways of scholarly inquiry. We are also grateful to those who helped us to capture a snapshot of these many conversations in the form of this book. Our deepest thanks to Davíd Carrasco (series editor) and Michael Millman (senior acquisitions editor) for their steadfast support, Sadman Rahman and Michelle Benavente for their reliable research assistance, and Allison Tirres and Benjamín Valentín for their constructive feedback and suggestions.

INTRODUCTION

# Religion in the Américas

CHRISTOPHER D. TIRRES AND JESSICA L. DELGADO

"Religion" in "America." At first glance, these two terms might strike many readers as self-evident. "Religion," as most dictionary entries would suggest, refers to a particular system of faith and worship in which adherents profess belief in certain religious tenets. "Religion" in this sense is something that one "belongs to" and "believes in." For its part, "America" sometimes refers to the continent of North or South America, though for many in the Americas (and especially for those who reside in the United States) "an American" refers more narrowly to a citizen of the US.

While these meanings are widely used and accepted, both tend to hide other significant meanings. This is especially true when one begins to grapple with the colonial histories of the terms themselves, neither of which was indigenous to this continent prior to European colonization in the fifteenth century. "America," after all, was named after Amerigo Vespucci, an Italian merchant and navigator, who insisted as early as 1501 that Brazil was not part of the eastern part of India (as many European explorers at the time erroneously assumed), but was instead part of a continent that was altogether new to Europeans. Vespucci's insight was validated in 1507 by a German cartographer, Martin Waldseemüller, who promoted the idea that the continent be named after Vespucci's first name. "Amerigo" was Latinized into "Americus," from which we now have "America." Thus, the name "America" can largely be credited to two Europeans—one from Italy and the other from Germany.

This story is both Eurocentric and limited, especially when we consider that America—a presumed "New World"—was, in fact, anything but new. As Charles C. Mann makes clear in his marvelous book, *1491: New Revelations of the Americas before Columbus*, the continent was teeming with 90 to 112 million inhabitants who spoke more than a thousand languages and were engaged in agricultural practices and other technologies far more advanced than anything in Europe at the time. Nevertheless, the history and continued vibrancy of these ancient and flourishing civilizations were conspicuously erased as early European explorers and colonists won the continent's naming rights.

In a similar way, whereas in the sixteenth century "an American" would have referred to anyone residing in North or South America, the phrase began to take on a much narrower meaning over the centuries, especially in the United States. Although the United States began as a fledgling set of British colonies, over the course of its relatively short 250-year history, it quickly emerged as a colonial power in its own right. Guided by Manifest Destiny, which was as much a colonial mindset as it was a theological one, the United States expanded westward, forcibly removing Indigenous peoples from their native lands. The United States continued its program of expansionism through the Mexican-American War (1846–1848), which seized roughly half of Mexico's land, and the Spanish-American War (1898), which seized territories in Latin America (Cuba and Puerto Rico) and the Western Pacific (Guam and the Philippines). It is not surprising that as the United States flexed its colonial muscles over the nineteenth and twentieth centuries, the very meaning of what it means to be "an American" would increasingly center around the United States. Thus, the terms "America" and "American" are hardly neutral; rather, they enshrine histories of imperialism and reflect the power and sway of colonial relations to determine political boundaries and language.

A similar historical freight surrounds our modern concept of "religion." As is widely accepted among scholars of religion, the term "religion" is itself a colonial invention. In many cases, the term was used by colonizers to signal a difference between "civilized" people, i.e., those who had "a religion," and "primitive people," i.e., those who did not. Such distinctions helped to legitimize policies that benefited the colonizers. For their part, native peoples in the Western hemisphere did not understand themselves as belonging to or practicing "a religion." Rather, a sense of what we might call religiosity or spirituality imbued everything that they did. European Christianity's distinction between God and nature made little sense to them. Instead, Native peoples in the Americas understood the natural world as being inherently infused with the sacred. Similarly, rather than approach the universe in terms of opposing (and value-laden) forces of good versus evil, Indigenous cosmologies pointed to a universe in which natural forces hung in a delicate balance and were always complementary: order *and* chaos, day *and* night, man *and* woman, sun *and* moon. Furthermore, *both* sides of these pairings were understood to be alive with sacred power. As a consequence, whereas colonizers saw a sharp distinction between God and human beings, Indigenous peoples believed that human beings played a crucial role in helping to maintain the cosmic balance in the ever-present struggle between the various opposing forces. In short, what today we refer to as "the sacred" was, for Native peoples, a fundamental part of the natural world, and their own relationship to the sacred was one of interdependency and reciprocity.

European colonizers also brought with them an idea of conversion that demanded belief in "the one true God" and the disavowal of all other ways of naming and understanding the sacred. Indigenous people on the continent were not strangers to empire; many Native American empires had risen and fallen across the continent, even long before the rise of the Triple Alliance (often referred to as the Aztec Empire) and the Inca. Theirs were merely the most recent large empires to hold power at the time of Iberian expansion. But unlike colonial Christianity, Indigenous conquerors did not require their new subjects to abandon their own rituals and ways of naming and understanding the sacred. Local and regional sacred places, deities, and "religious" practices coexisted alongside compulsory participation in imperial rites and rituals. In other words, the idea of true and false religions—or of "conversion" for that matter—was completely foreign to Native peoples. The idea of adherence to a particular religion—along with the notion of "religion" as something distinct from humanity and nature—did not square with the complex and highly interwoven ritual practices and Native understandings of humanity, nature, and the cosmos.

Today, scholars of religion (who represent a wide variety of academic fields, including religious studies, theology, anthropology, sociology, and history, among many other fields) acknowledge the problematic colonial roots of our shared scholarly endeavor. There is no way of getting around the fact that in the context of the Americas, "religion" was a tool of colonialism. European colonists divided the world into civilized Christians who "had" religion, and those who did not, and they used this division to justify waging war against those who were deemed to be "without" religion. As such, scholars of religion have had to grapple seriously with the meaning of core terms and ideas like "religion," "faith," "religiosity," "spirituality," and "the sacred."

At the same time, while it is clear that the idea of "religion" has been used to justify colonial incursions, it is equally clear that people throughout the Americas had complex rituals, symbols, myths, and cosmologies that more general anthropological terms like "culture" or "social organization" cannot easily capture. Like people everywhere, Native people used these meaning-intensive practices, ideas, and stories as ways of answering existentially significant human questions like the following: How did humans and the observable world come to be? What happens after death? What is the relationship between humans, the natural world, and unseen forces? What are humans' ethical responsibilities to each other and to the nonhuman world? And how should responsibilities guide human action in the here and now? When we focus especially on the *function* and *effects* of Native practices and cosmologies, we can begin to imagine anew what we might refer to today as their "religious" or "spiritual" significance. But this is only possible so long as we approach "religion" in a critical and self-reflexive way.

What we might imperfectly call the "religious history of the Americas" became even more interesting—and complicated—as European, Native, and African worldviews came into contact and began to inform one another in the context of colonial rule. In spite of the unequal and hierarchical relations of power, including the forced slavery of over ten million African men, women, and children, mutual learning took place, and a process of cultural and religious hybridity unfolded. While colonial authorities and missionaries certainly attempted to subsume and assimilate Native and African cosmologies into a European Christian worldview (if not eradicate them altogether), in practice, more often than not, dynamic cultural transformations went both ways. Cuban anthropologist Fernando Ortiz describes this process as "transculturation," a concept that has been important for subsequent scholars. As Robert Carlsen describes it, "Transculturation recognizes that although subjugated peoples cannot readily control what emanates from the dominant culture, they do determine to varying extents what they absorb into their own and what they use it for."[1] Furthermore, we know that the religion of the colonizers was also forever transformed through cultural contact. As a result, altogether new forms of religious expressions emerged in the Americas that reflect a diversity of European, Indigenous, and African practices, histories, and ideas.

As such, the study of religion in the Americas can largely be understood as a study of religious transculturation. It is a study of how different orientations toward the cosmos, and their related practices, have interacted with one another in the context of asymmetrical relations of power. It is also a study of how new religious sensibilities, rituals, and structures have functioned—and continue to function—in very concrete and particular cases. In some instances, hybrid religious sensibilities may reinforce and legitimize existing social hierarchies. In other cases, however, they may break open new ways of relating to one's self, one's community, the world, and the cosmos. In this sense, this volume approaches "religion in the Américas" as a dynamic, contested, and ever-shifting field of study that demands attention not only to those things that we normally associate with religion and spirituality (such as myths, symbols, and rituals) but also to other intersecting domains of culture (such as politics, economics, aesthetics, gender, language, technology, kinship ties, and, of course, general worldviews connected to time, space, and the cosmos).

# Rethinking "Religion in America"

This volume moves beyond the narrow renderings of "religion" and "America" that are commonplace today. Instead, we seek more capacious and generative interpretations that reflect their complexity, diversity, and dynamism. While our modern understanding of "America" has clear colonial roots, there are countless ways to read the term against the colonial grain. The essays in this volume thus present the Americas in a more decolonial and autochthonous light. Toward this end, we approach "America" not as a reference to the United States, in particular, but rather, in terms of *the Americas*, which is to say, as both North and South America. As many of the contributions here attest, there has been and continues to be a significant and steady flow of ideas, practices, and people across the Americas. The continued migration of human bodies in the Americas reminds us how arbitrary political and geographical boundaries can be. As human bodies travel, so do their ideas, customs, and worldviews.

Notably, a somewhat similar dynamic takes place at the level of scholarship. Many scholars in this volume have spent time, both in their home countries and abroad, learning and writing about countries and cultures that may not be directly their own. As this volume shows, scholars working in the United States and Canada have learned much from the histories, languages, and scholarship of Latin Americans, just as Latin American scholars have benefitted from their engagement with scholarship from their northern neighbors. As the reader will see, the footnotes in this volume, which often toggle back and forth between sources in Spanish and Portuguese, on the one hand, and English, on the other, are a testament to this ongoing exchange of ideas and interpretations.

This volume seeks to privilege the histories and experiences of communities that have their origins in what we now understand as "Latin America." Some of the essays in this volume deal directly with people and communities in this part of the world, whereas others focus on diasporic communities whose historical roots may be traced back to the region. For this reason, we have chosen to use the term "América" in the book's title—the accent indicating a shared experience of Iberian colonialism, irrespective of particular (and artificially constructed) political boundaries and borders. This choice is also meant to reflect the diversity of experiences within the Latin American diasporic community at large.[2] The prefix "trans-" in the subtitle ("Trans-hemispheric and Transcultural Approaches") points to a state of being "both/and" as well as to the active, liminal journeys that individuals and communities take, thereby positioning themselves betwixt and between. In various ways, the meaning of these terms reflect the histories, traditions, and cultural practices represented in this volume.

There are other terms presently being used that reflect this diasporic existence—such as Latinx, Latina/o, and Latine—and there are strong cases to be made about the use of each. We have left it to our authors to decide which of these terms (or combinations thereof) work best for them. No doubt, all of these terms reflect particular moments, orientations, and political/intellectual approaches to the linguistic challenges of representing shared historical and cultural experiences. Such diversity is emblematic of *América* itself.

As for the term "religion," we approach the concept less in terms of a particular system of belief (as important as this dimension is) and more in terms of a particular posture, sensibility, or orientation that individuals and communities assume in making sense of the world around them. As such, instead of focusing on the formal and official aspects of institutional "religions," the essays in this volume tend to focus more on what we can loosely call the religious dimension of human experience at large. Along these lines, historian of religion Charles H. Long, who was particularly interested in the religious dimensions of enslaved peoples from Africa, speaks of religion in terms of a basic human "orientation" toward ultimate reality. For Long, orientation refers broadly to "the meaning that human communities give to the particular stances they have assumed in their several worlds." Furthermore, it refers to the "actual situation" of particular stances and to "the reflections and imaginations attendant to it."[3]

We find Long's discussion of religious orientation helpful for at least three reasons. First, Long does not restrict the religious dimension of human experience solely to the realm of institutional "religions." Instead, he foregrounds how humankind's proclivity toward a sense of ultimate reality is "a basic element in the constitution of human consciousness and human community."[4] Second, he underscores the importance of one's "actual situation"—which is to say, one's specific *context*—for any discussion of religious orientation. To fully appreciate the religious quality of human experience, we must attend to how human beings orient themselves in light of the unique constraints and possibilities of their *particular* environments. And, lastly, Long reminds us that there are always *multiple* "reflections and imaginations" that inform one's orientation toward ultimate reality. In this way, "religious experience" is never a wholly unique, or *sui generis*, human phenomenon. Instead, it is always informed by other dimensions that speak to basic human needs and desires, such as those connected to our material, psychological, and sexual well-being. When we turn our attention to the Américas, we also see that we must attend to the persistent inequalities of power that lie in colonialism's wake, including racism, sexism, and classism. As such, the study of the religious quality of human experience in the Américas is not only a highly transcultural affair, but also a consummately intersectional one.

If the study of religion in the Americas entails close attention to questions of orientation and place, as Long suggests, so, too, does it demand a sensitivity to questions of mobility and fluidity. In his influential *Crossing and Dwelling: A Theory of Religion* (2006), Thomas Tweed articulates a theory of religion that is attentive both to "world-centering" and "world-traveling." Tweed's principle point of departure is his own ethnographic fieldwork on the adoration of Our Lady of Charity/*La Caridad del Cobre* among Cuban Americans in Miami, which is itself an exemplary transnational ritual practice. As Tweed defines them, religions can be understood as "confluences of organic-cultural flows that intensify joy and confront suffering by drawing on human and suprahuman forces to make homes and cross boundaries."[5] As Tweed suggests here, religion is something that both centers people in a meaningful space (or "home") and aids them in traveling across myriad boundaries (including geographical, emotional, symbolic, and ritualistic ones). In this sense, religion is as much about *dwelling* in a particular space as it is about *crossing*—and perhaps even *transgressing*—accepted social boundaries.

*Religion in the Américas* picks up on several of these themes. As volume editors, we, too, appreciate the religious dimension of human experience as a powerful cultural construction that confronts suffering and ushers forth joy through human and suprahuman means. To be sure, these are fairly familiar assumptions within the academic study of religion. What is perhaps less common, however, is the attention that Tweed gives to spatial and aquatic metaphors in understanding religion as a "confluence of organic-cultural flows." To underscore how religions are not reified substances but rather complex and ever-shifting processes, Tweed draws, among others, on the work of anthropologist Arjun Appadurai (who speaks of "global cultural flows"), historian Paul Carter (who proposes a "migrant perspective"), and anthropologist James Clifford (who uses "travel" and "routes" as orienting metaphors for understanding theory and culture).[6] Such scholars help us to see religion not so much as a discreet "entity" but rather as an ongoing dynamic *flow* between individuals and their communities, between nature and culture, between mind and body. These kinds of spatial and aquatic metaphors are especially useful for a trans-hemispheric and transcultural study of religion such as ours, given the steady and ongoing stream of religious practices and ideas across the Americas.

## Organization of the Volume

*Religion in the Américas* features fifteen chapters divided into five thematic sections consisting of three chapters each.[7] These sections cross and challenge traditional scholarly divisions of geography, periodization, and discipline. They strive to create space for conversations, as well as productive tensions, for future trans-hemispheric and transcultural approaches to the study of religion.

The first section, "Fluidity in the Afro-Latine Diaspora," features contributions that explore the hybrid nature of Afro-Latine religiosity. In Chapter 1, Michelle Gonzalez Maldonado surveys the transcultural significance of Marian figures from Cuba and Haiti for the Latinx population of South Florida. Her interdisciplinary study—which draws from theology, ethnographic research, and history—demonstrates the ways in which institutional Catholicism, everyday Catholicism, and Black Atlantic religions have intertwined in South Florida, a fascinating region of the country that remains considerably understudied among scholars of religion. Focusing on two Caribbean immigrant Maries, Cuba's Our Lady of Charity and Haiti's Our Lady of Perpetual Hope, Gonzalez Maldonado shows how immigrant communities have reimagined Mary in myriad ways, demonstrating the hybrid and ever-changing nature of religious symbols.

Chapter 2 focuses on the trans-religious aspects of Quimbanda ("black magic" or "left-handed") ritual practices in Minas Gerais, a state in southeastern Brazil. The essay is itself an exercise in trans-hemispheric collaborative research between Steven Engler (Canada) and a group of Brazilian scholars—Cristina Borges, Alexandre F. S. Kaitel, Guaraci M. Dos Santos— who are also Umbandist practitioners. The chapter inquires how we should understand a multilayered community practice like Quimbanda, which involves interaction between multiple and distinct religious traditions whose boundaries are kept noticeably intact. Rather than appeal to notions of "syncretism," "hybridity," or "juxtaposition," these authors argue that "ritual polyphony" is a better interpretive category for understanding how "different religions are practiced at different times, in the same physical space, with the same leaders, and attended by mainly the same group of members."

In Chapter 3, Alejandro Escalante offers a nuanced look at the gendered paradoxes that arise in a popular festival in Puerto Rico, the Fiesta de Santiago. In this fiesta, men perform their masculinity in ways that are different from their usual laborious and physically intense work. As Escalante explains, men also display masculinity not only through raucous displays of femininity, which includes cross-dressing, but also through a noticeable "suspension" of labor outside of their public performances. This includes nothing more than sitting, drinking, and eating, while women do the work of fundraising and cooking. But as Escalante shows, women also help to create an environment for this masculine forgetfulness: they, too, create social space for men to play and rest. Thus, while ritual performances in this festival creatively queer gendered divisions of labor, these same performances, at times, simultaneously sustain them.

The second section, "Aesthetics in Las Américas," explores the ethico-political significance of religiously inflected art forms. These chapters underscore the socially transformative potential of lived religion as it is manifested in everyday forms of art. In Chapter 4, Joel Morales Cruz looks at the religious and liberating dimensions of *La Borinqueña*, an independently published comic book that features a Puerto Rican female superhero by the same name. In particular, Cruz explores *La Borinqueña's* cultural motifs, its decolonial dimensions, and its capacity to serve as a diasporic theology that helps to address the island's historic and present challenges. As Cruz demonstrates, La Borinqueña "represents an authentic voice of the Puerto Rican diaspora who serves as a source of decolonial religious reflection."

Chapter 5 offers an analysis of a Peruvian nuns' rock 'n' roll band, the Siervas. Author Ann Hidalgo demonstrates how the Siervas "attract attention by defying audience members' expectations of who nuns are and can be." After situating the group within the male-dominated world of rock music, Hidalgo draws on the work of sociologist Danielle Giffort to explore how the Siervas may engage in a kind of "implicit feminism" that "conceal[s] feminist identities and ideas while emphasizing the more socially acceptable angles of their efforts." The chapter ends with a discussion of how the Siervas' music offers a distinctly different theological position than much of the evangelically driven contemporary Christian music scene. Rather than emphasize the fallenness of the world and claims to Christian uniqueness, for example, the Siervas offer a "positive valuation of people's typical daily activities," and they "promote solidarity with good people found in all walks of life."

In Chapter 6, Axel Presas explores how Osha-Ifá, or Santería, is reflected in Cuban visual art and literature. Drawing inspiration from the philosophical work of Wole Soyinka and Kwasi Wiredu, as well as Susan Greenwood's understanding of magic as a universal mode of human perception, Presas frames Osha-Ifá as a form of Afro-Cuban magic that transmits African philosophical wisdom through legends and mythologies. As Presas notes, African histories and stories have been largely passed down by means of the spoken word, but Cuban literature also plays an important role in transmitting traditional philosophical wisdom. This chapter offers insight into the significance of Afro-Cuban magic in the literary work of Alejo Carpientier and Lydia Cabrera and the poetry of Nicolas Guillén.

Picking up on Hidalgo's initial discussion of feminism in Chapter Five, the three chapters in "Critical Feminist Epistemologies and Activism" dive further into the significant contributions of activists and scholars who help to draw connections between spiritual imaginaries and North and South American expressions of feminism. In Chapter 7, co-authors Lloyd Barba and Tatyana Castillo tell the story of immigrant leaders within the Sanctuary Movement whose activism is guided by religious motifs. Whereas much existing scholarship on the Sanctuary Movement has looked at sanctuary leadership in terms of (documented) citizens who offer sanctuary *to* undocumented immigrants, Barba and Castillo take a more internal and organic look at the political activism of sanctuary seekers themselves. The authors show how these immigrant female leaders often appeal to motherhood and family unity through their use of Marian imagery, particularly Nuestra Señora de Guadalupe. The authors note that such appeals "buttress the Sanctuary Movement's claims of sacrality and reinforce its image as a family rights movement." As they further observe, "Guadalupan images accomplish this in ways that few others can."

Chapter 8 brings to light the significant contributions of a number of Indigenous scholar-activists from the Andes and other parts of Latin America who are actively pursuing decolonial articulations of indigenous feminist epistemologies. Author Cecilia Titizano, who is herself closely associated with an Andean network of Indigenous female scholar-activists, points out that much of this scholarship, which is in Spanish, has yet to be translated into English. Titizano offers valuable insight into this scholarly terrain. She does so by first establishing the Andean *Mercado/quathu* as a privileged space inhabited by Indigenous women that does not presuppose a common Eurocentric ideal of rationality. Instead, the *Mercado/quathu* is an intercultural and interspiritual space that reflects a cosmic interrelationship between thinking, feeling, acting, and being. With this interpretive frame in place, Titizano then offers a provisional overview of the scholarly work that is being done by indigenous scholar-activists, all of which point to non-dualistic cosmologies and serve as an important corrective to more reductionistic and androcentric approaches to Christianity.

In Chapter 9, author Laura E. Pérez challenges facile "cut-and-paste" interpretations of the work of Chicana feminist theorist Gloria Anzaldúa by venturing into what many interpreters often overlook: the psychic and spiritual dimensions of her thought. These dimensions enable Anzaldúa to rethink reality, being, and identity in radically novel ways. As Pérez notes, the "beyond" in Anzaldúa is "probably most literally her reports of the psychic, as in psychic readings, extraterrestrial trysts, the channeling of disembodied entities, and the Jungian collective unconscious beyond rational awareness. . . ." Pérez gives special attention to the Jungian influence in Anzaldúa's thought—owing most likely to Anzaldúa's reading of James Hillman—and she shows how the Jungian concept of the human actually points to the "non-human, to the beyond-human, through the individual psyche." In such a case, the human is conceived as a portal to that which actually lies "beyond" the human, as well as other forms of being.

The three chapters in "Complicating Institutional Religion" offer a critical interrogation of institutional religion in the Americas. In Chapter 10, Matthew Casey-Pariseault examines how the rural Southern Andes of Peru served as pivotal site of liberation theology between 1968 and 1975. Casey-Pariseault draws on a range of pamphlets, newsletters, and internal documents from the Catholic Church to show how during these years "Catholic activists built a complex politico-religious project that . . . threatened to upend the reigning social order in Peru's southern Andes." That said, institutional changes at the Vatican and within the Peruvian civil society (including the rise of Sendero Luminoso) forced Andean liberation theology to the margins. Internal challenges within the movement, such as the difficulty that some missionaries had in fully embracing an Andean worldview, also thwarted its progress. Casey-Pariseault offers a nuanced, on-the-ground look at both the successes and setbacks of grassroots Andean liberation theology in the 1970s.

Chapter 11 addresses Argentina's military dictatorship and its ensuing Dirty War (1976–1983), which led to criminal acts of state violence and the "disappearance" of thousands of individuals, many of whom were young men and women. As is widely known, a group of mothers of the disappeared, known as the *Madres de Plaza de Mayo*, came together to stand witness to these assassinations. As is also well documented, certain layers of the Catholic Church in Argentina implicitly sanctioned state violence through their inaction and/or silence. This said, popular and scholarly memory-making about both of these realities often rest on a set of opposing binaries, such as Catholic versus subversives, victimizers versus victims, hierarchy versus people, and ruling men versus vulnerable women. Author Ernesto Fiocchetto problematizes such dichotomies by focusing on an in-depth interview with a leading activist of the group. Drawing on the work of Danièle Hervieu-Léger, Fiocchetto shows that church leadership and Catholic women alike evinced a range of oftentimes competing positions within which opposing "chains of memory" vied for interpretative legitimacy and hegemony.

Chapter 12 examines the tangled dynamics of religious conversion in Peruvian jails. As author Véronique Lecaros points out, many incarcerated gang members are attracted to Pentecostalism, which, with its strict obedience to rules, promotes a radical change of life. Formerly incarcerated people who become Pentecostal church leaders often "capitalize on their past to present spectacular testimonies of conversion." And yet, existing scholarship on this population has yet to explain why many people convicted of crimes eventually leave churches and return to gangs after leaving prison. Drawing on firsthand research, Lecaros points out that gangs and Pentecostal churches in Peru often share a similar ethos, one that privileges hierarchy and authority (both human and divine) and one that frequently appeals to machismo. While Peruvian Pentecostalism affords formerly incarcerated people a new start in life, it is easy for many to slide back into gang life, given that a shared logic informs both.

Finally, the three chapters in "Spiritual Invasions and Contagions" explore the political and intersectional aspects of spirituality in situations of injury and harm. Chapter 13 looks at what is considered to be the first global public health campaign, the Spanish Smallpox Vaccine Expedition of 1803–1813. Author Paul Ramírez focuses on the ways that the Spanish government used religious ceremonies and norms to carry out this task. As he explains, whereas early advocates proposed having priests administer the vaccine using Catholic ceremonial life as a central conduit for Spain's vaccine expedition, the official plan "expunged all references to liturgical practice and vaccinating priests." Nevertheless, many ceremonial considerations were eventually restored. As Ramírez, shows, "The vaccination expedition drew on many rituals and routines that were a familiar component of local life," religious life included.

Chapter 14, by Jessica L. Delgado, analyzes how women's status in colonial Latin America was determined not only by intersectional factors such as race, class, sexuality, and gender, but also by their "spiritual status," wherein women's sin, and under certain circumstances, virtue, was understood to be "contagious." As Delgado argues, spiritual status is not simply an additional "add-on" to intersectional dimensions, but, rather, a central vehicle by which race, class, sexuality, and gender were co-constituted in the Spanish American colonies. Very often, spiritual status was coded for whiteness and wealth, but Delgado gives special attention to how poor and non-white women found ways of redefining virtue and piety using concepts of contagion to claim higher levels of spiritual status.

The final chapter, co-authored by Daisy Vargas and Jennifer Scheper Hughes, looks at the ways in which the annual celebration of *Noche de Altares*, or Day of the Dead, in Santa Ana, California, serves as a religio-political battle for geographical and spiritual territory wherein ghosts and spirits are deployed as "spectral comrades" whose haunting makes spatial claims to the city center. The chapter draws on the authors' own ethnographic work in Santa Ana, a supermajority Mexican city that hosts one of the largest community-sponsored Day of the Dead celebrations in Southern California, with almost two hundred individual altars and upwards of 40,000 visitors. Vargas and Scheper Hughes tease out a critical Marxist and Zapatista ethos that informs activist founders and organizers of the event. The authors also draw on the work of Jacques Derrida, who himself had significant links to Southern California, to underscore how ghosts and spirits function in Santa Ana to resist gentrification, displacement, commercialization, secularization, racialized policing, and border enforcement.

## Origins of the Volume

*Religion in the Américas* has been assembled with three objectives in mind: 1) to forge a much-needed space for Latin Americanists and scholars of US Latinx religion to think and work together; 2) to provide a model for other scholars to engage this kind of interdisciplinary and trans-hemispheric work, and 3) to offer multiple entry points for theorizing the fluid and ever-shifting nature of religion in the Americas. But these goals did not emerge solely from our commitments as editors. Anthologies such as this one often grow out of the exchanges and practices of specific intellectual communities, and yet, these origins are often not made transparent. The context that gave birth to this interdisciplinary volume is an important part of its contribution. For this reason, it might be helpful for readers to know its origin story.

The five themes outlined above were not arbitrarily chosen. Rather, these are themes that emerged over several years in the context of a concrete, embodied community of thought and practice. Religious studies scholars—particularly those working in the context of the United States—will be familiar with the professional academic organization called the American Academy of Religion (AAR), but this may not be the case for readers outside of this guild. Among other things, the AAR hosts an annual conference that boasts roughly 10,000 participants each year and approximately 1,000 panel presentations and other events. Unlike many other academic organizations that rely on a single program committee that reviews all conference proposals, the AAR is instead organized into over 150 individual program units, each of which is overseen by two co-chairs and a steering committee. These program units develop their own call for papers, and they receive, rank, and accept or reject submissions. From those proposals that are accepted, the program units both develop panels out of individual paper submissions and make space for pre-organized panel submissions.

These program units represent all sorts of overlapping divisions and categories. Some are organized around particular themes or topics, others around disciplines, others around geographical locations, and yet others around specific time periods. For the fields represented in this volume, these divisions had both intellectual and practical consequences. Prior to 2017, there existed within the AAR a unit called "Latino/a Critical and Comparative Studies Group" (which Tirres co-chaired) and another unit known as "Religion in Latin America and the Caribbean" (which Delgado co-chaired), and our two units occasionally shared ideas and co-sponsored panels.[8] Nonetheless, in 2017, our two units decided to join forces. In the meetings that followed, new paths were envisioned, but more importantly, shared legacies and commitments were revealed. Thinking together about diaspora—which can carry many names, including Latinx, Latina/o, Latine, and Latin American—made us see the ways that colonial boundaries had imposed separations between our intellectual communities that—much like the arbitrary political boundaries of "borders"—had far more to do with external forces than real differences. We asked ourselves: What would happen if we prioritized our shared histories and experiences while also honoring the differences in these lived realities as shaped by structural forces and constraints? Out of these conversations, a new unit emerged: the "Religion in the Latina/o Americas" unit, which combined our two previous units. With a trans-hemispheric and transdisciplinary framework in mind, our new scholarly community embarked on a fresh era of intellectual dialogue and imagination.

The immediate result was an onslaught of submissions. Our unit grew exponentially, and the richness of submissions representing all fields, time periods, and geographical locations was quite striking. The first decision we made was *not* to follow conventional colonial, national, or disciplinary divisions, but rather to organize our panels based on thematic connections that emerged out of the submissions themselves. Thus, every panel had papers from both north and south of "the border," from a variety of historical periods, and from a variety of disciplines. The conversations that emerged were incredibly rich and inspired further collaboration and creative transgressions of time, place, and scholarly disciplines. This anthology captures the spirit of creativity and growth that characterized this dialogue, and the organizing themes reflect the intellectual priorities and curiosities that organically emerged once the conversation was allowed to take place in ways that did not adhere or conform to colonial, national, and disciplinary divisions.

## A Turn to Experience

If geography, political boundaries, periodization, and disciplinary differences are *not* the organizing factor for this volume, what makes *Religion in the Américas* distinct? Or put another way: What, if anything, *unites* the histories, stories, and areas of inquiry found in the work of scholars in this volume?

As we gathered and organized essays that represented the vibrant new directions we were witnessing in our panels, "experience" began to emerge as a central conceptual anchor. However, more than simply a broad or general term referring to a generic trait of existence, the concept of experience we saw emerging within our group attested to the complex and multilayered ways people have made sense of their realities within the unique particularities of their historical and social contexts. And though these contexts varied widely, they were nevertheless linked by shared legacies of the forces of colonialism, imperialist aggression, migration and immigration under politically fraught and unequal political relations, as well as the shared inheritances of languages, cultures, and spiritual traditions those histories have left in their wake.

Within this context, experience is not a politically neutral term, nor one that implies a lack of agency in the face of power. Rather, experience here names not only what happens *to* people, that is, how they might be "passively" impacted by their realities, but also how human beings continue *actively* to understand, interpret, and shape their realities. It is often easier to account for the forces acting upon people than to see the ways people engage with and make sense of these forces. Scholars like Inga Clendinnen have offered inspiration for reading power-laden sources in ways that critically imagine the possibilities of human experience buried within them.[9] Many of the authors in this volume are engaged in similarly innovative practices from within their own disciplinary perspectives, holding in tension both senses of "experience."

It is also worth noting that, from a scholarly perspective, the study of experience as actively "making sense of reality" cuts in at least two directions. On the one hand, those who study religious cultures and practices must continually strive to understand how the peoples and cultures who they study have *themselves* made sense of their reality. What words, symbols, myths, rituals, and worldviews did they employ to make sense of their reality? Or, in an even more general sense, how did their daily "practices" inform their "theories" of the world and the cosmos, and vice versa? Such questions point to what anthropologists refer to as an "emic" approach of study: it is the attempt to see—and perhaps even "sense"—experience from an *insider* perspective. On the other hand, those of us who study religious and cultural practices also bring to the table our *own* concepts and theories—both scholarly and personal—that help us make further sense of what we are studying. This is what scholars often refer to as an "etic" approach. The essays in this volume engage in both emic and etic approaches in ways that invite critical reflections of both.

An emic approach, or the quest to make visible the ways the people we study make sense of their own realities, is always an imperfect endeavor. This is particularly true when faced with sources, contexts, and dynamics that are shaped by colonial legacies. Here William Taylor and Inga Clendinnen's concept of "exact imagining" can help us; we must remain critically aware of and tethered to the imperfect sources of information with which we work, and yet, we must attempt to stretch beyond them, interrogating the silences and absences, asking questions about our own assumptions as well as those of our sources and interlocutors. From an emic perspective, the essays in this volume attempt to critically imagine and honor insider perspectives in ways that are transparent to the reader and thus credible, even if they are ultimately at best an informed approximation.

The etic approach also implies difficulties and requires care. As scholars drawing on conceptual frameworks that are often foreign to the peoples, cultures, and contexts we study, we must be constantly self-reflective about how these frameworks are shaping our interpretation. One of the great dangers of following an exclusively etic approach is falling into the mentality that an outsider approach somehow gives a "more accurate" or "truer" interpretation of experience than any insider perspectives. Such a stance can fall quickly into a kind of intellectual paternalism. To be clear, the essays in this volume do engage etic perspectives. They draw on scholarly categories and frameworks that are part and parcel of the intellectual and scholarly communities of which contributors in this volume are a part. But, as the reader will find, this use of "outsider" theories and concepts is not meant to replace insider perspectives, but rather, to complement them in a respectful and cautious way.

As should be clear by now, this volume does not approach studying "religion in the Americas" through an encyclopedic point of view. This would largely be a fool's errand, given that "the Americas" is more than 16 million square miles, and the cultural histories of *homo sapiens* in North and South America date back to more than 13,000 years. Attempting to capture the diversity of religious expressions in such vast frames of space and time would not only require multiple volumes but would also suggest that such a task was finite.

Instead, this volume points readers in an altogether different direction, one that is ever-expanding and intentionally self-reflexive. We seek to honor knowledge as it emerges in at least four intersecting levels of inquiry: a) *local knowledge* that emerges from the religious insights and perspectives of those we study; b) *analytical interventions* that we, as academics who have been trained in a variety of disciplines, bring to our study of local knowledge, c) *new forms of inquiry* that arise when we transgress our traditional fields of study and move into more experimental spaces of transhemispheric and transdisciplinary conversation and practice; and finally, d) *the new knowledge that you, as a reader of these essays, bring to the table* in light of your own conceptual frameworks, questions, and tools of interpretation.

Significantly, at all of four levels, "we," as interpreters of religious practices (which includes, you, the reader), are intimately connected to the knowledge we produce, a knowledge that is never exhaustive or final. Indeed, there will always be new problems and circumstances that guide the direction of our inquiry, new points of entry and interpretive tools that we can use to help guide our inquiry, and new opportunities for revising our "conclusions," which, are themselves, merely the best hypotheses that we can put forward at a given time.

But all inquiry needs to start somewhere. And a good place to begin, we believe, is to squarely acknowledge our own role in helping to create knowledge. It is our hope that such an approach, along with this volume's interdisciplinary, trans-hemispheric, and transcultural orientation, will help readers to think beyond conventional scholarly and geopolitical boundaries in order to creatively reimagine and further enliven the study of "religion in the Américas." We invite students and scholars of this vast and shifting field of study to challenge, expand, and build upon the conversation begun here.

# Notes

1. Robert Carlsen, "Transculturation," in *The Oxford Encyclopedia of Mesoamerican Cultures* (Oxford, 2006).
2. A trans-hemispheric approach to Latin America and the Latin American diaspora in the Americas ought to include attention to these communities in Canada. We hope our approach here inspires scholars to venture further into this neglected area of study. One notable contribution in this direction is Néstor Medina and Becca Whitla, "(An)Other Canada is Possible: Rethinking Canada's Colonial Legacy," *Horizontes Decolonialies* 1 (2019), 13–42.
3. Charles H. Long, *Significations: Signs, Symbols, and Images in the Interpretation of Religion* (Philadelphia: Fortress Press, 1986), 97.
4. Long, *Significations*, 97.
5. Thomas A. Tweed, *Crossing and Dwelling: A Theory of Religion* (Cambridge: Harvard University Press, 2006), 54.
6. Tweed, *Crossing and Dwelling*, 57–9.
7. Short biographies of all the authors in this anthology may be found at the end of this volume.
8. It should be mentioned that there was (and still is) an important third Latine-related unit within the AAR called the "Latina/o Religion, Culture, and Society" group, with which the two groups also collaborated. Prior to 2017, the differences between the three groups were largely disciplinary and geographical ones. Whereas the Latina/o Religion, Culture, and Society Group tended to highlight theological themes and questions from within the Christian tradition, the Latino/a Critical and Comparative Studies Group tended to pursue a more pluralistic religious-studies approach that explored "non-Western beliefs and practices, including the Indigenous, the African-diasporic, Buddhist, and Islam, as well as those that advance a more complex understanding of culturally hybrid Christianities." For its part, the "Religion in Latin America and the Caribbean" group was largely constituted around the geography of Latin America and the Caribbean.
9. Inga Clendinnen, "Ways to the Sacred: Reconstructing 'Religion' in Sixteenth Century Mexico," *History and Anthropology* 5, no. 1 (1990): 105–41.

# References

Carlsen, Robert. "Transculturation." In *The Oxford Encyclopedia of Mesoamerican Cultures*, edited by Davíd Carrasco. New York: Oxford University Press, 2006.

Clendinnen, Inga. "Ways to the Sacred: Reconstructing 'Religion' in Sixteenth Century Mexico." *History and Anthropology* 5, no. 1 (1990): 105–41.

Long, Charles H. *Significations: Signs, Symbols, and Images in the Interpretation of Religion*. Philadelphia: Fortress Press, 1986.

Medina, Néstor, and Becca Whitla. "(An)Other Canada is Possible: Rethinking Canada's Colonial Legacy." *Horizontes Decolonialies* 1 (2019): 13–42.

Tweed, Thomas A. *Crossing and Dwelling: A Theory of Religion*. Cambridge: Harvard University Press, 2006.

PART I

*Fluidity in the Afro-Latine Diaspora*

FIGURE 1. Interior of la Ermita. Shrine to La Caridad del Cobre in Miami. Courtesy of Michelle Maldonado.

CHAPTER 1

# Our Ladies of the 305

*MICHELLE GONZALEZ MALDONADO*

In Miami, Florida, images of Mary reflect the cultural and religious tapestry of the city. Around the corner from El Palacio de los Jugos, a Miami institution where you can get your lechon (pork) for Christmas Eve and daily doses of croquetas (croquettes), mango juice, and agua de coco (coconut water), sits the Assumption of Our Blessed Virgin Mary Ukrainian Catholic Church. Nestled in an overwhelmingly Cuban neighborhood, this Catholic church has been ministering to the South Florida Ukrainian community since the 1950s. Catholics of all backgrounds are welcome to worship in the Byzantine tradition, but it is its distinctive architecture and its masses in Ukrainian that attract the Ukrainian community, some of whom live hours away.

Nestled on the shores of Biscayne Bay is La Ermita de la Caridad, a shrine dedicated to La Caridad del Cobre, the patron saint of Cuba. It is a powerful site of diasporic nationalism for the Cuban American and Cuban exile communities. In Miami, La Caridad symbolizes a preferential option for the exile community, one that has been wrongly forced to leave Cuba. This community is constructed as the marginalized, whom La Caridad accompanies. As the pamphlet detailing the history of the shrine outlines, La Caridad entered into exile with the Cuban people who were escaping Cuba's totalitarian government. She stands in solidarity with this community.

In the late nineteenth century, an image of Our Lady of Perpetual Help arrived in Port-au-Prince, Haiti, in the midst of a smallpox epidemic. The day after the archbishop lifted her image in a petition to end the epidemic, the illness ceased, and six decades later, she was made the patroness of the nation. She was said to have been brought to Haiti to cure any superstitions associated with Vodou.[1] Similar to the language we will see associated with La Caridad del Cobre, ecclesial leaders saw Our Lady as a tool of evangelization. Our Lady of Perpetual Help Catholic Church was dedicated in 1958 in Opa Locka, Florida. The name came with a new church building that replaced a mission school that began in 1954. The church was closed in 2009, merging with St. James Parish. However, the closing of the church did not lead to Our Lady's absence. Notre Dame d'Haiti Catholic Church serves as an epicenter of the Haitian Catholic Community in South Florida, and its name bears witness to Our Lady of Perpetual Help.

In all of these churches and many more throughout South Florida (including Our Lady of Czestochowa Polish Mission, Our Lady of Guadalupe Church, Our Lady of La Vang Mission, and St. Mary's Cathedral), Mary marks the Roman Catholic landscape of the region. While one of the most racially, ethnically, and religiously diverse parts of the country, South Florida remains a considerably understudied region for scholars of religion. Anecdotally referred to as the most northern city in Latin America, Miami represents the crossroads of the Americas. A key religious symbol that inhabits the region, both within and outside of Roman Catholicism, is Mary, the Mother of Jesus. Mary is a marker of South Florida's religious landscape. While you can find her within the institutional spaces of the Catholic Church, she also appears in yard shrines, murals, and cemeteries. Mary is also a key presence in the Black Atlantic religions that shape the region, most notable in Vodou and Santería. Mary represents not only the Roman Catholic community, but also the complexity of religion in South Florida. Though Mary is often identified as a Roman Catholic symbol, immigrant communities have reimagined her in myriad ways, demonstrating the dynamic, hybrid, and ever-changing nature of religious symbols. She accompanied these immigrant communities to Miami, and here the manner in which she has been transformed speaks to the ways in which religious symbols cross borders, both national and religious. She also reveals the complexity of religious identity in the region, reflecting the intersection of race, nationalism, and religion for Caribbean peoples.

This chapter examines the Marys of South Florida, arguing that they, like the region, are a gateway into the Americas as a whole. I focus on two Caribbean immigrant Marys: Our Lady of Charity from Cuba and Our Lady of Perpetual Hope from Haiti. This interdisciplinary study draws from theology, ethnographic research on their devotions, and history, demonstrating the ways in which institutional Catholicism, everyday Catholicism, and Black Atlantic religions have interwoven in South Florida. The hybridity that Mary symbolizes is representative of the religions and communities that claim her as their own. In this way, Mary is clearly a cultural symbol. The power of Mary's presence within these communities demonstrates both her accompaniment of them here in the United States and the ways in which she serves as a bridge between the United States and her devotees' homelands. Studying Our Ladies of the 305 shows us the personal, communal, and hybrid ways in which religious identity is constructed and the manner in which religious symbols give life and are given life by communities of faith.

# Our Lady of Perpetual Help

Our Lady of Perpetual Help is the patron saint of both Haiti, the country, and Little Haiti, the area in Miami that is the heart of the Haitian community. Her icon is a lithograph, not a statue. As noted by Terry Rey and Alex Stepick in their definitive study of Haitian religion in South Florida, "'Pepetyèl,' as she is affectionately called in Haitian Creole, is the most important symbol in Haitian religion. She is the saint most ardently prayed to by poor and wealthy Haitians alike, and by many Haitian immigrants in their journey to and settlement in the United States. For Haitian Catholics, this is Pepetuèl's church in the diaspora."[2] Housed in Notre Dame d'Haiti Catholic Church, Our Lady of Perpetual Help is a unifying image for the Haitian diaspora.

In Little Haiti, her feast day includes a reenactment of the annunciation and a procession. "Besides being an expression of genuine religious devotion, the feast-day celebration at Notre Dame is an attempt to re-create a sense of being Haitian and of being in Haiti."[3] She moves between the past and an imagined future, the homeland and the diaspora. She is the Mother of Haiti, who has chosen to protect the Haitian people. Notre Dame d'Haiti Catholic Church provides the Haitian community in Miami a sense of home and belonging. The Archdiocese of Miami played a significant role in receiving and supporting Haitian immigrants in the 1980s, particularly through the Notre Dame church and the adjacent Pierre Toussaint Haitian Center. The Center was established by Archbishop Edward McCarthy in 1978. Fr. Thomas Wenski, who was pastoring at nearby Corpus Christi Catholic Church, was named director of the archdiocesan Haitian apostolate. In 1982 Notre Dame church was consecrated. Devotion to Our Lady of Perpetual Help unites the Haitian people across time and space. At Notre Dame, parishioners celebrate her on numerous feast days, including Our Ladies of the Immaculate Conception on December 12, the Assumption on August 15, Mount Carmel on July 16, and the feast of Perpetual Help on June 27.

Religious rituals and practices centered on Our Lady of Perpetual Help must be contextualized in light of broader Haitian devotions to saints and the manner in which they reveal an understanding of the sacred that is in solidarity with the marginalized. Deborah O'Neil and Terry Rey's study of devotion to St. Philomena in northern Haiti reveals a liberationist theology underlying popular religious practices. In the Haitian devotion, St. Philomena has sacred power. She gives what O'Neil and Rey describe as a liberation hagiography (study of the saints) that emphasizes survival, resistance, and self-determination. In a similar manner to the function of the preferential option for the poor in liberation theology, "Liberation hagiography is motivated by the conviction that Catholic saints exercise just such a preferential option, as is so clearly on display among St. Philomena's devotees in Haiti."[4] Her relationship with the Vodou loa Lasyrenn demonstrates the manner in which Catholicism and Vodou enrich each other. In Vodou, loas are spirits that mediate one's relationship with God, serving similar, though not identical, intercessory roles as we see with Mary and the saints in Catholicism. Loas serve as mediators between humans and the Supreme Being. "Although there is a distinct monotheism in Vodou, despite its henotheism and pantheon of divinities and ancestral spirits, God is not the focus of worship in a service; people typically pray to Bondye through the spirits."[5] Associating the loa with images of Mary and saints was an intentional strategy slaves used to mask their beliefs in practices in the faces of slavery and colonialism.

O'Neil and Rey define popular religious practices as expressions of liberation theology and connect the demise of liberation theology in Haiti to the deterioration of the cult of the saints. This runs counter to the narrative that liberation theology is reduced to social justice action and that popular devotions somehow undermine liberationist impulses. Their study offers a significant contribution to this conversation. On the one hand, their criticism of liberation theology's inability to connect with lived religious expressions is sound. On the other hand, they open up the field of liberation hagiography to the study of American religion as a whole. Research on liberation hagiography is a much-needed avenue of study that would unite concrete investigations of religious devotions with liberationist movements and studies of African diaspora religions.

Rey rightfully points out in his own study of the cult of the Virgin Mary that Catholicism in Haiti is marked by Marian devotion, going so far as to say that Haitian culture as a whole is marked by Marian devotion.[6] The same can be said of Mexican and Cuban Catholicism, as well of Catholicism in many other countries in the Americas. Columbus, Rey points out, arrived in the Americas on the Santa María and named the first two ports in Hispaniola after Mary. I would add devotion to saints and folk saints as another defining element of Catholicism in the Americas. Although Mariology in particular has been a wellspring of liberationist impulses, it has also been a source of misogyny and oppression, creating unrealistic ideals within the construction of Catholic womanhood. Devotion to Mary is also not exclusively found in the realm of the poor, but rather crosses class lines. However, the Mary of the poor bears little resemblance to the Mary of the rich. The notion of liberation hagiography introduces a fruitful avenue for exploring the connection between lived religious practices and liberationist impulses in Marian and other folk devotions, particularly among the disenfranchised.[7] Such an analysis should examine not only symbol and culture but also class and power in Christian, Indigenous, and African religions.

Rey argues that Notre Dame du Perpétuel Secours has the same prominence among Haitians and Haitian Americans as Guadalupe for Mexican and Mexican-Americans.[8] She has been Haiti's patron saint since 1942. She "eclipses God, the Holy Spirit, Jesus Christ, and the community of saints in popular Haitian Catholic consciousness, is considered accessible for miraculous intervention in the people's daily lives, and plays a leading role in the guardianship of the nation," and "is the most often addressed spiritual being in the Catholic pantheon in Haitian religion, both popular and intellectual, petitioned constantly and widely in the supplicative prayers of Haitians of all social strata."[9] Her visible and central presence in the 305 among Haitians speaks to her privileged role within Haitian Catholicism, both on and off the island. She also reveals the way in which a liberationist interpretation of religious symbols can impact both Catholicism and Black Atlantic religions in the region.

## La Caridad del Cobre

The most prominent symbol of Cuban exile—and Cuban American religion—is La Caridad del Cobre. La Ermita de la Caridad is a national shrine in the United States, and on his last visit to the island of Cuba, Pope Francis offered a mass at her shrine in Santiago de Cuba. It is important to highlight there are two Caridads: one on the island and another in Miami, where we find the largest Cuban diaspora community. Devotion to La Caridad began locally within a community of royal slaves in the seventeenth century and grew until she became the national patroness of the island. She is revered both on the island and among Cubans in the diaspora. Throughout Cuban history, the image and story of La Caridad has been vastly transformed within Cuban oral tradition, so much so that the narrative and iconography surrounding her today is distinct from historical accounts of her historical arrival to the slave community in Cobre. Much of this transformation occurred during Cuba's wars of independence from Spain, during which she became a unifying national symbol that intertwined religious and national identity. La Caridad, therefore, is not only a symbol of Cuban identity; she represents the Cuban process of identity making, Cubans' self-construction as they articulated a distinctive identity from Spain, one that incorporated and challenged the legacy of slavery on the island.

If one looks at a prayer card or statue of La Caridad del Cobre in a Cuban-American's home, one finds a representation of Mary filling the sky above three men in a rowboat. She is dressed most often in blue, and she is carrying the baby Jesus as she floats over the three helpless men. Her skin is a light brown. The three men appear to be struggling in the midst of a storm. The man in the middle, of African descent, is holding his hands in prayer. The two other men, appear to be white (Spanish?) and brown (biracial? Indigenous?) and are gripping the oars. In Cuban folklore, these men are known as the "three Juanes." A quick interpretation of this image seems to imply Mary appeared over these three men during a storm as a result of their prayers for help. And while La Caridad did materialize before three men in a rowboat on the Bay of Nipe, she was a small statue floating in the water, and the skies were not stormy when they found her. The men were not all named Juan, and none of them were white or of European descent. The actual date of this discovery is contested, though scholars today agree that it occurred in the first fifteen years of the seventeenth century.[10]

The earliest written account of the circumstances that led to La Caridad arriving in Cobre is a 1687 interview of Juan Moreno, an African slave who claimed to be one of the three who discovered the statue. Moreno played an active political role amongst the Cobre slaves and was, for some time, seen as their leader and representative to the Spanish. The recording of his testimony and his prominent position occur around the same time period. In addition to the narrative told by Juan Moreno, Onofre de Fonseca, who was chaplain of the shrine in El Cobre from 1683 to 1710, adds the story of a girl named Apolonia to the narrative history. Apolonia was the daughter of a miner and on her way to visit her mother when La Caridad appeared before her, telling her where she wanted her temple built. This second "apparition" story is not as well-known within Cuba, and its later date, coupled with a lack of firsthand testimony, makes its historical validity questionable.

Moreno describes how he and two Indigenous brothers, Rodrigo and Juan de Hoyos, were searching for salt in the Bay of Nipe one early morning. In the distance, they saw an object floating on the water that they first mistook for a bird. Instead, they realized it was a statue floating in the water with the words "Yo soy la Virgen de la Caridad" ("I am the Virgin of Charity") attached to it. They took the statue with them and quickly turned it over to Spanish authorities. Devotion to this image of Mary began first among slaves in the region of El Cobre. At the time of her discovery, Cobre was primarily a copper-mining community of slaves. During Cuba's wars for independence from Spain, devotion to her began to spread nationally. When La Caridad's prominence grew beyond the Afro-Cuban community and she became the official patroness of Cuba, her narrative was altered to accommodate the racial make-up and history of the broader Cuban population.

No one knows exactly when the race of the three men in Juan Moreno's account was transformed. La Caridad's story and her iconography were whitened as her prominence among all Cubans grew. Much of this occurred when she was transformed into a symbol of Cuban nationalism during the Cuban armed struggles against Spanish colonial rule. The intersection of nationalism and religion that marks post-independence devotions to La Caridad has not disappeared in the diaspora, but has been rewritten once again to the political consciousness of the Cuban-American community. As a result of this, La Ermita has become a powerful site of diasporic nationalism. In the eyes of the diaspora community, La Caridad has come to symbolize a preferential option for those who have been wrongly forced to leave Cuba. She stands in solidarity with this community. Similar to the transformation of her historical narrative and presence throughout the history of Cuba, this is yet another rewriting of her history by Cubans in the United States.

Henry B. Lovejoy explores the ways in which nationalist discourse surrounding La Caridad have impacted orisha worship. "The transformation of Òsun into Ochún, also known as the Virgen de la Caridad del Cobre, occurred within the anticolonial discourse of the mulata as expressed in Cuban popular culture of the mid-to-late nineteenth century."[11] Lovejoy reminds us that it was not until the nineteenth century that the Yorùbá began to associate the two, for "To consider Ochún and the Virgen de la Caridad del Cobre fusing together in Cuba's early colonial history is ahistorical because few Yorùbá speakers from the Bight of Benin, if any, could have inhabited El Cobre before the nineteenth century."[12] La Caridad del Cobre's rise as a national symbol coincides with the mulata emerging as a symbol of independence.

La Caridad and Our Lady of Perpetual Help are not the only two Marian devotions that embody how religious images can also be expressions of national identity, though they are perhaps the most prevalent in South Florida. For both Cubans and Haitians, these Marian symbols become cultural and national repositories that allow for each community's particularity to survive in the diaspora. They are also not the only images whose narratives are framed by a theological interpretation that claims that Mary reveals a God who is on the side of the oppressed and marginalized. St. Ann Mission was established in November 1961 to serve the farmworker community in Homestead, south of Miami. The church has a shrine to Our Lady of Guadalupe. Her devotion allows Mexican-American farmworkers to connect to their Mexican and Catholic identity. "Not surprisingly, then, for St. Ann's Mission's congregation the feast of Our Lady of Guadalupe is the most important religious and cultural event of the year."[13] Mary, however, is not just limited to churches or even Catholicism exclusively. As the following section indicates, Mary's presence extends far beyond institutional Roman Catholicism.

## Not Just Jesus' Mother

While Marian devotions have their roots in institutional Catholicism, Our Ladies of the 305 show us the ways in which as symbols they become much more complex and elaborate, particularly in light of Black Atlantic religions. The presence of Mary in religions such as Santería and Vodou has been well documented in the study of these religions for decades, as is the local South Florida Catholic Church's efforts to disassociate Mary from Black Atlantic religions. Thomas Tweed's singular scholarship on La Ermita emphasizes that religious identity is a dynamic and hybrid process. For him, this shrine is a site of struggle, where the Cuban-American community negotiates a Catholic identity shaped by the intersection of Spanish and African religiosity. The clergy are at the forefront, striving to define authentic Catholicism against the influences of Afro-Cuban religions. The purpose of the shrine was evangelization. However, Tweed notes, many lay visitors have resisted this effort by the clergy to evangelize nominal Catholics. This "nominal Catholicism" is characterized, in the clergy's eyes, by ignorance about the true nature of Catholicism. Visitors to the shrine do not come overwhelmingly to be evangelized; they come to petition and pay tribute to La Caridad.

As exemplified by Tweed's interview with Bishop Agustín A. Román, the former pastor of the shrine, the institutional church sees evangelization as a central challenge within the local Catholic community. Román divides the community into three categories, from smallest to largest: the liturgical community, nominal Catholics, and those who were not "officially" Catholic. This is what leads to the confusion of the saints with the orishas. The shrine is an instrument to rectify nominal Catholic's "false" association of Caridad with the orisha Oshun. Orishas are supernatural beings that mediate our relationship with the sacred. Similar to the loas in Vodou, while not identical, they have parallel roles to the saints and Mary in Catholicism. This Afro-Cuban practice of associating or masking an African deity behind a Catholic image dates to the colonial era. Most Cubans and Cuban-Americans, despite their religious affiliation, are well aware of the relationship between Oshun and La Caridad, demonstrating the manner in which this Afro-Cuban devotion has saturated the Cuban cultural and religious history. Strong devotions to Our Lady of Charity, as well as other popular religious practices, are in part a result of Cubans' lack of historical ties to the institutional church. Mary becomes a shared symbol around which unchurched and churched Cubans and Haitians gather and construct a national identity in exile and in the diaspora.

La Caridad and Our Lady of Perpetual Help are not the only images of Mary that appear in South Florida and are connected to Black Atlantic religions. The Black Madonna, Our Lady of Czestochowa, who was brought to Haiti by Polish legionaries that were recruited by Napoleon to fight in the Haitian revolution, also became incorporated into the Vodou pantheon, connecting her to Erzulie Dantor. La Virgen de Regla, who is venerated in Regla, right outside of Havana, is associated with the orisha Yemayá, the great mother. She is the orisha of the sea and salt waters. It is said that she gave birth to the sun and the moon, as well as all of the orishas. It should not surprise us that she is associated with La Virgen de Regla, the patroness of the Bay of Havana, a Marian devotion associated with the ocean. "Affectionately called La Negrita, Regla is the only Marian image in Cuba considered to be Black, and Yemayá is the only spirit, or oricha, explicitly described as such by devotees.... In the eyes of her followers, the Virgin of Regla has remained miraculous not just by retaining her color in a literal sense, but also—through her alter ego, Yemayá, by bearing witness to the horrors visited on Afro-Cuban bodies, both enslaved and free."[14] La Virgen de Regla and Yemayá's black skin bears witness to suffering Black bodies.

These associations between the orishas, loas, and Mary should not be interpreted as devotee ignorance regarding religious systems and symbols. As noted by Stephan Palmié, while Roman Catholic images, rituals, and symbols are incorporated into Afro-Cuban religions, this is not a result of any confusion on the part of the practitioner. "Santeros observe a relatively clear-cut 'praxeological' distinction between 'African' and 'Catholic' cultural forms which—to a certain extent—corresponds to metonymical and metaphorical modes of representing the sacred. The otanes and those other objects which go into the making of what Santeros refer to as the fundamento (foundation) of an oricha are often talked about as containing the deity's powers, as serving as its abode. Catholic images, however, are generally regarded as images symbolizing its attributes."[15] These Roman Catholic images are not what contain the core of the spiritual power and theology of religions such as Vodou and Santería. In other words, these Roman Catholic images do not, strictly speaking, contain the core of the spiritual power, but rather re-present them in symbolic form. One can therefore not just look at incorporation of these symbols into Black Atlantic religious practices and claim theological syncretism; one must also look at their function and representation.

Similarly, it is also important that we not set up a Catholic-African binary when discussing syncretism. In his essay, "On Hearing Africas in the Americas," Michael Iyanaga "revises the historical binary and a priori interpretive position that nothing Catholic can also be African or Afro-American. Instead, I argue, many Catholic traditions of the Americas are themselves 'African,' or at least Afro-Diasporic in the same sense that orisha/orichá/orixá veneration is believed (and understood) to be. After all, Catholicism was already a relatively widespread 'African religion,' primarily in central Africa, generations before the transatlantic slave trade evolved into the insatiable funnel for human chattel that would eventually allow the Atlantic system to dominate global trade routes and transform the world."[16] In other words, we must not eclipse the presence of Roman Catholicism on the African continent prior and during the transatlantic slave trade.

Roman Catholicism was brought to Haiti by the slaves themselves, who were forcibly transported to the island. As Hein Vanhee rightly points out, Portuguese and Italian missionaries were extremely active in the Congo region beginning in the fifteenth century. As part of their missionary enterprise, they employed maestros de igrejas, lay assistants who served as catechists and at times even held political offices. These lay African missionaries, who are estimated to have numbered in the thousands, traveled to remote areas and instructed potential converts.[17] Individuals traveled great distances to be baptized. The French followed with heavy missionary activity in the Congo region in the eighteenth century. King Nzinga, a Nkuwu of the Congo, was baptized voluntarily in 1491 by Franciscan priests, though he did not place a heavy Christian emphasis upon his leadership and the kingdom's identity. Though his rule was short-lived, his son Afonso, who ruled from 1506 to 1543, affirmed Christianity as central to the Congo kingdom. Missionaries adopted Congolese ritual language to name and categorize Christian rituals, erasing the linguistic distinctions between Congolese religion and Christianity.[18] They seemed to have accepted the inevitable association of Catholicism with traditional Congolese religion. The existence of Catholicism in the Congo region in the early sixteenth century is well documented.

John Thornton's scholarship offers a fresh way of viewing the encounter between Catholicism and traditional Congolese religion by reminding us that it did not occur initially in the Americas. He argues that there was a particular Christianity that developed in Africa prior to the transatlantic slave trade. There existed in the Kongo kingdom, and in parts of Western Africa, an African Catholic Church that became the philosophical foundation of the evangelization of slaves in the New World. "The clergy in America, overworked and lacking opportunities to engage in substantial teaching in any case, found African Christianity acceptable, while Africans who came from non-Christian parts of Africa found it comprehensible and adapted it easily."[19] Thornton argues that clergy in Western and Central Africa in the sixteenth and seventeenth centuries were much more tolerant of syncretism than clergy today. This work is extremely important for understanding Catholicism in Haiti, for it debunks the myth that Catholicism arrived on the island exclusively through European missionaries. This is far from the case. This African Catholicism, with its underlying African worldview at its core, set the stage for the creation in the Americas of religions such as Vodou that draw from both African and Catholic worldviews.

A helpful framework to understand Marian devotions in the Caribbean is found in J. Lorand Matory's broad discussion of Black Atlantic religions. He explores three metaphors commonly used to discuss Black Atlantic religions: survival, creolization, and memory. The survival metaphor implies that a past African artifact has survived in the present in the Americas. The creolization process refers to the theory that African religious practices combined in the Americas in altogether new ways. Linked to this is a notion of collective memory. While Matory acknowledges the significance of studies of collective memory in shedding light on the dynamic and strategic nature of cultural forms, he takes issue with the use of the word memory. "This analytic metaphor implies the organic unity of the collective 'rememberer,' anthropomorphizing society rather than highlighting the heterogeneity, strategic conflicts, and unequal resources of the rival agents who make up the social life."[20] The word memory also implies a single agent and downplays the collective nature of remembering. Instead of drawing on these common three tropes, Matory proposes the metaphor of dialogue, which "instead highlights the ways in which the mutual gaze between Africans and African-Americans, multidirectional travel and migration between the two hemispheres, the movement of publications, commerce, and so forth have shaped African and African-American cultures in tandem, over time, and at the same time."[21] To situate dialogue in light of South Florida, we must not only look at the historical complexity of the relationship between Roman Catholic and traditional African worldviews, we must also examine the current dynamic relationships that continue between populations in Caribbean nations and the United States.

We must be careful, however, not to overemphasize the presence of Black Atlantic religions in Cuba, Haiti, and South Florida. Rey and Stepick, for example, are critical of the exaggeration of the influence of Vodou on Haitian religion and culture as a whole. "Although Vodou does remain the religion of the Haitian majority, and although Vodou has been strongly influential on the reception and shaping of Christianity in Haitian history, there are very good reasons to believe that the number of practitioners of Vodou has been on the decline since the 1940s, a decline that may be accelerating in the wake of the tragic earthquake of January 2010, which many Protestant preachers have blamed on Vodou, and which was prophesized months earlier by Fr. Jules Campion as being punishment for the sins of Vodou and homosexuality."[22] Demographics show us that Protestantism, particularly evangelical Protestantism and Pentecostalism, is growing considerably in Cuba, Haiti, and South Florida. Within the United States, the number of Catholics is declining.

In spite of waning institutional affiliations among US Catholics of Caribbean descent, Mary continues to mark Miami's landscape. We find her in altars in the front yards of homes and inside houses tucked away with candles, offerings and a community of saints. Images of her are sold in Catholic bookstores and in botánicas, where practitioners of Vodou and Santería buy ritual supplies. She is perched on gravestones, tattooed on bodies, dangling from heavy gold chains around the necks of believers. She saturates the 305. Her presence reminds us of the religious complexity of the region and the long and painful histories of the communities that have carried her image with them just as she has carried them through her intercessory prayers. Our Ladies of the 305 remind us that South Florida is a region marked by Marian devotions that remember communities, religions, and identities, all under her watchful gaze.

# Notes

1. Terry Rey, "The Politics of Patron Sainthood in Haiti: 500 Years of Iconic Struggle," *The Catholic Historical Review*, 88, no. 3, (July 2002): 519–45.
2. Terry Rey and Alex Stepick, *Crossing the Water and Keeping the Faith* (New York: New York University Press, 2013), 92.
3. Rey and Stepick, 101.
4. Deborah O'Neil and Terry Rey, "The Saint and the Siren: Liberation Hagiography in a Haitian Village," *Studies in Religion*, 41, no. 2 (2012): 170.
5. Claudine Michel, "Of Words Seen and Unseen: The Educational Character of Haitian Vodou," in *Haitian Vodou: Spirit, Myth, and Reality*, edited by Patrick Bellegarde-Smith and Claudine Michel (Bloomington, IN: Indiana University Press, 2006), 38.
6. Terry Rey, *Our Lady of Class Struggle: The Cult of the Virgin Mary in Haiti* (Trenton, NJ: Africa World Press, 1999).
7. Michelle A. Gonzalez, *Embracing Latina Spirituality: A Woman's Perspective* (Cincinnati, OH: Franciscan Media, 2009).
8. Rey, *Our Lady of Class Struggle*, 2.
9. Rey, *Our Lady of Class Struggle*, 162.
10. Olga Portuando Zuñiga dates the apparition at 1613. María Elena Díaz, in her excellent study of the slave community in El Cobre, dates the apparition at 1604. Olga Portuondo Zúñiga, *La Virgen de la Caridad del Cobre: Simbolo de la Cubanía*, rev. ed. (Madrid, Spain: Agualarga Editores, 2002), 75; María Elena Díaz, *The Virgin, the King, and the Royal Slaves: Negotiating Freedom in Colonial Cuba, 1670–1780* (Stanford, CA: Stanford University Press, 2000).
11. Henry B. Lovejoy, "Òsun Becomes Cuban: The Nationalist Discourse Over the Mulata in Cuban Popular Culture and Religion During the Nineteenth Century," *Atlantic Studies* 16, no. 2 (2019): 222.
12. Henry B. Lovejoy, "Òsun Becomes Cuban," 9.
13. Noemí Báez, María de los Angéles Rey, and Terry Rey, "Faith in the Fields: Mexican Marianism in Miami-Dade County" in *Churches and Charity in the Immigrant City: Religion, Immigration, and Civic Engagement in Miami*, edited by Alex Stepick, Terry Rey, and Sarah J. Mahler. (New Brunswick, NJ: Rutgers University Press, 2009), 198.
14. Elizabeth Pérez, "The Virgin in the Mirror: Reading Images of a Black Madonna through the Lens of Afro-Cuban Women's Experiences, *The Journal of African American History* 95, no. 2 (2010): 202.

15. Stephan Palmié, "Against Syncretism: 'Africanizing' and 'Cubanizing' Discourses in North American Òrìsà Worship" in *Counterworks: Managing the Diversity of Knowledge*, edited by Richard Fardon (New York, NY: Routledge, 1995), 82.
16. Michael Iyanaga, "On Hearing Africa in the Americas: Domestic Celebrations for Catholic Saints as Afro-Diasporic Religious Tradition," in *Afro-Catholic Festivals in the Americas: Performance, Representation, and the Making of Black Atlantic Tradition*, edited by Cécile Fremont (University Park, PA: The Pennsylvania State University Press, 2019), 167.
17. Hein Vanhee, "Central African Popular Christianity and the Making of Haitian Vodou Religion" in *Central Africans and Cultural Transformations in the American Diaspora*, edited by Linda M. Heywood (New York: Cambridge University Press, 2002), 243.
18. Jason R. Young, *Rituals of Resistance; African Atlantic Religion in Kongo and the Lowcountry South in the Era of Slavery* (Baton Rouge, LA: Louisiana State University Press, 2007), 50.
19. John Thornton, "On the Trail of Voodoo: African Christianity in Africa and the Americas," *The Americas* 44 (1988): 262.
20. J. Lorand Matory, "From 'Survival' to 'Dialogue': Analytic Tropes in the Study of African-Diaspora Cultural History" in *Transatlantic Caribbean: Dialogues of People, Practices, Ideas*, edited by Ingrid Kummels et al. (Germany: Transcript Verlag, 2014), 43.
21. J. Lorand Matory, "From 'Survival' to 'Dialogue,'" 47.
22. Rey and Stepick, *Crossing the Water and Keeping the Faith*, 88–89.

# References

Báez, Noemí, and María de los Ángeles Rey. "Faith in the Fields: Mexican Marianism in Miami-Dade County." In *Churches and Charity in the Immigrant City: Religion, Immigration, and Civic Engagement in Miami*, edited by Alex Stepick, Terry Rey, and Sarah J. Mahler. New Brunswick, NJ: Rutgers University Press, 2009.

Díaz, María Elena. *The Virgin, the King, and the Royal Slaves: Negotiating Freedom in Colonial Cuba, 1670–1780*. Stanford, CA: Stanford University Press, 2000.

Gonzalez, Michelle A. *Embracing Latina Spirituality: A Woman's Perspective*. Cincinnati, OH: Franciscan Media, 2009.

Iyanaga, Michael. "On Hearing Africa in the Americas: Domestic Celebrations for Catholic Saints as Afro-Diasporic Religious Tradition." In *Afro-Catholic Festivals in the Americas: Performance, Representation, and the Making of Black Atlantic Tradition*, edited by Cécile Fremont. University Park, PA: The Pennsylvania State University Press, 2019.

Lovejoy, Henry B. "Òsun Becomes Cuban: The Nationalist Discourse Over the Mulata in Cuban Popular Culture and Religion During the Nineteenth Century." *Atlantic Studies* 16, no. 2 (2019).

Matory, J. Lorand. "From 'Survival' to 'Dialogue': Analytic Tropes in the Study of African-Diaspora Cultural History." In *Transatlantic Caribbean: Dialogues of People, Practices, Ideas*, edited by Ingrid Kummels et al. Transcript Verlag, 2014.

Michel, Claudine. "Of Words Seen and Unseen: The Educational Character of Haitian Vodou." In *Haitian Vodou: Spirit, Myth, and Reality*, edited by Patrick Bellegarde-Smith and Claudine Michel. Bloomington, IN: Indiana University Press, 2006.

O'Neil, Deborah, and Terry Rey. "The Saint and the Siren: Liberation Hagiography in a Haitian Village." *Studies in Religion* 41, no. 2, 2012.

Pérez, Elizabeth. "The Virgin in the Mirror: Reading Images of a Black Madonna Through the Lens of Afro-Cuban Women's Experiences." *The Journal of African American History* 95, no. 2 (2010).

Palmié, Stephan. "Against Syncretism: 'Africanizing' and 'Cubanizing' Discourses in North American Òrìsà Worship." In *Counterworks: Managing the Diversity of Knowledge*, edited by Richard Fardon. New York: Routledge, 1995.

Rey, Terry. "The Politics of Patron Sainthood in Haiti: 500 Years of Iconic Struggle." *The Catholic Historical Review* 88, no. 3 (2002).

Rey, Terry. *Our Lady of Class Struggle: The Cult of the Virgin Mary in Haiti*. Trenton, NJ: Africa World Press, 1999.

Rey, Terry, and Alex Stepick. *Crossing the Water and Keeping the Faith: Haitian Religion in Miami*. New York: New York University Press, 2013.

Vanhee, Hein. "Central African Popular Christianity and the Making of Haitian Vodou Religion, Central Africans and Cultural Transformations." In *The American Diaspora*, edited by Linda M. Heywood. New York: Cambridge University Press, 2002.

Young, Jason R. *Rituals of Resistance: African Atlantic Religion in Kongo and the Lowcountry South in the Era of Slavery*. Baton Rouge, LA: Louisiana State University Press, 2007.

Thornton, John. "On the Trail of Voodoo: African Christianity in Africa and the Americas." *The Americas* 44 (1988).

Zúñiga, Olga Portuondo. *La Virgen de la Caridad del Cobre: Simbolo de la Cubanía.* Rev. ed. Madrid, Spain: Agualarga Editores, 2002.

CHAPTER 2

# Quimbanda and Ritual Polyphony in Minas Gerais, Brazil

CRISTINA BORGES, ALEXANDRE F. S. KAITEL,

GUARACI M. DOS SANTOS, AND STEVEN ENGLER

This chapter looks at what we call *ritual polyphony* in Afro-Brazilian religions in the state of Minas Gerais, Brazil.[1] This is when distinct religious traditions are performed by one group in a way that keeps the boundaries between different traditions intact. Different religions are practiced at different times, in the same physical space, with the same leaders, and attended by mainly the same group of community members. Each religion has its own ritual calendar, its own beliefs, rituals, songs/chants, artifacts, modes of dress, and offerings.

We propose this new concept because existing terms do not capture what we found. We did not observe a mixture of religious or cultural elements, as signaled by "syncretism" or "hybridity." Ritual polyphony is not juxtaposition, the presence of distinct elements from different religions within a tradition, separate in time and space; it is not bricolage, *créolité*, mestizaje, third-space or transculturation.[2] It is not an eclectic toolbox; though, for some members, it is a set of distinct toolboxes. Rather, ritual polyphony involves not the mixture or superposition of elements, but the co-presence—with temporal and sometimes partial spatial separation—of distinct "religions" (if that is even the right word). It is the performance of distinct ritual and belief systems, practiced by the same core group of members.

The ten *terreiros* ("grounds" or houses) that we studied in the cities of Belo Horizonte and Montes Claros alternate regularly between the rituals of two or three distinct religions, which includes always Umbanda, almost always Candomblé (Angola [central African] or Nagô [west African]), and sometimes also Quimbanda (in Montes Claros) or Congado, also called Reinado (in Belo Horizonte). Ritual polyphony in Afro-Brazilian groups is found in other regions of Brazil, for example in the southern city of Porto Alegre, where Umbanda, Quimbanda, and Batuque are practiced in many terreiros.[3]

There is a range of modes of affiliation in these groups. Some marginally affiliated members come only to observe or for ritual services. Some members do not incorporate any entities (usually serving as *cambones*, or ritual assistants).[4] Some incorporate entities from only one of the religions. And some (always the leaders) incorporate entities from all the traditions (except Congado, which is not a spirit-incorporation tradition). We interviewed over fifty leaders and core members of these terreiros. Mediums usually speak of reliably different experiences of trance when incorporating the entities of different religions in the same terreiro. Each of the religions is considered by participants to be African.

Various forms of mixture are found in Afro-Brazilian traditions. For example, Umbandaime is a mixture of Umbanda and the ayahuasca tradition, Santo Daime. To give a more complex example, rituals that work with the *caboclo* (Indigenous) spirits (prominent in Umbanda and other Afro-Brazil and Afro-Indigenous traditions) are found in many terreiros of Candomblé, with these rituals being subordinated and even hidden, in order to preserve the perception of authentic and authoritative relations to African roots.[5] In all the terreiros we studied, with the exception of one, both Candomblé and Umbanda are practiced and kept distinct. Ritual polyphony is not simply a calculated commodification of religions and spirituality, as if ritually polyphonic groups attract members simply by offering one-stop-shopping for ritual services. To be sure, many of our interviewees do value the broad palette of spiritual services, but for many, their leaders' status reflects a mastery of distinct traditions. These points hint at the complexity and variability that we found.

There is a range of views of the relation between distinct religions or traditions among members of the groups we studied, including perceptions of unity, overlap, mixture, hierarchy, and difference. But all the people we talked to agree on two things: first, there are different experiences going on as they gather together to participate in distinct ritual forms (traditions, types of entities, modes of energy etc.) and, second, these experiences are similar yet different from each other. The fact that scholars of religion/s would call these different experiences "religions" offered a starting point, but we bracketed that concept, to test its value. Not surprisingly—at least for those who do fieldwork in Brazil—the concept of "religion" turned out to be of little value, beyond the most general of gestures toward the complex forms of practice that we encountered. The concept of ritual polyphony is meant to remain open to the different voices of practitioners as they make sense of the multifaceted nature of their joint practice. Commonality and overlap within multiplicity and difference remain a constant, despite the fact that practitioners label things in different ways.

This chapter focuses on one significant finding: the impact of regional characteristics. Differences between Belo Horizonte (the state capital and fourth most populous city in Brazil, with 2.7. million people) and Montes Claros (the pole city of one of the poorest regions in the state, with 420,000 people) help explain distinct forms of ritual polyphony. To develop this theme, we focus on the important but little-studied Afro-Brazilian tradition of Quimbanda.

Quimbanda is often considered the "left-handed" path of Umbanda (*a linha da esquerda*) and is popularly seen as a dangerous source of black magic. Among other things, it offers, for a price, transgressive ritual "works" (*trabalhos*) that aim, for example, to influence romantic partners, give advantages in business, or weaken political rivals. Quimbanda is rooted in an African conception of the universe, in which positive and negative forces coexist in tension. This has led to the perception that it runs counter to or undermines dominant Christian norms. This misleading perception contributes, in a vicious circle, to its denigration and marginalization as nothing more than black magic.

Quimbanda is understudied in part because some scholars share this prejudice. Quimbanda is disparaged in most of Brazil, including in Belo Horizonte, one of our two field sites. However, there are places where the tradition is seen positively and where it plays a central role in local ritual ecosystems. The north of the state of Minas Gerais is one of these places. Quimbanda's distinct place in this region illustrates how historical and geographical contexts modify the organization and development of polyphonic Afro-Brazilian traditions.

## Candomblé, Congado, Umbanda, Quimbanda

This section offers a descriptive overview of relevant aspects of the vast and diverse Brazilian religious landscape. Cultural-religious knowledge from different regions of Africa came to this part of the Americas during and after the forced transmigration of enslaved African people. Mutual influences with Indigenous cultures, Iberian Catholic settler culture, and European esoteric traditions led to increasing diversity. There are many Afro-Brazilian religious traditions, with porous doctrinal/ritual boundaries, regional variants, and mutual influences.[6] Most have some degree of

Indigenous, Catholic, and/or esoteric elements. A partial list includes Candomblé and Umbanda (each with several distinct forms), Batuque, Cabula, Mesa de Santa Barbara, Jarê, Omolocô, Quimbanda, Tambor de Mina, Tambor de Nagô, Xambá, and Xangô. Some traditions are further along a spectrum characterized by the presence of Indigenous cultures, for example, Babaçuê, Batuque Paranaense, Candomblé de Caboclo, Catimbó, Jurema, Pajelança, Terecô and Toré de Xangô. At the more Indigenous end of this spectrum of traditions are ritual forms that overlap less with Afro-Brazilian traditions, such as Toré and Ouricuri. There is also a spectrum between "religions" and ritual forms of dance and procession. Congado/Reinado (one of the traditions in polyphonic terreiros in Belo Horizonte) is situated at this blurry boundary. Afro-Brazilian dance/religious traditions include Candombe, Canjerê, Caxambu (Cucumbi), Carimbó, Jongo (Bendenguê), and Suça.

In most Afro-Brazilian religions, initiated participants enter altered states of consciousness, as tradition-specific spirits, entities, forces of nature or deities incorporate in them. ("Incorporation" is a more useful concept than "possession" because it leaves open the issue of agency. It underlines the empirical nature of the question of who, if anyone, is actively driving the process: supranatural entities, mediums or both.) These incorporation trances have tradition-specific characteristics that are learned and embodied over time, in a long process of enculturation.[7] For example, umbandist mediums in training report that they begin to act in new ways in their everyday lives, consistent with the characteristics of particular spirits that they are learning to incorporate.[8]

Candomblé is an Afro-Brazilian religion that has maintained a great degree of continuity with African traditions.[9] It is present in different variants or nations in Brazil: especially west African (e.g., Nagô/Yoruba and Jeje) and central African (e.g., Angola and Congo). It honors a supreme being—Olorum, Zambi, or Olodumaré, depending on the nation—and it cultivates the forces of nature and ancestors, as personified by anthropomorphic deities who coexisted with human beings in Africa. These deities, alongside the divinized ancestors, are called Orishás, Inquices, or Voduns, depending on the nation. In the 2010 census, 0.2 percent of Brazil's population self-identified as *candomblecista*.[10]

Congado or Reinado is an urban, Afro-Brazilian processional tradition derived from lay brotherhoods that began in the early colonial period.[11] Congados have declined in many parts of Brazil but remain strong in the south of Minas Gerais and in parts of the interior of the state of São Paulo. They began with "colonial rosary brotherhood traditions in Minas Gerais in which African- and Brazilian-born slaves and free blacks formed communities, celebrated their saints, and helped one another on to the other world through rituals of death."[12] Each group celebrates an annual multi-day festival, centering on a procession, often to and from the local parish church. A central ritual involves the raising of a "mast" (a pole decorated with the flags of the different participating sub-groups, a practice found in popular processional traditions throughout Brazil). This is the culmination of a year-long series of rituals. Congado is related to local popular celebrations in various parts of (especially southeastern) Brazil, like the "August festivals" in Montes Claros.[13] Unlike the other traditions in the terreiros that we studied, there is no incorporation of spirits in Congado.

Umbanda first appeared in the historical record in the early twentieth century in the large cities of southern Brazil, especially São Paulo and Rio de Janeiro. Its origins are unclear, and it is characterized by fluidity and variability in belief and practices.[14] It invariably incorporates basic theological (or spiritological) ideas from Kardecist spiritism, a European esoteric tradition: in this tradition, all spirits seek spiritual evolution over many reincarnations; the spirits that incorporate during rituals were previously incarnate as humans; they are more spiritually evolved and appear in order to help less developed spirits as an act of charity.[15] However, Umbanda also usually (but not always) incorporates elements drawn from Afro-Brazilian traditions, primarily Candomblé.[16] The two most important types of spirits are *caboclos* (usually Indigenous spirits) and *pretos velhos* ('old black' spirits, usually identifying themselves as former slaves). Exus (a powerful, morally ambivalent, transgressive type of entity) incorporate in some terreiros on a regular basis: for example, once per month, to spiritually cleanse and protect the house. Umbanda's rituals involve the incorporation of spirits who offer religious services to largely non-Umbandist (mostly Catholic and Kardecist) clients. Clients come for advice, medical and spiritual diagnoses, healing rituals, purifying and protecting blessings, and other religious services. Umbanda varies regionally within Brazil and in other ways: from relatively Afro-Brazilian *terreiros* (grounds) to relatively Kardecist *centros* (centers) of "white Umbanda"; from terreiros/centros focused primarily on ritual consultation with spirits to those working with "spiritual surgery" techniques (the latter groups overlapping with "Esoteric Umbanda," which offers various healing rituals drawn from New Age traditions); and from traditional to Neo-Umbanda, the latter characterized by more reflexive and dynamic innovation in basic doctrine.[17] For Renato Ortiz, "If 'Candomblé' and 'Macumba' are African religions, the Spiritism of Umbanda is, on the contrary, a—I would say *the*—national religion of Brazil."[18]

Quimbanda is often seen as "black magic" or as the "left-hand line" associated with Umbanda.[19] Its main characteristic is the moral ambivalence of its spirits, the masculine exus and feminine pombagiras, as well as other morally ambivalent entities such as the *exu-mirins* ("mirim" being a Tupi Guarani word for "little") and *escoras* (protective exu-like entities).[20] Unlike Umbanda, Quimbanda charges for services and magical works that address emotional and sexual problems, remove personal or professional rivals, neutralize spiritual enemies, and ward off magical attacks. Quimbanda's entities can do both good and evil.[21] They are powerful protectors of people and of ritual spaces. Exus are believed to have lived previous incarnations marked by violence (as fighters, police officers, and law-breakers); pombagiras lived as strong, self-confident seductresses, concubines, and prostitutes. Both types of spirits offer their acquired powers in the service of good, helping clients to appreciate the energy of life and to achieve their goals.[22] Their negative impacts are sometimes seen as karmic responses in the lives of affected people, who have themselves transgressed in this or previous lives.[23]

Quimbanda in the north of Minas Gerais is supported in part by outside money. Its magical works are secretly sought by important politicians, business leaders and professionals, even by Evangelical Christians on occasion. Rich and important people from cities outside the region, especially Rio de Janeiro, fly in to pay for *quimbandista* rituals in Montes Claros.

Umbandists often seek to distinguish their religion from Quimbanda by suggesting that their exus are entirely positive, whereas those of Quimbanda are negative. This serves the purpose of positioning themselves in the religious marketplace. The *quimbandista* view differs, of course. As Borges explains:

> Quimbanda, with its pantheon of Exus and elements from the depths, does not represent evil itself but rather defense against it. Ontologically, the Exus are not evil; they know of the good. But it is necessary to work with them in Quimbanda rituals in order for them to acquire discernment and so not to harm human beings.[24]

This marks a key difference between Umbanda and Quimbanda. Umbandists see their spirits as higher, more spiritually evolved, wise, patient, and charitable (marking a closer relation to Kardecism). *Quimbandistas* see their spirits as being "from the street," more ambivalent, more fallible, less predictable. Umbanda's spirits reach down from above to help us. The spirits of Quimbanda are like the mediums and clients who attend

FIGURE 2. Assentamento (ritual seat) of Exu. Roça Ngunzokaiala Mazambi, Montes Claros, Minas Gerais, Brazil. Courtesy of Steven Engler.

their rituals. Given this similarity between Quimbanda's spirits and the people who seek them out, it is not surprising that this tradition is particularly sensitive to local historical and cultural contexts, as we find in the north of Minas Gerais.

## Ritual Polyphony in Afro-Brazilian Terreiros

The terreiros that we studied engage in ritual polyphony. In Belo Horizonte, the religions are Candomblé and Umbanda, sometimes with Congado (one terreiro practices only Umbanda and Congado). In Montes Claros, the religions are Candomblé and Umbanda, often with Quimbanda.

Ritual polyphony in Afro-Brazilian traditions in Minas Gerais seems to reflect three motivating factors. First, religious practitioners and clients see a commonality between the various religions. Crucially, this varies by location. Members in Belo Horizonte emphasize African identity, and those in Montes Claros focus more on the pragmatic outcomes of the services of a particular spiritual entity, Exu. Second, ritual polyphony indexes the expertise and status of leaders: new religions, expanding the palette of ritual services, were added historically as leaders gain more ritual and doctrinal knowledge. Leaders thus earned greater respect in the community. Third, in many cases, there is a perceived progression of spiritual expertise: working with (incorporating) the entities of one tradition serves as preparation and training for working with the entities of another. Mãe C., the leader of a terreiro practicing Candomblé, Umbanda, and Quimbanda in Montes Claros, says,

> I have a lot of respect for Umbanda, because that's where I began. ... [T]here you develop all your Umbanda lines [incorporating usually seven types of spirits] so that in the future you can go to Candomblé already developed. Your mediumship is already well established, and you have no difficulty in becoming [incorporating] your Saint or Inquice [called an *orixá* in Candomblé Nagô]. ... Sometimes, the person who hasn't passed through Umbanda, who comes straight to Candomblé, has a certain difficulty with incorporation. ... Not those who come from Umbanda.[25]

This hierarchy of skill and technique illustrates how the category of ritual polyphony acknowledges a range of perspectives: that of the broader community, of non-initiated members who attend for religious services, of initiated members, and of leaders.

Umbanda is present in all the terreiros we studied in both cities. In the city of Belo Horizonte, the state capital, all but one include Candomblé Angola; and some include, as a second or third tradition, Congado (or Reinado). None of the terreiros in Belo Horizonte include Quimbanda. All but one of the interviewees in Belo Horizonte rejected Quimbanda as an immoral, even demonic, tradition. In Belo Horizonte, acceptable ritual work with the "phalanx of the left" (exus and pombagiras) was reserved for Umbanda. By contrast, in Montes Claros, Quimbanda is the most popular religion and an essential element in the ritual offerings of terreiros that also integrate Umbanda and Candomblé (Angola or Nagô). None of the terreiros in Montes Claros included Congado. Most of the people we talked to in Montes Claros had never heard of it. This reflects the history of that tradition in the south of the state.

In our interviews, we discovered a variety of sometimes overlapping views when we asked people if they saw the different ritual forms that they practiced as one "religion" or two (or three). (1) The various traditions form one religion: "For me, it's one religion"; "Umbanda, Quimbanda and Candomblé form a group, you are automatically connected to all three already." (2) They are aspects encompassed by a higher-level tradition (almost always "Spiritism"): "I tell people I am a Spiritist, which includes all of them." (3) They are functionally equivalent, having "the same energy," or unified by their focus on spiritual training or healing or a basic moral stance of respect: "Umbanda is heart and so is Candomblé. It is the energy of the saint, right?" (4) Only one interviewee used the language of "mixture": "Here it's Umbanda and Candomblé, the mixture right ... due to the death of the mother saint's father was just Umbanda, so when he died, she also joined Candomblé, so that's why we're mixed here. . . ." (5) Some see the traditions in their house as different but still insist on their close relations: "They are different from each other, but it's like they form a group, each complementing the other." (6) A minority see Umbanda is a point of entry, leading on to Candomblé and Quimbanda. (7) Many interviewees see all these traditions as aspects of one, because they all originate in West Africa: "the three religions . . . have the same starting point, right, Bantu people. I don't believe that they are different if they can stay united, without one running over another. [This is] is a sign that they have a common point." This variety of ways of perceiving what is related and how—one tradition, multiple religions, overlapping spiritualities, etc.—underlines the value of the concept of ritual polyphony. "Polyphony" implies harmonization between different lines, and the lines here are not just different religions, traditions or ritual forms but also between practitioners' ways of seeing these as related to each other. The nature of the multiplicity is framed in different ways, but a core focus on practice and a sense of unity amidst difference remain.

At the same time, our fieldwork revealed one especially prominent difference between the two cities. A common theme among members of multi-ritual houses in Belo Horizonte is that the traditions present in those houses—Umbanda, alongside Candomblé Angola and/or Congado/Reinado—are unified in their Africanness. All our interviewees pointed to prejudice against African cultures in the city, especially on the part of the evangelical community. In sum, a key factor leading to perceptions of unity among these traditions in Belo Horizonte is their status as marginalized, oppressed, and rejected—sometimes in ways that include violence against ritual spaces and artifacts. The various religions, beyond their intrinsic similarities, are unified by their racist objectification under the biased gaze of others.

The case in Montes Claros is different. Prejudice against Afro-Brazilian traditions is certainly present, as some interviewees emphasize. However, the factor that most leads people to underline the unity of the traditions present there—Umbanda,

Candomblé (Angola or Nagô), and Quimbanda—is their common "energy." This is rooted in the presence of the Exu spirit in all three, and it reflects an emphasis on pragmatic results. All but one of the interviewees in Belo Horizonte dismiss Quimbanda as "dark," "black magic," and unacceptable. All interviewees in Montes Claros see it as a valuable Afro-Brazilian tradition, above all due to the worldly benefits that it provides.

## Magic in the Sertão

The Afro-Brazilian terreiros of the north of Minas Gerais are Afro-sertanejo, reflecting this historical and geographical context, with an emphasis on magic and its pragmatic results.[26] Exu characterizes the Afro-sertanejo universe, providing coherence in its ritually polyphonic religious continuum. Exus and pombagiras *sertanejos* offer human beings the freedom to transform their lives through magic.

In the northern part of the state of Minas Gerais, Quimbanda's magical-religious rituals are more popular than Candomblé and Umbanda. The appeal of Quimbanda's pragmatic and therapeutic services sustains Afro-religious traditions in a region characterized by ritual polyphony. This region is one of few in Brazil—along with, for example, the interior of the state of Ceará—where Quimbanda is prominent and popularly accepted. Historical, geographical, and cultural factors have led to a resonance between the people of this region of Brazil and Quimbanda's pragmatic ritual focus. This region—poor and neglected by governments—has always valued the practical benefits of magic.

This is not unique to this region of Brazil, but the north of Minas Gerais had and has a unique geographic situation: it is exiled in the backlands, yet it sits between and is influenced at a distance by the two great poles of Afro-Brazilian culture and religion in Brazil, Bahia and Rio de Janeiro. The north of Minas Gerais lies to the south of the state of Bahia, traditionally considered the heartland of Brazilian Candomblé, and to the north of the large southeast cities of Rio de Janeiro and São Paulo, where Umbanda developed and grew, reflecting processes of urbanization.[27] The formation of Afro-Brazilian traditions, especially Umbanda, in this part of the dry interior followed the line of settlement: traditions from the northeast and southeast met in the regional center of Montes Claros, before moving out to smaller communities.[28]

Crucial factors in the regional culture, and in the importance of Quimbanda, are the concepts of *sertão* (the dry "backlands" in the interior of Brazil's northeast, including the northern part of Minas Gerais) and *sertanejo* (the adjective describing the plants, people, and culture of this challenging landscape). Euclides da Cunha, in *Os Sertões*, his classic study of the millenarian movement of Canudos, described the region this way:

> At the height of the droughts they are most certainly a desert, but when these do not reach the point of bringing on a painful exodus, men, like the trees, struggle along with the reserves stored up during the times of plenty and in that fierce, nameless, terrible dark battle, engulfed in the solitude of the flats, [they] are not completely abandoned by nature. She takes care of them for quite a time beyond the desperate hours when the last waterholes have dried up. With the coming of the rains, the land . . . is transformed. . . . Dry gullies become rivers. The once bald hillocks stand out in a sudden green color. . . . Without the intense heat of the sun, the abnormal dryness of the air is no more. . . . The backlands have become a fertile valley. They are a vast orchard that has no owner. And then all this comes to an end. The time of torture returns.[29]

Ambiguity and ambivalence characterized this region, which remained outside the modern European project during the Portuguese colonial period. Far from the coast and devoid of riches, the northern backlands became a space of freedom for those who sought to avoid the eyes of power. This led to a relatively unconstrained society based on the logic of opposites, arid as the soil of the dry *caatinga* area and solitary as the more fertile *cerrado*, with moments of fluorescence and festival. These comments are not an attempt to reduce religion to a reflex of climate and geography, nor are they a romanticized celebration of *sertaneja* culture. *Sertanejo* freedom, with its marginal status, was not a conquest: it is a contingent historical construction shaped by the requisites of survival, in the absence of effective governmental structures.

By developing independent economic practices—primarily mining and agriculture—the *sertanejos* constituted territories under the command of rural potentates: strong men and "colonels" ruled over a social order founded on the tension between local patron-client solidarity and moments of harsh violence.[30] Seditious movements were repressed by the Portuguese state, and the *sertão* was decreed a forbidden zone. Isolation, now official, accentuated freedom and contributed to the permanence of a *sertaneja* order based on tensions between good and evil, violence and solidarity. João Guimarães Rosa, in his experimental modernist classic, *Grande Sertão: Veredas*, captured the resulting culture: "*Sertão* is where the strong are in charge, with their schemes."[31] *Sertão* is "penal, criminal"; it is "where a man has to have a stiff neck and a square hand"; it is "the loner" and is "inside of us." "The *sertão*," Guimarães Rosa adds, "made me, swallowed me, and spit me out of its hot mouth."[32]

Religion and magic played central roles in *sertaneja* culture. The arrival of enslaved Africans in the seventeenth century further contributed to this development. Misfortunes and failures were attributed to the actions of dark magic. Magic became a powerful tool for gaining pragmatic results in a society with little formal order:

> Violence in the *sertão* was not limited to the use of weapons. It extended to magic and spells, a disguised and hidden form of violence. Spells manifest cunning, the ability to influence behavior by invisible means... with the intention of obtaining practical and material results. Magic is symbolic violence.... Its power is psychological, acting on the unconscious, ... which, consequently, acts on the consciousness, in the way one perceives and acts in the world.[33]

Catholicism's vision of a contrast between God and the devil resonated strongly: "We [*sertanejos*] come from hell, all of us.... From a lower place, so monstrous and dreadful that Christ himself could only send down in a glance his illustrious sustaining grace, there in the darkness of the Third Day's eve."[34] Magic emerged as a middle path in the *sertão*, a winding track that sticks closer to the harsh landscape than God's righteous way or the devil's deviation.

Popular magical traditions go back centuries in the region. Umbanda and Quimbanda arrived only in the late 1940s and Candomblé in the 1950s.[35] Historical, geographical, and cultural factors provided conditions that help us understand why ritual polyphony in the north of Minas Gerais emphasizes pragmatic, magical benefits, centering on the figure of Exu. In recent decades, a continuum has been established: Umbanda, Quimbanda, and Candomblé in the region have formed a ritual polyphony that centers on a particular type of *exu*.

FIGURE 3: Image of Exu Zé Pilintra. Associated with the pombagira Maria Padilha, this Exu heads the line of *malandros*—embodying craftiness, roguish charm, and trickery—in Quimbanda and Umbanda. A distinct figure, "Master" Zé Pilintra, is important in the healing traditions of Catimbó and Jurema. Roça Ngunzokaiala Mazambi, Montes Claros, Minas Gerais, Brazil. Courtesy of Steven Engler.

## Quimbanda Sertaneja, Exu Sertanejo

Quimbanda stands out in Montes Claros and the surrounding region, but it bears a close relation to Umbanda and Candomblé. Exu serves as a common theme in all these traditions. The primary assistant-leader in a terreiro in Montes Claros says,

> Each [tradition] has its own particularities ... but they all are connected.... From the moment you are initiated into Candomblé, you need the Exus. They are the Quimbanda entities who will clear your way for you to have a good harvest.... You need *caboclos* [Indigenous Umbanda spirits] to place protection around your house, to give good energies in the house. So everything is connected, everything is connected to Olodùmare [the supreme deity in Candomblé].

As this religious leader notes, ritual polyphony in Montes Claros is based on more than participation in distinct religions: it reflects the presence of the same entities across these traditions in the context of practice. Ritual distinctions between the traditions are preserved, but the ability to work with entities that are "from" or "originate in" a given tradition stays with practitioners as they develop their mediumship in other traditions. The same entities appear in different traditions, or not, with differences in how they are conceived. For example, the roles of exus and caboclos differ: in Umbanda and Quimbanda, they attend to people, and in Candomblé, they "open the path" for those moving toward initiation, and they protect the house. But exus and related entities provide a form of continuity linked to ritual services and pragmatic benefits. The lines between traditions are both preserved and blurred, and practitioners have different perspectives on just how this is the case—another dimension of polyphony.

Exu is central to understanding the place of Quimbanda in the *sertão*. This requires moving past a generic Afro-Brazilian to an Afro-Sertanejo cosmology. Brazilian and *sertanejo* contexts have given the figure of Exu a degree of hybridity that makes it open to constant resignification. In the north of Minas Gerais, Exu has become Exu Sertanejo:

> In Quimbanda Sertaneja, there is a pantheon of Exus Sertanejos. ... There are the Exus Sertanejos who live in the depths of the earth, in cemeteries, in the bush, in fire, in the wind, in storms, in swamps, in mud, in garbage and in the crossroads. The Exus Sertanejos, according to Quimbanda Sertaneja, are beings in evolution. They leave the infernal world of darkness and torment and come to the light. In Quimbanda Sertaneja, there are still Exu Sertanejos who live in twilight, neither darkness nor light. The Exus Sertanejos ... are those of the Lucifer, Maioral, Caifaz, Satan and Beelzebub lines, classified as kings that command Quimbanda Sertaneja. It is understood in this ritual context that some types of Exus are spirits of people who lived here on earth, but who did not follow the laws or moral behaviors of their time, like corrupt people or bandits. On the other hand, the Exu Kings or Maioral appear. They are angels expelled from God's army—Catholic, according to the adepts.[36]

The difference we found between negative views of Quimbanda in Belo Horizonte and positive views of Quimbanda Sertaneja in Montes Claros reflects differing views of Exu. A member of a terreiro in Belo Horizonte told us, "For me,

Quimbanda is like a mixture of Candomblé and Umbanda. I prefer to stay with Umbanda and not mess with Quimbanda . . . because . . . I saw things that made me think that the religion was not for me. . . . I saw things that I did not like." The difference in feeling is widely recognized, but the valuation of that difference varies. A member of a terreiro in Montes Claros said,

> Umbanda . . . let's simplify, is that soft part . . . You leave with that feeling of inner peace and greater calm. . . . But Quimbanda is heavier, because of Exu and Pombagira. Depending on the line [of spirits] that we work with, sometimes we get very tired. It takes a lot of energy out of us, you know? So, as we have an *escora* [a protective entity] to stand in front for us. It comes and makes us calmer.

In the context of ritual polyphony, exus and pombagiras come to be situated hierarchically in relation to the entities of Candomblé and Umbanda. This reflects a hierarchy of spiritual authority and evolution among the entities themselves, as expressed by a religious leader in Montes Claros:

> Mediums have a spiritual current, below the orishas. . . . Below the orishas, the most important entity is the [Umbanda spirit] Preto Velho, who is directly connected to the orixá. Below the Preto Velho we find the Caboclo, the Cowboys [both Umbanda spirits], Ogum [a Candomblé orisha] and Cosmas and Damion [Catholic saints prominent in the of Umbanda that works with "Children" spirits], and these are the Angola Boys. Then below that come the Exús and Pombagiras and whatever comes at the end.

This hierarchy also reflects the relative positioning of human beings in relation to these entities, as expressed by a Pai de Santo (leader) of a tri-tradition terreiro in Montes Claros:

> When you talk about this Exu line, many people are prejudiced, because for many it is a backward line, a line of perversity. But it's a line! These are spirits like any others, right? I came to understand this only through great difficulty, because my first

encounter was not good. But as we live alongside each other, as we live these moments together, we have to understand that they are spirits. Of course, they have a little lesser light, let's say. Exu is actually the spirit closest to people, because Exu feels all human needs! Think for example of an Exu smoking, drinking, wearing luxurious clothes..., he is already expressing human characteristics.

Within its polyphonic context, Quimbanda is sometimes seen as requiring a separate location within the house. This again reflects the nature of Exu. As a Quimbanda Sertaneja leader says,

The same space that we use for Umbanda, we use for Candomblé as well. But Quimbanda needs another space.... We know of Quimbanda as the left-hand line, the line of Exu! It stands, let's say, in *aversion* to Umbanda. There are practices in Quimbanda that Umbanda rejects! Candomblé, in its own way, also reproves these. Elements used in these rituals ... are aggressive to these other two energies.

Quimbanda Sertaneja has many ritual variations. Some sessions—especially those celebrating key dates in the ritual calendar—are open to the public. Anyone can consult with the Exus and Pombagiras. Alcohol, music, dance, and laughter create a relaxed and joyful environment, where themes of debauchery and social transgression are expressed in songs and chants. A popular chant says, "I drink because I have a head. I only go home when the cabaret closes. I drink, because I have sense. It's my money, and nobody has anything to do with it." More often, the rituals of Quimbanda Sertaneja are restricted to members of the terreiros and have specific purposes, including protecting and cleansing the house and providing services to individual clients. The greater frequency of these rituals underlines their pragmatic value.

Exu is willing to enter into a relationship with those who cry out for help. Exu Sertanejo locates adepts in the *sertão*, where, in the words of a ritual chant, "The doctor trained in the crossroads carries on working. He works to help. He has a happy life, working and enjoying the good things in life." But Exu, when not respected, can turn solidarity to violence. This is a common theme in Afro-Brazilian—as in

FIGURE 4. Quimbanda shrines, placed at the front of the *terreiro*, in a protecting position near the street entrance. Rituals of Candomblé and Angola are performed in a separate space at the back of the *terreiro*. Roça Ngunzokaiala Mazambi, Montes Claros, Minas Gerais, Brazil. Image courtesy of Steven Engler.

many other—religions: "The basis of African sects [in Brazil] is faith. Faith in the all-powerful orishas, in the supernatural sanctions that punish those who violate taboos, a faith grounded on the thousands of cases and stories of the children of the gods who were punished for their disobedience."[37] The connection between Exu and those who attend *quimbandista* rituals is less a formal pact than a flexible relation of patron-client solidarity.

The elements that make up Afro-Brazilian rituals—gestures, dance, rhythms, and words—are not simply repetitions of the deeds of the deities; they are expressions of everyday life. The songs of Quimbanda Sertaneja reflect and shape the daily life of *sertanejos*, how they perceive and react to the obstacles they face. Those who attend the rituals of Quimbanda Sertaneja seek help in living trouble-free, and they believe that the transgressive nature of Quimbanda, with its relation to magic, will assist in this. They desire defense and the promise of support; they find this in a guardian capable of warding off conflicts and traps, and who can open paths for professional and personal success. Respect for Exu Sertanejo symbolizes and addresses these goals. As Exu proclaims, in a popular chant:

> I unroll, unknot, unroll everything. When I get to the trouble/crossroads (*encruza*) I unroll everything. Exu is no joke, no game. He ties a safe knot. He uncovers the blow that threatens. Seek him out if a hot coal burns you, because Saint Anthony is greatest! Pay attention, *cambones* [ritual assistants]! Exu is going to walk!

In sum, the historical, geographical, political, economic, and cultural context of the north of Minas Gerais helped foster an emphasis on magic and worldly benefits. This in turn led to the growing importance of the figure of Exu Sertanejo. This pragmatically oriented power of this regional variant of the Exu entity provides the unifying focus for the ritually polyphonic Afro-Brazilian traditions of the region. Exu—seen as threatening, dangerous, immoral, and even demonic throughout most of Brazil—has come to be seen here as positive. Its ambiguity and transgression resonate with regional cultural history and with the lived experience of religious practitioners.

## Conclusion

The divergence we found in views of ritual polyphony, especially in terms of relations between the different traditions, has two main takeaways. On the one hand, the concept of "religion" is of little help. Regardless of whether members accept this academic category—that their terreiro practices different "religions"—they all agree that there are multiple and distinct *somethings* taking place at different times: traditions, ritual forms, types of entities, or modes of energy or spirituality. The multiplicity that is ritual polyphony remains, regardless of the fact that the constituent things are labeled in different ways, with relations between them seen in a variety of manners.

On the other hand, members' kaleidoscopic views of ritual polyphony underline the importance of specific contexts. In ritually polyphonic groups, we can find sharp distinctions between the ritual forms in terms of when and how they are practiced: days and times, artifacts and clothing, entities and discourses about these, subjective perceptions of the incorporation of entity types, and so on. These tend to be the sorts of things that, as scholars of religion/s, we prioritize in our analyses. But it turns out that other issues, those about which members diverge in their views, are more important for understanding how and why ritual polyphony comes about and continues to be so prominent in parts of Brazil. What matters is not, for example, similarities in ritual form between Umbanda ritually polyphonic and monophonic groups. What matters are factors that vary between terreiros and between the members of each, all *within* the ritually polyphonic context: the social dynamic of the growing status of founders and leaders; the provision of ritual services (offered and appropriated in a multitude of ways); varying perceptions of spiritual growth and evolution; divergent views of disease and healing; different accounts of relations to Africa; and changing relations between distinct entity types. Ritual polyphony offers a larger tent within which members' volatile views find common grounds.

At a more general level, the differences we found between terreiros in Belo Horizonte and Montes Claros—especially in attitudes to Quimbanda and its central entity, Exu—underline the contextualized and relative nature of ritual polyphony. Ritual polyphony points to unity in difference, but the natures of the unity and the difference are not built into the concept. This is one of the many things that fieldwork slowly reveals. The polyphonic nature of what we found, as we talked to practitioners in Minas Gerais, extends to almost every aspect of our conceptual work. Generalizations are valuable, but a chorus of member voices offers multiple perspectives at each step. This is the most interesting result of our conversations and our own participation in rituals. It has the potential to destabilize many of our assumptions about "religions" and the boundaries between them.

## Notes

1. This chapter is part of a joint project by the four authors, with Steven Engler as lead researcher. The project, Ritual Polyphony in Afro-Brazilian Religions, was supported by an Explore grant from the Social Science and Humanities Research Council of Canada and an International Collaboration grant from the American Academy of Religion. Ethics approval was granted by HRC processes at both Mount Royal University (Calgary) and the Pontifícia Universidade Católica de Minas Gerais (Belo Horizonte). All translations are by Steven Engler, except where noted. Thanks to the book's reviewers and editors for valuable comments.

2. Christina Borges et. al., "Ritual Polyphany in Afro-Brazilian Religions: A Report on Research in Progress," 2020; Steven Engler, "Umbanda and Hybridity," *Numen* 56, no. 5 (2009): 545–77; Steven Engler, "Feijoada as a Concept of Cultural/Religious Mixture," *Religion* 52, no. 1 (2022a): 25–47; Steven Engler, "Grounded Theory," in *Routledge Handbook of Research Methods in the Study of Religion*, edited by Steven Engler and Michael Stausberg (London and New York: Routledge, 2022b), 300–313; Steven Engler, "Umbanda: Hybridity, Tradition and Semantic Plurality," *Interdisciplinary Journal for Religion and Transformation in Contemporary Society* (forthcoming). Roger Bastide, *Les religions africaines au Brésil: vers une sociologie des interpretations des civilisations* (Paris: Presses Universitaires de France, 1995 [1960]), 305, 362, 380, 419; Stephen D. Glazier, "Syncretism and Separation: Ritual Change in an Afro-Caribbean Faith," *The Journal of American Folklore* 98, no. 38 (1985): 49–62.
3. Marc Gidal, *Spirit Song: Afro-Brazilian Religious Music and Boundaries* (New York: Oxford University Press, 2016), 33–39.
4. "Incorporate entities" refers to practices sometimes referred to as possession, channeling, or otherwise bringing or receiving spirits into one's physical presence.
5. Tromboni, "A Jurema," 98–99; Santos, *O dono da terra*; Tall, *O papel do caboclo*; Engler, "Umbanda: Hybridity," 326–28.
6. Francisco van der Poel, *Dicionário da religiosidade popular: cultura e religião no Brasil* (Curitiba: Editora Nossa Cultura, 2013); Engler and Brito Ênio, "Afro-Brazilian and Indigenous-Influenced Religions," in *Handbook of Contemporary Religions in Brazil*, edited by Bettina E. Schmidt and Steven Engler, (Leiden and Boston: Brill, 2016), 142–69.
7. Arnaud Halloy, *Divinités incarnés: l'apprentissage de la possession dans un culte afro-brésilien* (Paris: Editions Petra, 2015).
8. Alexandre F.S. Kaitel, *Não chuta que é macumba: processos de subjetivação em médiuns desenvolventes na Umbanda*, Ph.D. diss., (Pontifícia Universidade Católica de Minas Gerais, 2019), 212.
9. Vagner Gonçalves da Silva and Fernando Giobellina Brumana, "Candomblé: Religion, World Vision and Experience," in *Handbook of Contemporary Religions in Brazil*, edited by Bettina E. Schmidt and Steven Engler (Leiden and Boston: Brill, 2016), 170–85.
10. Reginaldo Prandi, "As religiões afro-brazileiros em ascensão e declínio," in *Religiões em movimento: o censo de 2010*, edited by Faustino Teixeira and Renata Menezes (Petrópolis: Editora Vozes, 2013), 203–218.

11. Elizabeth W. Kiddy, *Blacks of the Rosary: Memory and History in Minas Gerais, Brazil* (University Park, PA: University of Pennsylvania Press, 2005); Poel, *Dicionário da religiosidade popular: cultura e religião no Brasil* (Curitiba: Editora Nossa Cultura, 2013), 241–3; Rubens Alves da Silva, *Negros católicos ou Catolicismo negro: um estudo sobre a construção da identidade negra no congado mineiro* (Belo Horizonte: Nandyala, 2010).
12. Kiddy, *Blacks of the Rosary*, 4.
13. Denilson Meireles Barbosa, "Religiosidade, festa e devoção no sertão do São Francisco," in *Sertão: tradição, cultura e poder*, edited by Carla Cristina Barbosa and Cesar Henrique de Queiroz Porto (Montes Claros: Editora Unimontes, 2018), 225–50.
14. Engler, "Esoteric Umbanda."
15. Engler, "Umbanda: Africana or Esoteric?" *Open Library of Humanities* 6, no. 1, (2020): 1–36.
16. Engler, "Umbanda and Hybridity"; Engler, "Umbanda," in *Handbook of Contemporary Religions in Brazil*, edited by Bettina E. Schmidt and Steven Engler (Leiden and Boston: Brill, 2016), 204–24.
17. Engler, "Umbanda," in *Handbook of Contemporary Religions in Brazil*; Engler, "Umbanda: Hybridity, Tradition and Semantic Plurality"; Lindsay L. Hale, *Hearing the Mermaid's Song: The Umbanda Religion in Rio de Janeiro* (Albuquerque: University of New Mexico Press, 2009); Diana Espírito Santo. *Fluid Spirits: Cosmology and Change in Contemporary Brazilian Umbanda.* (Pompano Beach, FL: Caribbean Studies Press, 2018).
18. Renato Ortiz, "A morte branca do feiticeiro negro," *Religião e Sociedade* 1 (1977): 43; Maria Helena Villas Bôas Concone, *Umbanda: uma religião brasileira* (São Paulo: Editora FFLCH/USP-CE, 1987).
19. Ortiz, "Umbanda, magie blanche. Quimbanda, magie noire," *Archives de sciences sociales des religions*, 47, no.1 (1979): 135–46; David J. Hess, "Umbanda and Quimbanda Magic in Brazil: Rethinking Aspects of Bastide's Work," *Archives de Sciences Sociales des Religions* 37, no. 79 (1992): 135–53.
20. Vagner Gonçalves da Silva, *Exu: o guardião da casa do futuro* (Rio de Janeiro: Pallas, 2015).
21. Sonia R.C. Lages, *Exu: luz e sombras: um estudo psico-junguiano da linha de Exu na Umbanda* (Juiz de Fora: Clio Edições Eletrônicas, 2003).
22. Alexandre Kaitel and Guaraci M. Dos Santos, "Conhecendo a Umbanda: uma tipologia sob o prisma Bantu," *Diversidade Religiosa* 7 (2017): 60–87.
23. Matta E Silva, Woodrow Wilson da, *Umbanda de todos nós* (São Paulo: Ícone, 2009), 318.

24. Cristina Borges, *Umbanda, Quimbanda e Candomblé: tensão moral produtora do novo religioso*. In *Sociabilidades religiosas: mitos, ritos e identidades* (Goiânia: Associação Brasileira de História das Religiões, XI Simpósio Nacional Da Associação Brasileira de História das Religiões, 2009), 3.
25. Cited in Engler, "Grounded Theory," 303.
26. João Batista de Almeida Costa, "O ser da sociedade sertaneja e a invisibilização do negro no sertão norte dos gerais," in *Cerrado e Desenvolvimento: Tradição e Atualidade*, edited by Claudia Luz and Carlos Dayrell (Montes Claros: Editora Unimontes. 2000) 107–140; Borges, "Umbanda, Quimbanda e Candomblé: tensão moral produtora do novo religioso" in *Sociabilidades religiosas: mitos, ritos e identidades* (Goiânia: Associação Brasileira de História das Religiões, XI Simpósio Nacional Da Associação Brasileira de História das Religiões, 2009).
27. Diana Brown, *Umbanda: Religion and Politics in Urban Brazil* (New York: Columbia University Press, 1994 [1986]); Lísias Nogueira Negrão, *Entre a cruz e a encruzilhada: formação do campo umbandista em São Paulo* (São Paulo: Edusp, 1996).
28. Borges, *Umbanda Sertaneja: cultura e religiosidade no norte de Minas Gerais* (Montes Claros: Editora Unimontes, 2011).
29. Euclides da Cunha. 2010 [1902]. *Backlands: the Canudos Campaign*. London: Penguin, Ch. 1, §5.
30. Carla Maria Junho Anastasia, *A geografia do crime: violência nas minas setecentistas* (Belo Horizonte: Editora UFMG, 2005), 69; Alysson Luiz Freitas de Jesus, *No sertão das Minas. escravidão, violência e liberdade (1830–1888)* (São Paulo: Annablume, 2007).
31. João Guimarães Rosa, *Grande Sertão: Veredas*, 22nd ed. (Rio de Janeiro: Campanhia das Letras, 2019 [1956]), 21.
32. Guimarães Rosa, *Grande* Sertão, 113, 315, 593, 793.
33. Admilson Eustáquio Prates, *Exu, a esfera metamórfica* (Montes Claros: Editora Unimontes, 2010) 41–42; Carla Maria Junho Anastasia,. *A geografia do crime: violência nas minas setecentistas* (Belo Horizonte: Editora UFMG, 2005).
34. João Guimarães Rosa, *Grande Sertão: Veredas*, 22nd ed. (Rio de Janeiro: Campanhia das Letras, 2019 [1956]).
35. Borges, *Umbanda Sertaneja: cultura e religiosidade no norte de Minas Gerais* (Montes Claros: Editora Unimontes, 2011); Anderson Marinho Maia and Amauri Carlos Ferreira, "A Umbanda na região metropolitana de Belo Horizonte: tradição e contemporaneidade," *Ciencias Sociales y Religión/ Ciências Sociais e Religião* 21 (2019): 1–21.

36. Prates, *Exu, a esfera metamórfica* (Montes Claros: Editora Unimontes, 2010), 104.
37. Bastide, *Les religions africaines au Brésil: vers une sociologie des interpretations des civilisations* (Paris: Presses Universitaires de France, 1995 [1960]), 310.

## References

Anastasia, Carla Maria Junho. *A geografia do crime: violência nas minas setecentistas.* Belo Horizonte: Editora UFMG, 2005.

Barbosa, Denilson Meireles. "Religiosidade, festa e devoção no sertão do São Francisco." In *Sertão: tradição, cultura e poder,* edited by Carla Cristina Barbosa and Cesar Henrique de Queiroz Porto, 225–50. Montes Claros: Editora Unimontes, 2018.

Bastide, Roger. *Les religions africaines au Brésil: vers une sociologie des interpretations des civilisations.* Paris: Presses Universitaires de France, 1995.

Borges, Cristina. "Umbanda, Quimbanda e Candomblé: tensão moral produtora do novo religioso." In *Sociabilidades religiosas: mitos, ritos e identidades. XI Simpósio Nacional Da Associação Brasileira de História das Religiões.* Goiânia: Associação Brasileira de História das Religiões, 2009.

Borges, Cristina. *Umbanda Sertaneja: cultura e religiosidade no norte de Minas Gerais.* Montes Claros: Editora Unimontes, 2011.

Borges, Cristina, Guaraci M. Dos Santos, Alexandre F.S. Kaitel, and Steven Engler. "Ritual Polyphony in Afro-Brazilian Religions: A Report on Research in Progress." Paper presented at the annual conference of the *American Academy of Religion,* 2020.

Brown, Diana. *Umbanda: Religion and Politics in Urban Brazil.* New York: Columbia University Press, 1994.

Concone, Maria Helena Villas Bôas. *Umbanda: uma religião brasileira.* São Paulo: Editora FFLCH/USP-CE, 1987.

Costa, João Batista de Almeida. "O ser da sociedade sertaneja e a invisibilização do negro no sertão norte dos gerais." In *Cerrado e Desenvolvimento: Tradição e Atualidade,* edited by Claudia Luz and Carlos Dayrell, 107–40. Montes Claros: Editora Unimontes, 2000.

da Cunha, Euclides. *Backlands: the Canudos Campaign.* Translated by Elizabeth Lowe. London: Penguin. E-book, 2010.

Engler, Steven. "Umbanda and Hybridity." *Numen* 56, no. 5 (2009): 545–77.

Engler, Steven. "Umbanda." In *Handbook of Contemporary Religions in Brazil*, edited by Bettina E. Schmidt and Steven Engler, 204–24. Leiden and Boston: Brill, 2016.

Engler, Steven. "Umbanda: Africana or Esoteric?" *Open Library of Humanities* 6, no. 1 (2020): 1–36.

Engler, Steven,. "*Feijoada* as a Concept of Cultural/Religious Mixture." *Religion* 52, no. 1 (2022a): 25–47.

Engler, Steven. "Grounded Theory." In *The Routledge Handbook of Research Methods in the Study of Religion*, edited by Steven Engler and Michael Stausberg, 300–13. London and New York: Routledge, 2022b.

Engler, Steven. "Umbanda: Hybridity, Tradition and Semantic Plurality." *Interdisciplinary Journal for Religion and Transformation in Contemporary Society* 9, no. 2 (2022): 311–34.

Engler, Steven. "Umbanda." In *Brill Dictionary of Contemporary Esotericism*, edited by Egil Asprem. Leiden and Boston: Brill, forthcoming.

Engler, Steven, and Ênio Brito. "Afro-Brazilian and Indigenous-Influenced Religions." In *Handbook of Contemporary Religions in Brazil*, edited by Bettina E. Schmidt and Steven Engler, 142–69. Leiden and Boston: Brill, 2016.

Espírito Santo, Diana. *Fluid Spirits: Cosmology and Change in Contemporary Brazilian Umbanda*. Pompano Beach, FL: Caribbean Studies Press, 2018.

Gidal, Marc. *Spirit Song: Afro-Brazilian Religious Music and Boundaries*. New York: Oxford University Press, 2016.

Glazier, Stephen D. "Syncretism and Separation: Ritual Change in an Afro-Caribbean Faith." *The Journal of American Folklore* 98, no. 38 (1985): 49–62.

Guimarães Rosa, João. *Grande Sertão: Veredas*, 22nd ed. Rio de Janeiro: Campanhia das Letras, 2019.

Hale, Lindsay L. *Hearing the Mermaid's Song: The Umbanda Religion in Rio de Janeiro*. Albuquerque: University of New Mexico Press, 2009.

Halloy, Arnaud. *Divinités incarnés: l'apprentissage de la possession dans un culte afro-brésilien*. Paris: Editions Petra, 2015.

Hess, David J. "Umbanda and Quimbanda Magic in Brazil: Rethinking Aspects of Bastide's Work." *Archives de Sciences Sociales des Religions* 37, no. 79 (1992): 135–53.

Jesus, Alysson Luiz Freitas de. *No sertão das Minas: escravidão, violência e liberdade (1830–1888)*. São Paulo: Annablume, 2007.

Kaitel, Alexandre F.S. "Não chuta que é macumba: processos de subjetivação em médiuns desenvolventes na Umbanda." Ph.D. diss., Pontifícia Universidade Católica de Minas Gerais, 2019.

Kaitel, Alexandre and Guaraci M. Dos Santos. "Conhecendo a Umbanda: uma tipologia sob o prisma Bantu." *Diversidade Religiosa* 7 (2017): 60–87.

Kiddy, Elizabeth W. *Blacks of the Rosary: Memory and History in Minas Gerais, Brazil*. University Park, PA: University of Pennsylvania Press, 2005.

Lages, Sonia R.C. *Exu: luz e sombras: um estudo psico-junguiano da linha de Exu na Umbanda*. Juiz de Fora: Clio Edições Eletrônicas, 2003.

Maia, Anderson Marinho, and Amauri Carlos Ferreira. "A Umbanda na região metropolitana de Belo Horizonte: tradição e contemporaneidade." *Ciencias Sociales y Religión/ Ciências Sociais e Religião* 21 (2019): 1–21.

Negrão, Lísias Nogueira. *Entre a cruz e a encruzilhada: formação do campo umbandista em São Paulo*. São Paulo: Edusp, 1996.

Matta E. Silva, Woodrow Wilson da. *Umbanda de todos nós*. São Paulo: Ícone, 1974.

Ortiz, Renato. "A morte branca do feiticeiro negro." *Religião e Sociedade* 1, no. 1 (1977): 43–50.

Ortiz, Renato. "Umbanda, magie blanche. Quimbanda, magie noire." *Archives de sciences sociales des religions* 47, no. 1 (1979): 135–46.

Prandi, Reginaldo. "As religiões afro-brasileiros em ascensão e declínio." In *Religiões em movimento: o censo de 2010*, edited by Faustino Teixeira and Renata Menezes, 203–18. Petrópolis: Editora Vozes, 2013.

Prates, Admilson Eustáquio. *Exu, a esfera metamórfica*. Montes Claros: Editora Unimontes, 2010.

Santos, Jocélio Teles dos. *O dono da terra: o caboclo nos Candomblés da Bahia*. Salvador: Editora Sarah Letras. 1995.

Silva, Rubens Alves da. *Negros católicos ou Catolicismo negro: um estudo sobre a construção da identidade negra no congado mineiro*. Belo Horizonte: Nandyala, 2010.

Silva, Vagner Gonçalves da. *Exu: o guardião da casa do futuro*. Rio de Janeiro: Pallas, 2015.

Silva, Vagner Gonçalves da, and Fernando Giobellina Brumana. "Candomblé: Religion, World Vision and Experience." In *Handbook of Contemporary Religions in Brazil*, edited by Bettina E. Schmidt and Steven Engler, 170–85. Leiden and Boston: Brill, 2016.

Tall, Emmanuelle Kadya.. "O papel do caboclo no Candomblé baiano." In *Índios e caboclos: a história recontada*, edited by Maria Rosário de Carvalho and Ana Magda Carvalho, 79–93. Salvador, BA: EDUFBA, 2012.

Tromboni, Marco. "A Jurema das ramas até o tronco: ensaio sobre algumas categorias de classificação religiosa." In *Índios e caboclos: a história recontada*, edited by Maria Rosário de Carvalho and Ana Magda Carvalho, 95–125. Salvador, BA: EDUFBA, 2012.

van der Poel, Francisco. *Dicionário da religiosidade popular: cultura e religião no Brasil.* Curitiba: Editora Nossa Cultura, 2013.

CHAPTER 3

# Playful Masculinity

## Labor, Relaxation, and Gender Formation in Loíza's Las Fiestas de Santiago Apóstol

ALEJANDRO S. ESCALANTE

"Just come by and enjoy!" María said with a big smile.[1] Partway through my conversation with Padre Barranca of La Parroquia Santiago Apóstol in Loíza, Puerto Rico, María walked up to us to chat with Barranca about the ongoing preparations for the festivities in honor of Santiago. When she approached, she did not initially say anything but instead seemingly waited for a lull in the conversation so she could speak to Barranca for a moment. I turned to her and stopped talking, thinking she needed something more urgently from Barranca than me; however, she did not say anything but instead redirected me back to the parish priest, using her lips to point. "Don't worry," she said. "*No se preocupe*," addressing me formally. She was holding a massive yellow Styrofoam tray, the kind that comes with pre-packaged meat from grocery stores. She smiled and nodded along as Barranca and I spoke, her hands shiny and dyed a burnt orange from working with *sazón*, a staple seasoning now made with artificial food coloring.

This was my first conversation with Barranca after introducing myself over email and being introduced earlier by my aunt, Mónica. Not wanting to take too much of his time, I intended this conversation to be informal and brief, but as so often happened in Loíza, time slowed down, and our conversation unfolded in new ways. By this point, my introduction turned into a conversation about the history of Loíza, of Santiago, and the schedule of events and festivities to be held in his honor. One of the events caught my attention, and I asked for further details. He paused, narrowed his eyes, and tried to remember. A lull. María found her opportunity: "Come by tomorrow! We are going to be cooking all day and raising money for the church," she said. It was not clear who "we" referred to, but as it would turn out, it was María along with a few other women from the church who took it upon themselves to sell Puerto Rican delicacies as a way of fundraising for the parish during the city-wide celebration in honor of their patron saint. I asked what time they would start cooking and offered my assistance, albeit limited. She smiled at the offer but told me with a welcoming smile to "just come by and enjoy!"

This chapter considers the role of play, theorized as unproductive action, as part and parcel to masculine gender formation. In the context of Puerto Rico, masculinity was routinely measured through a combination of social identities, including worker who should be seen being a "financially successful patriarch."[2] Moments of unproductivity, rest, and relaxation hinged on the presumption that men require rest to return to their gendered role as "breadwinner." I unsettle this notion of so-called "industrious masculinity" by examining labor's gender in contrast to the gendered division of labor, which is the implicit way play has been understood in this context. I take up an argument by renowned Puerto Rican anthropologist Ricardo Alegría as the starting point for thinking about the relationship between labor, gender, and *las fiestas en honor a Santiago Apóstol* (*las fiestas*) and connect this with my own fieldwork in Loíza, comparing and contrasting two experiences of labor's gender. I demonstrate that work is already understood to be a masculine category such that even chronically underemployed men are considered the breadwinner of their home. As such, the relaxed and pleasurable atmosphere of las fiestas is not a distinct period of time but is rather a continuation of the social and political landscape of Loíza. Willian, a Loiceño who costumed as *la loca*, one of the processional personages I introduce below, demonstrated the way that play hinges on perceptions of non-festal productivity. It was assumed, in this daily life, that Willian was a hard worker (and he was!), who had earned the chance to play through his labor. However, as I show, there is never any accounting for labor; rather, it is understood vis-à-vis one's gender. Thus, what I theorize as "playful masculinity" is a way of accounting for how men were socialized through enjoyment and relaxation as much as they were through work.

## Las Fiestas

Loíza is a coastal city in northeastern Puerto Rico. It sits about fifteen miles east of the capital, San Juan. Its first residents were Taínos, the Indigenous people who inhabited large parts of the western Caribbean. In the early parts of the sixteenth century, the area was settled by Spaniards and the enslaved Africans they brought with them to toil on agricultural plantations in Loíza and other parts of the island. As a result of enslavement, Loíza possessed a large Afro-Puerto Rican population and is called "Capital of the Tradition" because of the ways residents have preserved their African heritage, including las fiestas.

Las fiestas are one of many patronal celebrations in Puerto Rico that honor important Catholic figures who are feted with special masses, prayers, and other community events. Over the years, the celebrations have grown beyond Santiago's official feast day, July 25, and las fiestas now lasts a carnivalesque ten days. For three of these days, sacred images of Santiago are processed through the city, accompanied by a massive crowd of devotees, some of whom don one of four traditional festival personages. In addition to the special religious events, there were several other elements that helped to inspire a convivial atmosphere, including art exhibitions, film screenings, workshops, and even concerts downtown featuring some of Puerto Rico's top musical artists. People happily waited—taking the day in slowly—for hours for their favorite band to play and lined the streets hours before the procession started so they could get the best view.

The city's official patron saint is San Patricio, to whom the church in the city center, Pueblo, is dedicated. However, the city's unofficial patron saint is Santiago, who appears on the city's municipal crest and whose sartorial color, red, can be seen throughout the city. Of the numerous stories that circulate that explain devotion to Santiago, one was the most popular and tells the story of Atilano Villanueva, a peasant farmer on the estate of Juana Lanzó and José María Villanueva.[3] According to this account, Atilano was tilling the ground, preparing it for planting when he discovered a curious figure at the base of a cork tree (*el árbol de corcho*) near where he was working. The figure was a small statue of Santiago that is lovingly called "Santiago de los Niños" and sometimes "Santiago de los Muchachos" (Children's Santiago).[4] Atilano took the image to the church in Pueblo, now called La Parroquia del Espíritu Santo y San Patricio. However, Santiago would not stay there long: the next day, as Atilano was working in the field, he again saw Santiago at the base of the cork tree, and he again trekked him to the church in Pueblo, approximately a five-kilometer walk westward from where he was working in the Medianía Alta area of Loíza. This same thing occurred on the third day, and Loiceños took his insistence on staying in Medianía Alta, the historical periphery of the city, as a sign of his special dedication to them. Santiago's movement between Pueblo and Medianía Alta gave rise to the tradition of processing his image between the two locations during las fiestas.

In many ways, the procession of Santiago's image was the central, culminating event of las fiestas. Of the ten days dedicated to las fiestas, the procession of Santiago de Los Niños is the last day of the festivities and does not align with his proscribed feast day. Despite this, his procession drew the largest crowd of revelers and celebrants. As the small image is carried eastward toward Medianía Alta, the processional crowd grows larger and larger, and more and more raucous. Trucks and Jeeps outfitted with bands and large speakers meander down Carretera 187, playing some of the latest musical hits for people to sing and dance to. Along the way, people stop off at roadside bars and restaurants to get something to drink and eat before rejoining the crowd, which makes its way to the memorial set up at el árbol, the final destination for Santiago.

Among the mobile musical ensembles are a group of costumed celebrants that help tell the story of Santiago and draw our attention to the social and political realities wherein. Chief among them are *el caballero, el vejigante, la loca,* and *el viejo*. El caballero (the knight) is the avatar of Santiago who was historically understood to be the foil of el vejigante (the devil-like trickster character).[5] These two costumes are the most ornate and costly costumes, which are made by artisans and craftspeople; they emphasize the Spanish history of Santiago, drawing from histories of the Reconquista and subsequent colonization of the Americas, with el caballero dramatizing Santiago and el vejigante his Moorish counterpart.[6] La loca (the madwoman) and el viejo (the old man), on the other hand, were introduced post-colonization and are manifestations of the colonizer's imagined other: the inappropriate woman and the lazy man. Unlike el caballero and el vejigante, la loca's and el viejo's costumes are cheap and can be constructed ad hoc with no real foresight.[7] Over the years, the performers and impetus to perform have changed. Today, for example, the historical and theological antagonism between el caballero and el vejigante has disappeared and both characters process together, and, in some cases, are played by members of the same family. Further, la loca, who typified ill-constructed and inappropriate Black femininity, was reclaimed by performers who use the costuming to remember the matriarchs of their families.

In his seminal text on las fiestas, *La fiesta de Santiago Apóstol en Loíza Aldea* (1954), Ricardo Alegría argues that las fiestas provided an opportunity for men to relax. Specifically, he shows that the tradition of men costuming was rooted in the fact that most of the work of organizing and participating in las fiestas was taken up by women while men were presumably working. Thus, the celebrations gave men who worked in cane and palm fields, fishing, and other labor-intensive industries the opportunity to "forget their work and daily hardships and actively participate in different ways."[8] Las fiestas were one way that men could pause their labor and enjoy themselves, just as María has instructed me to do. Importantly, as Alegría notes, is the gendered division of roles: costuming was seen as men's role in las fiestas; the other roles, particularly those seen as more associated with religious activities, such as fundraising and praying, were women's roles. Alegría later added the additional observation that it was women who made the costumes for men but that it was men who exclusively wore the outfits.[9] This means that women and their labor provided the space for men to participate in las fiestas. Masculinity, then, is formed in two complementary ways during las fiestas: firstly, via a work-stoppage and, secondly, via costuming. Through both actions, men's role in society is shaped by their ability to play—indeed, in the presumed necessity to play based on their labor.

## Willian, La Loca

I met Willian through mutual friends while attending a workshop in Piñones, the barrio west of Pueblo. He was an immediately gregarious and larger-than-life personality who was mischievous and liked to play around. As with so many Loiceños, he was a jack-of-all-trades: he knew a bit about car maintenance and repair, construction, and even accounting; but he was also a well-known musician, poet, and historian. To make ends meet, he worked as a part-time Pizza Hut delivery driver. It was meant to be a job between jobs, but it ended up allowing him to make a bit of money but still have enough flexibility to create his own schedule and be relatively free during the day to take up small jobs that would come his way. On top of all of this, he was also one of the few remaining performers of la loca.[10]

La loca is a festival character that accents las fiestas in the carnivalesque. The character is played by men who dress in women's clothing and flirtatiously—and frustratingly—engage with festival spectators and participants through parodic and exaggerated performances. Unlike el caballero and el vejigante, their role during las fiestas is not always clear, making their winks and suggestive gestures as charming as they are vexing. Alegría notes that the traditional loca would go through the streets of Loíza with a tree branch used as a broom, sweeping people's homes and porches, conducting unrequested domestic work.[11] Along with their makeshift broom, they carried a large aluminum can with which they collected the dust and debris from people's homes. The can had a secondary use, though: it could be primed with coins to create a rattle to draw people's attention and even used to request payment for their service. This, Alegría says, is their "'work.'"[12] Using quotation marks, Alegría signals that this is not *really* work but rather parodic labor; real labor is produced in the field and produces something useful.

Complementing and further complicating their feigned industriousness was their off-kilter appearance. Locas painted their already dark skin black and their lips red using makeup. The effect is a disarming and shocking look that is not dissimilar to American minstrel-style blackface. Performers stuffed their shirts and trousers to give the impression of ludicrously large breasts and buttocks, using them to humorously flirt with unsuspecting (and mostly uninterested) festival attendees. Most often, la loca was played wearing a *bata*—a nightgown typically worn by older women—and slippers. Their gender-bending performance was less concerned with passing than it is with ridiculousness, hence their name.

In Spanish, "loca" literally means "madwoman"—as in, "a crazy woman." In Puerto Rico, the term comes with sense of incongruity with ostensible gender norms.[13] For men, it is usually used to refer to "feminine men who are typically assumed to desire other men."[14] Notice the use of the grammatical feminine ending ("loc*a*" as opposed to "loc*o*") to describe men who are presumed to be effeminate. "Loca" implies a slippage between one's gender and sexuality wherein one's assumed sexuality is determinant of one's gender and vice versa. In this sense, gender and sexuality are inextricably connected in "loca" and failure to meet gendered standards is a kind of mental illness.[15] Thus, as Melissa González notes: "loca reflects parallels in the biopolitical management of both craziness and homosexuality, two subjectivities that have been historically relegated to a position of otherness."[16]

Women can also be assailed as locas, of course. Whereas masculine forms of madness hinge on incomplete masculinity, feminine madness hinges on excessive performances of gender that are tied to respectability read through behavior, dress, and sexuality. Colloquially, it can be used to describe a woman who "doesn't behave well, dances a lot, goes out a lot."[17] Still further, a loca is "disorganized, messy, dirty, stupid, unpredictable, dangerous, out-of-control, and out of her mind. A 'loca' was rejected and looked down upon. 'Loca' acts as a label for a specific form of 'craziness' that contradicts gender expectations."[18] The festival personage of la loca plays with both ends of this spectrum. At once, she is a man feigning femininity and a hyper sexual, unrespectable woman. La loca is both insufficiently and excessively gendered; as such, she causes great consternation among those whom she visits during las fiestas.

For several years, Willian had been playing la loca at various festivals and events throughout Puerto Rico. He drew inspiration for his costume from family and found it to be a meaningful opportunity to both participate in the festivities surrounding Santiago but also honor those who came before him. It was also a chance for him to cut loose and be transgressive. Over the years I have known him, I have seen him cross all kinds of social boundaries while performing la loca: picked his nose and ran around trying to wipe the boogers on festival attendees; once, he even picked a wedgie and upon smelling his fingers, pretended to collapse in the street from the stench. He was an excellent performer who knew how to rile up an audience and who played his role with humor and ease.

As he showed me the process for how he gets ready and his sartorial choices, Willian told me the inspiration for performing la loca. "*¡Me gusta joder!*" he told me and let out a deep chuckle. "Joder" has a range of usages in Puerto Rico. When talking about behavior, as Willian did, it meant failure to comport with standards, walking the line between innocent "mischievous play" and transgressive "fucking around." Exotic animal prints topped his list for go-to batas. However, Alegría's faux buttocks were not a necessary component of his outfit because *"ya tengo nalgas suficientes,"* he said with a wry smile as he smacked his hip and blew me a kiss. He did not need to stuff his trousers because he "already has a large enough ass." He doubled over laughing after provocatively offering his behind. Even not in costume, Willian was playful and transgressive; he was testing boundaries and crossing others. I asked Willian why he liked to mess around. He looked at me confused. "I just like to have fun," he said. The shrug of his shoulders and the puzzled look on his face suggested he had never been asked this question. "Ever since I was a kid, I liked to have fun," he continued, pausing momentarily only to wink. "In school, the teachers used to tell my parents that I couldn't sit still. I was always getting into trouble doing little things, getting in trouble at school." He looked up, as if seeing a memory in the clouds. He laughed to himself. "I guess dressing up as a loca is no different?" he surmised, shrugging slightly.

## Gender and the Labor of Playfulness

When I arrived at La Parroquia Santiago Apóstol, as invited by María, I found the church's parking lot abuzz with music, people chatting and laughing together, and the smell of fried food in the air. I approached the *kiosko* (a pop-up-style food stall) where María and a few other women making and selling *alcapurria* (stuffed yuca meat fritter) and *bacalaíto* (crispy codfish fritter), both Loiceño culinary staples called *"frituras"* or fried foods. "Everyone comes out," María later told me as we caught up and I placed an order for some alcapurria and a soft drink. During the week, she is an office manager for a doctor's office in Río Grande, the city just east of Loíza, but she lives in Medianía Alta. She does everything: accounting, appointment scheduling, and even some light cleaning and organizing. However, on Sundays, she is entirely devoted to the church, coming early to say the rosary and staying late to help sell the local Catholic paper, which helped raise money for the church. Summers in Puerto Rico can be aggressive, with temperatures easily reaching over 90 degrees Fahrenheit and beyond, but this did not deter María from doing what she saw as her duty to the church. Enclosed in the kiosko, the temperature inched higher and higher with the stoves working overtime to get each order out, and María was fanning herself and dabbing herself with a cool towel to offset the heat. "People get dressed up, play music, dance; it's like a big party!" she said, beaming with pride as she wrapped up an order fresh out the fryer in a few napkins and handed it off to a young boy, who ran off giddily. Again, I offered to help. Having never made alcapurria or bacalaíto before, I told María: "Just tell me what to do and I will do it." I meant it: I wanted to make myself useful. But also, following Elizabeth Pérez, I understood the kitchen to be a place of teaching and learning by doing, and the impartation of (sacred) knowledge through the butchering, seasoning, and cooking of animals.[19] I thought I might be able to help contribute to the community I was visiting *and* learn at the same time. She chuckled this time, politely brushing off my offer. "Don't worry, just enjoy!" she said.

"At least let me help clean up, then," I said. This offer for help caused one woman, Cely, to laugh. She comedically imitated how I would wash the dishes by lazily moving her hands over the air. She said she would have to go back over them and clean them again, essentially doubling the work, and the amount of soap and water used. *"Los hombres no saben cómo limpiar,"* she said exchanging a knowing look with María. "Men don't know how to clean." As quickly as she had said it, Cely returned to her work and dropped another order of battered codfish into the hot oil.

While María and her colleagues were literally sweating over open-flame wood fires, men were sitting at tables or on the ground, eating and drinking. María and her colleagues were crowded into the small kiosko, hidden away. Men were out in the open, enjoying and relaxing. María and her colleagues cooked. Men ate. Men were playing while women were being productive. If, as Alegría argued, las fiestas gave men the opportunity to forget their work, there was notably no such season of forgetting for women. María was always on the move, always doing some kind of work—even outside of las fiestas, her weekly schedule was jam packed with work and familial obligations. More than this, though, women are the ones who create the environment for masculine forgetfulness through both their production of festival garments *and* through taking on the labor of food preparation and service. It was because of María's and Cely's labor (cooking) that men were able to relax (consume and costume). Thus, it is not only men's presumed labor that forms the possibility of men's enjoyment but also women's continuous labor.

Alegría's conclusions regarding the division of labor were written as Puerto Rico underwent tremendous economic and social change at the end of the Second World War and the implementation of Operation Bootstrap (Bootstrap). Bootstrap was designed in part to deal with an economic problem: the presumed financial burden of unincorporated territories like Puerto Rico on the United States. Officially commenced in May 1947, Bootstrap initiated certain tax eliminations and leniencies in order to attract new industries from the United States to Puerto Rico as a means of transforming the island's economy from agrarian to industrial. These incentives were particularly attractive to textile and garment manufacturing that in turn created new opportunities for women to enter the workforce and subsequently slowly changed the worker demographic.[20] This shift, however, rested on the idea that women would take on these new positions that were poorly compensated and left men undercut and chronically unemployed.[21] Whatever benefits could be said to have originated from Bootstrap were decades later undone by the development of non-US-aligned unions and worker organizing: "As Puerto Rican workers' demands for higher wages increased in the 1980s . . . many of these enterprises, notably garment businesses, began reducing operations in Puerto Rico."[22] This left Puerto Rico, and Loíza, one of those places affected by Operation Bootstrap, in financial hardship. According to recent US Census data, approximately half of the city's population is unemployed and experiencing poverty.[23] Those who are employed are often precariously so and many residents, like Willian and María, have to travel to neighboring cities—and even farther in some cases—in order to find employment.[24] Because of his proximity to the implementation of Bootstrap, it was impossible for Alegría to see the consequences of the professional and gendered economic changes surrounding him, though. Even still, scholars have not been attentive to the shifting economic landscape of las fiestas and have taken it for granted, still drawing from Alegría's gendered division of labor for their studies decades later.[25]

The current economic climate is slightly more complex. The previously imagined physically grueling agricultural work no longer exists, and the employment that does exist is meager.[26] Moreover, it is not so much that labor is divided by gender but rather that work is already a gendered category. In Puerto Rico, labor, which is understood as public and economically productive, is presumed to be masculine; women, on the other hand, are assumed to be household caretakers—and mothers, especially—which certainly takes effort but is not labor, per se. At the same time, women who work and are financially successful are often viewed as usurping men's role as "breadwinner."[27] As anthropologist Helen Safa notes, even while men suffer from chronic underemployment, they are still considered the financial and economic head of house; women's income, on the other hand, is considered "supplemental."[28] Though the labor market has changed—and with it, household structures and economics—las fiestas are still imagined to be a space of male rest. As such, it is not so much that men needed opportunities to rest from labor but that men were perceived to need rest because of labor's gender. Part of masculine identity formation, then, is the understanding that men *require* moments of relaxation—or even transgression, as la loca demonstrates.

Indeed, this was even the case for me, a researcher and guest in Loíza, who did not do any kind of visible labor and who was not known to be involved in any physical work. My ability to relax and enjoy was read through my gender instead of the other way around, as Alegría found. My experiences with María and Cely showed me that my gender prohibited me or, at the very least, informed my ability to perform certain domestic tasks, like cooking and cleaning. María undoubtedly could have simply been being nice to me: a guest in her country and in her city. However, María's coworker, Cely, made this clear when she said that as a man, I fit into a specific category—foreigner or not. Her generalization, "los hombres no saben cómo limpiar," indicated how she read me through my gender.

Play, as Alegría theorized, is thought of as a release valve for the labor that men do throughout the year, which is understood as their quotidian behavior. During las fiestas, there is no specific requirement for men to produce any labor. Instead, men's work is postponed, and they enter into a time of play that is supported by women's labor. While men's playfulness was constructed during these periods of celebration, these moments of escape actually served to reinforce their position as laborers. Meaning, men deserve to play during las fiestas, despite no visible work being done (as was the case for me) because it was assumed that throughout the celebrations men would otherwise have been working. "Playful masculinity" is a way of understanding labor's gender and attending to the nuances of gender construction via rest and relaxation. María's and her colleague's responses to my offer of help illustrate this. Two times, María told me to just "enjoy" myself without knowing whether I was productive or not. Cely's comment that I, and other men, are not thorough enough to wash dishes further shapes how the perception of enjoyability is matched with a blasé attitude toward certain kinds of work. Men's labor was not domestic but public and physical—or so it is assumed. Though this is no longer the case in Loíza, the perception abounds.

## Conclusion

After my interview with Willian as he showed me his outfits, I asked him what his plans were for the rest of the day. "I don't know," he said. "Maybe going to see La Tribu de Abrante later but other than that, I don't know." He let out another dismissive "Heh!" as he did a miniature basic salsa step in place. La Tribu de Abrante is a musical group that combines bomba and salsa to produce a style all its own. They were closing out the evening's festivities, playing in the plaza near La Parroquia del Espíritu Santo y San Patricio at around 1 a.m. on Sunday morning. No plans, he said, except to go to a concert, dance, and enjoy himself. This was the flexibility that his patchwork employment allowed him: he could make decisions about shifts to take or give up on a whim; he could decide to stay out all night and party; or he could decide to stay in and rest.

This chapter explored the longstanding notion that Puerto Rican masculinity is based on one's productivity and labor or ostensible "industrious masculinity." Though this is certainly true, it is not the only way in which to understand masculinity. Through a combination of examination of labor and play, I offer "playful masculinity" as a theory of men's gender formation as inherently tied to relaxation as much as it is to industriousness. Whereas anthropologists like Ricardo Alegría argued for a gendered division of labor whereby men earned the right to relax through their daily physically exhausting work, I argue that instead labor is already a gendered category. The presumption is that men are doing *real* work and women, "supplemental." Thus, it is not so much that men require these moments of respite because of labor but simply deserve them for being men.

Las fiestas provided an opportunity for Willian to relax and enjoy himself. Dressing in women's clothing, singing, and dancing during the procession of the images of Santiago down Carretera 187 were all ways that Willian found time and space to relax and enjoy himself. Play, however, was not so much a release valve from physically demanding work; instead, it was a continuation of the way that men were perceived to be the economic heads of households despite that not always being the case. Willian demonstrated how play was not secondary to masculine gender formation but was built into it. While it was understood that Willian deserved to play because of his work, women in Loíza, like María, did not find the same respite from work despite their household and other economic contributions, which were understood to be domestic and supplemental to men's work and, therefore, they did not need the same rest from their labor.

Before I left Loíza, María invited me to her home for a meal with friends from church. She was busy in the kitchen moving with speed and urgency between stirring, frying, checking, and serving up food for her husband and guests. She wiped her brow and greeted me with a hug, telling me to sit and eat. Music was playing, and a few men were sitting around a domino table, playing and drinking. After preparing a plate, she brought it and a beer she had retrieved from a cooler to her husband, who was playing dominos. "Ma!" her husband cried out, "could you bring me some napkins?" "Yes, my love," she said, hurrying back to the kitchen. Passing me by, she rolled her eyes slightly and said, "My work is never done!"

## Notes

1. Some personal details about my research participants, such as names, have been changed.
2. Eileen J. Suárez Findlay, *We Are Left Without a Father Here: Masculinity, Domesticity, and Migration in Postwar Puerto Rico* (Durham: Duke University Press, 2014), 3.
3. There are usually no dates given for the miraculous discovery of the image of Santiago; however, some residents date this to the late nineteenth century. Loiceños would often use sayings like "*cuando Dios andaba por el mundo*" "*en tiempos pasados*" ("when God walked on year" [referring to the Genesis account of creation] and "many years ago") to give historical context. Given some of the details of the story, it is likely that Atilano was a manumitted slave or descendent of slaves (Figueroa 2005, 244n17).
4. Other versions of the events of Santiago's epiphany include his being found on the shore by an elderly woman bathing in the sea and, similarly on the shore, by a fisherman working early in the morning. During my fieldwork in Loíza, I heard

these versions of events less frequently than the Atilano Villanueva version. These other versions are recorded elsewhere more explicitly. See Alegría 1954; Ungerleider Kepler 2000; Zaragoza 1995.
5. Lowell Fiet, *Caballeros, vejigantes, locas y viejos: Santiago Apóstol y los performos afropuertorriqueños* (San Juan: Terranova Editores, 2007).
6. See Max Harris, *Carnival and Other Christian Festivals: Folk Theology and Folk Performance* (Austin: University of Texas Press, 2003).
7. There are performers who take their work very seriously, though, and take the time to seriously consider how to put together an outfit for la loca and el viejo.
8. Ricardo E. Alegría, *La Fiesta de Santiago Apóstol en Loíza Aldea* (Madrid: Artes Gráficas, 1954).
9. Ricardo E. Alegría, "The Festival of Santiago Apostol (St. James the Apostle) in Loíza, Puerto Rico," *Journal of American Folklore* 69, no. 272 (1956): 129. This exclusivity is no longer the case and women have begun to take part in the tradition of costuming, developing new characters such as *La Vejiganta*.
10. Lowell Fiet (2022) notes the decline of la loca performers.
11. Alegría, *La Fiesta de Santiago Apóstol en Loíza Aldea*, 61.
12. Alegría, *La Fiesta de Santiago Apóstol en Loíza Aldea*, 61.
13. In Latin America more broadly, "loca" indexes a range of pejorative uses. In addition to the discussion here, it is also used to describe trans people and sex workers. See La Fountain-Stokes 2021 and Lara 2021.
14. Melissa M. González, "La Loca," *Transgender Studies Quarterly* 1, nos. 1–2 (2014): 123–25.
15. Indeed, one Loiceño told me that the inspiration for la loca was a woman who lost her mental faculties, became homeless, and began wandering the streets looking for domestic work.
16. González, "La Loca," 25.
17. Collins, Pamela Y., Hella von Unger, and Adria Armbrister, "Church Ladies, Good Girls, and Locas: Stigma and the Intersection of Gender, Ethnicity, Mental Illness, and Sexuality in Relation to HIV Risk," *Social Science and Medicine* 67 (2008): 392.
18. Collins et al., "Church Ladies, Good Girls, and Locas," 392.
19. Elizabeth Pérez, *Religion in the Kitchen: Cooking, Talking, and the Making of Black Atlantic Traditions* (New York: New York University Press, 2016).
20. Surendra Bhana, *The United States and the Development of the Puerto Rican Status Question, 1936–1968* (University Press of Kansas, 2023); James W. Russell, "Operation Bootstrap and NAFTA: Comparing the Social Consequences," in *Critical*

*Sociology* 21, no. 2 (1995): 91–108. It should be noted that Bootstrap, in additional to other policy decisions, left Puerto Rico's economy in dire straits. By the 2015, the country had amassed an eye-watering $121-billion debt that it could not repay and as a result, still more legislation was implemented to ensure debt holders were be repaid at the expense of the populace. See Zambrano (2021) and Klein (2018).
21. Altagracia Ortiz, "Introduction," in *Puerto Rican Women and Work: Bridges in Translational Labor,* ed. Altagracia Ortiz (Philadelphia: Temple University Press, 1996), 29–30 n61.
22. Ortiz, "Introduction," 16.
23. US Census Bureau, n.d. "Loíza Municipio, Puerto Rico," Quick Facts, accessed May 6, 2024, https://www.census.gov/quickfacts/loizamunicipiopuertorico.
24. Moira Alexandra Pérez, "The Place of Abandonment: Geography, Race, and Nature in Puerto Rico" (PhD diss., The University of California, Berkeley, 2002), ProQuest (AAT 3063517).
25. A notable exception to this is David Ungerleider Kepler (2000), who nevertheless takes the effects of capitalist expansion and globalization as givens rather than points of analysis.
26. Today, Loíza's economy is driven by las fiestas related tourism and its reputation as the "Capital de la Tradición."
27. Ortiz, "Introduction," 21. Women who overstep these social norms of becoming "breadwinners" themselves are liable to being labelled as "locas" for exceeding the boundaries of their gender.
28. Helen I, Safa, *The Myth of the Male Breadwinner: Women and Industrialization in the Caribbean* (London: Routledge, 1995), 69.

# References

Alegría, Ricardo E. *La Fiesta de Santiago Apóstol en Loíza Aldea*. Madrid: Artes Gráficas, 1954.

Alegría, Ricardo E. 1956. "The Festival of Santiago Apostol (St. James the Apostle) in Loíza, Puerto Rico." *Journal of American Folklore* 69, no. 272 (April–June): 123–34.

Bhana, Surendra. *The United States and the Development of the Puerto Rican Status Question, 1936–1968*. University Press of Kansas, 2023.

Collins, Pamela Y., Hella von Unger, and Adria Armbrister. "Church Ladies, Good Girls, and Locas: Stigma and the Intersection of Gender, Ethnicity, Mental Illness, and Sexuality in Relation to HIV Risk." *Social Science and Medicine* 67 (2008): 389–97.

Fiet, Lowell. *Caballeros, vejigantes, locas y viejos: Santiago Apóstol y los performos afropuertorriqueños*. San Juan: Terranova Editores, 2007.

Fiet, Lowell. 2022. "Las Fiestas de Santiago Apóstol de Loíza, 2022: ¿Dónde se encuentran las Locas y los Viejos?" *Claridad*, August 16, 2022, https://claridadpuertorico.com/las-fiestas-de-santiago-apostol-de-loiza-2022-donde-se-encuentran-las-locas-y-los-viejos/.

Figueroa, Luis A. *Sugar, Slavery, and Freedom in Nineteenth-Century Puerto Rico*. Chapel Hill: The University of North Carolina Press, 2005.

Findlay, Eileen J. Suárez. *We Are Left Without a Father Here: Masculinity, Domesticity, and Migration in Postwar Puerto Rico*. Durham: Duke University Press, 2014.

González, Melissa M. "La Loca." *Transgender Studies Quarterly* 1, nos. 1–2 (2014): 123–25.

Harris, Max. *Carnival and Other Christian Festivals: Folk Theology and Folk Performance*. Austin: University of Texas Press, 2003.

Klein, Naomi. *The Battle for Paradise: Puerto Rico Takes on the Disaster Capitalists*. Chicago: Haymarket Books, 2018.

La Fountain-Stokes, Lawrence. *Translocas: The Politics of Puerto Rican Drag and Trans Performance*. Ann Arbor: The University of Michigan Press, 2021.

Lara, Ana-Maurine. *Streetwalking: LGBTQ Lives and Protest in the Dominican Republic*. New Brunswick: Rutgers University Press, 2021.

Ortiz, Altagracia. "Introduction." In *Puerto Rican Women and Work: Bridges in Translational Labor*, edited by Altagracia Ortiz. Philadelphia: Temple University Press, 1996.

Pérez, Elizabeth. *Religion in the Kitchen: Cooking, Talking, and the Making of Black Atlantic Traditions*. New York: New York University Press, 2016.

Pérez, Moira Alexandra. "The Place of Abandonment: Geography, Race, and Nature in Puerto Rico." Ph.D. diss., The University of California, Berkeley, 2002. ProQuest (AAT 3063517).

Russell, James W. "Operation Bootstrap and NAFTA: Comparing the Social Consequences." *Critical Sociology* 21, no. 2 (1995): 91–108.

Safa, Helen I. *The Myth of the Male Breadwinner: Women and Industrialization in the Caribbean*. London: Routledge, 1995.

US Census Bureau, n.d. "Loíza Municipio, Puerto Rico," Quick Facts, https://www.census.gov/quickfacts/loizamunicipiopuertorico.

Ungerleider Kepler, David. *Las Fiestas de Santiago en Loíza: La Cultura Afropuertorriqueña Ante los Procesos de Hibridación y Globalización*. San Juan: Editorial Isla Negra, 2000.

Zambrana, Rocío. *Colonial Debts: The Case of Puerto Rico*. Durham, NC: Duke University Press, 2021.

Zaragoza, Edward C. *St. James in the Streets: The Religious Processions of Loíza Aldea, Puerto Rico*. Lanham, MD: Scarecrow Press, 1995.

PART II

*Aesthetics in Las Américas*

CHAPTER 4

## *¡Mira, pa ya en el cielo!*

### The Amazing Decolonial and Theological Adventures of *La Borinqueña*

*JOEL MORALES CRUZ*

> *Our people will never be defeated, for generation after generation will give birth to heroes and heroines.*
> —PEDRO ALBIZU CAMPOS

For much of their existence, superhero comics have been considered intellectual junk food, devoid of depth. Impossibly powered heroes fight mad scientists, killer clowns, and giant robots across the urban and cosmic landscape. Yet, as its earliest fans became its modern writers and artists, and as the once crudely drawn characters morphed into universally recognized icons, many have discovered that these heroes who can lift mountains can also shoulder complexity. As Frederick Luis Aldama observes, while comic books and comic strips "can be as uninteresting, sophomorically self-absorbed, and flat" as other storytelling media, they can also be "aesthetically complex, self-aware, and emotionally engaging."[1]

Far from mindless entertainment, comics can be deciphered in ways that reveal participation in or resistance to patriarchy, racism, sexism, or other ills. As a form of sequential art (i.e., storytelling presented in a sequence of separate works of art), they can also represent and reframe in powerful ways all aspects of the everyday world. Comics can serve to bolster the imagination to help us envision a reality different from our own.[2] Considering the monumental impact of films such as *Wonder Woman* (2017), *Black Panther* (2018), and the HBO *Watchmen* series (2019), which are all based on comic books that feature female and black protagonists, Latinx scholars of religion should take a closer look at the comic book genre. This chapter will build on Aldama's work by exploring the religious dimensions of a significant recent contribution to the pantheon of Latinx superheroes.

La Borinqueña is a character who made her debut in 2016's New York Puerto Rican Day Parade and now stars in an independently published comic book of the same name.[3] Created by writer and activist Edgardo Miranda-Rodríguez, the series gives voice to the Puerto Rican diaspora and serves as a source of decolonial religious reflection. *La Borinqueña* subverts imperial myths and dominant discourses of power, pointing to an alternative decolonial and liberating praxis.[4]

In what follows, I look at *La Borinqueña* through four interrelated lenses: the historical context of Latinx comics, its cultural motifs, its decolonial dimensions, and, finally, its capacity to serve as a diasporic theology that helps to address the island's historic and present challenges while emphasizing empowerment and community.

## Latinx Superheroes in Comics

Comic books in the United States emerged as a means of repackaging and reselling the Sunday newspaper comics pages into a book format. Their association with superheroes began in Action Comics #1 (1938) with the debut of Superman. Publishers such as Detective Comics (later DC), All-American, Timely (later Marvel), Fawcett and others sought to capitalize on the success of Superman and opened the floodgates to the creation of both unforgettable and forgotten superheroes and the Golden Age of Comics, which lasted roughly through the end of World War II. With few exceptions, those in charge of creating and publishing superhero comics tended to be straight white men. The representation of ethnic characters skewed toward the stereotypical and ancillary. Black people were depicted with exaggerated features drawn from blackface and other Jim Crow images, Asians as bucktoothed threats, and Latin Americans as lazy or festive stereotypes with over-pronounced accents.[5] Change at the major publishers did not begin until the 1970s, when creators like Stan Lee, Jack Kirby, Denny O'Neill, and Neal Adams sought to have their stories more grounded in everyday reality. At Marvel Comics, characters such as the Black Panther introduced readers to an African nation without colonialism while the Falcon fought urban crime. Meanwhile, at DC Comics, Green Lantern and Green Arrow were forced to look into the problems of urban decay, overpopulation, and drug addiction. During this time, the predominant model governing the industry was work-for-pay, and it afforded creators little voice or rights given the enormous control publishers had over the comics. In the 1990s, with the emergence of creator-owned publishers such as Jim Lee's Image Comics and the move toward giving artists and writers more credit and voice in their art, we begin to see more authentic representations of diverse populations, including ethnic minorities, women, and LGBTQ people. This diversification of representation was also aided by the fact that publishing houses recognized that they could appeal to more varied demographic audiences.[6]

Latinx superheroes in mainstream US comics have existed almost as long as the genre itself, appearing a mere two years after the first appearance of Superman eight decades ago. The Whip/El Castigo debuted in *Flash Comics* #1 (1940) as the secret identity of Don Fernando Suarez, a copy of the original Latinx hero, Zorro, who first battled colonial evildoers in Johnston McCulley's 1919 pulp novel, *The Curse of Capistrano*. Beginning in 1942, Brazilian movie star Rita Farrar fought crime and served as US secret agent Senorita Rio during the war in Fiction House's *Fight Comics*. She was often drawn by Lily Renée, one of the few women working in the fledgling comics industry at that time. Latinx heroes all but disappeared until 1975 when Marvel Comics introduced the urban Puerto Rican hero White Tiger. Bushmaster and Green Fury represented Venezuela and Brazil, respectively, starting in the late 1970s, with Green Fury, now renamed Fire, joining the Justice League in the 1980s. In the Saturday morning cartoon *Super Friends*, El Dorado joined other ethnic heroes to better reflect the diversity of American society. These early Latinx heroes were followed by characters such as Sunspot (1982), Vibe (1984), and Extraño, comics' first queer Latinx superhero (1988). Recent entries in this history include Dominican police officer Renee Montoya, who would later become the Question after being outed as a lesbian (1992); Kyle Rayner (1994) and Jessica Cruz (2013), both Green Lanterns with Hispanic roots. Similarly, three other superheroes made their debut in 2011: America Chavez, the first Latin American LGBTQ character to be introduced by Marvel Comics; Bunker, DC Comics' gay Mexican teenage superhero; and Marvel's biracial Spider-Man (Miles Morales).[7]

Aldama provides points of contrast between Latinx heroes and their Anglo counterparts. Anglo superheroes, typically characterized as recast Manifest Destiny cowboy-types with invincibility thrown in, tend to defend the nation or the world but simultaneously stand apart from it. In their books on popular culture and the formation of monomyth in the United States, Robert Jewett and John Shelton Lawrence see this aspect as a distinctly US reformulation of the hero's journey made popular by Joseph Campbell, a scholar of comparative mythology and comparative religion. Whereas many myths and legends from around the world link the hero's journey to ancient and traditional rites of initiation that serve to transition the child into adulthood and into the community's full privileges and responsibilities, the US version, in contrast, stresses the power of individual redemption. Anglo heroes are crusaders against evil and are seen as the selfless servants who give their life for others. They live apart or above the community and tend to renounce the everyday pleasures of sex, marriage, or family while serving as extralegal heroes who use redemptive violence to fight for law or justice outside democratic institutions.[8] Anglo superheroes are often born or gifted with special abilities (Superman, Thor)—or come to them through an entitled meritocratic or classist rise to power (Batman, Iron Man). The focus is often on their intellect or abilities. They lead with their heads, not their emotions. They are independent, self-sufficient, and have few ties to history or spirituality. Community seems to be limited to a few close associates or a benevolent paternalism ("This is my city. I must protect it"). This echoes common ideas of redemption within US Christianity since the Second Great Awakening of the early 1800s. Here, redemption is conceived as an individual salvation from one's personal sins, a one-on-one relationship with God and the resulting struggle to fight temptation and increase in holiness.

By contrast, Latinx superheroes, particularly those created by non-Latinx writers and artists, tend to be identified by their bodies and emotions rather than their intellect—the "hot-blooded," "hot-tempered" stereotype. And in this genre controlled predominantly by straight white men, Latinx superheroines are usually featured as "hot-bodied." Latinx heroes' abilities and knowledge do not always come naturally to them. Latinx heroes often must earn their powers and work at learning how to become heroes, running a gauntlet of personal and super-powered challenges to become who they are meant to be. Significantly, Latinx superheroes, especially those by Latinx creators, are rooted in community—be it the pre-Columbian past, big-city barrios, or the border towns of the Southwest. They often come from working-class communities, have large family networks, and are tied to traditional Latinx religions, usually Catholicism or Santería. Rather than facing global or cosmic threats, it is these communities of family and neighbors that they are most committed to protecting and that are often pivotal to the hero's growth.[9]

## La Borinqueña's *Bona Fides*

In interviews, Edgardo Miranda-Rodríguez has stated that he wanted to create an authentic Puerto Rican superhero that would resonate with a Puerto Rican audience.[10] In what follows, I look at the ways that he accomplishes this in the debut issue of the comic.

FIGURE 5. La Borinqueña cover. Image courtesy of Edgardo Miranda-Rodriguez.

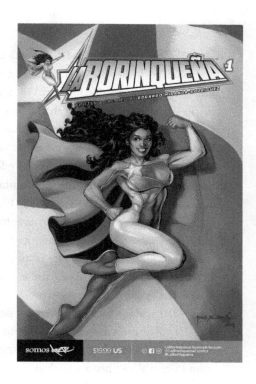

FIGURE 6. La Borinqueña History. Courtesy of Edgardo Miranda-Rodriguez.

For starters, Miranda-Rodríguez's use of the term "La Borinqueña," which describes both the title of the series as well as the main protagonist, makes an unmistakable connection to Puerto Rico, as the term is the Indigenous Taíno name for the island, Boriken. Rather than calling her "Rican-Woman," Miranda-Rodríguez chooses a name that distances the heroine from the island's more recent colonial history and that, instead, identifies her with the island's native inhabitants. Most Puerto Ricans will also recognize the reference as being the title of the national anthem, whose original, more confrontational lyrics were written by the poet/activist Lola Rodríguez de Tió (1843–1924).[11]

The front cover introduces one to the character and conveys important information about her. Her clothing and pose (she is in flight, flexing her right arm) identifies her as a superhero. Her costume is made up of the stripes, colors, and star of the Puerto Rican flag. In case these details are lost on the readers, there is also a Puerto Rican flag in the background.

Alternate (or variant) covers deepen the character's identification with the island. One features distinguished Puerto Ricans like Supreme Court Justice Sonia Sotomayor and social activist Oscar López Rivera, and another has various scenes from Puerto Rican history such as the Grito de Lares and activist Pedro Albizu Campos. Other covers show Carnaval, or La Borinqueña flying over El Yunque or El Morro, two of the island's landmarks.[12] Even before readers open the book, Miranda-Rodríguez establishes and privileges a Puerto Rican setting and culture. The first several pages of this debut issue introduce us to this new superheroine, her powers, and her motivations. She is Marisol Ríos De La Luz—another nod to her Puerto Rican identity—Marisol (Mar y Sol, Sea and Sun). Her name echoes the line from the chorus of the anthem and ties it to another part of her identity, that of a university student majoring in environmental science.[13] La Borinqueña identifies with Puerto Rico, referring to her homeland as "my island" and concludes that "as Puerto Ricans we have always had a rich history of fighting for our right [sic], our culture, and our future...."[14]

La Borinqueña's splash page—that very first full-page image inside the book that is so important in establishing the setting or character of the series—shows us that when the superhero's job is done, La Borinqueña doesn't fly off like Superman or brood in the dark like Batman. Instead, she dances! Miranda-Rodríguez's splash page features the first full view of our dancing hero as one onlooker comments that "*Negrita, tu si que tienes ¡tumbao!*" ("Sister, you got rhythm!"). This interaction signals to the reader that she is not an isolated loner but part of a larger, vibrant community.

A character's physical characteristics, or phenotype, is also important in telling the reader something about her. She is dark-skinned, reflecting the African roots of the people, and in a stark departure from how women are often depicted in superhero comics, La Borinqueña is more full-figured. She is beautiful, she is athletic, but not hypersexualized. Miranda-Rodríguez has been clear about instructing artists to not portray his creation for the pleasure of the heterosexual male gaze.[15] This was important to him when creating the character: he wanted a hero who would reflect the strong women who helped raise him.[16] This sentiment seems to have found a receptive audience.

> We've never seen ourselves as the protagonist, we've never seen ourselves as the hero of the book, especially women, especially dark-completion (sic) women and so oftentimes when I hear overwhelmingly from these women from different stories events and social media, "Oye pero se parece a mi." They say it in a coy way but I tell them you're right. She does look like you. She looks exactly like you. She looks like your mom, your sister, your best friend and like your cousin.[17]

The rest of the story in this first issue is a flashback to her origin. Marisol is a Nuyorican from Brooklyn—connected to both the island and the diaspora. Marisol is interested in the "Estrella del Camino," the Star of the Way. It is a plot point created for the story, a crystal star said to appear throughout important events in Puerto Rico's history. While studying it she makes mention of the Taíno people and the Defender of the Indians, Bartolomé de Las Casas.[18]

Marisol is an ordinary student who bikes to school through familiar New York neighborhoods and struggles with asthma. Her parents are supportive of her plans to travel to Puerto Rico to complete her graduate studies. Like the Marvel superheroes who were celebrated early on for being set in actual cities like New York instead of imaginary places like Metropolis or Paradise Island, Marisol and her super-powered alter ego are rooted in the real world and the real history of the Puerto Rican communities on the island and the diaspora. The themes of community, history, and social challenges are developed throughout her series. These connections to real-life events such as fiscal crises, environmental hazards, and prejudice are invaluable in helping readers relate to the characters and stories.

Before she leaves, her mother presents her with a family heirloom, "something she can draw strength from." It is a ribbon made from the fabric of the flag that flew throughout the Grito de Lares, the 1868 rebellion against the Spanish colonial government. She mentions how the flag was created by Mariana Bracetti and that the ribbon has been handed down from mother to daughter throughout the last century and a half. The artwork focuses on Marisol and her mother as she receives the ribbon—an intimate snapshot of the larger role women have played in handing down tradition and history through our families.[19] The importance of women in the island's history is underlined further in the variant cover Miranda-Rodríguez issued to commemorate the 150th anniversary of the Grito de Lares in 2018, where women are featured front and center.

The graphic novel is also filled with various "Puertoricanisms," those visual and written cues that inform the reader that this character and story is seasoned in Boriqua culture. As Marisol leaves for the island, her parents give her *la Bendición*, the blessing that many Puerto Ricans have heard from their parents and relatives. "*Dios te bendiga!*" ("God bless you!"), they tell her.[20] When the plane arrives in San Juan, the passengers erupt into applause, and after her grandparents pick her up at the airport, they take her to the café they own to savor traditional *pasteles*, *guineos*, and *malanga*.[21] Throughout the issue, real place names are used, like Loíza, Río Piedras, and Arecibo. These touches, along with how Spanish is used occasionally without translation, privilege an insider knowledge of the experiences, culture, and history of the Puerto Rican people. By giving voice to an insider view, Miranda-Rodríguez flips the dominant script found throughout Anglo-centered US entertainment. It is now the Puerto Ricans who center the narrative and others who have to imagine themselves in it.

But not everything is paradise on the Island of Enchantment. While Marisol helps her grandparents in their café, Sofía, who is blond and light-skinned, enters and, alluding to a popular soap opera trope often found in Spanish-language telenovelas, belittles Marisol as the "black cook." Later, Marisol confronts Sofía about this incident not through violence but in a dance-off.[22] Sofía's classism and racism are not fully addressed at this point, though she becomes a more complex character in the next issue.

To complicate matters, when Marisol goes to the University of Puerto Rico in Río Piedras, she discovers that her classes have been canceled due to faculty cuts, an allusion to the very real problems affecting the university for the past several years. Unwilling to let these setbacks deter her, she begins studying soil samples on her own from the caves of Puerto Rico, including Cueva del Viento, las Cavernas de Camuy, and the Cueva del Indio—all real places.[23] In these locales, she discovers various crystals but before she can study them further, a tropical storm begins to batter the island, one made worse by the municipal cuts that austerity measures have forced on services.[24] Marisol races against the rising waters to Cueva Ventana in Arecibo to gather her last soil samples and discovers yet another crystal. The crystals call out to her. Coming together with those she had already discovered, the crystals form the five-pointed star of the Puerto Rican flag—"the Star of the Way." And that's when all Heaven breaks loose.[25]

## Goddess of Our Mothers

In a full-page spread, we encounter Marisol floating in mid-air, dwarfed by the Taíno goddess Atabex in front of a technicolor psychedelic background. This altered state of consciousness is indicated by swirling shapes and colors. It contains a theophany, a pulling apart of the curtains of perception to reveal the ancient goddess. Marisol gasps, "*Ay Dios mío.*" "Yes," Atabex replies, identifying herself as the "Mother of Boriken. I am the ancient spirit of your deep past. I am the water that flows through your consciousness. I am the love of my people, mar y sol, my sea and sun."[26]

Atabex tells Marisol that her island is suffering, and that when the island suffers, her children suffer. They need a champion, a symbol of hope. At this point, the ribbon that Marisol has been wearing begins to transform, weaving and expanding itself over her body to form the blue, red, and white costume reminiscent of the Puerto Rican flag. Earlier we learned that this ribbon is made from the flag that flew during the Grito de Lares, an enduring symbol of Puerto Rican resistance to colonial imperialism both then and now. La Borinqueña literally wears her politics on her sleeve.[27] Atabex then informs Marisol that her sons, Huracán and Yúcahu, will gift her with powers. Huracán teaches her to fly and control the winds, while Yúcahu gives her power over the seas and earth.[28] As Marisol soars above the mountain, we see it transformed into a giant version of the *zemis*, or religious statues of the Taíno.[29]

From a religious point of view, this exchange resonates deeply. For the Taínos, caves served as shelters from storms and shelters from colonists. They may have been used for ritual purposes, including burials and galleries for petroglyphs. Caves also often represented the womb of the earth, the place from where the sun, moon, and the people emerged from darkness into light.[30] As religious spaces that symbolize

*¡Mira, pa ya en el cielo!*

FIGURE 7. La Borinqueña Zemi. Courtesy of Edgardo Miranda-Rodriguez.

both the cosmic uterus and the cosmic tomb, the caves serve as powerful liminal spaces for Marisol: she enters the caves as a struggling university student and is reborn, transformed into much more.

Seen from another religious angle, the Abrahamic faiths repeatedly make mountaintops and the caves they form the loci of revelation, where human beings meet God. Examples include the giving of the Covenant in Exodus on Mount Sinai; the still small voice of Elijah on Mount Horeb; and the Temptation, Transfiguration, and Ascension of Jesus on various hills and mountains. In Islam, the angel Gabriel meets Mohammad on Mount Hira to give him the Quran. However, the closest Abrahamic analog to this sequence in *La Borinqueña* might be the calling of Moses in Exodus 3 on Mount Sinai. The table below highlights these similarities.

Like Moses, Marisol experiences a theophany—a visible manifestation of a god. Atabex reveals herself to Marisol and calls her to become a symbol of hope and resistance to her people. La Borinqueña joins the pantheon of superheroes who receive their powers from the god(s). Nonetheless, she stands out from these in her connection to a specific land and people. Wonder Woman is an Amazon gifted

TABLE 1. CRUZ, LA BORINQUEÑA

|  | La Borinqueña | Moses |
|---|---|---|
| The Place | Cueva Ventana | Mount Sinai |
| The Call | Star calls her | The Burning Bush |
| The Query | "What's going on?" | "I will turn and see" |
| The Introduction | "I am the Mother of Boriken" | "I am the God of your fathers" |
| The Name | "I am Atabex" | "I AM THAT I AM" |
| The Crisis | "My island/children suffer" | "I have seen the suffering of my people" |
| The Mission | "They need a champion" | "I send you" |
| The Objection | "I can't fight" | "What shall I say?" |
| The Resolution | "You will know" | "I will teach you" |

by the Greek pantheon, but she has no connection to modern Greek people. Thor is a Norse god, but he is not seen flying over Sweden eating lutefisk and drinking glogg. But La Borinqueña is connected to the entire history and struggle of the Puerto Rican people. We follow the Estrella del Camino as it shoots across the sky, lighting the way throughout our history. Then, in the next few pages we witness the Taínos; Mariana Bracetti, who sewed the flag for the Grito de Lares; and the 65th Infantry Borinqueneers, a Puerto Rican regiment that fought during the two World Wars and the Korean War. We also encounter independence leader Pedro Albizu Campos suffering radiation burns in a US jail, and the Young Lords, who called for Puerto Rican liberation and self-determination for all Hispanics. In the next few pages, we encounter Agueybana II leading the 1511 revolt against the Spanish, the Grito de Lares, the mourners of the 2016 Orlando Pulse Shooting, and the Ponce Massacre of 1937 when unarmed men and women protesting the US occupation of the island were gunned down.[31]

The rest of the issue follows our hero as she rescues people through a tropical storm and blackout that appears prophetic of the destruction wrought by Hurricane Maria a year later. A second short story in the first issue addresses the dumping of toxic waste in the city of Peñuelas, a case of art imitating life. Beginning in 2014, several communities on the island protested against energy producer AES Puerto Rico. The company had been dumping coal ash in landfills around Peñuelas, exposing nearby residents to inhalation of toxic dust.[32] More recently, the hurricane-relief fundraiser *Ricanstruction* has her teaming up with several DC Comics superheroes in various post-Maria episodes that range from the silly to the empowering to the reflective. In the second issue of her book, Marisol struggles with her powers and her dual identity, one that finds its source not only in the superhero narrative itself but in those of many throughout the diaspora who ask themselves whether they are a New Yorker or a Chicagoan or a Puerto Rican, and whether one identity will subsume the other. In the meantime, a shadow corporation, claiming to "own" everything on the island for their own profit (including, apparently, people) seeks to further division and chaos and exploit our hero as a potential weapon of mass destruction. This issue is set within the context of nonviolent protests held by university students against austerity measures and anticipates the historic demonstrations of the people in Old San Juan that resulted in the resignation of Governor Ricardo Roselló in July 2019.

## A Graphic Decolonial Theology

Aldama notes that comic book creators organize visual and verbal elements in ways that guide and educate readers in how to engage with their storyboards. They set the tone, pace, and focus of the story and lead the reader to the desired end.[33] This is not a passive process. Taking what writers and artists present, readers co-create stories and characters, putting themselves in the characters' shoes. As readers, we fill in the gaps between the panels and pages, making static images and words dynamic in our imaginations. Taking cues from the art and script, we use emotion and thought to fill in gestures, movement, dialogue, and interactions. We do this without altering what the original creators have given us. When encountering minority characters, we may ask whether the parts that comprise the characters make up an integrated whole or whether they are examples of tokenism. The difference between these extremes will enhance or diminish one's engagement with the character as a fictional reconstruction of real-life Latinx experiences. While some characters may reaffirm stereotypes of Latinx life, others can challenge racism and colonialism and help us imagine another, liberating form of being.[34]

Puerto Rican theologian and ethicist Teresa Delgado elaborates on the need for theological reflection from a Puerto Rican perspective in order to address contemporary issues. Delgado sees literature as a valuable starting point for this kind of thought, given that it is "both descriptive and prescriptive of the experiences of the

Puerto Rican people." Literature, according to Delgado, serves as a reflection of the cultural, spiritual, and political realities of the Puerto Rican people, including our colonial relationship to the United States. As Delgado explains, "The writer whose work reflects a desire for freedom from the context of a condition of non-freedom (i.e., colonization) offers a prophetic vision for that which is not yet fully realized." From this perspective, literature serves as a well that can be accessed to develop a Puerto Rican theological perspective that is "freedom-centered and decolonized."[35]

Although she does not write about graphic novels specifically, Delgado can help us see how comics, which combine word and image, do not simply exist to point to a truth outside of the text but have the potential to contain and convey truth precisely *through* the interaction between text, image, and reader. This dovetails well with Aldama's understanding of how readers of comic books and graphic novels become co-creators of the story when they fill in what happens to the characters in those empty spaces on the page between panels. In doing so, one can enter into an act of receptivity to the author's prophetic vision and to a transcendent reality that nonetheless remains rooted in a specific worldly context—a time and place and a people. The divine revelation arrives within the theater of creation—the sacred attaching itself to both the works and the experience of beauty, whether in nature or created by human hands. Like the home altars of Catholic popular spirituality, they presuppose the divine in the everyday.[36] In a similar way, the four-color graphic novel of an Afro-Boriqua superheroine—an expression of a diasporic Puerto Rican community identifying with both mainland and island—can serve as a specific contextual expression while still retaining a connection to the spiritual or transcendent in a post-Christian world that has largely divorced truth and justice from religious discourse. This aesthetic expression has the potential to reveal both ecstasy and consolation.

Miranda-Rodríguez is able to convey this vision by returning to the history of Puerto Rico. He draws on the island's geography, its Taíno roots, the star of its flag, the Grito de Lares, and its original spirituality to create a symbol that will remind Boricuas of their strength and encourage them in their pursuit of justice and hope for the future. He creates more than a superhero in blue, red, and white. By making her a symbol of the history and resilience of the Puerto Rican people, he presents La Borinqueña as she sums up the people themselves. In her shining star on blue, she draws the vision of the community to something beyond themselves. Simultaneously, she fulfills the role of consoler by calling the people to reflect on their achievements and fortitude, particularly during the present environmental crisis and political and fiscal disasters. In short, La Borinqueña helps create community.

*¡Mira, pa ya en el cielo!*

In *La Borinqueña* we find a decolonial theology that reimagines the traditional symbolism of the Christian faith with religious imagery of the original Taíno inhabitants and the modern superhero template. There is Atabex, the Mother and Lover of Creation and her comic-book emissary who represents the people of Boriken, past and present.[37] Instead of the Christian Jesus, the story of La Borinqueña focuses on the community nailed to the cross of colonialism, imperialism, and vulture capitalism. It is also a risen community united in a common history of suffering, resistance, and resilience that calls for unity with one another by reclaiming that history. La Borinqueña's connection to the Creator-Mother also spurs an environmental urgency to care for the island and its irreplaceable creatures beset by disasters both natural and human-made.[38] As her adventures attest, the fate of the island's environment and creatures is inseparable from the well-being of its people.

*La Borinqueña* eclectically draws on various religious symbols, particularly those that represent the divine feminine in her various guises. When our heroine rescues a gay couple in Brooklyn from violence, one of the men gratefully greets her as Yemayá, the Yoruba orisha or spirit of the living Ocean, considered the mother of all, the source of all the waters, and whose ritual color is blue. Readers will recall that the Virgin Mary's color is also blue, and that Our Lady of Providence in San Juan Cathedral, Puerto Rico's patron saint, like our comic book superheroine, is also draped in the flag of the island. The symbolic significance of all these features point to the fact that La Borinqueña, like many Marian devotions in Latin America and the Caribbean, is on the side of the marginalized and oppressed.

The decolonial narrative presented in *La Borinqueña* overturns the relationship between center and margin that has existed in the modern world for the past five centuries. For Spain and the rest of Europe to establish itself as the center of the world after 1500, it was necessary for Africa and the Americas to serve as its margins.[39] Likewise, for the United States to become the center of economic, political, and cultural life from the late nineteenth century onwards, it needs its far-flung holdings—the Indian Territories, Guam, Puerto Rico—to define itself.[40] On a smaller scale, the United States and its urban centers, whether real or imaginary, serve as the center of the modern superhero universe. *La Borinqueña* reverses this vision, re-centering it on Puerto Rico and its people.[41]

Moreover, as it is represented in the comic, Puerto Rico is not simply an imperial territory, nor a half-forgotten appendage to the United States.[42] The mountain where Marisol receives her calling to be a Taíno *zemi* is a place of divine revelation, and in portraying it as such, the book's creators upend the imperial myth, portraying the island itself as literal holy ground. Boriken becomes an *axis mundi*, a navel of the world foundational to the transformation of its people and from where a message of environmental stewardship and mutual support spreads to the diaspora and beyond.

This re-centered worldview has far-flung implications. In *Ricanstruction*, various writers envision a post-Maria future where Puerto Rico will reject the empire and its empty promises. Inspired by the strength that La Borinqueña reveals, Puerto Ricans will look to their own Taíno and African heritage to become responsible stewards of the island's natural resources and learn to live in harmony with the created world in their architecture, technology, and relationships. These writers imagine a future where Puerto Rico will bring light and inspiration to other parts of the world beset by the ravages of unheeded climate change.[43]

This emphasis on modern social justice issues is not new in comics but harkens back to the origins of the superhero genre itself where, during the Depression, Superman fought domestic violence and corrupt corporate bosses, Captain America punched Adolf Hitler in the face months before the United States entered World War II, and Wonder Woman turned the tables on toxic masculinity. The success of *La Borinqueña* has transcended its own comic book roots to become tangible in our real world. It is visible in the *Ricanstruction* fundraising effort, which to date has resulted in over $200,000 in grants to local grassroots organizations working to help Puerto Rico.[44] Lately, Miranda-Rodríguez has teamed up with Masks for America to send protective gear to healthcare workers across the island during the COVID-19 crisis.[45] And as noted above, a woman took inspiration from *La Borinqueña* to dress as the titular hero during 2019's successful nonviolent uprising against the governorship of Ricardo Roselló.[46]

## What If?

In La Borinqueña, Edgardo Miranda-Rodríguez creates a modern figure that confronts five centuries of colonization and the individualism of modern existence. As a character that evokes the entire history of Puerto Rico from the Taíno uprisings to the recent protests against government corruption, La Borinqueña serves as an antidote to the perpetual problem faced by colonized people everywhere, the challenge of being a people whose histories are suppressed by colonial powers in the interests of creating a loyal, subservient, and unrooted subaltern. La Borinqueña's links to the history of the island and its spirituality has the potential not only to draw the curious to study history, but also to bring forth that sense of connection and pride among those whom she reflects. She connects Puerto Ricans to their land and to their history, and in doing so, she helps create a consciousness that resists the dominant myths of US society.

These dominant myths—which privilege capitalist and urban mainland settings and as well as a white male savior, "go it alone" mentality—have long been reflected in the modern superhero genre. La Borinqueña, however, serves as an icon of social justice and cultural pride, as evidenced by the way in which she has aided grassroots organizations in times of national crises. She spurs readers to ask, "What if?" What if Puerto Ricans can imagine a decolonized society where its history and people are perceived of as blessings to the world rather than as the marginalized Others? What if our religious traditions would cast off fundamentalism and division and encourage love, dialogue, and mutual respect for the betterment of all society? What if we could cultivate the environment responsibly rather than exploit it and envision a community in harmony with nature rather than at odds with it? What if the descendants of the Taíno, the Africans, and the Europeans could see themselves as the diverse children of Boriken and reject the racist, patriarchal, and heteronormative caste labels imposed on them throughout their colonized history?

Miranda-Rodríguez created a superhero to inspire Puerto Ricans, to raise contemporary issues facing the island and the diaspora, and to inspire readers to imagine a future by rooting them in the past. When read in light of its religious overtones, *La Borinqueña* presents a vision of the divine united in love with the island and its people, a vision that extends all the way back to the island's original inhabitants.

*La Borinqueña* bids Puerto Ricans to believe the unbelievable and to reclaim that which colonization has sought to suppress for over 500 years. In the best traditions of liturgy, music, art, and literature, this graphic novel and its hero seek a subjective response that engages in acts of creation and redemption: *La Borinqueña* invites the community to engage with one another and their history and to reclaim the symbols of their past as vessels of hope. Through this decolonial process, Puerto Ricans learn that their strength doesn't come from Wall Street, FEMA, colonial structures, or the governor's mansion, but resides deep within themselves and their history. Miranda-Rodríguez's *La Borinqueña* helps inspire Puerto Ricans to enter a future where "what ifs" are transformed into reality.

# Notes

1. Frederick Luis Aldama, *Your Brain on Latino Comics: From Gus Arriola to Los Bros Hernández* (Austin: University of Texas Press, 2012), 2. Examples of comics and graphic novels that have explored the depths of human experience in a meaningful way include *Watchmen*, *Fun House*, *X-Men: God Loves, Man Kills*, *Persepolis*, and *Maus*.
2. Aldama, *Your Brain on Latino Comics*, 2.
3. Throughout this chapter, the character of La Borinqueña will not be italicized whereas the book as a published object will be written in italics.
4. As an independently published work by SomosArte, *La Borinqueña* is not released on a monthly schedule. To date there have been three issues featuring the character, her first two issues (2016 and 2018) as well as a longer anthology, *Ricanstruction* (2018), a fundraiser for recovery efforts in Puerto Rico after Hurricane María. Issue #3 of her own series, unavailable at the time of this writing, was released in 2021. While most monthly titles feature about twenty-three pages, *La Borinqueña* averages about sixty-four pages per issue, providing an adequate introduction to the character and the book's themes.
5. See, for example, the characters of Ebony White in the Spirit, Chop-Chop, the Asian cook to the Blackhawks, or the *Whip* who debuted in Flash #1 (1940).
6. For a more extensive history of comic book history see Gerard Jones, *Men of Tomorrow: Geeks, Gangsters, and the Birth of the Comic Book* (New York: Basic Books, 2004); Bradford W. Wright, *Comic Book Nation: The Transformation of Youth Culture in America* (Baltimore: Johns Hopkins University, 2003); and Adilifu. Nama, *Super Black: American Pop Culture and Black Superheroes* (Austin: University of Texas, 2011).
7. Aldama, *Latinx Superheroes in Mainstream Comics* (Tucson: University of Arizona Press, 2017). Renee Montoya first appeared in the Batman animated series in 1992 and made the jump to comics later that year.
8. John Shelton Lawrence and Robert Jewett, *The Myth of the American Superhero* (Grand Rapids: Eerdmans Publishing, 2002), 6–8; *Captain America and the Crusade Against Evil: The Dilemma of Zealous Nationalism* (Grand Rapids: Eerdmans Publishing, 2003), 29.
9. For example, Fire from Brazil in the *Justice League International* comics (DC) was often portrayed as the stereotypical "Latin spitfire" in the 1980s. Aldama, *Latinx*, 7.
10. *Edgardo Miranda-Rodríguez on Creating a Superhero for Puerto Rico, What's Good with Stretch and Bobbito*, Season 2, Episode 4, September 5, 2016. www.npr.org/2018/30/643326450/edgardo-miranda-Rodríguez-on-creating-a-superhero-for-puerto-rico

11. The concept of a national anthem arose during the nineteenth century when independence movements, exuberant over their successful revolts against Spanish control, anticipated in hope that the island would also see her independence. As the anthem predates the US conquest in 1898 and since Puerto Rico is regarded as a "Free Associated State" rather than an actual state of the "United States," the directives for the anthem's use are spelled out in the Puerto Rican Constitution. The original 1866 lyrics to the anthem read "Arise, boricua!/ The call to arms has sounded!/ Awake from the slumber/ it is time to fight!" By contrast the 1903 lyrics still officially in use go "The land of Borinquén/ where I was born/ is a flowery garden/ of magical beauty." The changes were made in light of the takeover and occupation of the island in 1898.
12. Carnaval is the traditional festival that precedes Ash Wednesday. The El Yunque National Forest is the only tropical rainforest in the national forest system. El Morro is a citadel built between the sixteenth and eighteenth centuries in San Juan.
13. *La Borinqueña*, (Vol.1 No.1), 1. "Es Borínquen la hija/ la hija del mar y el sol/ Del mar y el sol, del mar y el sol."
14. *La Borinqueña*, (Vol.1 No.1), 3.
15. Mariza Bafile, "Edgardo Miranda-Rodríguez: la Borinqueña es un símbolo de esperanza," (*ViceVersa Magazine,* October 22, 2018). https://www.vicerversa-mag.com/edgardo-miranda-rodrigues-la-borinquena-es-un-simbolo-de-esperanza/ Accessed October 23, 2018.
16. *Edgardo Miranda-Rodríguez on Creating a Superhero for Puerto Rico, What's Good with Stretch and Bobbito,* Season 2, Episode 4, September 5, 2016. www.npr.org/2018/30/643326450/edgardo-miranda-Rodríguez-on-creating-a-superhero-for-puerto-rico.; Isabel Dieppa, *La Borinqueña Is the Puerto Rican Superhero We Need Right Now,* (October 17, 2017). www.bust.com/books/193640-la-borinquena-edgardo-miranda-Rodríguez-interview.html. Accessed October 16, 2018.
17. Damaly González, *La Borinqueña: A Female, Puerto Rican Superhero* (January 11, 2017), https://hiplatina.com/la-borinquena-comic-book-puerto-rican-superhero/ Accessed October 16, 2018; "This is the World's First Afro-Latinx Comic Book Superhero" by Devri Velázquez (March 24, 2017), www.naturallycurly.com/curlreading/curly-kinky-hair-type-3c/this-is-the-worlds-first-afro-latinx-superhero. Accessed October 16, 2018; "New Mural Underscores Hunts Point's Puerto Rican identity" in *Hunts Point Express;* June 14, 2017. https://huntspointexpress.com/2017/06/14/new-mural-underscores-hunts-points-puerto-rican-identity/ Accessed October 18, 2018.

18. *La Borinqueña* (Vol. 1 No.1), 8.
19. *La Borinqueña* (Vol. 1 No.1), 14.
20. *La Borinqueña* (Vol. 1 No.1), 9.
21. *La Borinqueña* (Vol. 1 No.1), 15.
22. *La Borinqueña* (Vol. 1 No.1), 16, 20–21.
23. *La Borinqueña* (Vol. 1 No.1), 18.
24. "Puerto Rico Needs Both Fiscal Austerity and Pro-Growth Tax Cuts" by Ryan Ellis in *Forbes*, March 15, 2016. https://www.forbes.com/sites/ryanellis/2016/03/15/puerto-rico-needs-both-fiscal-austerity-and-pro-growth-tax-cuts/#7ab11483b2e7. Accessed July 26, 2019;

    University of Puerto Rico Student Shut Down Continues, *Democracy Now!*, March 17, 2016. https://www.democracynow.org/2016/3/17/headlines/university_of_puerto_rico_student_strike_continues. Accessed July 26, 2019; "The 1 percent declares war on Puerto Rico: The austerity push that unmasks neoliberalism" posted by korzen.1 in *Ohio State University*, October 26, 2016. https://u.osu.edu/korzen.1/2016/10/26/the-1-percent-declares-war-on-puerto-rico-the-austerity-push-that-unmasks-neoliberalism/. Accessed July 26, 2019.
25. *La Borinqueña* (Vol. 1 No.1), 23–4.
26. *La Borinqueña* (Vol. 1 No.1), 25.
27. *La Borinqueña* (Vol. 1 No.1), 29.
28. As in many Indigenous oral traditions, there are many ways in which the stories of the deities and their relationships are told and retold. For more on Taíno mythology, see, Sebastián Robiou Lamarche, *Taínos y Caribes: Las Culturas Aborígenes Antillanas* (San Juan: Editorial Punto y Coma, 2003).
29. *La Borinqueña* (Vol. 1 No.1), 30–32; cf. "Taino Perseverance" in *Smithsonian*, August 8, 2018; www.si.edu/newsdesk/photos/taini-perseverence-5. Accessed October 17, 2018.
30. Shawn Gregory Morton, *The Taino Use of Caves: A Review*. https://fieldresearchcentre.weebly.com/uploads/1/8/0/7/18079819/morton_a_2015.pdf. Accessed October 16, 2018. The Pueblo, Choctaw, and Aztec/Mexica are among those American Indigenous peoples for whom caves feature prominently in their origins.
31. *La Borinqueña* (Vol. 1 No.1), 26–8.
32. Ruth Santiago, "Coal Ash Contamination in Puerto Rico," *openDemocracy* (November 25, 2016), https://www.opendemocracy.net/en/democraciaabierta/coal-ash-contamination-in-puerto-rico/. Accessed January 18, 2021.

33. Aldama, *Brain*, 103.
34. Aldama, *Latinx*, 91, 94ff.
35. Teresa Delgado, *A Puerto Rican Decolonial Theology- Prophesy Freedom* (New York: Springer International, 2017), 11–2.
36. cf. Orlando Espín, *The Faith of the People: Theological Reflections on Popular Catholicism* (Maryknoll: Orbis Books, 1997).
37. Miranda-Rodríguez's use of Taíno myths can be seen as an example of the reclaiming of Taíno identity among Puerto Ricans and other Caribbean peoples. For more information see, "Taino Affirmation in the 21st Century" by R. Múkaro Agüeibaná Borrero at www.tainolegacies.com/170582894. Accessed October 19, 2018. Indeed, a page from *La Borinqueña* is featured as part of the exhibit on Taíno heritage at the Smithsonian Museum of the American Indian. "Taíno: Native Heritage and Identity in the Caribbean/ Taíno: herencia e identidad indígena en el Caribe," *Smithsonian: National Museum of the American Indian*; https://americanindian.si.edu/explore/exhibitions/item/d=966. Accessed October 19, 2018.

    See also: "Born Puerto Rican, born (again) Taino? A resurgence of indigenous identity among Puerto Ricans has sparked debates over the island's tri-racial history," Christina Veran at https://www.thefreelibrary.com/Born+Puerto+Rican%2C+born+(again)+Taino%3F+A+resurgence+of+indigenous....-a0108693833. Accessed October 19, 2018.
38. On the use of Indigenous spirituality as a foundation for environmental care, see Mary Judity Ress, *Ecofeminism in Latin America* (Maryknoll: Orbis Books, 2006), 68–73.
39. Goizueta, Roberto S. *Christ Our Companion: Toward a Theological Aesthetics of Liberation* (Maryknoll: Orbis Books, 2009), 147.
40. See for example, Daniel Immerwahr, *How to Hide an Empire* (New York: Farrar, Straus and Giroux, 2019).
41. cf. *Ricanstruction*, 68.
42. Kyle Dropp and Brendan Nyhan, "Nearly Half of Americans Don't Know Puerto Ricans are Fellow Citizens," *The New York Times*, September 26, 2017. https://www.nytimes.com/2017/09/26/upshot/nearly-half-of-americans-dont-know-people-in-puerto-ricoans-are-fellow-citizens.html. Accessed November 8, 2018.
43. *Ricanstruction*, 105–7, 152–54, 155–7, 158–160, 164–9, 170–172; cf. Christina M. González, "Abuelas, Ancestors and Atabey: The Spirit of Taino Resurgence," *American Indian Magazine*, (Fall 2018/Vol. 19 No. 3); https://www.americanindianmagazine.org/story/abuelas-ancestors-and-atabey-spirit-taino-resurgence/. Accessed October 19, 2018).

44. J. K. Parkin, "Watch Edgardo Miranda-Rodriguez's Full Eisner Acceptance Speech," *Smash pages: The Comics Super-Blog* (July 20, 2019). http://smashpages.net/2019/07/20/watch-edgardo-miranda-rodriguezs-full-eisner-acceptance-speech/. Accessed October 29, 2019.
45. https://www.la-borinquena.com/. Accessed June 5, 2020.
46. From Edgardo Miranda-Rodríguez's Twitter account, July 22, 2019: https://twitter.com/mredgardonyc/status/1153386863320850433. Accessed June 5, 2020.

## References

Aldama, Frederick Luis. *Latinx Superheroes in Mainstream Comics*. Tucson: University of Arizona Press, 2017.

Aldama, Frederick Luis. *Your Brain on Latino Comics: From Gus Arriola to Los Bros Hernández*. Austin: University of Texas Press, 2012.

Delgado, Teresa. *A Puerto Rican Decolonial Theology- Prophesy Freedom*. New York: Springer International, 2017.

Espín, Orlando. *The Faith of the People: Theological Reflections on Popular Catholicism*. Maryknoll: Orbis Books, 1997.

Goizueta, Roberto S. *Christ Our Companion: Toward a Theological Aesthetics of Liberation*. Maryknoll: Orbis Books, 2009.

Immerwahr, Daniel. *How to Hide an Empire*. New York: Farrar, Straus and Giroux, 2019.

Jones, Gerard. *Men of Tomorrow: Geeks, Gangsters, and the Birth of the Comic Book*. New York: Basic Books, 2004.

Lamarche, Sebastián Robiou. *Taínos y Caribes: Las Culturas Aborígenes Antillanas*. San Juan: Editorial Punto y Coma, 2003.

Lawrence, John Shelton, and Robert Jewett. *Captain America and the Crusade Against Evil: The Dilemma of Zealous Nationalism*. Grand Rapids: Eerdmans Publishing, 2003.

Lawrence, John Shelton, and Robert Jewett. *The Myth of the American Superhero*. Grand Rapids: Eerdmans Publishing, 2002.

Miranda-Rodríguez, Edgardo, et al. *La Borinqueña*. New York: Somos Arte. 2016–present.

Miranda-Rodríguez, Edgardo. *Ricanstruction: Reminiscing & Rebuilding Puerto Rico*. New York: Somos Arte, 2018.

Nama, Adilifu. *Super Black: American Pop Culture and Black Superheroes.* Austin: University of Texas, 2011.
Picó, Fernando. *Historia General de Puerto Rico, 4ta ed.* San Juan: Ediciones Huracán, 2008.
Ress, Mary Judity. *Ecofeminism in Latin America.* Maryknoll: Orbis Books, 2006.
Wright, Bradford W. *Comic Book Nation: The Transformation of Youth Culture in America.* Baltimore: Johns Hopkins University, 2003

CHAPTER 5

# Rockin' the Habit

## Colliding Cultural Identities and a Peruvian Nuns' Rock Band

*ANN HIDALGO*

> *We like to see people's faces when our songs play because most people are surprised. Many times, they come to a concert without knowing what they are going to hear and, suddenly, the drums crash!*
> —SISTER MÓNICA, PERCUSSIONIST AND VOCALIST FOR SIERVAS

In 2014, a group of Catholic nuns in Lima, Peru, formed the rock band Siervas (Spanish for 'Servants') to communicate their message of joy and hope to the world. By virtue of their musical talents and savvy use of social media, the nuns have become a viral sensation and have toured across Latin America and around the world. The religious order in Lima to which they belong, the Siervas del Plan de Dios (Servants of the Plan of God), operates nursing homes and a school for children with disabilities, and the sisters are active in hospital chaplaincy and providing resources for people who are poor. The nuns began playing music together in small settings, such as masses and other devotional services, and while visiting nearby schools and women's prisons. Media coverage of their 2016 performance in Ciudad Juárez, Mexico, at a liturgy celebrated by Pope Francis, introduced them to an audience worldwide that was captivated by the image of a group of nuns wearing traditional habits, playing in a rock band. The group credits Pope Francis with inspiring their public work, and, following his pastoral style, they chose popular music as an avenue to reach audiences of believers and nonbelievers alike.

This chapter examines the Siervas, first, as women successfully performing in the male-dominated world of rock music by exploring the impact of gender on audience perceptions of genre, performance style, training, and entry into the public sphere. Next, it engages sociologist Danielle Giffort's term *implicit feminism* to see if it is an appropriate description of the Siervas' behavior. Finally, a textual analysis of the Siervas' lyrics highlights some key contrasts with the broader field of contemporary Christian music. The Siervas' public performance of their Catholic identity, a performance which thrives on contradictions, appeals to audiences with originality, enthusiasm, and joy.

## Women in Rock

In popular news media coverage, the Siervas are called "las monjas del rock,"[1] "las religiosas roqueras," and "monjas rockeras"[2] (all of which roughly translate to "the nuns of rock"), and their musical genre is described as rock, pop rock, *rocanrol*, and *pop latino*.[3] Starting from a United States–based perspective, this article analyzes their music as Latin pop, using the term Latin to indicate that this music comes from Latin America and is sung in Spanish (rather than identifying the use of particular rhythms or instrumentation), and considering pop as a subset of rock music. These classifications are important because they are embedded in a web of gendered connotations that shape how listeners hear and experience the music. As they listen to music, audiences, often unconsciously, tap into preconceived notions about who is capable of performing rock music successfully. If part of the Siervas' popularity comes from the unexpected juxtaposition of nuns in habits playing rock music, examining these gendered connotations is crucial. Why are we surprised to see them perform? What unwritten rules of the genre are they transgressing?

To say that the recording industry and commercial popular music culture are male-dominated is an understatement. While women have always been involved in popular music, they are a minority among performers and occupy an even smaller percentage of positions in music management and production. As philosopher Alison Stone notes in "Feminism, Gender and Popular Music," as of 2008, women comprised only 39 percent of those working in the music industry, 23 percent of those in music promotion and management, and less than 5 percent of music producers and engineers.[4] Likewise, across the industry, predominantly female bands are much less common than predominantly male bands, and women are more likely than men to perform music written by others.[5] These numerical imbalances in the industry and the gendered characteristics that are built into the rock genre require women who are active in the industry to navigate complicated sets of expectations.

FIGURE 8. Concert in El Salvador. Facebook post, September 24, 2018.

Because the rock star persona is characterized by traits that have been socially coded as masculine, namely a rebellious nature, overt sexuality, aggression, and association with hard drinking and drug use, women in rock are often considered outsiders or are seen to belong only if they act like one of the boys.[6] The pop star persona, on the other hand, is typically more socially acceptable, de-emphasizing rebellion, aggression, and substance abuse (at least in intentional presentation). While this is a generalization, typical female pop stars are more likely be objectified for the pleasure of their audience than they are to express sexual agency themselves.[7]

Stone goes a step further in identifying pop music as a feminized subset of rock. She explains that audience perception of popular music conforms to a hierarchy that privileges "qualities deemed masculine—authenticity, original vision, innovation" over those "deemed feminine—the formulaic, inauthentic, superficial and banal."[8] In turn, she traces the origins of this hierarchy to centuries-old, gendered contrasts that map the masculine and the feminine dualism to spirit and body, as well as art and entertainment, valuing the first of each pair over the second.

Musically, pop is associated with several characteristics: a strong emphasis on the vocals at the foreground of the texture, the use of synthesized instruments, clearly identifiable song structures (verse/chorus/bridge), and an overall sound that is highly produced. These common traits are often criticized as formulaic elements of a "pop machine" that churns out singles that are immediately accessible because they neatly fulfill the pop listener's expectations. If rock is seen as the outpouring of a soul-searching, countercultural artist, pop is more often characterized as the trite commercial endeavor of a performer who obediently complies with the rules of the music industry to produce (yet another) hit. According to Stone, the facts that there are more women performers in pop than in rock, and that women in the role of vocalist frequently perform songs written at least in part by others, accentuate the tendency to assign a lower artistic value to pop.[9]

The audience member's experience of popular music, however, is shaped by more than the auditory act of listening to a piece of music. A performer or band communicates their identity through cover art, fashion, performance style, dance routines, music videos, and their online presence. These elements shape how a listener receives and understands a piece of music, as well as how the listener identifies the genre of the piece. Through the act of identifying and classifying the music by genre, the listener also taps into the socially constructed gendered meanings that are associated with each genre.[10] The Siervas' visual presentation in their live performances and also in their music videos and online presence (on Facebook, Twitter, Instagram, YouTube, etc.) is an important driver of their popularity. Their identity as nuns—signaled visually by their habits—immediately sets them apart in the field of popular music performers. Their comportment is consistent with their sense that the band is part of their religious ministry, and their performance style and limited choreography convey modesty and emphasize a friendly engagement with audiences. None of these visual elements communicate the rebelliousness or overt sexualization of rock.

If the Siervas are perceived as transgressive of traditional boundaries, their act of transgression comes through the use of the pop rock genre and its typical instrumentation. It is no accident that popular media coverage describes the Siervas as "rockers" rather than "pop musicians," which would be a more accurate description of their musical genre. Using the term "rockers" sets up the series of expectations that are in the greatest contrast with the Siervas' presentation.

While the use of the pop genre downplays some of the harder-edged, more objectionable elements of the rock persona and makes it more compatible with the

FIGURE 9. Las Siervas rooftop concert.

objectives of ministry, the Siervas nevertheless complicate some elements of the dichotomies Stone describes between rock and pop, and thus between the male and female domains. First, the Siervas are both vocalists and instrumentalists. Specifically, instruments that are typically associated with men, including the lead electric guitar, bass, and drums are featured prominently in their music. Second, the Siervas write their own songs. While the songs are not credited with individual bylines, the Siervas relate in interviews and through social media that they write their own music.[11] Some songs are written as a group, but many sources indicate that Sister Andrea writes many of the lyrics and Sister Ivonne composes much of the music.[12] Finally, all of the proceeds of their live concerts and albums go toward the ministries of their religious order.[13] To broaden their outreach to the widest audiences possible, they do not charge admission for their concerts; rather, they accept voluntary donations.[14]

## Gender and Training

Many women musicians struggle to find opportunities to develop their skills and to perform. Sociologist Mary Ann Clawson studies how gender influences whether or not children or young adolescents will aspire to be musicians, will learn to play an instrument, and will become part of a band.[15] Specifically, she demonstrates that teenage girls "have a harder time translating their desire to become rock musicians into the practical experience that was readily available to boys."[16] Beginning in childhood or early adolescence, boys typically form bands in their preexisting network of friends. This allows friends who lack musical skills to participate and to develop their skills as the band progresses. If girls are included in a band, however, they generally have to demonstrate musical competence before being accepted into the group.[17] Clawson highlights adolescence as a crucial time for developing musical skills and confidence but notes that young adolescents are likely to socialize in same-gendered groups. She explains: "During the crucial high school years when aspiring musicians form these bands, boys tend to exclude girls from participating, which limits their ability to learn how to play rock music."[18]

Similarly, sociologist Diana Miller focuses on the accessibility of learning spaces in which an aspiring musician can develop skills and gain valuable performance experience. Miller coins the phrase *performance capital* to describe "the instrumental and interpersonal skills required to perform music."[19] Expanding on Pierre Bourdieu's field theory in an article on gender and performance capital, Miller examines the ways in which gender-specific access to learning spaces enhances or limits one's potential. Specifically, she analyzes the opportunities for new musicians to enter a local music scene by contrasting the learning spaces available in the folk and metal music genres. Because metal groups typically form out of preexisting social networks and rehearse in private spaces (garages, basements), women are often excluded. By contrast, folk musicians often develop their skills in workshops and open stages at local clubs. Anyone who attends and wishes to participate is welcome. According to Miller, these differences in access to the spaces and opportunities in which one builds skills and confidence "can lead to greater or lesser opportunities for women to become cultural producers."[20]

For the Siervas, it is likely that liturgical settings provided a significant training space for their musical abilities. While some of the members of Siervas had previously studied classical music, it is likely that all of them benefitted from singing and playing their instruments in liturgies and other devotional contexts prior to forming the band. Some may have begun liturgical music making prior to joining the order, while others may have begun in the convent. In a video clip from the news website América Vive, Sister Ivonne relates that she learned to play the guitar at age twelve in the music group at her parish, and she studied music education after entering the community.[21] Although the Siervas are currently in their twenties and thirties, many joined the convent in their late teens, allowing them to take advantage of performing opportunities at the formative age that Clawson identifies as crucial for the development of musical skills and confidence.

Furthermore, in a religious context, music making serves a role as a form of worship, giving it a purpose beyond the solely aesthetic. Although some individuals might be designated as music leaders for a mass or other worship service, everyone in attendance is invited to participate in the singing, which allows individuals without formal training to participate in the music making. While musical proficiency is certainly appreciated, especially among the music leaders, the liturgical context encourages participation of all. If the primary goal of music making is worship, then a genuine desire to worship can be considered more important than musical proficiency. Similarly, the group dynamic often present in choirs or church music ensembles encourages lesser-skilled members to develop their skills, learn the repertoire, and assimilate the performance practice by imitating the more experienced members of the group.

The following comments from three of the Siervas illustrate how the idea of forming a band and performing in public grew out of their musical experiences within the private sphere of the convent. Sister Daniela, the drummer, described the formation of the group in this way:

> From the beginning of the community, we made music, but four years ago, we started to live together in the same house. There was one who lived in Colombia and went to live in Lima, later I entered the community, another who plays the violin entered and, in that way, we started to make music differently than had been done previously. Later the idea arose to make our music known to the public outside [of the convent].[22]

Sister Arisa describes a similar experience:

> One day in 2014, in the local congregation of the Siervas del Plan de Dios in Lima, a group of nuns of diverse nationalities who played musical instruments or sang came together.... When we recognized our instrumental abilities, we asked ourselves why not form a band. It was God's design to bring us together.[23]

Similarly, Sister Mónica notes the following:

> At first, we were not formalized at all. We were eleven sisters with musical talents: some composed, others had studied music in conservatories since they were small. . . . We made music about our experiences in the community and later, we sang these songs on visits to the jail, on the street, in the elementary schools, when we visited. . . . It was something natural. Later, when we had a wide repertoire, we released the album and officially formed the band.[24]

As various YouTube recordings show, the Siervas perform in small settings, such as the convent and small gatherings, as well as their larger concert settings. These publicly archived performances likely represent the tip of the iceberg of the many hundreds of hours that the Siervas have spent rehearsing and performing in liturgical settings or informal concert settings. This experience of singing and playing provides opportunities to develop what Miller describes as performance capital, the combination of musical proficiency and—although the phrase seems awkward with respect to liturgical music—their "performing personas." For those who lacked formal musical training, these steadily recurring opportunities to rehearse and perform, perhaps several times each week, allowed them to build individual skills and confidence, as well as to develop group cohesion. Over the years, the many smaller performance opportunities were likely crucial steps in building the polished image visible and audible in the professionally produced videos.

## Implicit Feminism

Given their success in a male-dominated field, it would be easy to see women's empowerment as part of the Siervas' social message. Asking whether or not the Siervas consider themselves feminists, however, is a more complicated question. To the best of my knowledge, the Siervas have not used the term *feminist* in any of their interviews and promotions of the band, and the content of their lyrics is seldom explicitly feminist. (The lyrics to "Mi comunidad," celebrating life in a women's religious community, are perhaps an exception.) Complicating this evaluation is the song "Dame la Oportunidad," a single released in 2018, with a clear anti-abortion message. For many feminists, this religiously based, pro-life posture would place the Siervas solidly outside the feminist camp.

FIGURE 10. Las Siervas singer.

Following the broad feminist practice of self-naming and self-identification, I am inclined not to describe the Siervas as feminists if they do not use the term themselves, but it is still possible to identify feminist elements in their artistic output and their public image. Sociologist Danielle Giffort has coined the term *implicit feminism*, which may be helpful for understanding the Siervas. In her article "Show or Tell? Feminist Dilemmas and Implicit Feminism at Girls' Rock Camp," Giffort analyzes the behavior of the volunteers of a summer day camp for young girls that focuses on rock music as a way to bolster the girls' self-esteem and empower them as cultural producers. She notes that despite the seemingly feminist mission of the camp, volunteers carefully avoided using the word feminism when describing the program. Giffort develops the term implicit feminism to describe "a strategy practiced by feminist activists within organizations that are operating in an anti- and postfeminist environment in which they conceal feminist identities and ideas while emphasizing the more socially acceptable angles of their efforts."[25]

Rockin' the Habit   113

Drawing on earlier research on feminist organizations, Giffort notes that organizations tend to "practice feminism in less visible and disruptive ways within mainstream institutions" and at times "ton[e] down feminist ideologies in order to obtain the resources that keep these organizations running."[26] This perspective may shed light on the Siervas' stance, given that they are members of a religious community within the Catholic Church and they consider their music to have an evangelizing role. Adopting a clear feminist posture would put them at odds with their church and current interpretations of its pro-life teachings. As Giffort reminds us, however, "Not claiming a feminist identity ... does not mean that individuals are not engaging in what can be interpreted as feminist activism."[27] The title of Giffort's article, "Show or Tell," allows for the possibility that the Siervas may communicate more through their actions than can be identified looking solely at their lyrics and public announcements in print.

## Siervas in the Christian Music Ecosystem

Music, as a medium for both expressing and experiencing emotions, has the capacity to connect disparate groups of people across time and space. As such, it has been a primary component of Christian worship for centuries. The physical act of singing together requires people to breathe in unison, connecting them through that most fundamental human activity. Likewise, through their lyrics, songs serve an instructive function and can shape believers' theological imaginaries.[28] While the practice of Christianity has never been limited to events taking place within houses of worship, religious music is notable for its ability to transcend the boundary between spaces that are traditionally considered sacred and those that are seen as secular.

In his analysis of Christian music, theologian Brian Nail highlights the ways in which the emergence of social media in the twenty-first century has greatly expanded the possibilities for forming religious community outside of church spaces. The near ubiquity of digital devices allows people to access the music of their choice anytime, anywhere, to accompany their work, commute, and everyday tasks. In fact, Nail explains, mobile devices can come to function as devotional objects, like rosaries or Bibles, creating portable, personal religious experiences.[29] In addition, social media platforms facilitate the encounter with new songs and performers, while services such as YouTube, Spotify, and other streaming platforms place a wide range of recordings at listeners' fingertips that might otherwise remain obscure or difficult to access.[30]

Locating the Siervas within today's Christian music ecosystem requires taking a step back to understand some broader trends within Christian popular music.

The genre known as contemporary Christian music (CCM) grew out of the US–based evangelicalism of the 1960s, specifically the conservative Christian efforts of the Jesus Movement.[31] Musician and scholar of music industry studies Shawn David Young, however, traces the roots of CCM back to the early 1900s and the rise of radio broadcasting. Young contrasts the approaches of fundamentalists and evangelicals with respect to emerging media, explaining that the former positioned themselves firmly in opposition to the cultural mainstream, while the latter "sought to sanctify culture with their own version of pop media."[32] At the heart of this evangelical approach is a tension between the desire to connect with a mass audience and a religious critique of secular society.

It was not until the 1960s, with the rise of youth-based popular culture, protest movements, and the so-called "Jesus freaks" that the commercial pop recording industry was firmly established as a tool of evangelism.[33] The Christian hippies of the Jesus movement married aspects of the 1960s counterculture (long hair, informality, focus on youth culture) with literal interpretations of the Bible and a theologically conservative Christianity. Significantly, the Jesus movement had little interest in activism relating to the present world, favoring instead an apocalyptical view and a focus on personal piety and the salvation of souls.[34]

One aspect of its enduring legacy is the creation of the evangelical popular media industry. The music of the Jesus movement laid the foundation for the development of CCM, which Young describes as a commercially successful "hybrid of rock 'n' roll and Jesus music."[35] Early performers, such as singer Larry Norman, whose 1969 album *Upon This Rock* is considered the world's first Christian rock album, laid the groundwork for the emerging CCM pop stars of the 1980s, including Amy Grant, Michael W. Smith, Rich Mullins, and many others.[36] The growing Christian media industry included bookstores, publishers, record labels, conferences and festivals, and even theme parks. These corporate relationships, Young explains, "helped seal the deal between establishment evangelicalism and capitalism," making CCM "the most extensive attempt to merge religious music with commercialization and industrialization of the popular entertainment industry."[37]

These commercial developments as well as the theological underpinnings of CCM are relevant to understanding how the Siervas differ from mainstream Christian popular music groups. The following analysis of Siervas lyrics from their 2014 and 2016 albums, *Ansias que queman* and *Hoy despierto*, illustrates this contrast with CCM.

The stress of modern life is a recurrent theme in Siervas' lyrics. While the lyrics acknowledge that some people suffer material poverty and lack adequate food and shelter, they also spend a significant amount of time talking about anxiety, loneliness, depression, fear, and discouragement. For example, "Confía en Dios," perhaps their most popular single, sets the stage with the phrase: "When the future is uncertain and fear weakens your confidence...."[38] Similarly, in "Junto a mí," the soloist sings of being "imprisoned by fear" with "sadness that drowns me" in "tears as bitter as bile."

The first part of the Siervas' response to this condition of anxiety and fear is perhaps predictable for any Christian song: if individuals are overwhelmed and anxious, God can help. God is good, powerful, and loves all people deeply. It is the second part of their response, however, that most strongly characterizes the work of this group, namely that God needs people on earth to help others who are suffering. Drawing from biblical language, the central image of one of their songs claims, "The harvest is plentiful but the workers are few." God works through believers to act in the world. Rather than claim that their religious vocations give them special status as God's envoys to modern society, the Siervas highlight the fact that the responsibility for transforming and humanizing the world belongs to everyone. In one particularly memorable phrase, they pray that we "at once—men, women, children, the elderly—rise from our comfortable armchairs and move from being resigned spectators to being protagonists, protagonists of the great change." This posture is a far cry from the Jesus Movement's focus on saving individual souls and waiting for the end times.

In several of their songs, the Siervas emphasize the difficulties they personally encounter in living a life of faith. In "Reencuentro," they use imagery from the biblical story of the prodigal son, casting themselves in the role of the prodigal: "I felt a deep emptiness. I didn't even recognize my own voice. I was a stranger to myself." Similarly, in the song "Mi encuentro con el Señor," the soloist admits "at times, I don't know how to talk to you; I don't know what to say, what to ask of you." By sharing their moments of uncertainty, the sisters emphasize that they are not different from laypeople and that everyone struggles in the walk of faith. They admit to their own struggles as a way of providing encouragement to others, and they reassure their listeners of God's mercy and patience, insisting that God understands even when they cannot find words to express their deepest longings.

The song "Gente más que buena" further extends this idea. In it, the sisters admire the actions of ordinary people who go about their days doing God's work.

Specifically, they compliment the good people whose smiles are contagious, who love intensely even though they are suffering, who sow kindness in the midst of discord. The sisters note that these people are students and workers, farmers and business owners, grandparents, self-sacrificing parents ... in short, they are "santos de lo cotidiano"—everyday saints. In the refrain, the sisters thank these people and sing: "I want to be one of them, these people who are more than good, to build a world that is just and good, and to encourage hope to grow." In this seeming reversal, a nun—arguably someone who can be confident in her status as a holy person—is suggesting that she wants to be like an honest business owner or a dedicated parent—ordinary, worldly people.

This positive valuation of people's typical daily activities signals a distinctly different theological position than much of the CCM repertoire, which emphasizes the fallenness of the world—out there—and suggests that only the Christian insiders have any hope of salvation.[39] In fact, ethnomusicologist and theological ethicist Nathan Myrick explains that evangelicalism "considers itself inherently dissenting in sinful societies" and "thrives on social conflicts that strengthen the identity of the 'saved.'"[40] By contrast, the Siervas' predominant view of the world is one of goodness, and they promote solidarity with good people found in all walks of life.

Returning to the theme of the Siervas as women in a man's industry, it is helpful to examine one of several of their songs that feature Mary, the mother of Jesus. "El sí de María" describes the Annunciation scene found in the first chapter of Luke's gospel (Lk 1:26–38). In it, a soloist narrates in Mary's voice in the verses, and the whole ensemble responds in the refrain. The first verse creates a backstory, a persona for Mary. She sings: "I always wanted to give myself to You, I had longings for greatness. My life was not enough for me. I wanted to give my whole life for others. I always dreamed of a new world where everyone finds the truth. Where those who cry may be happy and the captives find liberty." This characterization of Mary is largely extra-biblical with hints of the Magnificat, from the latter part of Luke's first chapter (Lk 1:45–55). It paints a picture of Mary with far greater agency than she receives in official church piety, where she is often cast as a passive vessel and obedient servant.

In the second verse, Mary narrates the visit from the angel Gabriel, and the verse concludes with "And he invites me to collaborate in this adventure." This Mary seems neither meek nor mild. The third verse builds on Mary saying, "I said yes," with the chorus responding, "She said yes." Again, this seems to highlight her agency and choice. "I said yes for those who came yesterday, for those today, and for those who are to come." There is intentionality and purposefulness to her words.

In their treatment of this traditionally Catholic theme, the Siervas empower Mary by envisioning her as an individual with strong personal agency in the imagined conversation with Gabriel. By honoring Mary for her active participation with God's plan rather than for her passive acceptance, the Siervas open a space for themselves and for the women of their audience to likewise take active roles in bringing about a better future.

Although CCM's marketing strategy is targeted at their ideal listener, a woman code-named "Becky," who is a white, middle-aged housewife, the patriarchal masculinity commonly associated with evangelicals in North America heavily influences the lyrics of CCM songs.[41] The majority of songs that speak with the voice of a gendered protagonist are articulated from a man's perspective, and, more significantly, the "symbolic representation of good [is] consistently coded as masculine."[42] By speaking for themselves as women of faith and by shading the Marian tradition to give greater agency to women, the Siervas sidestep the patriarchal masculinity associated with the Catholic hierarchy and follow a different path in their lyrics. In the theology of the Siervas repertoire, women are never considered lesser than men (literally or symbolically), and they have an equally important role to play in the unfolding of God's plan.

As women performing in the male-dominated world of rock music, the Siervas attract attention by defying audience members' expectations of who nuns are and can be. Although aspects of their Catholic tradition might seem to limit their options as performers, the Siervas have successfully navigated their religious tradition as well as the gendered expectations that govern the rock genres, the difficulties of entry into the public sphere, and the challenge of cultivating an audience for their music. By leveraging positive elements of their Catholic heritage and their personal skills as composers, lyricists, and performers, the Siervas stand out from the broader field of contemporary Christian popular music.

Although the Siervas themselves might not acknowledge this possibility, one could suggest that their musical performance as evangelism works on two levels. The first corresponds to evangelism as it is commonly understood: the Siervas' stated goal of bringing a positive expression of the Christian message to the public. In this respect, they use the skillful performance of tuneful, accessible music to share lyrics that convey particular ideas about who God is and what it means to be a believer.

FIGURE 11. Las Siervas. Facebook post, March 3, 2018.

In contrast to a popular piety that would only look inward, the Siervas' message suggests that it is by reaching out to others who are struggling and by relying on the support of the community to get through hard times that people most strongly experience God's love. No one needs to feel inadequate because people from all walks of life are holy.

On a second level, the Siervas may communicate something equally profound through their actions rather than their words. Their embodied presence on the stage challenges preconceived notions and proves that women can be rockers who compose, arrange, and perform their own music. Likewise, their smiling faces and evident joy in performing belie the stereotype that nuns (or Christians at large) are dour, stern, and judgmental. While not claiming to be feminists, the Siervas' successful participation in the male-dominated music industry and their presence on stage and social media consistently communicate a message that is empowering to women and to all people: they are capable of fulfilling their dreams.

# Notes

Epigraph: "Grupo Musical Siervas," Catholic.net, accessed August 23, 2021, https://es.catholic.net/op/articulos/70486/cat/171/grupo-musical-siervas.html#modal. Translations from Spanish are mine unless otherwise indicated.

1. "Dayana Cobos, de Ecuador, es vocalista de Siervas, las monjas del rock," *El Comercio*, January 12, 2019, https://www.elcomercio.com/tendencias/entretenimiento/dayana-cobos-ecuador-vocalista-siervas.html.
2. "Siervas, el grupo de monjas rockeras que quieren hacer bailar al Papa," *Clarín*, January 17, 2019, https://www.clarin.com/mundo/siervas-grupo-monjas-rockeras-quieren-hacer-bailar-papa_0_QeUYVfjQG.html.
3. "Dayana Cobos," *El Comercio*; "Siervas, el grupo," *Clarín*.
4. Alison Stone, *Feminism, Gender and Popular Music, The Bloomsbury Handbook of Religion and Popular Music*, edited by Christopher Partridge and Marcus Moberg (New York: Bloomsbury Academic, 2017), 54. Stone cites these statistics from the Performing Rights Society for Music's 2008 report on its 95,000 members.
5. Stone, *Feminism, Gender and Popular Music*, 54.
6. Stone, *Feminism, Gender and Popular Music*, 57.
7. Stone, *Feminism, Gender and Popular Music*, 58.
8. Stone, *Feminism, Gender and Popular Music*, 56.
9. Stone, *Feminism, Gender and Popular Music*, 57.
10. Stone, *Feminism, Gender and Popular Music*, 55.
11. In this video, which is typical of the Siervas promotional style, Sister Mónica explains that members of the group write both lyrics and music (2:15). Siervas, "América Vive," September 6, 2016, Video, YouTube, 5:48, https://www.youtube.com/watch?v=OpEAaeJf2Hs.
12. See, for example, Silvia Núñez, "Hermana Daniela y su grupo Siervas están ansiosas por cantarle por primera vez a los romeros," *La Teja*, July 31, 2018, https://www.lateja.cr/farandula/hermana-daniela-y-su-grupo-siervas-estan-ansiosas/NS5VNMV35RBY5M5XFP2C5OE2OE/story/. Producing and recording are unknown pieces of this puzzle. I have not been able to find clear information to document the Siervas' move from talented local performers to a polished recording ensemble. While it is documented that producers Joe Martlet and Francisco Murias worked on the music video for "Confía en Dios," it is unclear if they or other producers have managed the production of the two albums. (See "Las

Siervas: Singing Nuns Selling Out Concerts," Catholic Outlook, January 19, 2016, https://catholicoutlook.org/las-siervas-singing-nuns-selling-out-concerts/). Similarly, the band's carefully constructed social media image may be handled in-house or by outside advertising professionals.
13. "Las Siervas: Singing Nuns Selling Out Concerts," Catholic Outlook, January 19, 2016 https://catholicoutlook.org/las-siervas-singing-nuns-selling-out-concerts/.
14. "Dayana Cobos," *El Comercio.*
15. Mary Ann Clawson, "Masculinity and Skill Acquisition in the Adolescent Rock Band," *Popular Music* 18, no. 1 (1999): 99.
16. Clawson, "Masculinity and Skill Acquisition," 102.
17. Diana L. Miller, "Gender and Performance Capital among Local Musicians," *Qualitative Sociology* 40 (2017): 265.
18. Miller, "Gender and Performance Capital," 266.
19. Miller, "Gender and Performance Capital," 263.
20. Miller, "Gender and Performance Capital," 263.
21. Siervas, "América Vive."
22. Núñez, "*Hermana Daniela y su grupo Siervas.*"
23. "Siervas, el grupo," *Clarín.*
24. "Grupo Musical Siervas," Catholic.net.
25. Danielle M. Giffort, "Show or Tell? Feminist Dilemmas and Implicit Feminism at Girls' Rock Camp," *Gender and Society* 25, no. 5 (October 2011): 569.
26. Giffort, "Show or Tell?," 571.
27. Giffort, "Show or Tell?," 572.
28. Brian W. Nail, "Music," *The Bloomsbury Handbook to Studying Christians*, ed. George D. Chryssides and Stephen E. Gregg (London: Bloomsbury Academic, 2020), 192.
29. Nail, "Music," 194.
30. Nail, "Music," 193–4.
31. Shawn David Young, "Contemporary Christian Music," *The Bloomsbury Handbook of Religion and Popular Music*, ed. Christopher Partridge and Marcus Moberg (New York: Bloomsbury Academic, 2017), 101.
32. Young, "Contemporary Christian Music," 102.
33. Young, "Contemporary Christian Music," 103.
34. Young, "Contemporary Christian Music," 104.
35. Young, "Contemporary Christian Music," 105.
36. Young, "Contemporary Christian Music," 105.
37. Young, "Contemporary Christian Music," 108.

38. Given that digital purchases of the Siervas' albums do not contain liner notes, I rely in this section on my own transcription and translation of the lyrics.
39. Consider, for example, the Not of This World merchandizing (bumper stickers, t-shirts, jewelry, etc.) currently distributed by Mardel Christian & Education.
40. Nathan Myrick, "Todd and Becky: Authenticity, Dissent, and Gender in Christian Punk and Metal," in *Christian Punk: Identity and Performance*, ed.Ibrahim Abraham (London: Bloomsbury Academic, 2020), 120.
41. Myrick, "Todd and Becky," 129.
42. Myrick, "Todd and Becky," 130.

## References

Catholic.net. "Grupo Musical Siervas." Accessed August 23, 2021. https://es.catholic.net/op/articulos/70486/cat/171/grupo-musical-siervas.html#modal.

Catholic Outlook. "Las Siervas: Singing Nuns Selling Out Concerts." January 19, 2016. https://catholicoutlook.org/las-siervas-singing-nuns-selling-out-concerts/.

Clawson, Mary Ann. "Masculinity and Skill Acquisition in the Adolescent Rock Band." *Popular Music* 18, no. 1 (1999): 99–114. https://www.jstor.org/stable/853570.

"Dayana Cobos, de Ecuador, es vocalista de Siervas, las monjas del rock." *El Comercio*, January 12, 2019. https://www.elcomercio.com/tendencias/entretenimiento/dayana-cobos-ecuador-vocalista-siervas.html.

Giffort, Danielle M. "Show or Tell? Feminist Dilemmas and Implicit Feminism at Girls' Rock Camp." *Gender and Society* 25, no. 5 (October 2011): 569–88. https://www.jstor.org/stable/23044173.

Miller, Diana L. "Gender and Performance Capital among Local Musicians." *Qualitative Sociology* 40 (2017): 263–86. https://link.springer.com/article/10.1007/s11133-017-9360-0.

Myrick, Nathan. "Todd and Becky: Authenticity, Dissent, and Gender in Christian Punk and Metal." In *Christian Punk: Identity and Performance*, edited by Ibrahim Abraham, 119–36. London: Bloomsbury Academic, 2020.

Nail, Brian W. "Music." In *The Bloomsbury Handbook to Studying Christians*, edited by George D. Chryssides and Stephen E. Gregg, 191–94. London: Bloomsbury Academic, 2020.

Núñez, Silvia. "Hermana Daniela y su grupo Siervas están ansiosas por cantarle por primera vez a los romeros." *La Teja*. July 31, 2018. https://www.lateja.cr/farandula/hermana-daniela-y-su-grupo-siervas-estan-ansiosas/NS5VNMV35RBY5M5XFP2C5OE2OE/story/.

Siervas. "América Vive." September 6, 2016. YouTube video, 5:48. https://www.youtube.com/watch?v=OpEAaeJf2Hs.

"Siervas, el grupo de monjas rockeras que quieren hacer bailar al Papa." *Clarín*. January 17, 2019. https://www.clarin.com/mundo/siervas-grupo-monjas-rockeras-quieren-hacer-bailar-papa_0_QeUYVfjQG.html.

Stone, Alison. "Feminism, Gender and Popular Music." In *The Bloomsbury Handbook of Religion and Popular Music*, edited by Christopher Partridge and Marcus Moberg, 54–64. New York: Bloomsbury Academic, 2017.

Young, Shawn David. "Contemporary Christian Music." In *The Bloomsbury Handbook of Religion and Popular Music*, edited by Christopher Partridge and Marcus Moberg, 101–110. New York: Bloomsbury Academic, 2017.

CHAPTER 6

# The Afro Cuban Sense of Magic in Osha-Ifá

Its Representation in National Literature and the Visual Arts

*AXEL PRESAS*

Cuban aesthetics are distinctively Afro Cuban. Africans and their descendants have shaped the island's national culture with their music, cuisine, traditions, mores, and religious systems from the colonial era to the present. Cuban literature and visual arts offer unique insight into Afro Cuban aesthetics and their ties to Afro Cuban religious traditions. The African sense of magic is still very much present in Afro Cuban religions, specifically in Osha-Ifá, which is also pejoratively known as *Santería*.

To introduce the subject of this chapter, I begin here with Cuban visual artist Wifredo Lam (1902–1982) because his representations of Afro Cuban themes and magic in his paintings are also key to a broader understanding of a Cuban national cultural aesthetics. Lam is a pioneer in the development of Afro Cuban visual arts. His personal life is a Cuban paradigm of diverse cultural influences, which he brought to bear in his work, as his father was a Chinese immigrant and his mother the daughter of a former Congolese slave. Several cultural traditions were integrated into Lam's work. From the time he was a small child, he was very close to Afro Cuban religious practices, and although he only participated indirectly, he become acquainted with a complex system of traditions that enriched his understanding of Cuban culture and influenced his work.

Lam's notable 1943 piece, *La Jungla*, is a work in which the sense of magic in Cuban culture expands. His mythical representation of people, nature, and spirituality captivates the inquisitive imagination of his admirers and art enthusiasts alike. Lam decided to incorporate all sorts of magical and mythical figures into this painting to illustrate a symphony of collected images, bodies, and plants, which are representative of Afro Cuban traditions and culture. A Cuban urban legend tells the story that when Lam was painting *La Jungla*, a neighborhood kid, peering in a window, enjoyed watching him work at his studio in La Habana, but the boy's mother called out a warning not to look because the artist in that house was painting "the Devil." This anecdote is relevant to understand both the obviously affluent sense of magic in *La Jungla*, although it was unfinished at the time of the episode, and Lam's commitment to an art that portrayed the African legacies and traditions that pervaded Cuban culture, yet were often misunderstood. Beyond her interpretation, the mother's first impression of *La Jungla* that prompted her to warn her son exemplifies how intensely Lam's work represented Afro Cuban culture; certainly, her apprehensive reaction to the portrayed images in *La Jungla* reinforce the impact of Lam's work at that time.

Upon his return from Paris to Havana in 1941, Lam became a fervent advocate of Afro-descendent art and culture in Cuba, while also working tirelessly to produce his own art that he felt represented Afro Cuban culture. Lam's connections to European artists and familiarity with their ideas about the avant-garde influenced his work as well, leading him to explore these concepts within the context of Cuban culture. His friendships with Lydia Cabrera and Max-Pol Fouchet were particularly significant for these explorations. As Paulette Richard indicates, Lam expressed to Fouchet that he wanted to portray the drama of his country "by painting the beauty and the spirit of the negro, the power of African aesthetics present in Cuba."[1] To this end, Lam articulated a critique of the cultural trivializations of capitalism and flattened stereotypes of Afro Cubans through his quest for a new "genuineness" in modern national art that would center Afro Cuban culture and capture its complexities. Being one of only a few Cuban artists and intellectuals at the time and with this purpose in mind, Lam was decolonizing Afro Cuban culture. *La Jungla* set in motion new ways to understand the aesthetics of *AfroCubaness*. With his work, Lam restored Afro Cuban multicultural traditions, spiritual worlds, and legacies by representing the vivid, the mystic, and the divergent in natural aesthetics. Lam's works illustrate a multifaceted Cuba through interconnected cultural images of the Afro Cuban, the Chinese, and the Spanish as part of the collective values that comprise Cuban transcultural identity. He opened the path for the next generation of creators and for novel depictions of the Cuban visual arts. However, throughout this time of finding himself in his own creative expression, Lam associated himself with the group of intellectuals and writers that were the new renaissance of literary, visual, and musical Afro Cuban aesthetics. In particular, Nicolás Guillén, Marcelino Arozarena, Fernando Ortiz, Alejo Carpentier, and Lydia Cabrera were transforming the ways in which Afro Cuban culture was represented and understood on the island.

It is essential to consider that Cuban literature and visual arts frequently represent magic as preserving the wisdom of old African legends, mythologies, and

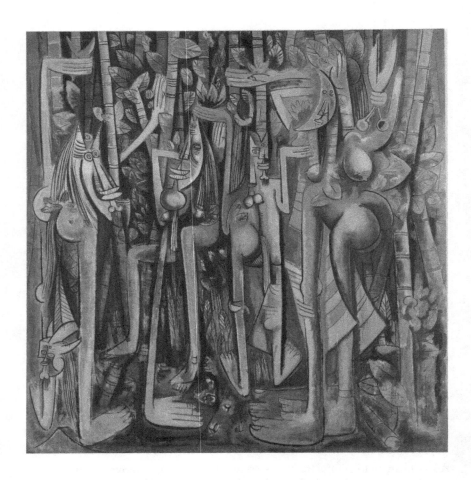

*FIGURE 12.* Wilfredo Lam, La Jungla (1943). Courtesy of MOMA.

stories within Cuban culture. Here, I examine the ways the Afro Cuban Osha-Ifá religion has influenced the work of writers in the nation. African ideas of magic in Osha-Ifá have shaped the artistic imaginaries of a good number of Cuban writers. Specifically, I analyze how writers draw on the particular sense of magic in Osha-Ifá in attempting to represent and celebrate an Afro Cuban identity. Wole Soyinka's claims about the ontology of Yoruba art are helpful in tracing the relationship between African traditions of magic and Cuban aesthetics, and Alejo Carpentier's prologue to his novel *The Kingdom of This World* (1949) personifies magic as something deeply rooted in the cultural philosophy of the particular African traditions influencing Caribbean culture.

## The Philosophy of Magic in Afro Cuban Art

Cuban visual art draws from sacred and secular knowledges articulated by Afro Cuban collective oralities. Hence, both *history* and *story* are foundational parts of this visual tradition. The former registers and chronicles the forced expatriation and enslavement of Africans in Cuba.[2] The latter articulates the vast oral corpus of ethical, religious, and traditional knowledges that accompanied these enslaved women and men, and which they passed on to their descendants via the spoken word. In art, these two categories often converge, and this convergence bestows Afro Cuban aesthetics with a metaphysical quality experienced as part of Afro Cuban social identity. This aspect of Afro Cuban identity encompasses collective experiences of the sacred and is, in turn, reflected in the symbology of magic in artistic representation of such experiences.

Put another way, a collective effort of remembrance has been central to the development of Afro Cuban aesthetics. This effort includes a retelling of history and the struggle to shape national memory and historical narrative. The representation of African magic, mysticism, and religious thought in Cuban popular culture appears as both subversive and liberatory. One of the significant manifestations of orality in Afro Cuban culture is an understanding of human experience as being rooted in the magic of an ancestral communication of knowledge. People's everyday struggles and affairs are understood through the lens of a spirituality shaped by these ancestral invocations—the magic of passing down knowledge. Magic, understood in this way, is not related to superstition or illusion. Nor am I using the term *magic* as related to the adjective "magical," as in something pleasant, sparkly, or exciting. Rather, I offer the term as a cultural element that is effective in its ability to construct—to conjure—a national identity. Through a collective representation of African metaphysical legacies, Afro Cuban artists have constructed Cuba's national identity.

While examining the notion of tragedy in Yoruba art, Wole Soyinka distinguishes it from the notion of tragedy in Hellenic aesthetics:

> Yoruba traditional art is not ideational however, but "essential."
> It is not the idea (in religious arts) that is transmitted into wood

or interpreted in music, or movement, but a quintessence inner being, a symbolic interaction of the many aspects of revelations (within a universal context) with their moral apprehension.[3]

Cuban art has inherited this essence of "inner being" from Yoruba art. In this peculiar ontology of "inner being," spirituality, orality, and magic conform to an African cultural presence within Cuban visual art. An aspect of "revelation" also emerges from the way Cuban art represents the human experiences as existing within a complex natural world. These "revelations" of Afro Cuban aesthetics represent the intimate distinction of the human self and its relationship with both spiritual and material presence in collective spaces.

In Cuba, Yoruba religious traditions account for philosophies of life as postures that contest the colonial mentalities that have permeated the national state of sociopolitical affairs. While analyzing the cultural authority of African systems of philosophy, Kwasi Wiredu writes:

> What has generally happened is that not only the genuine distinguishing features of African traditional thought but also its basic non-scientific, spiritistic tendencies have been taken as a basis for contrasting Africans from western peoples. One consequence is that many westerners have gone about with an exaggerated notion of the differences in nature between Africans and the peoples of the west.[4]

Wiredu's analysis elucidates commonplace Western assumptions that tend to misinterpret African thought and philosophy. If we understand Afro Cuban art as containing a corpus of African spiritual and philosophical traditions as well as historical legacies that have been gathered and preserved by means of the spoken word, then we can understand this transmission of knowledges as key to the formation of national identity. *Histories* and *stories* in Afro Cuban art are the emblematic recollections of ancestral African knowledges present in Yoruba traditions on the island.

The sense of magic within Afro Cuban art articulates the idea of powerful mysteries present in human affairs. Susan Greenwood writes that magic is a manifestation of human consciousness. As she puts it, "Magic is a universal mode of perception" because it is a vital fragment of the conscious processes that occur in our phenomenological understanding of the world. Greenwood claims that logical reason and magic are not necessarily in opposition, but rather are rational features in our human mental abstractions, which take part in our own understanding of metaphors, complex introspections, discernments, and beliefs, while also existing as legitimate forms of knowledge within a synthetic view of science.[5] Here, Greenwood's analysis is important because it underscores that in the oral communication of religious knowledge, the articulation of this sense of magic is present through the representation of peculiar experiences in a person's familiarity with the natural world. Said another way, in Osha-Ifá traditions, magic is part of the person's own spiritual relationship with nature. This experience of magic is not necessarily concomitant with religious belief because it exceeds particular forms of religiosity. Rather, it is an awareness of being in contact with the spontaneous challenges of the fluctuating living world.

Afro Cuban art represents the embodiment of all sorts of human experiences through this sense of magic, in particular transforming the experiential into an aesthetics of preserving all African mythologies that enrich Cuba's cultural history. Alejo Carpentier's prologue to his novel, *El reino de este mundo [The Kingdom of This World]*, explicates how people in the Caribbean and the Americas have assumed living an existence concomitant with what he defines as *lo real maravilloso*, "the marvelous real."[6] Carpentier says that lo real maravilloso is that thoughtful state in which people perceive, believe, and understand mythologies and the idea of magic as something natural. The Cuban writer says that the aesthetics of lo real maravilloso create a particular ontology, a way of genuinely living and articulating the existence of the surreal. Carpentier contemplates lo real maravilloso not only as an aesthetics but also as that sense of magic rooted in a way of understanding human existence as rooted in nature. Furthermore, he writes that lo real maravilloso is an innovative artistic expression that reveals complex human spiritual affairs more authentically than does European Surrealism. Carpentier thinks the aesthetics of Surrealism could not genuinely define the representation of people's dreams, visions, and spirituality as lo real maravilloso can. He writes:

> The marvelous begins to exist unequivocally when it surges from an unexpected alteration of reality (the miracle), from a privileged revelation of reality, from an unusual or singularly favorable illumination of the unsung riches of reality, perceived with particular intensity as a result of an exaltation of the spirit that leads it to a kind of "heightened state."[7]

This notion of "a privileged revelation of reality" expresses an understanding of a two-way process. It first grasps, then expresses the feeling of being in contact with and experiencing a peculiar sense of the natural world and its correlation to magic. This specific sense of a "privileged revelation" hails from an understanding that natural features still hold the doors open to unknown phenomena. I distinguish this peculiar idea of magic as a state of awareness in which individuals experience and understand their reality as concomitant with their idea of spirituality—a reality that originates in ancestral legacies, folklore, spiritual beliefs, collective stories, and ordinary events. These types of events also shape and give meaning to national culture. Carpentier adds:

> It's just that, given its virgin landscape, its formation, its ontology, the Faustian presence of the Indian and the black, the revolution brought about by its recent discovery, and the fecund racial mixtures it enabled, the Americas are far from exhausting their mythological riches.[8]

The sense of magic, in its artistic and literary sense, is not necessarily an approximation of mysticism. Instead, it is how a peculiar sense of the mystical casts an aesthetic veil on laypeople and artists alike. This sense of magic and the marvelous characterizes the creativity of Cuban authors and visual artists, imaginatively enlivening the corpus of popular, religious, and cultural epistemologies present in the collective oralities preserved in Afro Cuban artistic expression. In Afro Cuban art, magic is present in landscapes, the animal world, deities, human experiences, and bonds between humans and the natural world.

In "What Are Poets For?" Martin Heidegger writes that "we are unprepared for the interpretation of the elegies and the sonnets, since the realm from which they speak, in its metaphysical constitution and unity, has not yet been sufficiently thought out in terms of the nature of metaphysics."[9] In the realm of Afro Cuban aesthetics, artists and writers first acknowledge, then represent this sense of magic to illustrate a culture nourished by African religious traditions present on the island. Afro Cuban aesthetics represents the metaphysics of cultural occurrences, growing out of historical memory and practices of orality. It participates in the social mythologies that have shaped Cuba's national identity. Understood in this way, Afro Cuban aesthetics can be read as a communal consecration of diverse cultural legacies on the island, from which African metaphysical traditions emerge as central.

## Magic in Literature

Lydia Cabrera is one of the primary exponents of the representation of magic as characteristic of Afro Cuban identity. In both her fiction and scholarly writings drawing on ethnography and folklore studies, Cabrera writes about Afro Cuban religious themes in a way that situates magic as central to other sociocultural practices. *El Monte* (1954), *Yemayá y Ochún* (1974), and *Koeko Iyawó: Aprende Novicia* (1980) describe the structures of philosophies, legends, rituals, theologies, and gastronomies present in these African cultures. One of the most conclusive works of Cabrera's representation of magic and orality is her *Cuentos negros de Cuba: Afro Cuban Tales* (1972), published first in Paris by Gallimard and translated by Francis de Miomandre as *Contes nègres de Cuba* (1936). In *Cuentos*, Cabrera incorporates a broad representation of the universe of Afro Cuban culture that includes a vast array of both religious legends and human experiences central to African legacies in Cuba. It is worth noting that *Cuentos*, initially published in a foreign country and foreign language, intentionally offers the religious and oral philosophies of Afro Cuban peoples for the reading desires of French enthusiasts. The sense of magic in Cabrera's work stands as a reaffirmation of Afro Cuban existence; through the characters' stories, the situations they encounter, and the choices they make, magic operates as a window on broader Afro Cuban cultural philosophies. The *Cuentos* are, in fact, fictional short stories that reproduce the teachings of African religious tales, known as *Patakís*,[10] in Afro Cuban theology.

Cabrera's representation of women takes a progressive stance concerning the nature and agency of female authority. In her short story "Bregantino Bregantín," she writes,

> Sanune touched the earth and kissed it on her fingertips. Prostrate at the men's feet, she lost consciousness. When she opened her eyes, she was surrounded by night, in a room thick with the smell of warm foliage and guavas, as if a crowd of blacks had just gathered there a few minutes before. She found herself before an altar made of two wildcat skins and two freshly cut poplar branches popped against the wall.... Beside her, an old woman with her head wrapped in a veil held in her kerchief twenty-one little snails, all beautifully white like unpolished ivory, and she kept counting and re-counting them for fear that one might be

lost (specifically the one belonging to Elegguá). When she was convinced that none were missing, she touched Sanune's shoulder and sent her off, giving her a bundle of multicolored clothes.[11]

"Bregantino Bregantín" not only portrays the religious and communal relationship between these two women, but also depicts a Yoruba understanding of magic as a central part of Cuban cultural and religious affairs. In this context, magic is presented as a part of an interchange in which the powers of prophecy and divination are transferred from one woman to another as a distinctive cultural legacy. The handling of the twenty-one snails, or *cowries* (*Cypraea Moneta, Moneta Monetaria*), entails the formal delivery of a sacred Yoruba deity. The old woman specifically ensures that she "does not lose the one belonging to Elegguá," the god of fortune and communication in Afro Cuban theology, which will open spiritual and material prosperity to Sanune (the younger woman).

Cabrera represents feminine power as constituted through the closeness of communal bonds among women as well as through the protagonist's ability to alter her own destiny. In Afro Cuban culture, *cowries* represent the way of communicating with the Orishas. By casting the shells, Sanune can meet her own destiny and thus be prepared to face it. To a certain extent, this allows her to alter what she understands is unfavorable for her. The story of Sanune is a tale of sacrifice, as divination tells her that her son will become king and replace his tyrannical father. She hides the birth of her son and, after this event, dies. She faces her death with a smile, revealing her satisfaction with her own destiny and that of her son.

Cabrera's story about Sanune is an account of how feminine power has the capacity to challenge male control and authoritarianism. The birth of Sanune's son restores order in the town of Cocozumba. After killing his father, Sanune's son resolves that all women in their village should be free to decide their own well-being and destiny. Sacrifice and justice appear in Sanune's experience through the power of magic to pass on spiritual knowledge among women. Magic also becomes the vehicle by which feminine powers of creation can bring stability to society. Sanune's personal sacrifice is a form of magic through which her son will become the chosen one to overthrow Cocozumba's tyrant and eradicate male authoritarianism from their village. Thus, her sacrifice is not only for society in general but for the collective, communal well-being of women in particular. Cabrera's story embodies Afro Cuban religious values concomitant with the transmission of gendered moral and spiritual knowledges.

In "Arere Marekén," another story from *Cuentos*, the power of magic is expressed in the relationship of Hicotea ("Turtle") and the queen, Arere. Here, the love of Hicotea for the queen seals his death. Arere is a beautiful, sensuous woman married to the king. By contrast, her husband is a jealous old man. Despite her marriage, Hicotea persists in his courtship and desire to declare his love to the queen. His patience eventually pays off, and he has the opportunity to express his love to Arere. However, his audacity is discovered, and the king's soldiers club him to death.

Cabrera's short story about Hicotea and Arere is a homage to the relationship existing among humans and animals in Afro Cuban theology. Her fiction reintroduces the significance of the turtle's archetype in Afro Cuban religious culture. For example, Hicotea, the male character, possesses the qualities of patience and endurance. These are the same mystical features that turtles possess in African mythology. Arere and Hicotea fall in love because, in his persistence, he sees her true self, her authentic inner beauty. Hicotea's character is a poet who charms Arere with well-chosen words. He wins her heart, all while anticipating his own fate and demise. However, in this story, magic appears to bring Hicotea back from death. By the mystical powers of the night and the moon, he returns to become Arere's true love.

> And who could have imagined that Hicotea's body was no longer coarse, but was hard, smooth, and nice to touch.
> So many scars for Arere's love, Arere Marekén's love![12]

In *Cuentos*, the roles of women and men correspond to the representation of wisdom and perseverance. Cabrera's depiction of magic not only restores life and love between the characters of Arere and Hicotea, but it also illuminates the imaginary, mystical, and religious characteristics that African civilizations bestow to turtles. Through these elements, the stories in *Cuentos* reflect the living resonance of African traditions within Afro Cuban literary and cultural expression.

If magic in Lydia Cabrera's work shows up in the fictional retelling of African traditional oralities, then Nicolas Guillén's poetry positions magic as the affirmation of African communal legacies. Guillén's work is a poetic representation of Afro Cuban history, gestures, ways of being, and identity in which magic emerges as political. Guillén's poetry elevates Afro Cuban aesthetics by incorporating the distinctive oral expressions of the Afro Cuban peoples, their everyday vernacular, mannerisms and behaviors, social interactions, and their presence in Cuban society. He makes them visible in their ordinary ways of being.

The presence of an African aesthetic and understanding of magic in Guillén's poetry is political because it highlights the legacy and vibrant presence of people whose enormous significance in the cultural history of the nation has been under-recognized. Guillén's representation of magic is not separate from ordinary life and society. Rather, it infuses every collective space, every image, and every human experience represented in his poetry. Through this integrated approach to magic, Guillén leads the reader into an intuitive awareness of Cuban ontological diversity. When Heidegger examines Herder's thoughts on language as that "human breath that becomes the portrait of the world,"[13] he thinks about the audacity of poets, calling it "the venture." It is a daring stance by which poets communicate the innermost thoughts of human existence. In Heidegger's thoughts, to be a venturesome poet is to excel in saying that which has not yet been said; it is to outshine the ordinary margins of language with neatness and simplicity.[14] In his poetry, Guillén ventures into conversing about the presence of magic as part of a tradition of cultural expression that he posits is central to Cuban identity. He "converses" with everyone because his poems are in constant dialog with Cuban social history—they are a kind of poetic discourse for cultural illumination. His "breath" aims to make visible the popular, the authentic, the autochthonous of Afro Cuban culture.

In his "Son número 6" [Son number 6], Guillén writes:

> Here is the riddle
> of all my hopes:
> what's mine is yours
> what's yours is mine;
> all the blood
> shaping a river.
> The silk cotton tree, tree with its crown;
> father, the father with his son;
> the tortoise in its shell.
> Let the heart-warming *'son'* break out,
> and our people dance,
> heart close to heart,
> glasses clinking together
> water on water with rum!
> I'm Yoruba, I'm Lucumí,
> Mandinga, Congo, Carabalí,
> Listen my friends, to the *'son'* that goes like this:[15]

Guillén's "Son número 6" is a poetic testament to the value of social integration within Cuban cultural history. In Guillén's verses, the sentient and mystical combine to articulate a sense of Afro Cuban existence. Magic manifests in the "river of blood" uniting all sorts of people into one stream of social consciousness. The *hicotea* (turtle) also appears along with the Ceiba (*Ceiba Pentandra, Bombax Ceiba*) or silk cotton tree, reflecting the sacred connections humans have with nature and the religious significance of plants and animals in Afro Cuban theology.[16]

Guillén writes a poem with the image and composition of the *son* in mind. His poem resembles a popular song; it is an invitation to dance in unison, in kinship, commemorating the cultural heritages of the nation. "Son número 6" is a poem about how the Cuban nation belongs to all. The poem is published in the book, *El son entero [The Entire Son]* (1947), appropriately using the cultural expansion of this musical genre to address all Cubans in a collective dance of social reaffirmation. He continues:

> Come out Mulatto,
> walk on free,
> tell the white man he can't leave ...
> Nobody breaks from here;
> look and don't stop,
> listen and don't wait
> drink and don't stop,
> eat and don't wait,
> live and don't hold back
> our people's '*son*' will never end![17]

The last verses of Guillén's *son* end with an invitation to a collective celebration of national identity. Another Cuban poet, José Lezama Lima (1910–1976), wrote about Cuba that "nacer aquí es una fiesta innombrable," [to be born here is an unmentionable celebration,] indicating the character of the country's vibrant culture.[18] In Guillén's poem, the stanza "I'm Yoruba, I'm Lucumí, / Mandinga, Congo, Carabalí," frames the retracing of African lineages on the island as a cultural celebration. However, his *fiesta* is meant to celebrate the social acknowledgment and integration of Afro Cubans. Guillén's poetry is a narrative of Cuba's social history. Magic appears in his "Son número 6" within the precise understanding of these legacies and their cultural contribution to Cuban identity. For example, the mention of the Ceiba tree is significant as the most sacred tree in all African religious traditions present in Cuba. The images of both the *Ceiba* and the *turtle* emerge as representations of African traditions integrated into a celebration of the island's African traditions and cultural religiosity. They are symbols of belonging and speak to an understanding of Cuba's ancestral mysticism.

Part of a poet's value in a given society is intertwined with their ability to understand the cultural complexity within narratives of national history and origins. Guillén is a poet who captures the culturally specific senses of existence in his nation. His poetry contains references to the transcultural history of legacies, histories, and stories that have shaped Cuban social identity. Various images in his poetry present allegories and elegies to *lo popular*. The sense of magic in Guillén's poetry is expressed in an accessible Cuban vernacular that represents the mystical in everyday affairs. Magic in Guillén's poetry reflects sensibilities particular to the various African traditions that have shaped Cuba and its history. He preserves the cultural differences within Cuban culture, elevates the nation's African and Spanish historical origins, and celebrates the value of cultural integration. Part of the significance of his aesthetic contributions is to highlight the diversity of all Cuba's peoples. Guillén's poetry depicts the recognition of Cuba's foundational cultural legacies as key to social progress in the nation.

Exploring the particular representations of magic in Afro Cuban aesthetics requires attention to the historic and cultural legacies that have shaped Cuba as a nation and society. Many creators, writers, and intellectuals have identified an African-derived sense of magic as a distinct presence, an accumulation of behaviors and customs, and an identity present throughout Cuban history. The sense of magic in Afro Cuban aesthetics is a key part of an ontology in which existence is shaped by viscerally present legacies and knowledges that shape national culture. Cuban authors and artists see magic as central to the collective culture of African peoples on the island. Afro Cuban aesthetics are imbricated in the national formation of Cuban culture; its influence expands and resonates with the undisputable significance of Cuba's prospering national identity.

# Notes

1. Paulette Richards, "Wifredo Lam: A Sketch" *Callaloo*, no. 34. (1988): 91.
2. The first slaves (around three hundred) arrived from Africa to Cuba in 1517, and in 1527, they began arriving in larger numbers. However, a sudden change came with the Haitian Revolution in 1791, wherein thousands of African enslaved peoples arrived in Cuba to fuel a burgeoning sugar plantation economy.
3. Wole Soyinka, "The Fourth Stage: Through the Mysteries of Ogun to the Origins of Yoruba Tragedy," in *African Philosophy: An Anthology*, ed. Emmanuel Chukwudi Eze (Oxford: Blackwell, 1998), 438.
4. Kwasi Wiredu, "How Not to Compare African Thought with Western Thought," in *African Philosophy: An Anthology*, ed. Emmanuel Chukwudi Eze (Oxford: Blackwell, 1998), 194.
5. Susan Greenwood, "Magical Consciousness: A Legitimate Form of Knowledge," in *Defining Magic: A Reader*, ed. Bernd-Christian Otto and Michael Stausberg (New York: Routledge, 2013), 208–209.
6. Alejo Carpentier, Preface to *The Kingdom of This World*, trans. Pablo Medina (New York: Farrar, Straus and Giroux, 2017).
7. Alejo Carpentier, Preface to *The Kingdom of This World*, xvi.
8. Alejo Carpentier, Preface to *The Kingdom of This World*, xix–xx.
9. Martin Heidegger, "What Poets Are For?" in *Poetry, Language, Thought*, trans. Albert Hofstadter (New York: Harper and Row, 1971), 96.
10. In *Osha-Ifá*, the *Patakís* divination tales, articulated by Babalawos and Osha-Orisha priests and priestesses, become oral archives for the dissemination of moral knowledge. *Patakís* are narratives of knowledge; their epistemic reach is grounded in the oral accumulation and transmission of cultural ancestral experiences.
11. Lydia Cabrera, *Afro-Cuban Tales*, trans. Alberto Hernández-Chiroldes and Lauren Yoder (Lincoln: University of Nebraska Press, 2004), 13.
12. Lydia Cabrera, *Afro-Cuban Tales*, 121.
13. Johann Gottfried Herder, *Outlines of a Philosophy of the History of Man*, trans. T. Churchill, 2nd ed. (London: Luke Hansard, 1803), 418.
14. Martin Heidegger, *Poetry, Language, Thought*, trans. Albert Hofstadter (New York: Harper and Row, 1971), 137.
15. Nicolás Guillén, *Yoruba From Cuba*, trans. Salvador Ortiz-Carboneres (Leeds: Peepal Tree, 2005), 67.

16. It is vital to mention here the error in translation, since in Cuba there are no species of tortoises present in its fauna.
17. Nicolás Guillén, *Yoruba From Cuba*, 69.
18. José Lezama Lima, "Noche Insular: Jardines Invisibles," in *Antología de la Poesía Hispanoamericana Actual* (edición 8va), ed. Julio Ortega (México, D.F.: Siglo Veintiuno, 2001), 32.

## References

Bolívar, Natalia. *Los Orishas en Cuba*. Caracas: Ediciones CR, 1995.
Cabrera, Lydia. *Afro-Cuban Tales*. Translated by Alberto Hernández-Chiroldes and Lauren Yoder. Lincoln: University of Nebraska Press, 2004.
Carpentier, Alejo. Preface to *The Kingdom of this World*. Translated by Pablo Medina. New York: Farrar, Straus and Giroux, 2017.
Gottfried Herder, Johann. *Outlines of a Philosophy of the History of Man*, 2nd ed. Translated by T. Churchill. London: Luke Hansard, 1803.
Greenwood, Susan. "Magical Consciousness: A Legitimate Form of Knowledge." In *Defining Magic: A Reader*, edited by Bernd-Christian Otto and Michael Stausberg, 197–210. New York: Routledge, 2013.
Guillén, Nicolás. *Yoruba from Cuba*. Translated by Salvador Ortiz-Carboneres. Leeds: Peepal Tree, 2005.
Heidegger, Martin. *Poetry, Language, Thought*. Translated by Albert Hofstadter. New York: Harper and Row, 1971.
Lam, Wifredo. *La Jungla*. Gouache on paper mounted on canvas. The Museum of Modern Art, *MoMA*. New York, United States. 1943. https://www.moma.org/collection/works/34666.
Lezama Lima, José. "Noche Insular: Jardines Invisibles." In *Antología de la Poesía Hispanoamericana Actual*, edited by Julio Ortega, 8th ed., 30–34. Ciudad de México: Siglo Veintiuno, 2001.
Machado, Eloy. "Asere I Say." In *Afrocuba: An Anthology of Cuban Writing on Race, Politics, and Culture*, edited by Pedro Pérez Sarduy and Jean Stubbs, 157–158. London: Ocean Press, 1993.
Martínez Furé, Rogelio. *Diálogos Imaginarios*. Ciudad de La Habana: Editorial Letras Cubanas, 1979.

Ortiz, Fernando. *Contrapunteo Cubano del Tabaco y el Azúcar*. Ciudad de La Habana: Jesús Montero, 1940.

Richards, Paulette. "Wifredo Lam: A Sketch." *Callaloo*, no. 34 (1988): 90–92.

Soyinka, Wole. "The Fourth Stage: Through the Mysteries of Ogun to the Origins of Yoruba Tragedy." In *African Philosophy: An Anthology*, edited by Emmanuel Chukwudi Eze, 438–46. London: Blackwell, 1998.

Wiredu, Kwasi. "How Not to Compare African Thought with Western Thought." In *African Philosophy: An Anthology*, edited by Emmanuel Chukwudi Eze, 193–99. London: Blackwell, 1998.

*PART III*

# Critical Feminist Epistemologies and Activism

CHAPTER 7

# Sacred Motherhood in the Sanctuary Movement

## Marian Imagery and the Family Fight for Immigrant Justice

**LLOYD D. BARBA AND TATYANA CASTILLO-RAMOS**

*Therefore, I ask the President, please do us the favor of granting us our liberty and residency.... We've been here a long time.... We don't have criminal records. We are the ones who came to work and strive. I ask the President, please let me be happy with my family. I want to be with my family because that is something valuable that we have, a gift from God is our family, our children.... I wish to tell the President that we are also valuable. We are human beings. We have rights like all others. I wish to appeal to his good heart to please help us leave this shadow we are under. Our greatest desire is to enjoy our family, to make the most of the time we've since lost with them. I have been fighting since 2009 when I was deported for simply being too close to my husband's case. They already deported my husband. I only ask for the opportunity to have our case reopened and to get to know us to see who we really are. This I ask the President, and of the First Lady and Vice President—since you are mothers, you know the love of a mother. You know the love for children, the family's love; that's the reason we fight.*
—MARIA MÉRIDA, SANCTUARY SEEKER/LEADER

Less than a week after Donald Trump vacated the White House in 2021, the National Sanctuary Collective held an online press conference. The host of the meeting, Rosa Sabido, facilitated a storytelling session with former and current sanctuary seekers. Within the Sanctuary Movement, leaders are typically identified as those who *offer* sanctuary. Sabido, however, made it a point to recognize that sanctuary *seekers* were also leaders.[1] These seekers/leaders testified to a pervasive sense of confinement, precarity, and isolation. While rebuking the Trump administration for its handling of immigration, the speakers conveyed collective hope for brighter days ahead with Biden's recent inauguration. They called upon Biden to depart from the punitive status quo of the last four years and to empathize with their plight and deep longing to be free with their families. At the time of the press conference, over fifty "sanctuary families" were taking refuge in houses of worship. Some of those individuals had been in the United States for decades and reared children who, in many cases, knew no other country, yet many of these children entered into sanctuary with their parent.

While images and discussion of family are common in the public discourse about sanctuary, scholarship on the Sanctuary Movement has tended to understate both the critical nature of sanctuary seekers as leaders as well as the multilayered importance of family to this demographic. This chapter serves as a corrective to this underrepresentation. The scholarship on the Sanctuary Movement in the 1980s largely focused on the individuals and organizations who provided sanctuary to refugees. Over time, this focus led to the association of certain exemplary figures, such as pastors and other religious leaders, with the movement's efforts. As a departure from this older sanctuary narrative, the overwhelming consensus from participants in the January 26 press conference conveyed that their time as sanctuary seekers/leaders in houses of worship affected entire families that had put down roots in the United States. Stories of Latin American refugees undergoing traumatic, sometimes permanent, separation from their families—and their courageous responses to this trauma—are central to the US Sanctuary Movement. While the 1980s Sanctuary Movement was distinctly Central American, the New Sanctuary Movement includes refugees from beyond Latin America, including Asian, European, Middle Eastern, and African countries. However, migrants from Latin America still comprise the vast majority of those who took sanctuary during the Trump administration. Considering this, and in line with the focus of this edited volume, we focus on Latin American refugees and how their stories of undergoing traumatic, sometimes permanent, separation from their families—and their courageous responses to this trauma—are central to the US Sanctuary Movement.

The primacy of motherhood and discursive constructions of Latinx people as "family oriented" are highly visible within the narratives that sanctuary seekers/leaders tell about themselves and in various photographs publicized by media outlets. Those conveying these stories use the rhetorical appeal to families, the image of familial suffering, and the protective duty of motherhood to diffuse criticism and change hearts and minds.[2] In what follows, we show how sanctuary seekers/leaders creatively deploy Marian images (especially that of Our Lady of Guadalupe) to buttress the Sanctuary Movement's claims of sacrality and reinforce its image as a family rights movement. Guadalupan images accomplish this in ways that few others can.

This chapter begins by offering a broad overview of the Sanctuary Movement. It then notes the significance of activism and motherhood in Latin American and US Latinx contexts by emphasizing Guadalupe's paramount importance as mother to, protectress of, and advocate for Latinx immigrant justice causes. Finally, this chapter focuses on three highly publicized episodes of undocumented immigrants taking sanctuary in houses of worship and their invocation of Guadalupe's image and role as protectress and mother.

The first of these episodes occurred at the start of the Sanctuary Movement in Los Angeles in 1985, when Father Luis Olivares declared La Iglesia de Nuestra Señora la Reina de los Ángeles (La Placita) a sanctuary for Central American refugees fleeing civil war and violence. The second involves the launching of the New Sanctuary Movement in Chicago in 2006 when Elvira Arellano entered sanctuary at Adalberto United Methodist Church. The final episode transpired at a pivotal transitional moment when Trump left office and sanctuary seekers/leaders called upon the Biden administration to make good on the promises of immigration reform. In each of these three episodes, Marian imagery was used as a distinctly Latinx claim to religious capital. By using images of a divine mother—particularly Our Lady of Guadalupe, which has historical and cultural significance for Latinx communities—sanctuary seekers and leaders validated their cause by drawing comparisons (either subtly or explicitly) to Mary and her maternal love for her son, Jesus Christ. As they framed it, Mary approved of their valiant fight to support and keep migrant families together and, therefore, the general public should support these sanctuary efforts as well.

## The Sanctuary Movement in Historical Perspective

Displaced families have long been at the core of the Sanctuary Movement.[3] By the closing years of the 1970s, civil wars tore apart and threatened communities and families in El Salvador, Guatemala, and Nicaragua. The United States, following its imperative to root out communism wherever it could globally, but especially in

Latin America, offered military and financial aid in these proxy wars to overthrow regimes that acted against American capitalist interests and maintain those that furthered those interests. It is hard to overstate the brutality and pervasiveness of physical violence in these countries during this time, as death squads ravaged the country and disappearances plagued entire communities. The widespread violence sent millions north in search of safety, and by the 1980s, the consequences of these wars reached US soil as local aid groups in Arizona noted an uptick in persons from Central America. News of the horrors occurring in Central American civil wars soon reached the United States in unexpected ways. In July 1980, national headlines reported on the macabre details of thirteen survivors of twenty-six Salvadorans found in the Sonoran Desert, raising serious concern for everyday Americans.[4] After President Jimmy Carter signed the 1980 Refugee Act, the United States was ostensibly bound to offer (or at least consider) asylum to the incoming refugees. But the Reagan administration unequivocally framed Salvadorans and Guatemalans as "economic migrants," effectively denying their claims of asylum. To offer them asylum would have legitimated the reasons for leaving their home countries in the first place, which the United States could not afford to do, as they had backed those governments.[5] Forged under such conditions of duress, the Sanctuary Movement is representative of how hemispheric (even global) tensions remained at play in the difficult decision to offer, take up, and leave a house of worship as a sanctuary space.

Far from the Central American highlands or US Capitol Hill, the sunbaked Sonoran Desert became ground zero of the 1980s Central American refugee crisis. There, local Mexican and Latinx activists began to provide aid for the refugees who were gradually arriving under dire circumstances. Many emerged from the desert trek with little to no money, clothes, or connections to Americans, for fleeing violence was their main goal. Alongside the work of aid groups, in the summer of 1981, Quaker rancher Jim Corbett began housing migrants in his own home as well as those of concerned neighbors in the Tucson area. Corbett then turned to Southside Presbyterian Church pastor John Fife to petition for broader support from the Tucson Ecumenical Council. The combined efforts of various groups on the ground "laid the foundation" for the Sanctuary Movement to build up as quickly and become as widespread as it did.[6] In late 1981 Fife gained the support of his local church members to declare sanctuary, and they, in turn, partnered with churches in California to summon the longstanding biblical tradition and declare their houses of worship "sanctuaries" for the oppressed of Central America.[7] On March 24, 1982, which was the two-year anniversary of the assassination of

Salvadoran Bishop Oscar Romero, Fife issued a formal declaration of sanctuary.[8] Forty-five faith communities within the next year also declared sanctuary, and by the decade's end, nearly 500 churches declared sanctuary.[9] The Sanctuary Movement of the 1980s no doubt had various goals, but if we consider that the main goal was to bring about a reversal of US policy toward Central Americans, then the movement scored a clear victory in the early 1990s when the United States changed course following a settlement between *American Baptist Churches v. Thornburgh*. From this case, legal provisions such as Temporary Protected Status and Deferred Enforced Departure materialized.[10]

Outlined above is a rather condensed overview of the Sanctuary Movement.[11] More recent scholarship has brought to light the role of transnational and local Latinx actors, Catholic communities, and branches of the movement beyond Tucson.[12] This chapter builds upon the early scholarship and more recent work by analyzing public images of sanctuary: the locations where declarations and pleas for help happen, the people involved, the powerful images invoked, and the underlying resonance of motherhood. The following analysis will show how the Sanctuary Movement and New Sanctuary Movement's use of Marian imagery, particularly that of Guadalupe, builds upon larger claims to the sacrality of family and motherhood in Latinx and Latin American communities. Marian imagery transcends Latinx communities, as it invites a wider Christian audience that is familiar with the story of Mary's love for her son to support the plight of immigrants.

## Immigrant Activism: Of Mothers and Mary

Activist mothers in both Latin American and US contexts have leveraged the cultural capital of motherhood.[13] Across the board, the pathos of grieving mothers quickly grabs national attention, humanizing despair by making it relatable and forcing many to ask, "What if it were my child?" Mothers from around the world can sympathize with the measures migrant mothers are willing to take to protect their children. That narrative also leverages a great deal of capital in the United States[14] These appeals to motherhood are precisely the kinds that have been front and center in the Sanctuary Movement since the 1980s. Given that many sanctuary seekers arrived from Latin America, where Marian devotion is prominent, it is little wonder that the language of motherhood assumes an aura of divinity and conjures up images of the most famous Marian apparition in the Americas: Our Lady of Guadalupe.

Mary stands out as the most ubiquitous symbol of motherhood in Latin American and Latinx contexts.[15] In church art, Madonna imagery has occupied a special place for centuries, and it is deeply embedded into religious and popular culture throughout the broader Americas. Guadalupe has received and continues to receive widespread recognition from both the Catholic Church and the everyday faithful. Recognized as the Patroness of New Spain in 1754, she later became a symbol against Spanish rule during the Mexican War of Independence.[16] In 1895 Guadalupe's stature increased when she was offered a solemn coronation. Within the next fifteen years, her shrine in Mexico City was declared a basilica, and Pope Pius X proclaimed her Patroness of all Latin America. Adding honor to such high estimation, in 1945 Pope Pius XII declared her Queen of Mexico and Empress of the Americas.[17] For Americans, the tender motherly devotion of Guadalupe has become nearly synonymous with Latin American Christianity, as her image has long been a staple of Catholicism in the American Southwest.[18]

In addition to these formal recognitions by the Catholic Church, Guadalupe is popularly considered to be on the side of everyday people and immigrants. Vernacular art testifies to her prominence among laypeople. In California, where Chicano muralism has enjoyed over half a century of community protection, Guadalupe has made her presence visible as one of the earliest and most prominent figures depicted.[19] Guadalupe in public art is arguably the preeminent symbol of Mexican nationalism in the United States, surpassing even the Mexican flag.[20] Her imagery at once symbolizes a political, religious, and ethnic identity.[21] We may very well conceive of the Guadalupan image as a "hidden transcript," a term coined by political scientist James Scott to describe the covert ways subaltern groups make public statements that include layers of meaning clear to people within these communities but veiled to those outside of them in dominant positions of power. As biblical and Latinx studies scholar David Sánchez notes, Guadalupe's presence in the barrios of the Southwest indicates not just Latinx cultural presence but also acts as a "reclamation" of space.[22] Vernacular arts, as expressed through both covert and overt means, demonstrate that Guadalupe occupies a critical role as a symbol of peoplehood and protection in migrant narratives.

Migrants who have crossed through the desert have shared stories of Guadalupe appearing to them and providing help along the dangerous journey.[23] Such stories of Guadalupe as an immigrant protectress are reflected in the murals of San Diego's Chicano Park (Figure 13). Painted by artist Sal Barajas and located at Chicano Park in Barrio Logan of San Diego, this mural centers Guadalupe in the migrant experience of crossing the desert.

FIGURE 13. Chicano Park mural. Courtesy of Tatyana Castillo-Ramos.

Guadalupe's identification with the plight of immigrants is clearly displayed in this Chicano Park mural. Here, Guadalupe is holding a water jug and a cross that reads *"NO OLVIDADOS"* ("NOT FORGOTTEN"); the water jug on the upper left declares *"¡Ni una muerte más!"* ("Not one more death!") while the water jug on the upper right consoles *"el amor no tiene fronteras"* ("love has no borders").[24] The pink hearts above Guadalupe contain the word *"Paz"* ("Peace") underneath doves bearing olive branches. Across the mural, the text reads *"AMOR, SÍ SE PUEDE"* (LOVE, YES WE CAN"). Demonstrating the love Guadalupe is able to bring to fruition, on the left, notable activists and day laborers gather together and, on the right, a family stands reunited in a warm embrace.

As mentioned, among the most resonant of images in this mural is that of Guadalupe carrying a jug of water and embracing a cross declaring *"NO OLVIDADOS"* ("NOT FORGOTTEN") as she treks through the desert. The words on the cross are a clear reference to the multitude of migrants who lost their lives during the dangerous trek across the US-Mexico border. Enrique Morones, the commissioner of this mural and the head of the Border Angels (a humanitarian faith-based group that leaves water and supplies for migrants crossing the desert) shared that he wanted the mural to portray a strong message from "the saint and mother of all of Latin America."[25]

Guadalupe maintains a similar status as the migrant protectress in formal church settings as well. In Los Angeles, the 2012 California Catholic Conference of Bishops declared that Guadalupe was a "Mother Without Borders."[26] Such invocations resonated given the discursive affinity between Guadalupe, motherhood, and immigrant rights.[27] And thus it is this weighty history and sacrality that emerge in cases in which sanctuary activists invoke her.

## Marian Motherhood at the Sanctuary Declaration in Los Angeles

Throughout the Americas, there are countless testaments to the centrality of Guadalupe's motherly protection of immigrants. One exemplary case is the mural of Guadalupe at La Placita Church in Los Angeles, a major battleground for the Sanctuary Movement. The centerpiece of the mural is Guadalupe appearing to Juan Diego (Figure 14). The two figures are flanked by a US flag on the left and a Mexican one on the right. Flags of various Latin American countries form an arch above the patron saint of the Americas. Between the arch of flags and Guadalupe, the mural declares in simple, bold face font: *"REINA DE MEXICO Y EMPERATRIZ DE AMERICA"* ("QUEEN OF MEXICO AND EMPRESS OF AMERICA"). This declaration is flanked by Guadalupe's famous maternal refrain: "AM I NOT HERE, WHO AM YOUR MOTHER?" and *"¿NO ESTOY AQUI, QUE SOY TU MADRE?"*

Olivares invoked this maternal imagery in La Placita's 1985 declaration of sanctuary.[28] Just four years earlier, Olivares had assumed the pastorate of La Placita, located at the historic center point and birthplace of Los Angeles. The church, at the heart of Mexican Catholicism in Los Angeles, has long served as a Latinx community center. During the height of the 1980s refugee crisis, Olivares made a concerted effort to assist Central Americans. Although there had been efforts to privately help Central American refugees at other Catholic churches in Los Angeles, none of these churches were willing to make a public declaration of sanctuary, particularly in light of the FBI's investigation into the Tucson sanctuary workers earlier that same year.[29] Olivares proved to be particularly adept at curating a strong media presence. He not only adopted the deep symbolic tradition of sanctuary but also used Guadalupe as a way of presenting a familiar Latin American face and claiming space to unify immigrants. He declared sanctuary on December 12, 1985,

FIGURE 14. Mural of Juan Diego's encounter with Guadalupe on the exterior of La Placita Church. Courtesy of Nathan Ellstrand.

Guadalupe's feast day. In this move, Olivares linked his decision to offer sanctuary to Guadalupe's apparition and requests to Juan Diego. A press release on November 18 of that same year announced:

> On December 12, 1985, the feast of Our Lady of Guadalupe "La Placita" (Our Lady Queen of the Angels Church) will be the first Roman Catholic Church in the city of Los Angeles to offer PUBLIC SANCTUARY to Central American refugees. This is the fulfillment of Mary's mandate to Juan Diego at TEPEYAC: Build a temple "where I can demonstrate and impart all of my love, compassion, aid and defense." Later on she says, "Why is your heart troubled? Why are you afraid? ... Am I not here who am your mother?"[30]

Sacred Motherhood in the Sanctuary Movement 151

FIGURE 15. Guadalupe Mother of Sanctuary: Father Luis Olivares (farthest left) reads his official declaration of sanctuary on December 12, 1985, in La Placita church. Courtesy of Los Angeles Times Photographic Archive (Collection 1429). Library Special Collections, Charles E. Young Research Library, UCLA.

Olivares chose to decorate the walls of the church with an "immense" image of Guadalupe and other images of "renegade saints" and holy figures, such as Guatemala's and New Mexico's Black Christ of Esquipulas and the would-be saint Archbishop Oscar Romero.[31]

During this historic mass, two Central American families in sanctuary accompanied Olivares at the front of the church (Figure 15). The children held signs that stated the death tolls of their respective countries ("El Salvador, 70,000 Persons Killed, 1980–1985" and "Guatemala, 50,000 Persons Killed, 1980–1985"). The sanctuary seekers each held a red rose, which symbolized the roses that Guadalupe gave to Juan Diego to prove her apparition to Catholic Church officials. This visually linked Central Americans' plight to Guadalupe's concern for Juan Diego.[32]

At the declaration service, a Salvadoran couple, along with a Guatemalan woman and her three children, stood before the congregation, centering attention on a mother and her children and invariably shaping their image of those who sought sanctuary. The painful image of "non-people" dressed in all-black clothes and masks with only small slits in the eye area contrasted to the openness and warmth of Guadalupe. The juxtaposition, no doubt, served as a solemn reminder of how US policy dehumanized fellow brothers and sisters from Central America, while Guadalupe and those gathered wished to embrace them. Before the congregation and a robust media presence, the "non-persons" testified of the violence they beheld and the support they hoped to receive from the congregation in the spirit of Guadalupe's love. In this setting, Olivares powerfully articulated the violence against families wrought by the terror of US involvement in Central America and the nation's subsequent refusal to protect displaced people. Guadalupe, as a mother, *had* to get involved.

## Marian Motherhood in the New Sanctuary Movement

From the 1980s to the early 2000s, Guadalupe's role as an immigrant rights mediatrix and protectress continued to accrue more recognition, in good measure due to her frequent invocation by immigrant and Sanctuary Movement leaders. After several years (2005–2007) of witnessing Congress fail to pass comprehensive immigration reform, the New Sanctuary Movement (NSM) began to take shape. At the start of the NSM, mother, activist, and soon-to-be sanctuary leader Elvira Arellano invoked the power of motherhood and Guadalupe's instrumental role in mediation. Her groundbreaking 2006 case caught the public's attention and put the NSM on the map. After 9/11, stricter immigration regulations had led to Arellano's arrest in a sweep of employees at Chicago's O'Hare International Airport in 2002. She was sentenced to three years of probation and given notice of deportation. Nevertheless, she steadfastly remained committed to stay in the country and fight so that her US-born son Saul could have all the opportunities for which she worked.

An epic story of a mother fighting for her son's well-being largely framed the narrative around Arellano, who in the summer of 2006 was effectively kickstarting the NSM, which was officially declared in January 2007. By 2006, Arellano had officially expended all of her resources and in August of that year took sanctuary at

Adalberto United Methodist Church in Chicago as a last resort.[33] She specifically chose a church that honored Guadalupe and respected her Mexican Catholic traditions and practices.[34] Arellano remained active during her time in sanctuary, becoming an outspoken advocate for immigrant rights, particularly those of undocumented parents. Her influence and message of struggle involving motherhood attracted a national audience, resulting in *Time* magazine listing her on its annual list of "People Who Mattered" in 2006.[35]

In some significant ways, Arellano's example set a new tone for sanctuary seekers in the NSM in that they would become the faces and voices of the movement. Arellano's advocacy for undocumented parents facing separation from their children positioned her to effectively use maternal language in her activism. Much of her rhetoric revolved around her identity as a mother. When asked why she kept fighting to stay in the United States, she replied, "It's wrong to split up families. I'm fighting for my son, not for myself. It's a matter of principle. I don't want him treated like garbage. I am a mom and a worker. I am not a terrorist."[36] Arellano's appeal to motherhood, coupled with the fact that she was taking sanctuary with her son in a church, made her concerns resonant with those of Guadalupe. Throughout her time in sanctuary, Arellano drew on the trope of sacred motherhood to present herself and her cause in a favorable light to the media and the wider public. Scholar of religion Luis León explains that "the idea of sacred motherhood, symbolized by Guadalupe, resonates throughout Mexican culture."[37] As true as this is, Arellano was also making a wider appeal to white Christians who also understand Mary's central role as a mother and protectress.

To emphasize the connection between Guadalupe and herself, Arellano began to make purposeful appearances with images of Guadalupe.[38] Various photographs of Arellano in sanctuary capture Guadalupe strategically placed in the frame. This is not to suggest that Arellano's devotion to her was purely performative. Even before she entered sanctuary, she had been a longtime Guadalupan devotee. In fact, as Arellano notes, she first began attending Adalberto United Methodist Church because the leaders and congregation "honored the Virgin of Guadalupe and respected [Arellano's] Mexican Catholic traditions."[39] To be sure, some congregants were not entirely happy with the church's reverence of Guadalupe, as it departed from usual Methodist traditions. Nevertheless, the faithful did not abandon Guadalupe, as they felt she embodied the spirit of freeing "the most downtrodden of God's people," who in this context were undocumented immigrants in the United States.[40] The pastors and leaders of the congregation recognized parallels between Arellano and

Mary. In response to criticism that, as a single mother, Arellano was not the "right" public symbol for immigrant rights activism, her supporters would reply, "We did not choose Elvira; God did. And we reminded the activists that God had once chosen another single mother, to bring about the birth of Jesus."[41]

In her analysis of Arellano's activism, political scientist Amalia Pallares argues that a significant portion of Arellano's rhetoric and public image emphasized her identity as a mother trying to do best for her child, thus allowing onlookers to make an easy connection to Guadalupe. To strengthen this connection, Pallares further maintains that Arellano "[deemphasized] her sexuality while emphasizing her religiosity." Her clothes matched this as well, as Arellano began wearing more veils in her appearances. In addition to maternal rhetoric, she began referencing God and her faith in her justifications of her actions and the potential outcomes of her case. As her case continued, "she increasingly projected an otherworldly aura, of someone whose mission lay in the hands of God."[42] Arellano relied on a sacred motherly figure who would do anything to protect her children as a way of claiming spiritual legitimacy for her political actions.[43]

Motherhood continues to play a major role in public depictions of sanctuary and immigrant justice in the second wave of the NSM (2016–2021).[44] As most Americans have witnessed, Trump's presidency signaled a seismic shift against Latin American immigrants. For nearly three years, the Trump administration maintained a draconian zero-tolerance policy. This, in effect, gave little recourse to undocumented immigrants with active cases, as it suspended prosecutorial discretion. For this reason, longer periods of sanctuary stays became increasingly common, some lasting for several years. Some sanctuary seekers remained in sanctuary until the Biden administration countermanded Trump's policies and issued a moratorium on numerous deportations.[45] With little legal recourse during the Trump years, sanctuary seekers, on the one hand, tended to stay in sanctuary longer but, on the other hand, became bolder about their dreams, determination, and demands. With a political regime as patently xenophobic as the Trump administration, one did not need to look too hard for the voices of opposition.

Sanctuary leaders such as Jeanette Vizguerra have been among the most vocal and emboldened sanctuary seekers. In the Denver area after Vizguerra was out of sanctuary, four Coloradan sanctuary seekers—Sandra Lopez, Ingrid Latorre, Araceli Velazquez, and Rosa Sabido—launched the People's Resolution. Three of the four leaders of the People's Resolution emphasized their identity as mothers, and Sabido used more general family rhetoric. While it is customary for sanctuary seekers to fight for a simple stay of removal, the founders of the People's Resolution mounted a much larger platform, in which they also called for specific ways to advance immigration reform.[46]

Trump-era approaches to family unity had the unintended effect of emboldening sanctuary seekers/leaders to speak up. Some have carried their demands into the Biden era. The National Sanctuary Collective press conference on January 26, 2021, called on the Biden administration to implement swift action and to put together an exit plan for those in sanctuary as part of broader immigration reform. Three themes emerged from the oral statements of sanctuary seekers/leaders. First, sanctuary seekers/leaders established that Trump's presidency and harsh anti-immigrant policies negatively affected their lives and led them to take sanctuary. That said, they expressed hope that the Biden administration would set in place protections for undocumented immigrants and pathways to citizenship. Second, many emphasized their identities as law-abiding, tax-paying non-citizens. Finally, eleven of the thirteen sanctuary leaders on the panel mentioned family as a primary reason for staying in the United States.

Sanctuary seekers/leaders justified coming to and staying in the United States for the benefit of their families, emphasizing the struggle they endured as mothers and fathers just trying to seek out a better life with their children and not wanting to be separated from them. Juana Luz Tobar Ortega pointed out that "the fact that we are here in a sanctuary church is to keep our family together. We don't want to get separated from our family. That's why we are fighting: for our family." Some sanctuary seekers implored President Biden directly, emphasizing that his identity as a father should allow him to understand their pain and why they continue to fight for a path to legal residency. María Mérida, however, addressed First Lady Jill Biden and Vice President Kamala Harris as mothers, stating, "You know the love of a mother. You know the love for children, the family's love; that's the reason we fight." By framing demands in terms of motherhood, sanctuary leaders created a baseline emotional understanding that spans cultures, making an emotional appeal and calling upon the weight and sanctity of a mother's love in the face of the unfeeling state.[47]

Pressing the issue of motherhood further, Maria Chavalan Xut, a Maya woman who came to the United States to escape racism and injustice in Guatemala, centered her speech around familial relations and sacred motherhood. In her statement, she combined Maya spiritual worldview with Catholic theology, referring to the audience as her "brothers and sisters" and reminding them that, as a Maya woman who is indigenous to this continent, "this is my place. I want to share it with all of you."

Chavalan Xut also spoke of the racism she faced in Guatemala and why her name is so meaningful to her: "They call all of the Indigenous women in Guatemala City 'Maria.' They call them Maria as a mockery, but I feel very happy to be called Maria. I have the name of our celestial mother. I'm in my continent. I love my continent, my mother Earth. I haven't been out of my place, but I'm in my home."[48] She not only mentions the earth as a mother figure who deserves to be respected and shared, but she also identifies a connection to her "celestial mother," Mary. Fittingly, as Chavalan Xut delivered her remarks, one could not help but notice that in the meticulously staged background stood a painting of the "Guatemalan Madonna" by the artist John Battista Giuliani. The Madonna's presence looked over yet another sanctuary press conference. But instead of appearing as the mestiza protectress Guadalupe, the Guatemalan Madonna icon stood in solidarity with Chavalan Xut.

## Conclusion

In the weeks and months following Biden's inauguration, sanctuary seekers from all over the country began to leave the houses of worship with the hope that he would reverse former president Trump's anti-immigrant policies. Sanctuary had provided refuge from Trump's zero-tolerance deportation policy, and this refuge ultimately allowed sanctuary seekers to return home to their families after months—and in many cases, years—of living on sacred premises. On the day of Biden's inauguration, the Department of Homeland Security announced a 100-day moratorium on deportations. Shortly thereafter, a Trump-appointed federal judge in Texas blocked the administration from enforcing the moratorium. Despite this setback, the change in administration signaled some semblance of hope, at least for those in sanctuary. Some of those who left sanctuary received stays of deportation while others learned that the US Citizenship and Immigration Services reopened their cases. Nevertheless, immigration reform remains yet to be realized under Biden.

Fighting to keep families together has long been a staple in immigrant rights activism, especially with regards to the Sanctuary Movement, which supports individuals who sacrifice their personal freedoms in their fight to stay in the United States. And few relationships articulate the sacredness of these bonds than does motherhood. From the beginning of the Sanctuary Movement in the 1980s and continuing through the NSM, immigrants and families have invoked the close affinity between motherhood and Mary, summoning Mary's religious and cultural capital.

Guadalupe, to be sure, is not the only Marian apparition that consoles migrants. One could also point to the Cuban Our Lady of Charity, the Mexican Virgin of San Juan de los Lagos, the Guatemalan Madonna, and a host of other apparitions.[49] That said, Guadalupe is undoubtedly the most widely recognized and celebrated Marian symbol in the Americas. It is little wonder, then, why Sanctuary Movement leaders have turned to her sacred motherhood to support the family fight for immigrant justice.

Even if the practice of sanctuary fades both as a practice and from the public's memory, Latin American migration to the United States remains an ongoing phenomenon, one that is still hotly debated and will not end anytime soon. The public's attention remains captured by issues surrounding immigration, such as Central American migrant caravans, the further militarization of the US-Mexico border, and cases of family detention and separation. Given these circumstances, we should not be surprised to find migrants and activists seeking out help from a divine power that transcends the state. By focusing on Guadalupe and Marian symbols in the Sanctuary Movement as well as migrant-rights activism more broadly, researchers are able to examine historical continuities that speak to larger US-Christian sensibilities and connect the migrant rights activism of Latin America to US Latinx traditions. Significantly, migrants and pro-migrant activists have found a way to speak back to the largely anti-immigrant Religious Right by using religious rhetoric and capital to justify their actions and presence in the United States. The importance and power of religious imagery in this activism, particularly Marian imagery, must not be overlooked or underestimated.

## Notes

Epigraph: Maria Mérida quoted in Free Migration Project FMP, "National Sanctuary Collective January 26, 2021 Press Conference," January 26, 2021, YouTube, 58:24, https://www.youtube.com/watch?v=ESKNbuwr-RE**&feature=youtu.be.

    Most of the press conference speakers spoke in Spanish and captions allowed for English speakers to follow along. All translations are our own though many do match the captions.

1. On the framing of "leadership" in the sanctuary movement, see Lloyd D. Barba and Tatyana Castillo-Ramos, "Latinx Leadership and Legacies in the US Sanctuary Movement, 1980–2020," *American Religion* 3 no. (Fall 2021): 1–24.

2. Grace Yukich, *One Family Under God: Immigration Politics and Progressive Religion in America* (New York: Oxford University Press, 2013).
3. We recognize that the tradition of offering sanctuary is a much larger global phenomenon and bears deep ancient roots as well as antecedent ones in the United States (Vietnam War protesters, for example). Our study is limited to the Sanctuary Movement that developed in the 1980s and has continued, albeit differently, to present day.
4. Al Senia, "13 Smuggled Salvadorans Found Dead in the Desert" *Washington Post*, July 7, 1980, https://www.washingtonpost.com/archive/politics/1980/07/07/13-smuggled-salvadorans-found-dead-in-us-desert/06e736ff-07bd-4cc2-8695-374f839278ea/.
5. From 1983 to 1990, 2.6 percent of migrants from El Salvador and 1.8 percent from Guatemala received asylum, see María Cristina García, *Seeking Refuge: Central American Migration to Mexico, the United States, and Canada* (Berkeley and Los Angeles: University of California Press, 2006), 13–43, 86–87, 90.
6. Geraldo Cadava, *Standing on Common Ground: The Making of the Sunbelt Borderland* (Cambridge, MA: Harvard University Press, 2013), 201.
7. García, *Seeking Refuge*, 98–99. The act of declaring a house of worship as "sanctuary" principally draws upon the establishment of cities of refuge as described in the Hebrew Bible. In the cities of refuge, those who committed unintentional manslaughter could find safety in the designated cities of refuge and thereby legally evade the blood avenger. Sanctuary activists in the United States also invoked the longstanding practice of sanctuary as developed in the Christian European context from the fourth century onwards. These activists also invoked the Underground Railroad as righteous precedent for transporting undocumented Central American migrants into and throughout the United States, see Ignatius Bau, *This Ground Is Holy: Church Sanctuary and Central American Refugees* (Mahwah, NJ: Paulist Press, 1985), 124–71.
8. Quoted in Renny Golden and Michael McConnell, *Sanctuary: The New Underground Railroad* (Maryknoll, N.Y: Orbis Books, 1986), 48.
9. Hilary Cunningham, *God and Ceasar at the Río Grande: Sanctuary and the Politics of Religion* (Minneapolis: University of Minnesota Press, 1995). 35–43.
10. García, *Seeking Refuge*, 108–112.
11. For brief literature reviews, see Lloyd Barba and Tatyana Castillo-Ramos, "Sacred Resistance: The Sanctuary Movement from Reagan to Trump," *Perspectivas 16* (2019): 14–16; Sergio González, "The Sanctuary Movement," *Oxford Research Encyclopedia American History*, (2020): 15–18.

12. Carlos Ruiz Martinez, "The Question of Sanctuary: The Adorers of the Blood of Christ and the U.S. Sanctuary Movement, 1983–1996," *U.S. Catholic Historian* 38 no. 4 (Fall 2020): 53–70; Cadava, *Standing on Common Ground*; Sergio González, "Refugees, Religious Spaces, and Sanctuary in Wisconsin," in Theresa Delgadillo, Ramon H. Rivera-Sivera, Gerlado H. Cadava, and Claire F. Fox eds., *Building Sustainable Worlds: Latinx Placemaking in the Midwest* (Urbana-Champaign: University of Illinois Press, 2022).
13. For example, the "Mothers of the Disappeared" from Argentina's Plaza de Mayo, publicly organized a grassroots effort to demand accountability and answers from the Argentine government. They highlighted their grief as mothers of the 9,000 to 30,000 people who were abducted, tortured, and killed after the coup of 1976 and the eight years of state terrorism that followed known as Argentina's Dirty War. See Jo Fisher. *Mothers of the Disappeared* (Boston: South End Press, 1989), 10. See also Ernesto Fiocchetto's chapter in the present volume. Similarly, in her study of the Nicaraguan Association of Mothers and Relatives of the Kidnapped and Disappeared, anthropologist Sheila Tully notes that "recognizing the importance of family and motherhood in Nicaraguan society, the mothers publicly emphasize the suffering and pain which has been inflicted upon them *as mothers* . . . in so doing, the women adopt the state's own language of family and motherhood, and use it to demand information concerning the whereabouts of the disappeared." Sheila R. Tuly, "A Painful Purgatory: Grief and the Nicaraguan Mothers of the Disappeared," *Social Science & Medicine* (1982) 40 (12): 1602.
14. Shannon Watts, *Fight Like a Mother: How a Grassroots Movement Took on the Gun Lobby and Why Women Will Change the World* (San Francisco: HarperOne, 2019).
15. Eric R. Wolf, "The Virgin of Guadalupe: A Mexican National Symbol," *The Journal of American Folklore* 71, no. 279 (Jan–Mar, 1958): 34–39.
16. William B. Taylor, "Mexico's Virgin of Guadalupe in the Seventeenth Century: Hagiography and Beyond" in *Colonial Saints: Discovering the Holy in the Americas*, ed. Allan Greer and Jodi Bilinkoff, (New York: Routledge, 2003), 294.
17. Timothy Matovina, *Theologies of Guadalupe: From the Era of Conquest to Pope Francis* (New York: Oxford University Press, 2019), 159.
18. Timothy Matovina, *Guadalupe and Her Faithful: Latino Catholics in San Antonio, from Colonial Origins to the Present* (Baltimore: Johns Hopkins University Press, 2005); Luis D. León, *La Llorona's Children: Religion, Life, and Death in the U.S.-Mexican Borderlands* (Berkeley, CA: University of California Press, 2004), 91–126.

19. Shifra M. Goldman, "How, Why, Where, and When It All Happened: Chicano Murals of California," in *Signs from the Heart*, 2nd ed., ed. Eva Sperling Cockcroft and Holly Barnet-Sánchez (University of New Mexico Press, 1993), 29.
20. Roberto Lint Sagarena, "Making a There There: Marian Muralism and Devotional Streetscapes," *Visual Resources* 25, no. 1–2 (March-June 2009); David A. Sánchez, *From Patmos to the Barrio: Subverting Imperial Myths* (Minneapolis: Fortress Press, 2008).
21. Laura Pérez, *Chicana Art: The Politics of Spiritual and Aesthetic Altarities* (Durham, NC: Duke University Press, 2007), 257–96.
22. Sánchez, *From Patmos to the Barrrio*, 1, 111.
23. Jacqueline Maria Hagan, *Migration Miracle: Faith, Hope, and Meaning*, (Cambridge: Harvard University Press, 2010); Jorge Durand and Douglas S. Massey, *Miracles on the Border: Retablos of Mexican Migrants to the United States* (Tucson: University of Arizona Press, 1995).
24. Kate Morissey, "New Chicano Park Mural Will Celebrate Work of Border Angels," *The San Diego Union*, Published April 2, 2018, https://www.sandiegouniontribune.com/news/immigration/sd-me-new-mural-20180402-story.html
25. Enrique Morones, phone interview with Tatyana Castillo-Ramos, March 2019.
26. Catholic Review, "Our Lady of Guadalupe called 'Mother Without Borders,'" https://www.archbalt.org/our-lady-of-guadalupe-called-mother-without-borders/.
27. For an example outside of the Southwest, see Guadalupe's role as a protectress of immigrants in Alyshia Gálvez, *Guadalupe in New York: Devotion and Struggle for Citizenship Rights among Mexican Immigrants*, (New York: New York University Press, 2010).
28. Mario T. García, *Father Luis Olivares, a Biography: Faith Politics and the Origins of the Sanctuary Movement in Los Angeles*, (Chapel Hill: University of North Carolina Press, 2018), 320.
29. García, *Father Luis Olivares*, 320.
30. As quoted in García, *Father Luis Olivares*, 320.
31. León, *La Llorona's Children*, 113.
32. García, *Father Luis Olivares*, 329.
33. Wendy Cole, "People Who Mattered: Elvira Arellano," *Time*, December 25, 2006, http://content.time.com/time/specials/packages/article/0,28804,2019341_2017328_2017183,00.html.
34. Walter L. Coleman, *Elvira's Faith and Barrack's Challenge: The Grassroots Struggle for the Rights of Undocumented Families* (Ann Arbor, MI: Wrightwood Press, 2016), 41.

35. A list of over thirty of the year's most influential figures worldwide in politics, sports, and entertainment; Cole, "People Who Mattered: Elvira Arellano."
36. Elvira Arellano, as quoted in Cole, "People Who Mattered: Elvira Arellano."
37. León, *La Llorona's Children*, 78.
38. Arellano is a longtime devotee of Guadalupe and three years before entering sanctuary, partook in a Freedom Ride to New York City. For Arellano, the Freedom Ride was a "spiritual journey" in that she carried a statuette of Guadalupe with her, and once the organizers arrived at the final destination—the Statue of Liberty—Arellano approached the edge of water to hold up Guadalupe in juxtaposition to Lady Liberty. See chapter titled "The Virgin of Guadalupe" in Coleman, *Elvira's Faith*, 41–5.
39. Coleman, *Elvira's Faith*, 41–42.
40. Coleman, *Elvira's Faith*, 74.
41. Coleman, *Elvira's Faith*, 70.
42. Amalia Pallares, *Family Activism: Immigrant Struggles and the Politics of Noncitizenship* (New Brunswick, NJ: Rutgers University Press, 2015), 51.
43. Arellano's inclusion of Guadalupe in activism had been an aesthetic feature of her earlier work with immigrant rights groups, see Coleman, *Elvira's Faith*, 42.
44. On the second wave of the New Sanctuary Movement, that is, the wave of activism since Trump's election, see Barba and Castillo-Ramos, "Sacred Resistance."
45. Catherine E. Shoichet, "He took sanctuary in a church more than 3 years ago. He just returned home because of a new Biden policy." *CNN*, January 23, 2021, https://www.cnn.com/2021/01/22/us/north-carolina-jose-chicas-leaves-sanctuary/index.html.
46. The People's Resolution, (accessed January 8, 2021), https://web.archive.org/web/20210412214931/http://peoplesresolution.org/.
47. Free Migration Project FMP, "National Sanctuary Collective January 26, 2021, Press Conference," (accessed January 29, 2021): https://www.youtube.com/watch?v=ESKNbuwr-RE**&feature=youtu.be.
48. Quoted in ibid.
49. On the assistance offered by Mary and other saints, see Durand and Massey, *Miracles on the Border*, as well as Michelle Gonzalez's chapter in the present volume.

# References

Barba, Lloyd, and Tatyana Castillo-Ramos, "Sacred Resistance: The Sanctuary Movement from Reagan to Trump." *Perspectivas* 16 (2019): 11–36. https://perspectivasonline.com/wp-content/uploads/2019/06/P-E-R-S-P-E-C-T-I-V-A-S_2019.pdf.

Barba, Lloyd D., and Tatyana Catillo-Ramos. "Latinx Leadership and Legacies in the US Sanctuary Movement, 1980–2020." *American Religion* 3, no. 1 (Fall 2021): 1–24.

Bau, Ignatius. *This Ground Is Holy: Church Sanctuary and Central American Refugees.* Mahwah, NJ: Paulist Press, 1985.

Catholic Review. "Our Lady of Guadalupe called 'Mother Without Borders.'" January 19, 2012, https://www.archbalt.org/our-lady-of-guadalupe-called-mother-without-borders/.

Cadava, Geraldo. *Standing on Common Ground: The Making of the Sunbelt Borderland.* Cambridge, MA: Harvard University Press, 2013.

Coleman, Walter L. *Elvira's Faith and Barack's Challenge: The Grassroots Struggle for the Rights of Undocumented Families.* Ann Arbor, MI: Wrightwood Press, 2016.

Cole, Wendy. "People Who Mattered: Elvira Arellano" *Time*, December 25, 2006, http://content.time.com/time/specials/packages/article/0,28804,2019341_2017328_2017183,00.html.

Cunningham, Hilary. *God and Caesar at the Río Grande: Sanctuary and the Politics of Religion.* Minneapolis: University of Minnesota Press, 1995.

Delgadillo, Theresa, Ramon H. Rivera-Sivera, Gerlado H. Cadava, and Claire F. Fox, eds., *Building Sustainable Worlds: Latinx Placemaking in the Midwest.* Urbana-Champaign: University of Illinois Press, 2022.

Durand, Jorge, and Douglas S. Massey. *Miracles on the Border: Retablos of Mexican Migrants to the United States.* Tucson: University of Arizona Press, 1995.

Fisher, Jo. *Mothers of the Disappeared.* Boston: South End Press, 1989.

Free Migration Project FMP, "National Sanctuary Collective January 26, 2021 Press Conference." Video, 58 min., 24 sec. https://www.youtube.com/watch?v=ESKNbuwr-RE**&feature=youtu.be.

Gálvez, Alyshia. *Guadalupe in New York: Devotion and Struggle for Citizenship Rights among Mexican Immigrants.* New York: New York University Press, 2010.

García, María Cristina. *Seeking Refuge: Central American Migration to Mexico, the United States, and Canada.* Berkeley and Los Angeles: University of California Press, 2006.

García, Mario T. *Father Luis Olivares, a Biography: Faith Politics and the Origins of the Sanctuary Movement in Los Angeles.* Chapel Hill: University of North Carolina Press, 2018.

Golden, Renny, and Michael McConnell. *Sanctuary: The New Underground Railroad.* Maryknoll, NY: Orbis Books, 1986.

Goldman, Shifra M. "How, Why, Where, and When It All Happened: Chicano Murals of California." In *Signs from the Heart: California Chicano Murals,* 2nd ed., edited by Eva Sperling Cockcroft and Holly Barnet-Sánchez, Albuquerque: University of New Mexico Press, 1993.

González, Sergio, "The Sanctuary Movement." *Oxford Research Encyclopedia American History.* June 30, 2020; Accessed May 6, 2024. https://oxfordre.com/americanhistory/view/10.1093/acrefore/9780199329175.001.0001/aCrefore-9780199329175-e-790.

González, Sergio. "Refugees, Religious Spaces, and Sanctuary in Wisconsin." In *Building Sustainable Worlds: Latinx Placemaking in the Midwest,* edited by Theresa Delgadillo, Ramon H. Rivera-Sivera, Gerlado H. Cadava, and Claire F. Fox, 182–203. Urbana-Champaign: University of Illinois Press, 2022.

Hagan, Jacqueline Maria. *Migration Miracle: Faith, Hope, and Meaning.* Cambridge, MA: Harvard University Press, 2010.

León, Luis D. *La Llorona's Children: Religion, Life, and Death in the U.S.-Mexican Borderlands.* Berkeley, CA: University of California Press, 2004.

Martinez, Carlos Ruiz. "The Question of Sanctuary: The Adorers of the Blood of Christ and the U.S. Sanctuary Movement, 1983–1996." *U.S. Catholic Historian* 38, no. 4 (Fall 2020): 53–70.

Morones, Enrique. Phone interview with Tatyana Castillo-Ramos, March 2019.

Matovina, Timothy. *Theologies of Guadalupe: From the Era of Conquest to Pope Francis.* New York: Oxford University Press, 2019.

Matovina, Timothy. *Guadalupe and Her Faithful: Latino Catholics in San Antonio, from Colonial Origins to the Present.* Baltimore, MD: Johns Hopkins University Press, 2005.

Morissey, Kate. "New Chicano Park Mural Will Celebrate Work of Border Angels." *The San Diego Union,* April 2, 2018. https://www.sandiegouniontribune.com/news/immigration/sd-me-new-mural-20180402-story.html

Pallares, Amalia. *Family Activism: Immigrant Struggles and the Politics of Noncitizenship.* New Brunswick, NJ: Rutgers University Press, 2015.

Pérez, Laura. *Chicana Art: The Politics of Spiritual and Aesthetic Altarities.* Durham, NC: Duke University Press, 2007.

Sagarena, Roberto Lint "Making a There There: Marian Muralism and Devotional Streetscapes." *Visual Resources* 25, no. 1–2 (March-June 2009): 93–107.

Sánchez, David A. *From Patmos to the Barrio: Subverting Imperial Myths.* Minneapolis, MN: Fortress Press, 2008.

Shoichet, Catherine E. "He took sanctuary in a church more than 3 years ago. He just returned home because of a new Biden policy." *CNN*, January 23, 2021. https://www.cnn.com/2021/01/22/us/north-carolina-jose-chicas-leaves-sanctuary/index.html.

Senia, Al. "13 Smuggled Salvadorans Found Dead in the Desert." *Washington Post*, July 7, 1980. https://www.washingtonpost.com/archive/politics/1980/07/07/13-smuggled-salvadorans-found-dead-in-us-desert/06e736ff-07bd-4cc2-8695-374f839278ea/.

Taylor, William B. "Mexico's Virgin of Guadalupe in the Seventeenth Century: Hagiography and Beyond." In *Colonial Saints: Discovering the Holy in the Americas*, edited by Allan Greer and Jodi Bilinkoff. New York: Routledge, 2003.

The People's Resolution (accessed January 8, 2021) https://web.archive.org/web/20210412214931/http://peoplesresolution.org/.

Tuly, Sheila R. "A Painful Purgatory: Grief and the Nicaraguan Mothers of the Disappeared." *Social Science & Medicine*, 1995.

Watts, Shannon. *Fight Like a Mother: How a Grassroots Movement Took on the Gun Lobby and Why Women Will Change the World.* San Francisco: HarperOne, 2019.

Wolf, Eric R. "The Virgin of Guadalupe: A Mexican National Symbol." *The Journal of American Folklore* 71 no. 279 (Jan-March 1958): 34–39.

Yukich Grace. *One Family Under God: Immigration Politics and Progressive Religion in America.* New York: Oxford University Press, 2013.

CHAPTER 8

# Subversive Indigenous Feminist Epistemologies

## A Methodological Reflection on *El Mercado/Qhathu*

*CECILIA TITIZANO*

Across the Americas, which many Indigenous people refer to as the *Abya Yala* continent, native people are decolonizing the religious landscape, bringing to the theological table their philosophical and spiritual principles. The contributions of Indigenous women, many of whom are Christian, have been significant in this regard, though largely underappreciated. While Western decolonial theorists have made important strides in advancing decolonial epistemologies, many fall short in fully appreciating the actual voices and cosmologies of Indigenous people, especially Indigenous women. For example, Enrique Dussel, who has made significant contributions to decolonial thought at large, often glosses over the relational metaphysics of Indigenous thought. Similarly, even the work of Indigenous Christian theologians Roberto Tomichá Charupá, OFM and Fr. Eleazar Lopez fall somewhat short. I say this with the highest respect for their work, as both are tireless advocates of Teología India and have significantly contributed to its development. Tomichá Charupá endorses an "epistemological disobedience"[1] that, at first glance, would seem to foreground Indigenous ways of knowing, and Lopez wants to construct Indigenous Christian theologies based on an "intercommunication between the ancestral theology of the people and the official theology of the [Catholic] Church."[2] Yet, both advocate a purification process for theologies grounded on Indigenous cosmologies without indicating how the process would take place, what gets left behind, and who makes that decision.[3] Like Dussel, they seek to promote a decolonial theology at the service of subalterns, yet they shy away from placing Christian doctrines and their metaphysical roots on the table. It is not clear what good an epistemological disobedience would do if, at the end of the day, an Indigenous metaphysics is not seriously considered as a potential contributor to doctrinal development. It seems that despite their best efforts at decolonization, what is still lacking is a truly critical and decolonial intercultural dialogue. As this chapter shows, epistemological delinking is further hampered when Indigenous women's voices, and the particular ways in which they present their cosmologies, are left out of the dialogue. The results are androcentric interpretations of their cosmologies and an underappreciation of their integral *cosmovivencias*, which are grounded in harmonic relations and gender balance.

To challenge such androcentric approaches, some exemplary Indigenous Christian women are creating support groups that include Christian and non-Christian Indigenous women alike. These women are spiritual leaders in their own communities as well as women theologians who are committed to the decolonization and depatriarchalization of Christianity. The construction of Indigenous theologies requires a deep process of epistemic decolonization that demands revisions of androcentric readings of their ancestral cosmologies. In what follows, I lift up the perspectives of Indigenous women, many of whom simultaneously identify as community activists and scholars. Many are Christian, but not all. Despite their different positionalities, all the women share a deep love for ancestral cultures and worldviews. As I will show, their non-dualistic cosmologies serve as an important corrective to more reductionistic and androcentric approaches to Christianity.

In what follows, I first propose the Andean *Mercado/quathu* as a metaphor for an intercultural and interspiritual conversation to create a decolonial methodological space where non-Indigenous people can listen to Indigenous feminist voices as they articulate their *sentipensante cosmovivencias*, which can be roughly translated as relational and dialogical experiences with the cosmic community to transform, reconceptualize, and reconstitute ways of living/knowing/thinking/acting/being. The *Mercado/quathu* is a privileged space inhabited by Indigenous women, a muddy and hybrid place that does not presuppose a common Eurocentric ideal of rationality. Second, I highlight the important contributions of Indigenous women's work in epistemology. The scholars highlighted in this article are Mayas, Quechuas, and Aymaras, to name a few, each with their own millennial wisdoms. In an effort to lift up their communal and individual voices (as well as other Indigenous women's activist voices), this chapter organizes their writings—much of which have not yet been translated in English—into categories that contribute to the emerging and provisional systematization of Indigenous feminist epistemologies.

## Walking Toward *el Mercado/qhathu*

I grew up going to *el Mercado/qhathu* on Saturdays with my grandmother. Throughout Bolivia, el Mercado/qhathu is a vibrant marketplace full of splashing colors, different smells, and bustling crowds. Loud music competes with the noise from cars and the singing voices of vendors. During the colonial period, el Mercado was the last link in the production and sale of goods that were fully modern yet grounded in Indigenous technologies and knowledge.[4] For those who self-identify as *jaqi* and *runa* (which mean "person in relation" in both Aymara and Quechua, respectively),[5] el Mercado/qhathu was also a place to engage cosmic and spiritual energies and to harmonize life energies.[6] Both meanings of the Mercado/qhathu emerge in a contested exchange between two different *mythos*, or horizons of intelligibility.[7] For the jaqi/runa, this intercultural exchange is informed by decolonizing agendas that reshape interculturality and "make visible lived legacies and long horizons of domination, oppression, exclusion, and colonial difference (ontological, political, economic, cultural, epistemic, cosmological, and existence based)."[8]

I still remember the sweet smell of fresh herbs and fruit commingling with other odors. *El Mercado* is a large area where mouth-watering aromas of local dishes compete with foul smells of garbage and dark waters pullulating with decaying products. It is one of the rare places, in a society that is still very much colonial, where people from different walks of life intermingle. El Mercado/qhathu is where middle-class white and *mestizo* women shop, some of them followed by their maids, who are usually Indigenous young women, carrying bags full of products. In this sense, it is also a women's space, displaying large varieties of experiences based on their interstitial locations.

El Mercado/qhathu is also a contested space where categories usually kept separate and opposed interact. Clean and unclean, fresh and decomposing, urban and rural, *mestizo* and Indigenous, modern and premodern, a place where decent and vulgar engage each other. El Mercado/qhathu is an interlocking space where cultural, religious, social, and aesthetic categories fuse into an incarnational muddy place.[9] It defies a clean and detached encounter with the other. If people want to buy, they must converse with the sellers. My grandmother would refer to the sellers as *caseritas* (women from whom she bought often), indicating a relation of respect and friendship.

El Mercado/qhathu is, for many non-Indigenous people, the place where uncomfortable memories of an Indigenous and distant past are represented in the *qhateras*, the Spanish name that refers to the women merchants selling at the qhathu. Many mestizos would prefer to leave behind their Indigenous roots and the shame it produces. The Quechua and Aymara qhateras, who wear lively *polleras*, or wide embroidered skirts, capes, and shawls, offer their products while keeping an eye on their children. Their bodies bear the signs of hard work. Their skins are tanned by the Andean sun and dried by the cold winters. Their hands are cracked, their heels fissured, and their brown breasts chapped by their suckling infants. The buyers at the market—heirs of an entrenched colonial mentality—gaze upon them as smelly Indians, ignorant peasants, dark and ugly.[10] In the imaginary colonial landscape of whites and mestizos, Indigenous women's bodies and the repugnant wet, dark, and smelly side of el Mercado/qhathu are the same. Quechua and Aymara women are the "other"; they are targets of disgust and fascination. In the cultural and social imagination of the colonized mind, they are no longer humans; they occupy the imaginary space of un-ruled, instinctual, oversexualized creatures, incapable of reason and in constant need of guidance and control.[11]

Many qhateras engage with their clients on an equal basis, demanding respectful interactions such as not touching the merchandise if they do not intend to buy it; hence transforming el Mercado/qhathu into a place of resistance. Indigenous women demand to be treated as humans, deserving equal treatment and respect. They see themselves as the heirs of millennial wisdom, the daughters of *Pachamama* or Mother Earth.[12] They are heirs of Bartolina Sisa, Gregoria Apaza, and Micaela Bastidas, strong ancestors who were martyrs and fighters.

Early mornings, before opening their shops, qhateras give libations (*challar*) to the Creator, to *Pachamama*, and the protector spirits, transforming el Mercado/qhathu into a sacred space where humans encounter the divine amidst colorful fabrics and sweet fragrances of a *K'oa*,[13] yet they are never too far from purulent puddles of decayed products. The K'oa ceremony, something that my grandmother insisted on practicing during holy days, is an act of gratitude and reciprocity, as well as a request for blessings. The qhateras transform el Mercado into a qhathu, a sacred cosmic space to balance and reciprocate life energies. They are the ones dialoguing with the cosmos. The qhateras at el Mercado/qhathu are reclaiming their right to be epistemic subjects and putting forward categories of concern for them and the cosmic family.

El Mercado/qhathu is not unique to the Andean region; we can find it all over Latin America. As such, it serves as a metaphor for a methodological decolonial space that reflects the Latin American religious milieu (muddy, *hibrido*,[14] and contested). It also provides a heuristic device highlighting Indigenous women's active resistance against the triple axes of discrimination for being Indigenous, women, and poor. For community leader Julia Ramos (Quechua from Bolivia), racism causes Indigenous women to hate their roots and lose their identity and customs. It teaches them to "get away from their reality and see their people, their mothers [and] grandmothers as a synonym of backwardness, ignorance, and poverty."[15] In the 1990s, autonomy and cultural recognition in Latin America emerged as central topics to Indigenous decolonization projects. Within these projects, Indigenous women emerged as independent political subjects who shared the struggle with their peoples and organizations, simultaneously posing specific gender-based demands. They demand the recovery of their territories, which includes their first territory—their bodies—as well as their ancestors' embodied cosmic memories.

A growing number of Indigenous women, many of them activist/scholars who connect through various networks, center their spirituality as the origin of and motor for a new pan-Indigenous movement in which women's leadership is prominent. Their claims are rooted in their cosmologies, which also provide ways of naming and knowing reality. To claim epistemological agency is a subversive decolonial act. As epistemological subjects, Indigenous women claim authority to question and criticize lived historical oppressions while acknowledging that they belong to "original societies with millenary roots, with philosophies and ancestral cosmogonic paradigms."[16] From their perspective, despite the diversity of peoples in *Abya Yala*, they all share "sacred principles based on their cosmogonies."[17] These women draw on principles like reciprocity, complementarity, and duality "in order to regain equilibrium."[18]

As epistemological subjects, Indigenous women challenge the epistemic hegemony of dominant Western groups. Their epistemology may be described as *"sentipensante cosmo-cimientos,"* which translates to both "heartfelt-thinking" and "cosmic knowing." This epistemology, which is grounded in ancestral memories, moves beyond body/mind, subject/object, and human/nonhuman dichotomies. Ancestral memories and constant relations with the other-than-human community of beings stretches the Western notion of "body" out to a more cosmic understanding of cuerpo-territorio. A cuerpo-territorio, or "body-territory," provides the epistemological foundations to interpret and construct reality. But how can Indigenous women "name" and "know" (epistemology) reality when their spiritualities and philosophical assumptions of the nature of reality (ontology) are dismissed and their architectonic texts discharged?[19] As the influential feminist theologian and Aymara activist Sofia Chipana argues, epistemic decolonialization requires these women to drink from the well of their ancestral wisdom.[20]

Within Indigenous circles, decolonization involves healing the communal self by consciously reconnecting with their ancestral memory. In many instances, I have heard Indigenous women referring to themselves as embodied memories of their millennial cultures. The Aymara concept of memory (*amuyt'aña*) consists of looking, feeling, tasting, and remembering the past to theorize and construct the present.[21] For Silvia Rivera Cusicanqui, one of the most important Aymara scholars from Bolivia, embodying decolonial practices involves a communal cosmic praxis of *sentipensar*, or *feelingthinking*, with the *chuyma*, or lungs in Aymara. *Feelingthinking* with their chuyma refers to the act of engaging their hearts, livers, and lungs, including their communal memory (amuyt'aña) to feel and will the present.[22] For these women, decolonizing praxis is incomplete if it is not grounded in Indigenous epistemologies that value women's voices.[23]

## Indigenous Feminist Epistemologies

Latin America is home to an impressive group of Indigenous women activists and scholars. Although much of their work has not yet been translated into English, their significant contributions are worth noting. Prominent activists and some scholars include the following: Tarcila Rivera (Quechua, Perú), Julieta Paredes (Andean/Aymara, Bolivia)[24], Lorena Cabnal, Aura Cumes (kaqchikel, Guatemala), Dorotea Gomez (Quiche, Guatemala), Maya Cú Choc (Quiche, Guatemala), Sofia Chipana (Aymara) and Gladys Tzul Tzul (Quiche, Guatemala)[25], Alma López (Quiche, Guatemala), Vicenta Mamani Bernabé (Aymara, Bolivia), and Silvia Rivera Cusicanqui (Andean/Aymara, Bolivia). Not all of them self-identify as feminist, and yet all share a leading role in creating a good life for women.

Indigenous feminism is a controversial concept. Indigenous women's engagement with feminist theory ranges from rejecting it as a neocolonial imposition to adopting it in highly qualified ways.[26] Despite internal negotiations, all of the women listed above embrace their cosmological principles. They re-inscribe them in their contemporary struggles for justice for themselves, their people, and Mother Earth, and they embody them through their daily life and spiritual practices.

An important step in their struggles is to recognize that many communities do not embody their cosmological principles in relation to the role and treatment of women. Alma Lopéz, ex–council member of the City of Quetzaltenango, Guatemala, says with sadness that the "famous gender complementarity of the Mayan culture does not exist, and affirming the opposite constitutes an act of aggression."[27] Communitarian feminists Julieta Paredes and Lorena Cabnal respond to this reality and call for the recovery of ancestral cosmic memory of the foremothers. This recovery entails remembering their daily lives, wisdom, and struggles. Paredes and Cabnal are part of a movement that proposes an Indigenous feminism that speaks to the lived realities of the women in their collectives. They do not idealize the past as a perfect utopia where women flourished; instead, they call for a faithful and critical engagement with their ancestral cosmologies. Using what I call a "double-hermeneutical perspective," Paredes and Cabnal seek to "de-patriarchate to decolonize and to decolonize to de-patriarchate"[28] so that their cosmologies can recover the intrinsic dignity of women and Mother Earth.[29]

Indigenous women produce a wealth of materials during local, regional, and continental gatherings; some of these riches are systematized in *Memorias* (Memories) and *Palabras Vivas*—written declarations that emerge through shared consensus. Some scholarly reflections are starting to emerge as articles in newsletter and journals, as well as book chapters, but they are still very few. In what follows, I organize their contributions in sub-areas that reflect their analytic significance. To underscore the significance of their arguments, I will at times refer to the work of other scholars, mostly Native North American scholars, whose work on Indigenous epistemologies is well developed, having been produced over decades.

## Knowledge as Embodied and Cosmic

Dorotea Gomez, Blanca Chacoso, Sofia Chipana, Lorena Cabnal, and Julieta Paredes link together Indigenous female bodies, territory, Mother Earth, and the cosmos, and argue for the recovery and defense of their bodies and territories.[30] As Cabnal writes,

> [I] propose to recover and historically defend my territory/body/earth. I assume the recovery of my expropriated body, to give my body life, joy, vitality, and pleasure. I also give my body the capacity to construct a liberating knowledge for decision-making; and I add to this capacity the defense of my territory/earth, because I cannot conceive this woman's body without a *space* on earth that dignifies my existence and promotes my life in its fullness. The historical and oppressive violence exist in my first territory, my body, as well as in my historical territory, the earth.[31]

Space in the Andean culture has several meanings. According to Paredes, it refers to tangible or historical space such as territory, public spaces, neighborhoods, and homes. However, space also can be understood as intangible space, as in political and cultural space.[32] The well-being of Indigenous women, explains Blanca Chacoso (Quechua, Ecuador), depends on having ownership over their own spaces, for "violence not only originates from the husband or the father, but it also comes from those who have appropriated our land, and by the government because it does not let us use our authority." Quechua women must fight so that the land will be theirs, "but we must also fight so that we are not raped again [by the military]."[33] Chacoso thus links her body to territory.

Similar to Chacoso, Gomez, who is a pioneering exponent of the notion of the body as political territory, connects her brown body to the land to secure her historical survival and liberation. For Gomez, her body is a political territory constructed by colonization and historical violence. It is a territory with history, memory, and knowledge—both ancestral and personal.[34]

The connection between body/territory and Mother Earth/cosmos is possible because for Indigenous women, land is not an object. Rather, it is the cosmic Mother of Life, which in her most tangible form is Mother Earth. Chacoso explains: "We [Indigenous women] speak of land, even though other women do not need to talk about land. However, we do, because land for us is not only the parcel we work on; it is the *Pachamama*."[35] Indigenous women's bodies as *topos* take a cosmic dimension when interpreted through their cosmologies. In the specific example of the Andes, space takes a cosmic meaning when it is referred to as *Mama Pacha* (Mother/matter of all that is).[36] Indigenous feminist scholars locate their female bodies and territory/Mother Earth/cosmos as the places that engender knowledge.

## Knowledge as Cosmo-cimiento, or Cosmic Knowledge

For Vicenta Mamani Bernabé, the *jaqi/runa* lives his or her life listening to and conversing with *Pacha* (all that is).[37] Mamani is a Methodist Aymara theologian who has written about Aymara women's spirituality. She describes humanity as neither the apex of creation nor the center of reality.[38] In fact, the very notion of fullness of being comes from being able to relate to others. We find a similar concept among Native American communities, where personhood is based upon maintaining proper relationships with fellow creatures.[39] This relational accountability promotes reciprocity, which guides the construction of knowledge.

The Andean person as jaqi/runa has particular functions or responsibilities within the relational cosmic reality. The jaqui/runa serves as mediators or bridges between an unfolding cosmos, the creative advance of life, and the chaotic aspects of reality;[40] it is a *chakana* or cosmic bridge between the different aspects of reality. Their bodies function as chakanas, fostering a deep interconnection and harmonious relations between all members of the cosmos. In this sense, their bodies are permeable, and they are both objects and subjects of knowledge.[41] Andean Indigenous women, who locate their bodies/Mother Earth in relation to the cosmos, see themselves as chakanas. They are not dispassionate tools, mechanisms, or contrivances for knowing; they are embodied mediations. Ivone Gebara defines mediation as "a reality that is a means for knowing but at the same time a part of and constitutive purposes of the knowing subject. In this sense, a means is present in the beginning, the middle and the end of every aspect of the knowing process itself."[42]

As embodied mediations, Andean Indigenous women invite humanity to live the connectedness of matter, energy, and the Creator Spirit. The jaqi/runa deploy their sensual beings in the cognition process. They use their chuyma, or lungs, indicating a connection between body and mind. This action marks a departure from views of the mind that are dominant in traditional cognitive science.[43] There is no space for a narrow understanding of cognition, traditionally conceptualized as an "abstraction from bodily mechanisms of sensory processing and motor control."[44] As chakanas, humans think as much with their minds as they do with their hearts and bodies.

Patricio Guerrero (Quechua scholar, Ecuador) explains, for instance, that the jaqi/runa feel, prehend, and will reality as an energetic web of relations.[45] Using their chuyma, or lungs, and amuyt'aña, or communal memory, Indigenous women go beyond what Alfred North Whitehead calls "the sensationalist mythology."[46] Rather than restrict reality to what is experienced by the five senses, they experience multiple realities, materials, and energies. Knowledge is a matter of intuitive insight, similar to what Whitehead describes as "emotional tones."[47] Through their thinking-heart, Indigenous women experience reality through *intuitive reasoning*, bringing together subjectivity and objectivity.[48] As subjects and objects dancing in the matrix or web of life, a feelingthinking rises from it, helping redesign its elements, to then be woven back into the matrix.[49]

For Guerrero, knowledge is a process of self-in-relation. The jaqi/runa perceive concrete material reality as an aspect of a larger matrix of the energetic web of relations. Using their thinking heart, they open their whole bodies, tuning to the sacred truth or divine wisdom that sustains and creates *Pacha* (all that is). Through their sentipensante epistemology, they experience and relate to the Divine through an open corporality, where a chuyma and belly is the place where reality is continuously created and recreated. It means that the concrete materiality of Indigenous women's lives and bodies is the locus through which they constantly interact with the Divine and the cosmic reality.[50] It begins with a deeply shared awareness of the divine manifestation in matter. The cosmos pulses toward harmony and balance, and the human community, immersed in this relational and muddy reality, does the same.

Knowledge is embodied through an open corporality, a mode of feelingthinking (*sentipiensa*) that is woven into the very nature of the cosmos (*Pacha*). Women in their communities, through their open corporality and chuyma, actively collaborate in the ongoingness of the universe or creative advance of Pacha. The Mexican scholar Silvia Marcos maintains that Indigenous women's "skin does not separate the exterior from the interior, nor the material from the immaterial. Instead, there is a permanent and constant interchange, where all types of fluxes constantly cross the skin."[51] Corporality is thus open to the energetic fluxes of the cosmos.

## Knowledge as Relational

Just as the jaqi/runa understand being in terms of relations, so, too, do they understand knowledge in a relational and reciprocal way. Mamani Bernabé explains that Aymara people converse with Pachamama and all members of the cosmic family. All members, animals, plants, rivers, the Earth herself have knowledge; it is the role of the jaqi/runa to listen and enter in conversation with these other-than-human members.[52] Aymara epistemology goes beyond the idea of individual knowledge to the concept of relational knowledge. Reciprocal relations ground knowledge production. Shawn

Wilson (Opaskwayak Cree, Canada) shares this value when he says, "It is not the realities in and of themselves that are important. It is the relationship that I share with reality. . . . [This] includes interpersonal, intra-personal, environmental and spiritual relationships and relationships with ideas."[53]

Wilson maintains that knowledge comes from people's histories, stories, observations of the environment, visions, dreams, and spiritual insights.[54] "A lived, and creative relationship with the natural world cannot be underestimated in Native science."[55] Indigenous researchers observe and participate in reality with all their sensual being. This is what cognitive scientists often refer to as "embodied cognition." According to Robert Wilson and Lucia Foglia, "Cognition is embodied when it is deeply dependent upon features of the physical body of an agent, that is, when aspects of the agent's body beyond the brain play a significant causal or physically constitutive role in cognitive processing."[56] To put the matter another way, Gregory Cajete notes that as we experience the world, so we are also experienced by the world. In such a light, everything has its own energy and its own unique intelligence and creative process. This includes not only obvious animate entities, such as plants, animals, and microorganisms, but also what are often deemed "inanimate" objects, such as rocks, mountains, and rivers. Everything in nature has something to teach humans.[57]

The capacity to open ourselves to learn from non-humans requires a "practiced ability to enter into a heightened sense of awareness of the natural world, which allows the indigenous person intimate understanding of the process of nature."[58] As Margaret Kovach (Cree/Saulteaux, Canada) suggests, "Energy reveals itself as knowledge stored deep within a collective unconscious, which surfaces through dreams, prayers, ceremonial rituals, and other happenings."[59] In similar way, Chipana and Cabnal acknowledge that an Indigenous feminist epistemology entails the "recovery of the corporal cosmic memory of their female ancestors to support indigenous feminist efforts to weave their history grounded in the particularity of their own corporal memory."[60] Knowledge production is a relational activity grounded in the whole body.

One of the most striking aspects of Indigenous feminist epistemology is the proposal to recover the corporal cosmic memory of their female ancestors, present in an incarnational universe. The brutality of colonization hit women the hardest. A patriarchal Christianity decried the sacred feminine as diabolic, stripping the philosophical/spiritual grounding that supported women's economic, spiritual, and political power. By reclaiming the sacred feminine in their cosmologies, these women perform a subversive act of healing.

Indigenous women's ancestral concept of dual complementarity guides their gender analysis and feminist hermeneutics. Their conception of gender is based on fluid female and male cosmic principles dancing together in spaces beyond material procreation, opening spaces for fluid gender identities. In the first Continental Gathering of Indigenous Women that took place in Oaxaca, Mexico in 1993, more than 400 delegates from across *Ayba Yala* arrived to question the Inter-American Development Bank's (IDB) policies. The delegates discussed feminism and gender relations and defined gender equity as "respectful relationship . . . of balance, of equilibrium. It is a relationship of respect and harmony, where men and women have the same opportunity, without adding more work to women."[61] A harmonious gender relation ensures rightful and healthy relations with themselves, with other humans, and the cosmos. They support and value differences and embodied relations; there is no space for androcentrism. Indigenous women envision flourishing as relational, communal, in search of a cosmic equilibrium.[62]

## More Than Mere Translations at El Mercado-qhathu

Epistemological disobedience is an important step toward decolonizing Christianity, but it needs to espouse a critical interculturality moving beyond missiological goals. Theologians need to take Indigenous epistemologies seriously, many of which are being articulated outside ecclesial circles. It is preferable to err on the side of caution than to continue rushing inculturation projects. We need a critical and creative revision of inculturation projects from local perspectives, showing how colonized and silenced Christian communities have resisted and today continue to drink from their wells of millennial wisdom. A humbler approach that listens more attentively to Indigenous perspectives—and, especially, Indigenous women's perspectives—could open the door for deeper conversations between Christianity and Indigenous thought. Decolonizing Christianity entails an epistemological disobedience that is not afraid to address head-on onto-epistemological assumptions such as the anthropocentric understanding of *imago dei*, nature of God, and world-God relations.

The journeys of many Indigenous Christian women are guided by the soft breeze of *Ruah* and the strength of their female ancestors. As heirs of millennial-old cultures, members of *Comunidad de Sabias y Teologas de Abya Yala*, of which I am a part, "rescu[e] broken and burned threads and creatively weave them into multicolored cloaks."[63] These new theological cloaks result from what Chipana calls "a process of playful and creative creations, since the absence of sacred texts leads us to oral traditions, narratives, and myths that are reenacted, ritually and verbally."[64]

Using the muddy and hybrid space of el Mercado/qhathu as guiding metaphor, this chapter has shown how Indigenous Christians can engage Christianity on their own terms. The hybrid nature of el Mercado/qhathu provides a back-and-forth movement between the center and the margins. It is a contested space where Indigenous women have taken ownership and claim epistemological agency.

As we have seen, these women decenter Eurocentric conceptions of reality and knowledge. Their understanding of the world as a simultaneous expression of body, territory, Mother Earth, and cosmos serves as a corrective to the more reductionistic view that the world is simply a collection of raw materials, objects for human use and abuse. Like *Pachamama* herself, Indigenous female bodies are sacred. Their bodies are connected to all creation and transform *Pacha* (all that is) from a geographical place (*ubi*) into a place of meaning for the communal experience of Mother-Father Creator in history (*quid*).

In the Indigenous imaginary of el Mercado/qhatu, knowledge is a communal, embodied, and interconnected enterprise in a cosmos where everything is alive and requires respectful relations. Indigenous epistemology broadens sources of revelation to include other-than-human persons; they become active members at the theological table, each with their own voices. They will continue to challenge Christians to heal our relationship with Mother Earth, value the intrinsic dignity of Indigenous bodies and voices—especially women's—and build *un mundo donde quepan muchos mundos*, that is, a world where many worlds could fit.[65]

## Notes

1. Roberto Tomichá Charupá, "Diez consideraciones para una pneumatología cristiana en perspectiva indígena," *Revista Teología* LVI, no. 129 (agosto 2019): 132.
2. Eleazar López Hernández, "Hacia una teología del Espíritu de Dios en pueblos mesoamericanos," in *Espíritu Santo y pueblos originarios. Estudios preparatorios al VII simposio de Teología India* (Mexico: CEM, 2019), 103.
3. I am aware of the importance of doctrinal assessment of new theological developments. However, what is at play here is whether or not Indigenous cosmologies and its metaphysis would be considered as equal dialogical partners.

4. Simón Yampara Huarachi, *La cosmovisión y lógica de la dinámica socioeconómica del Qhatu/Feria 16 de Julio Investigaciones Regionales El Alto* (La Paz, Bolivia: Fundación PIEB, UPEA, 2007), xvi.
5. In Quechua, *runasimi* is also used to refer a person who speaks Quechua.
6. Yampara Huarachi, *La cosmovisión y lógica de la dinámica socioeconómica del Qhatu/Feria 16 de Julio Investigaciones Regionales El Alto*, xv.
7. Raimundo Panikkar, "What Is Comparative Philosophy Comparing?" in *Interpreting across Boundaries*, ed. Gerald James Larson and Eliot Deutsch (Princeton: Princeton University Press, 1988), 130, https://www.degruyter.com/view/books/9781400859276/9781400859276.116/9781400859276.116.xml.
8. Walter D. Mignolo, "Interculturality and Decoloniality," in *On Decoloniality. Concepts, Analytics, Praxis*, eds. Walter D. Mignolo and Catherine E. Walsh (Duke University Press, 2018), 57.
9. Peter Stallybrass and Allon White, *The Politics and Poetics of Transgression* (Ithaca, NY: Cornell University Press, 1986), 125–48.
10. Julia Ramos, an Aymara woman, remembers her father's tearful warning words: "Children you have to study, never be like me, a donkey, [an] Indian, a smelly peasant." Testimonio de Julia Ramos in Yuderkys Espinosa Miñoso, Diana Marcela Gómez Correal, and Karina Ochoa Muñoz, eds., *Tejiendo de otro modo: Feminismo, epistemología y apuestas descoloniales en Abya Yala* (Popayán, Colombia: Editorial Universidad del Cauca, 2014).
11. María Lugones, "Methodological Notes towards a Decolonial Feminism," in *Decolonizing Epistemologies. Latina/o Theology and Philosophy*, ed. Ada María Isasi-Díaz and Eduardo Mendieta, 1st ed. (New York: Fordham University Press, 2012), 68–86; Julieta Paredes, *Hilando fino, desde el Feminismo Comunitario*, Primera Edicion en Mexico, 2013. (Mexico: Creativa del Rebozo, 2013).
12. COTIAY, "Herederas de culturas milenarias," *Comunidad de teólogas del Abya Yala*, 2010.
13. Aromatic tree.
14. I use *hibridez* as a back-and-forth movement between the center and the margins (their identities as Christians and their otherness as Indigenous), moving between two different cultures, which have independently developed in different spaces (*topos*) their own methods of theologizing and ways of reaching intelligibility along with their proper categories.

15. Julia Ramos was a Congressional Representative (2006–2009) and later Minister of Land and Rural Development (2009–2010). Her interview is part of a chapter in Espinosa Miñoso, Gómez Correal, and Ochoa Muñoz, *Tejiendo de Otro Modo*.
16. Lorena Cabnal and ACSUR-Las Segovias, "Feminismos diversos: el feminismo comunitario," *ACSUR-Las Segovias* (2010): 13.
17. Cabnal and ACSUR-Las Segovias, "Feminismos diversos: el feminismo comunitario," 14.
18. *Mensaje de las Mujeres Indígenas Mexicanas*, 32–33.
19. Architectonic texts refer to the use of material constructions such as buildings, temples, statues, ruins and rock carvings to express ideas, concepts, and beliefs.
20. Sofía Chipana Quispe, "Desafíos y Tareas Desde La Teología India," in *Desafíos y Tareas de La Teología En La Región Andina* (Presented at the Conferencias Teológicas Andinas, Bogotá, Colombia, 2011), http://www.redescristianas.net/desafios-y-tareas-de-la-teologia-en-la-region-andina-desafios-y-tareas-desde-la-teologia-indiasofia-chipna-quispe/.
21. Silvia Rivera Cusicanqui, *Un mundo ch'ixi es posible. Ensayos desde un presente en crisis* (Buenos Aires: Argentina: Tinta Limón Ediciones, 2018), 84.
22. Silvia Rivera Cusicanqui, *Un mundo ch'ixi es posible*, 72.
23. Cutcha Risling Baldy, *We Are Dancing for You: Native Feminism & the Revitalizacion of Women's Coming-of-Age Ceremonies.* (Seattle, WA: University of Washington Press, 2018), 35.
24. Julieta Paredes Carvajal is a lesbian Andean/Aymara communitarian feminist. She is a founding member of Mujeres Creando, Mujeres Creando Comunidad, and the Assembly of Community Feminism. She is an anti-patriarchal writer, singer, and poet.
25. Gladys Tzul Tzul is an activist, public intellectual, sociologist, and visual artist who was one of the first to study indigenous communal politics and gender relationships in Guatemala.
26. Francesca Gargallo Celentani, *Feminismos desde Abya Yala: Ideas y proposiciones de las mujeres de 607 pueblos en nuestra América* (Mexico: Editorial Corte y Confección, 2014), http://francescagargallo.wordpress.com/.
27. Ángela Ixkic Bastian Duarte, "Conversación con Alma López, autoridad guatemalteca: La doble mirada del género y la etnicidad," *Estudios Latinoamericanos* 0, no. 18 (August 12, 2015): 178.
28. Paredes, *Hilando fino, desde el Feminismo Comunitario*; Cabnal and ACSUR-Las Segovias, "Feminismos diversos: el feminismo comunitario," 14–15.

29. Cabnal and ACSUR-Las Segovias, "Feminismos diversos: el feminismo comunitario," 19.
30. Cabnal and ACSUR-Las Segovias, "Feminismos diversos: el feminismo comunitario," 12–13; Paredes, *Hilando fino, desde el Feminismo Comunitario*, 95–109.
31. Cabnal and ACSUR-Las Segovias, "Feminismos diversos: el feminismo comunitario," 23.
32. Paredes, *Hilando fino, desde el Feminismo Comunitario*, 13.
33. Chacoso recalls how military gangs in Yara-Cruz, paid by the landowners to throw them out of their land, raped more than sixty women from her community. She adds: "Our partners were furious, but they said this has happened because of the struggle for land, that we had to stick to this. We said that it is true." Tarcila Rivera Zea, ed., *El andar de las mujeres indígenas*, Serie Palabra viva 4 (Lima, Perú: Chirapaq, Centro de Culturas Indias, 1999), 19.
34. Dorotea Gomez Grijalva, " Mi cuerpo es un territorio político," *Voces Descolonizadoras—Brecha Lesbitica* 1 (2012): 6.
35. Rivera Zea, *El andar de las mujeres indígenas*, 19.
36. Cecilia Titizano, "Mama Pacha: Creator and Sustainer Spirit of God," *Horizontes Decoloniales / Decolonial Horizons*, no. 3 (2017): 127–159.
37. Vicenta Mamani Bernabé, "Spirituality and the Pachamama in the Andean Aymara Worldview," in *Earth Stewardship*, ed. R. Rozzi et al., *Ecology and Ethics* 2 (Switzerland: Springer International Publishing, 2015).
38. Juvenal Quispe, *Ecosofía andina, instituciones ecológicas en la filosofía andina*, vol. 8, Texto Taller (Cochabamba, Bolivia: Verbo Divino, 2006), 23.
39. Bagele Chilisa, *Indigenous Research Methodologies* (Thousand Oaks, CA: SAGE Publications, 2012), 41.
40. Josef Estermann, *Filosofía andina: sabiduría indígena para un mundo nuevo*, 2 ed. (La Paz, Bolivia: ISEAT, 2006), 215; Quispe, *Ecosofía andina, instituciones ecológicas en la filosofía andina*, 8:23.
41. Sylvia Marcos, "Mesoamerican Women's Indigenous Spirituality: Decolonizing Religious Beliefs," *Journal of Feminist Studies in Religion* 25, no. 2 (2009): 25–45.
42. Ivone Gebara, *Longing for Running Water: Ecofeminism and Liberation* (Minneapolis, MN: Fortress Press, 1999), 58.
43. Francisco Varela, Evan Thompson, and Eleanor Rosch, *The Embodied Mind, Revised Edition: Cognitive Science and Human Experience* (Cambridge, Mass: MIT Press, 2017).

44. Robert A. Wilson and Lucia Foglia, "Embodied Cognition," July 25, 2011, accessed March 20, 2018, https://plato.stanford.edu/entries/embodied-cognition/#EmbVsTraCogSci.
45. Patricio Guerrero Arias, *La chakana del corazonar desde las espiritualidades y las sabidurías insurgentes de Abya Yala* (Quito, Ecuador: Universidad Politécnica Salesiana/Editorial Universitaria Abya-Yala, 2018).
46. Alfred North Whitehead, *Process and Reality: An Essay in Cosmology*, ed. David Ray Griffin and Donald W. Sherburne, Corrected ed., Gifford lectures 1927–28 (New York: Free Press, 1979), 141.
47. Whitehead, *Process and Reality*.
48. Elizabeth Kraus explains: "Just as conscious perception is a grasp and display of a past object and present experience with a view of future action, so the more fundamental process of prehension synthesizes the agency of the past factual world into the unity and immediacy of a new present. The past is lifted into, made operative in, the emergent now without losing its vector origin in the past." Elizabeth M. Kraus, *The Metaphysics of Experience: A Companion to Whitehead's Process and Reality* (New York: Fordham University Press, 1979), 20.
49. Catherine Keller reminds us that "matrix is always *mater*, mother. No inert matter here; there is no such thing. All beings come tied to the matrix of interconnection. ... The umbilical line, unwinding into meaning, transformation, a web of thought and caring and connection. Catherine Keller, *From a Broken Web: Separation, Sexism, and Self* (Boston: Beacon Press, 1986), 248.
50. Cecilia Titizano, "The Divine Feminine in the Andes: A Comparative Triadic Theology from an Indigenous Feminist Perspective" (Graduate Theological Union, 2020), 38–42.
51. Sylvia Marcos, "Descolonizando el Feminismo: la insurrección epistemológica de la diferencia," in *Siente pensar el género. Perspectivas desde los pueblos originarios*, ed. Georgina Mendez Torres et al. (Guadalajara, México: Red Interdisciplinaria de las Investigadores de los Pueblos Indios de México, Asociación Civil, 2013), 155.
52. Mamani Bernabé, "Spirituality and the Pachamama in the Andean Aymara Worldview."
53. Shawn Wilson, *Research Is Ceremony: Indigenous Research Methods* (Black Point, N.S: Fernwood Pub, 2008), 74.
54. Wilson, *Research Is Ceremony*.
55. Gregory Cajete, *Native Science: Natural Laws of Interdependence*, 1st ed. (Santa Fe, NM: Clear Light Publishers, 2000), 20.
56. Wilson and Foglia, "Embodied Cognition."

57. Cajete, *Native Science*, 21.
58. Cajete, *Native Science*, 22.
59. I would interpret "happenings" as events that happen to humans. Margaret Kovach, *Indigenous Methodologies: Characteristics, Conversations and Contexts* (Toronto: University of Toronto Press, 2009), 57.
60. Cabnal and ACSUR-Las Segovias, "Feminismos diversos: el feminismo comunitario," 22.
61. Bernardine Dixon and Nuria Gómez Barrio, eds., *Género desde la visión de las mujeres indígenas: Primera cumbre de mujeres indígenas de Las Américas, Oaxaca, México, 2002*, 1a ed. (Managua: Centro de Estudios e Información de la Mujer Multiétnica (CEIMM-URACCAN), 2005), 23.
62. "Equilibrium means taking care of life... when community values of our environment and social community are respected, there is equilibrium. Between one extreme and the other, there is a center. The extremes and their center are not absolute but depend on a multiplicity of factors... variable and not at all exact. [Duality] is an equilibrium at its maximum expression." *Memoria de La Primera Cumbre de Mujeres Indígenas de América* (México: Fundación Rigoberto Menchú Tum, 2003), 2.
63. Palabra viva de las Teólogas Indígenas de Abya Yala (COTIAY). Manifiesto del primer encuentro en el año 2009, en el Salvador.
64. Sofia Chipana, "El peregrinaje de las mujeres indígenas en el camino de la Teología India," in n.p., Itinerarios Editorial, n.p.
65. Ejército Zapatista de Liberación Nacional.

## References

Baldy, Cutcha Risling. *We Are Dancing for You: Native Feminism & the Revitalizacion of Women's Coming-of-Age Ceremonies*. Seattle, WA: University of Washington Press, 2018.

Bernabé, Vicenta Mamani. "Spirituality and the Pachamama in the Andean Aymara Worldview." In *Earth Stewardship*, edited by R. Rozzi et al., *Ecology and Ethics* 2. Switzerland: Springer International Publishing, 2015.

Cabnal, Lorena, and ACSUR-Las Segovias, "Feminismos diversos: el feminismo comunitario," *ACSUR-Las Segovias* (2010): 13.

Cajete, Gregory. *Native Science: Natural Laws of Interdependence*, 1st ed. Santa Fe, NM: Clear Light Publishers, 2000.

Celentani, Francesca Gargallo. *Feminismos desde Abya Yala: Ideas y proposiciones de las mujeres de 607 pueblos en nuestra América*. Mexico: Editorial Corte y Confección, 2014.

Charupá, Roberto Tomichá. "Diez consideraciones para una pneumatología cristiana en perspectiva indígena." *Revista Teología* LVI, no. 129, 2019.

Chilisa, Bagele. *Indigenous Research Methodologies*. Thousand Oaks, CA: SAGE Publications, 2012.

COTIAY, "Herederas de culturas milenarias." *Comunidad de teólogas del Abya Yala*, 2010.

Cusicanqui, Silvia Rivera. *Un mundo ch'ixi es posible. Ensayos desde un presente en crisis*. Buenos Aires: Argentina: Tinta Limón Ediciones, 2018.

Dixon, Bernardine, and Barrio, Nuria Gómez eds., *Género desde la visión de las mujeres indígenas: Primera cumbre de mujeres indígenas de Las Américas, Oaxaca, México, 2002*, 1a ed. Managua: Centro de Estudios e Información de la Mujer Multiétnica, 2005.

Duarte, Ángela Ixkic Bastian. "Conversación con Alma López, autoridad guatemalteca. La doble mirada del género y la etnicidad." *Estudios Latinoamericanos* 0, no. 18, August 12, 2015.

Estermann, Josef. *Filosofía Andina: sabiduría indígena para un mundo nuevo*, 2nd ed. La Paz, Bolivia: ISEAT, 2006.

Gebara, Ivone. *Longing for Running Water: Ecofeminism and Liberation*. Minneapolis, MN: Fortress Press, 1999.

Grijalva, Gomez. "Mi cuerpo es un territorio político," *Voces Descolonizadoras—Brecha Lesbitica* 1, 2012.

Guerrero Arias, Patricio. *La chakana del corazonar desde las espiritualidades y las sabidurías insurgentes de Abya Yala*. Quito, Ecuador: Universidad Politécnica Salesiana/Editorial Universitaria Abya-Yala, 2018.

Hernández, Eleazar López. "Hacia una teología del Espíritu de Dios en pueblos mesoamericanos." In *Espíritu Santo y pueblos originarios. Estudios preparatorios al VII simposio de Teología India*. Mexico: CEM, 2019.

Huarachi, Simón Yampara. *La cosmovisión y lógica de la dinámica socioeconómica del Qhatu/Feria 16 de Julio Investigaciones Regionales El Alto*. La Paz, Bolivia: Fundación PIEB, UPEA, 2007.

Huarachi, Yampara. *La cosmovisión y lógica de la dinámica socioeconómica del Qhatu/Feria 16 de Julio Investigaciones Regionales El Alto*, xv.

Kovach, Margaret. *Indigenous Methodologies: Characteristics, Conversations and Contexts*. Toronto: University of Toronto Press, 2009.

Lugones, María. "Methodological Notes towards a Decolonial Feminism." In *Decolonizing Epistemologies. Latina/o Theology and Philosophy*, 1st ed., edited by Ada María Isasi-Díaz and Eduardo Mendieta, New York: Fordham University Press, 2012.

Marcos, Sylvia. "Descolonizando el Feminismo: la insurrección epistemológica de la diferencia." In *Siente pensar el género. Perspectivas desde los pueblos originarios*, edited by Georgina Mendez Torres et al. Guadalajara, México: Red Interdisciplinaria de las Investigadores de los Pueblos Indios de México, Asociación Civil, 2013.

Marcos, Sylvia. "Mesoamerican Women's Indigenous Spirituality: Decolonizing Religious Beliefs." *Journal of Feminist Studies in Religion* 25, no. 2, 2009.

Mignolo, Walter D. "Interculturality and Decoloniality." In *On Decoloniality: Concepts, Analytics, Praxis*, edited by Walter D. Mignolo and Catherine E. Walsh. Duke University Press, 2018.

Panikkar, Raimundo. "What Is Comparative Philosophy Comparing?" In *Interpreting across Boundaries*, edited by Gerald James Larson and Eliot Deutsch. Princeton: Princeton University Press, 1988. https://www.degruyter.com/view/books/9781400859276/9781400859276.116/9781400859276.116.xml.

Paredes, Julieta. *Hilando fino, desde el Feminismo Comunitario*, Primera Edicion en Mexico, 2013. Mexico: Creativa del Rebozo, 2013.

Quispe, Juvenal. *Ecosofía andina, instituciones ecológicas en la filosofía andina*, vol. 8, Texto Taller. Cochabamba, Bolivia: Verbo Divino, 2006.

Ramos, Testimonio de Julia in Espinosa Miñoso, Diana Marcela Gómez Correal, and Karina Ochoa Muñoz, eds., *Tejiendo de otro modo: Feminismo, epistemología y apuestas descoloniales en Abya Yala*. Popayán, Colombia: Editorial Universidad del Cauca, 2014.

Stallybrass, Peter, and Allon White. *The Politics and Poetics of Transgression*. Ithaca, NY: Cornell University Press, 1986.

Titizano, Cecilia. "Mama Pacha: Creator and Sustainer Spirit of God." *Horizontes Decoloniales / Decolonial Horizons*, no. 3, 2017.

Titizano, Cecilia. "The Divine Feminine in the Andes: A Comparative Triadic Theology from an Indigenous Feminist Perspective." Graduate Theological Union, 2020.

Varela, Francisco J., Evan Thompson, and Eleanor Rosch. *The Embodied Mind: Cognitive Science and Human Experience*. Cambridge, MA: MIT Press, 2017.

Whitehead, Alfred North. "Process and Reality: An Essay in Cosmology." In *Gifford Lectures 1927–28*, edited by David Ray Griffin and Donald W. Sherburne, Corrected ed. New York: Free Press, 1979.

Wilson, Robert A., and Lucia Foglia, "Embodied Cognition," July 25, 2011. Accessed March 20, 2018. https://plato.stanford.edu/entries/embodied-cognition/#EmbVsTraCogSci.

Wilson, Shawn. *Research Is Ceremony: Indigenous Research Methods*. Black Point, NS: Fernwood Pub, 2008.

Zea, Tarcila Rivera, ed., *El andar de las mujeres indígenas*, Serie Palabra viva 4. Lima, Perú: Chirapaq, Centro de Culturas Indias, 1999.

CHAPTER 9

# Anzaldúa[2]

## Beyond (in) Anzaldúa

*LAURA E. PÉREZ*

As the title of this chapter suggests, I will examine the work of Gloria E. Anzaldúa in three ways. "Beyond in Anzaldúa," one of the two ways of reading the subtitle, refers to what Anzaldúa recognized as the most threatening to US academics: "the beyond," the liminal with respect to rationalist, empirical, materialist dominant cultural thought; that is, thought that is legible to dominating patriarchal, heteronormative, Eurocentric, and/or classist cultures.[1] The second way of reading the subtitle, "beyond Anzaldúa" is related to the first and refers to the reaction against Anzaldúa's work—the minimization or dismissal of it—and not simply the critique of it; the idea that her creative and intellectual work is not that important, is too flawed, or simply put, not good enough, hence the call to get over the excitement it was causing, especially among an already invisibilized body of thinkers: Chicana feminists. Finally, and in contrast to the idea that there isn't really that much to Anzaldúan thought, "Anzaldúa to the second power" notes the multiplication or growth in her thought, and its ongoing, exponentially generative effect on others.

### "The Beyond" in Anzaldúa

The psychic is central to Anzaldúa's thought. By the psychic I refer, first, to the psychological, following Carl G. Jung, MD (1875–1961), who reminded us that the ancient Greek root of psychology, "psyche," is "soul." Jung's own interest in the broadest sense of the psyche, as a researcher and practicing psychiatrist has, after one hundred years, still not found much favor among academics, unlike Freud's work, although the former has consistently impacted artists and creative thinkers, and most to the point of this essay, decisively so in Anzaldúa's case. The psychic in reference to paranormal, superhuman, and nonhuman phenomena is what remains most challenging in Anzaldúa's and Jung's thought, given the hegemony of materialist and empiricist thought from the twentieth century to the present. In Anzaldúa's case, the Eurocentric Christian bias against non-European spiritualities and philosophies or worldviews has further racialized the devaluation of her work, even when the critiques are coming from people of color. The psychic also most broadly encompasses the spiritual; that which is concerned with the idea of Spirit, spirit, or spirits, understandings that of course vary by culture and epoch but that in Anzaldúa largely follow Mesoamerican traditional thought, particularly that of the Mexica "Aztec," the Maya, and African-diasporic Santería, premised on the belief in the interconnection and interdependence of all life forms.[2]

Jung and the analysts he trained broke new ground in developing the concept of the collective unconscious as more than the site of an individual's hidden repressions. Parting ways with Freud, the concept of the collective unconscious allowed Jung to observe the recurrence of symbols and mythic narratives that he called "archetypal," which recur in different guises, seemingly across time and across cultures, such as the hero/ines journey: that is, the story of human life as a developmental process, particularly at the level of self-awareness and thereby self-realization that could be characterized by the birth-death-rebirth cycle. In Anzaldúa's "Toltec" terms, this process is called "making face, making soul," an attunement between our heartfelt desires and impulses, and the persona we have developed to face the world.[3]

As observed in other of my writings, in *Borderlands/La Frontera*, Anzaldúa acknowledged the importance of Jung and Jungian-trained James Hillman's *Re-Visioning Psychology* to her work.[4] Image-making and the power of the "imaginal" were important to her as prerequisites for bringing things into being, and not only art objects.[5] The imaginal was also the basis of what Anzaldúa considered real power in art objects, or "presence," versus the exercise of mere virtuosity of execution and form of objects/art objects. A deeper reading of Jung, his co-creators—many of whom were women—and of Hillman (1926–2011), whom he trained, is helpful to understand "the beyond" in its multiple meanings in Anzaldúa's ambitious life's work.

Jung's development of the field of psychology critiqued the limits of Freud's thought on the function of dreams, the unconscious, the role of sexuality, and the reality of psychic phenomena such as the paranormal.[6] Deeply uncomfortable as it was for him, Jung was after a more complex account of the human, and of the psyche in particular, in courageous defiance of the culture of empiricism that dominated his era. Images were natural to Jung as an artistically gifted person, but also were central to his methodology to explore and bring intrapsychic forces into visibility.[7] Further, he had witnessed and experienced paranormal and enigmatic psychic phenomena throughout his life and had a high tolerance for the unknown and unknowable, and the unknowable psychic terrain of the human. But what the human mind could not hope to fully understand about itself, Jung thought, could nonetheless be glimpsed in what resonated across different cultures in their myths, religions, cosmologies, arts, and other human records.

Jung observed that humanity had always concerned itself with notions of God or gods, Spirit or spirits, and therefore that the religious, seriously out of vogue in his scientific circles, was characteristic of humanity. Jung considered it a prejudgment lacking scientific objectivity and intellectual rigor to dismiss the religious and psychic functions of the human mind as unimportant, and he warned that such bias was dangerous and responsible for the cataclysmic and dehumanizing projections onto others that he witnessed in World Wars I and II.[8] The study and practice of psychology were in their scientific infancy in Jung's day, but he was convinced that it was a crucial field to develop to heal modern Europeans' increasingly split psyche, the repression of natural bodily instinct, and the denial of the spiritual nature of humans. He considered that these powerful repressions were reflected in the rise of neuroses and other mental illnesses and the projection of the repressed upon others.

The evils of war—of the rise of Hitler and Nazism, totalitarianism, and more simply, the dangers of socialization that repressed human nature in the name of "civilization" and "the modern"—led him as a medical doctor and researcher to venture into social theory.[9] Jung developed the idea of "the shadow" as the negated within one's culture and within individuals, which nonetheless emerges as unconscious projection upon others in a dehumanizing binary logic of mutually exclusive good versus evil, where I or we are the good, unlike the others, who are not. Jung's research led him to the conclusion that the repressed contents of the psyche had to be acknowledged, identified with, and integrated as the human. Hitler and fascists are not inhuman exceptions, he reasoned, but rather the consequence of repressing human nature, thoughts, feelings, and actions rewarded as "good" or punished as bad or evil. The shadowed or repressed side of the split psyche of the beholder was thus projected onto others as the bad, evil, or the undesirable denied within us.

The research and analytic collaboration of Jung's personally trained analysts, Toni Wolff, Marie-Louise von Frantz, and his wife, Emma Jung, resulted in work-in-progress concepts such as that of the "anima" and "animus" to describe the split in consciousness resulting from the internalization of painful and binary judgments regarding binary of good and evil. In European men, the "anima" represented the repressed dimensions of the human associated with the feminine, driven by punishing cultural norms into what Jung called the unconscious. In European women, the "animus" named the energies associated with masculinity that they were compelled to repress by their families and societies, and which they had therefore learned to repress themselves. Jung observed that the co-existence or integration of these intrapsychic energies was symbolized in European Medieval alchemy through the symbol of the process of the mystical union of opposites, and that this goal was a human one, and the same as that of what was then the new science of psychology. The figure of the androgyne, a symbol of the "mystical marriage" of parts of the self, was ancient knowledge based on the nature of the human and its soul or psyche.

The artistic as an expressed creative force was regarded by Jungians as a route to self-discovery, to the uncovering of an individual's more authentic and unique nature. An individual's instincts, desires, dreams, creative work, obsessions, illnesses, and accidents all helped reveal this more authentic but repressed nature. Reflecting upon dreams and journaling about the figures or energies, messages, and stories that surfaced there were part of the healing process of seeing, nonjudgmentally accepting, and hence, integrating the psyche. At the level of the species, it appeared that the symbolic language of dreams, art making, myths, and fairytales recur across time and cultures and somehow seemed to be a function of the human species' inherited knowledge of how to be or exist.[10]

Jung believed that the new mythologies of scientific progress, intellectual enlightenment, and cultural superiority over earlier Europeans and so-called primitive peoples were dangerous fantasies. He considered the mind of medieval Europeans, contemporary peasants, and tribal non-European peoples as healthier, to the degree they expressed human nature with less repression. Alchemy's language of the mystical union of opposites suggested a path to healing modern people from the cultural normalization of Christian repression of the body and instincts and of the overdevelopment of materialist rationalism and empiricism. These observations led to Jung's key concept of "individuation" as the work of the psyche throughout human life. It is here that through Jung and James Hillman, Anzaldúa found a powerful model by which to navigate her own instincts, intuitions, and desires; her artistic and spiritual vocation as a healer; and to theorize in her own terms the enigmatic nature of life as a becoming, and art-making as soul-making.

In Anzaldúa, the path of soul-making assumed historically and culturally specific contours. Because she was a Chicana queer writer from one of the poorest counties in the United States, psychic reintegration required confronting the experience and effects of anti-Mexican racial hatred; systemic political, social, and economic subjugation; systemic cultural and racialized disparagement; and recurrent, widespread racialized and gendered homophobic physical and psychological violence. Thus, the body was not abstract or secondary in the journey to psychological integration and soul-making; that is, the journey toward more authentic being and integrated Self.

The Jungian concept of the shadow allowed Anzaldúa to develop her concept of the "shadow-beast" as the specific effect of the internalization of the negatively gendered racialization created by Spanish, Mexican, and "Anglo" or Eurocentric patriarchal heteronormative classist colonization. As the brown queer female child of impoverished sharecroppers on land that had once been within her family, and as a child laborer in a violently anti-Mexican, homophobic, sexist, classist, and anti-intellectual place, she marveled that she had survived. Thus, in Anzaldúa, mental and physical well-being were crucial tools of decolonial struggle. In theorizing the internalization of subjection at the US-Mexico borderlands for people such as herself—impoverished, socially and culturally marginalized, queer, and furthermore psychic, spiritual, and artistic—Anzaldúa goes beyond Frantz Fanon's powerful analysis identifying the internalization of racism in colonial subjects as a crucial mechanism of colonialism, and she goes beyond Foucault's subsequent theory of the primarily class-based self-disciplining that characterizes European modernity's well-behaved normative citizens.[11]

On the ground of her own flesh, of her own embodied being and its historically and culturally specific social circumscriptions and interpellations, Anzaldúa analyzed and named the way political power operated through individual bodies, through her own history, that of five generations of her family in the US-Mexico borderlands and of Mesoamerican ancestors, some of whose homeland, Aztlán, was indigenous to the United States and not just Latin America. In this work, she engaged the rich living analyses of the US women of color of her generation and was deeply influenced by the more general counterculture of the sixties and seventies. Born in 1942, she was a little older than the first half of the Baby Boomer generation. Among many influences, including the emerging Chicana/o movement in its social movement work and literature, she was also influenced by and in co-creative dialogue with the feminist movements and the gay and lesbian movements. She recounted how her close friend Randy P. Conner encouraged her to go to her first lesbian meeting,[12] and Randy told me of recommending feminist and lesbian books to her. Her *Interviews/Entrevistas* (2000), as well as her collected writings published by Duke University Press, *The Gloria Anzaldúa Reader* (2009), tell of the influence of astrology, psychic training, Buddhism, feminist goddess and Wicca movements, the psychic channeled material of the *Seth Speaks* series, four near-death experiences, experiences with nonhuman entities (including extraterrestrials), and of her experiences of the supernatural in her own mind and body. Anzaldúa was very clearly enmeshed in the spiritual renaissance of the 1970s in the Bay Area after her arrival in 1977, if not before then.[13] This renaissance included the circulation among Latina/os of Andrés Segura Granados (1931–1997), who taught ritual "danza Azteca" and the teachings of his teacher, the Maya linguist, Dr. Domingo Martinez Paredez (1904–1983).[14]

Anzaldúa deepened the analysis of what US women of color contemporaries were calling in the late 1960s and early 1970s double, triple, and multiple oppressions and the simultaneity of oppressions. From Audre Lorde and the Combahee River Collective of Black queer feminists, Anzaldúa could center not just feminism in her decolonial analytic, but also what she very early on called the sexually and gender "queer," as Randy P. Conner (personal communication) and AnaLouise Keating have pointed out. In *Borderlands/La Frontera*, she developed the concept of queerness as a non-binary, "third" space of being, thought, and practice. She wrote that "lesbian" was what she called herself for want of a better word to describe her sexuality, eventually preferring the Nahua "*patlache*" as the word she most closely identified with. She wrote nonjudgmentally that she felt attraction for women, gay men, her father, her brother, children, and animals.[15] Queer was not a synonym of lesbian or gay for her; it marked transgression even within these already marginalized and repressed gender and sexual identities.

Through her concept of queerness, she could reapproach the culture of the US-Mexico borderlands, psychology, spirituality, and even the social role of the artist in contemporary society. The queer as a non-binary reality of lived experience became for her a way to make gender, sexuality, the psyche, spirituality, and the artist's way intelligible beyond a reigning, binary politics of reaction, of negating the negations of dominant cultures. She used the Jungian concept of the shadow to critique the cultural shadow-making of her *mexicano* culture, writing, "I do not buy all the myths of the tribe into which I was born" and "what I want is an accounting with all three cultures—white, Mexican, Indian";[16] that is, of the cultures that constituted her as a Chicana mestiza. She noted that the Indigenous, gendered and racialized negatively, was the shadow in her: "The worst kind of betrayal lies in making us believe that the Indian woman in us is the betrayer. We, *indias y mestizas*, police the Indian in us, brutalize and condemn her. Male culture has done a good job on us. *Son los* [sic] *costumbres que traicionan. La india en mí es la sombra: La Chingada, Tlazolteotl, Coatlicue.*[17]

This is quite remarkable and a deeper development of the already brilliant collection of analyses of the multiple and simultaneous oppressions that US women of color named in their theorization of the hostilities and violence that they experience daily, particularly the queer among them. What Anzaldúa deeply explored and presents in her writings is the psychic and the spiritual as part of the bodily experience of being human which Jung and the Jungians advised as an antidote to the dehumanizing mind-body-spirit splitting in modern Europeans (also observed in Euroamericans).

What Anzaldúa contributes to further developing US women of color theories is the implicit corollary to the theory of the "double," "triple," "multiple," and "simultaneity of oppressions," the last formulated by the Combahee River Collective. If women of color are oppressed by racialization, gender, class, and sexuality under the legacies of colonization of the Americas and slavery in ways that are complex and changing rather than simple or essential, it follows in her thought that subjectivity is also complex and that there are multiple, simultaneous aspects of the self.[18] W. E. B. Du Bois had long ago written of double consciousness as a Black man living in a society dominated by white men. And women of color had analyzed the multiple social and cultural forces that shaped and misshaped them, which Chela Sandoval (2000) captured in her theorization of the "differential consciousness" that this generation of US women of color expressed in their creative and intellectual work. Jungian psychology allowed Anzaldúa to formulate the idea of multiple selves from a psychological and spiritual perspective. In Anzaldúa, the self is multiply split, fragmented by the identities that are demanded by family and society to which she was supposed to be subservient as a female, then as a queer woman of color and artist who was also psychic and spiritual. What she adds to Jung's thought is the specific examination of psychic fragmentation and reintegration under conditions of further duress, those of racist patriarchal heteronormative cultures; and what she adds to Fanon is that psychic fragmentation is also caused by rationalist and materialist utilitarian classist dominations.

But in her thought, the multiplicity of selves resulting from the fragmentation that oppression causes is transformed as an act of ideological transformation, recuperated from the paralysis of victimhood to cross-cultural, human ancestral wisdom that life's purpose is the growth of consciousness, wherein the cycle of birth-death-renewal describes the process of development of a mature and more autonomous subjectivity. Like a medieval alchemist, Anzaldúa turns straw into gold, taking whatever lessons can be found in suffering and injustice about being human to empower the self through growth in self-awareness.

The generation to which Anzaldúa belonged, and that of the late 1980s and later feminisms, criticized the essentialism that rationalized racism, sexism, and homophobia. The publication of Anzaldúa's 1987 *Borderlands/La Frontera* is not a break with US women of color feminist thought of the 1960s and 1970s, but an intensification of it—the rejection of binary either-or thought, a sustained exploration of third spaces, options, and realities beyond mere negating reaction against dominating powers.

Anzaldúa deepened what Chicana feminists Anna Nieto Gomez and Elizabeth "Betita" Martinez described in the early and mid-1970s as a model of gender based on Hispanic European and Euroamerican binary patriarchal notions of machismo and *marianismo* (Marianism) that were culturally imposed on Indigenous and mestizo cultures through colonization and ongoing neocolonial domination. Anzaldúa wanted to get beyond binary oppositions to shifting terrain, beyond mere negation to creation of other ways of viewing difference and practicing a simultaneously plural identity and constantly transforming consciousness. The spiritual as the common identity of humans and other life forms was essential to thinking beyond colonially imposed identity dichotomies and hierarchies in her thought.

However, in an interview with Irene Lara published posthumously in 2005, Anzaldúa analyzed the rejection, criticism, and repression of parts of her book. In the earlier *Interviews/Entrevistas*, she had noted that even Chicana feminists chose to ignore the psychic and spiritual borderlands that she wrote from and that were a central part of the logic of *Borderlands/La Frontera*. In the interview, she noted that she had been panned since the 1981 National Women's Studies Association by one and all for her talk of spirituality, and that even the other women of color speakers and audience members were "horrified."[19] "It's tiring; even when they don't openly disagree there's this energy that says, 'You're not fighting for human rights. You're not fighting for civil rights. . . . The spirit is not basic to our struggle.' If you speak out like that too often, your body takes it on. I'm convinced that part of the reason I came down with diabetes is exhaustion from those situations."[20] She was forty-five when the book was first published in 1987. What she described as her untamable wild tongue was beyond playing to approval of hegemonic, academic feminist and queer compulsory atheism and the derision of spirituality as a primitive throwback.

She did not write for mainstream or even progressive academics, yet instead has impacted artists and the kind of reading public represented by *The UTNE Reader*, which named *Borderlands/La Frontera* as one of the one hundred most important books of the twentieth century. For all the multi-genre, nontraditional, experimental structure of *Borderlands/La Frontera*, it is an accessible piece of writing and stimulating in its innovative synthesizing of ideas about human subjectivity and its practice of what she later called "*autohistoria-teoría*," where the autobiographical and social and political analyses meet. Indeed, when one carefully reads Anzaldúa's pre- and post-*Borderlands* interviews and writings, it is clear that *Borderlands* is a studied piece of social analysis whose aesthetic innovation integrates multiple modes of knowing and whose expression performs third space or non-binary thought.

## "Beyond Anzaldúa"

The critique of Anzaldúa's use of the concepts of the "cosmic race" and of "mestizaje," and her identification with the Indigenous, have been the cause of rejecting her thinking as part of inherited nation-building discourses of racial hybridity that contribute to the genocide and cultural erasure of Indigenous peoples and cultures. However, her positionality was more complex than the simple adoption of disingenuous and secretly racist mestizaje discourse created by Mexican elites. Conner addressed the critique of her identification with the Indigenous in a plenary address that was published in 2010. As to her idea of the "new mestiza," Anzaldúa felt that her idea had been misunderstood. Apart from the fact that in 1987 understanding her concept required connotative thinking that placed it into conversation with her non-binary ideas of borders and the queer, it didn't help that *Borderlands/La Frontera* early on cited José Vasconcelos's idea of the "raza cósmica," widely circulating in the Chicano Movement of the late 1960s and 1970s, as if it meant a post-racist future human race. Unfortunately, Vasconcelos's idea of the cosmic race was the tortured product of an anti-imperialist who argued for improvement of the Mexican "race" through the reigning "science" of racism of his time, eugenics. Anzaldúa and her Chicano contemporaries are not likely to have celebrated *La raza cósmica* (1925) if they had read through to the point where the author argues for the voluntary non-breeding of the aesthetically unpleasing "races," which would have included dark Indigenous Chicana/os, like Anzaldúa, rather than white-passing mestiza/os. Anzaldúa did not conflate "*indios y mexicanos*,"

"Indians and mestizos," writing about them both as distinct peoples and of the Indigenous as ancestral to Chicana/os.[21] She is criticized for using an inherited discourse about mestizaje that was developed by settler colonial Mexican elites to deracinate and assimilate, and hence to disappear Indigenous peoples and cultures. However, while Mexico's elite intellectuals elaborated theories of mestizaje as part of their strategy to unify the nation, Chicana/os affirmed their own mestizaje as mixed peoples who were both Indigenous and European against prevailing views in Mexico and the United States that this mixture spoiled the pureness of European races, and that Mexicans and Mexican Americans were inferior half-breeds and mongrels. Chicana/os were not dominant cultural Latin Americans, but rather people subjugated and systematically disempowered since the conclusion in 1848 of the US-provoked Mexican American War, part of the United States' project of imperialist expansion across the continent ("Manifest Destiny").

*Borderlands/La Frontera* records Anzaldúa's confrontation with her internalization of the culture of loathing of the Indigenous, the Mexican, and the female in Texas, at the US-Mexico border. Unlike dominant cultural Latin Americans, as a survivor of systemic anti-Mexican racism exacerbated by the preceding anti-Spanish sentiment at the US-Mexico borderlands, Anzaldúa's identification with her Indigenous ancestry was circuitous, given the erasure of the Indigenous in her Mexican family's culture due to colonization. In this context, her resistance to Mexican and US anti-Indigeneity found expression indirectly through her study of and identification with Mesoamerican Mexica and Maya cultures. With all the flaws that such cultural removal would unsurprisingly give rise to, this study nonetheless constituted an effort to recuperate the broader contours of Mesoamerican Indigenous ontologies. For her and the Chicana/os of her generation, recuperation of the ancestral Indigenous constituted a rejection of the internalized anti-Indigeneity of dominant cultural Latin American (racial hybridity) and US (racial purity) nation-building discourses, in solidarity with the Northern Indigenous peoples' movements.[22] Her aim was to identity with the most repressed, shadowed aspect of her identity, the female and the ancestral Indigenous, as Alarcón observed.[23]

Anecdotal critique of Anzaldúa and her companion generation of US women of color thinkers as passé comes from those who have not studied the historical context and larger corpus of these thinkers' work and have instead absorbed the idea that post-structuralist thought regarding the instability of identity, authority, and truth are richer and more deeply theorized and relevant sources of critical thought to all of us, whether we are dominant cultural Euromericans or marginalized and oppressed people of color. Simultaneously, such derision has not prevented the strip mining of Anzaldúa's and other women of color's analyses, as if it were raw material requiring intellectual manufacture elsewhere to be sold back to the natives. These intellectual politics follow the economic model that created the narrative of a global order of so-called first versus third—and second—worlds. Well-known feminist philosophers and decolonial heterosexual male thinkers alike have appropriated concepts from the work of women of color without citation, or with minimal discussion, as if these concepts were self-evident and naturally produced for the taking, rather than painstakingly elaborated. Suffice it to say that this does not happen when cultural capital is to be gained by intellectual name-dropping as it continues to be of first world, Eurocentric and/or masculinist thinkers.

I have personally—and publicly—been instructed to read Giorgio Agamben and other more recently discovered contemporaries of the more famous post-structuralists. I do not assume that the new translations from the French of people in Audre Lorde and Gloria Anzaldúa's generation, or older writers from Europe or Latin America, have something more important to tell us about the experiences of people of color, especially women and queers of color in the United States, and therefore about what possible strategies and tactics we might adopt. I entertain it, I read it, but I do not assume, mystically, that progress must lie anywhere else but in the analyses, the theories, the practices gained from real-life experiences of suffering, negotiating, surviving, and analyzing in order to be well, and to envision other more just realities so that those who follow will not suffer what we have. The now fashionable dismissal of historic US women of color thought, with Anzaldúa's as a part of this devaluation, is anything but analytical and is intellectually irresponsible. Why do sister feminists trash brilliant feminists, such as the French philosophers Hélène Cixous and Luce Irigaray, on charges of seemingly unforgiveable essentialism, but overlook far worse in their famous androcentric counterparts?

Anzaldúa's observations regarding the marginalized role of the artist and of the disempowerment of art help us to further understand the devaluation of her own work among academics. The socially significant work of envisioning new social worlds and individual ways of being that are more liberatory was the focus of her analytical and theoretical labors, and tellingly were accomplished through creative work. For her, creativity was a technology, a tool, by which to bypass and short-circuit new and old orthodoxies, not least those of academia. In *Borderlands/La Frontera*, she theorizes the creative as another and a real borderland—a social one—where art and artist are devalued, stripped of historic and cross-cultural social relevance. That is, Anzaldúa rejects the disciplining of art as commodity by capitalist culture that values art for its virtuosity or style, as object of consumption to decorate with or to invest in financially. This is a historic redefinition and muzzling of the social role art that Anzaldúa resisted based on her study of the function of art in pre-Colombian Mesoamerican and traditional African cultures.

Anzaldúa was thereby able to rearticulate the role of art as socially powerful cross-culturally and now acutely necessary as a vehicle mediating the growth of self-awareness, self-integration, and healing. What is specifically decolonizing and particularly courageous about her work here is that she argues that art can literally be full of power if it contains such intent by the artist. All artwork for her is performative—indeed all writing is—and not just creative literature, if we follow her thought. Mere works of virtuosity of form and execution, however, she suggested, are defanged, socially disempowered objects. I will add that they serve dominant hegemonic state ideas of good citizenship as compliant and untroubled. Anzaldúa's critique of mere virtuosity is the critique of the seemingly cutting edge that is not, however, ideologically avant-garde, as were many of the historic avant-garde of the World War I and II periods full-scale social, political, ideological critique of the bankruptcy and hypocrisy of Western dominant culture. Next to them, I must confess that I find the development of post–World War II post-structural thought rather derivative and tame.

Anzaldúa's idea of the power and necessity of the creation of new images extended beyond art making to imagining new, more liberatory ways of being human and being together socially and environmentally with other life forms. Thinking creatively was central to imagining how to be and act beyond binary thought and beyond disciplinary regimes of truth, including those of the faux cutting edge. In her case, this of course took her ABD (all-but-dissertation completed) bad self beyond straight academic training.

In my own work, I have long argued that the visual and performative, as with other nonscriptural media, are forms of thought that often constitute philosophical reflection and are always ideological or political.[24] From this perspective, I want to argue that her corpus of writings constitute a body of thought and not just a literary, productive germ of what must be properly developed elsewhere, separate from art making and creative writing. It can be and has been, of course, further explored and developed at length and with careful attention to artistic or literary elements. Nonetheless, it is the product of highly complex and broad cultural syntheses of very important and still timely thought, and it is creative and generative.[25]

The creative for Anzaldúa was the path of self-awareness, the growth of human consciousness, a path she called "making face, making soul," that in *Borderlands/ La Frontera* is called the path of the red and the black inks and characterizes the movement "towards new mestiza consciousness." A path, that like all heroic journeys in mythology and in Jungian psychology, traverses the descent into the underworld or the unconscious on the one hand, and of personal social suffering on the other. She figured this through her concept of the Coatlicue State, the state of psychic fragmentation, disorientation, loss, disintegration of old ways of perceiving self or world: in short, of crisis, but leading to rebirth as same-yet-different.

The Coatlicue State figured Anzaldúa's analysis of the cultural and historic difficulties of the negatively racialized, gendered, sexed, and classed person to follow the human process of the growth of self-awareness and of consciousness that obeys the unique, unrepeatable elements natural to each individual as the ultimate purpose of life. But the Coatlicue State also described her plight as a writer and intellectual. She created maps of her experience, piecing together knowledge and wisdom that were resonant across history and cultures and fine-tuning these to allow her to objectify, to the degree it was possible, what she had experienced, yearned for, and hoped to become.

It is worth emphasizing that images, particularly symbols by virtue of being non-verbal, not fully narrated in our possible perception of them, function like the poetic in working through connotation, suggestion, and evocation. They invite interpretations in the plural, rather than denoting and defining meaning. They are also access points to deeper and hidden meanings in an individual's life and in life as humans, psychologically, as I have pointed out, but also ideologically. Images have the potential to act upon social discourses and logics of moments and to point elsewhere as well as to reveal the repressed and contradiction. Art and creativity can be methodologies beyond hegemonic regimes of truth and subjection.

"The beyond" in Anzaldúa is probably most literally her reports of the psychic, as in psychic readings, extraterrestrial trysts, the channeling of disembodied entities, and the Jungian collective unconscious beyond rational awareness to *conocimientos, la facultad*. The Jungian concept of the human collective unconscious posits the enigma of accessibility to the nonhuman, to the beyond-human, through the individual psyche. The human here is therefore conceived as a portal beyond the human, and therefore psychic faculties function as medium of interdependent relationship to other forms of being, and not just other humans. In beginning to close these ruminations, I want to also think of the beyond in Anzaldúa's thought by connecting the idea of expanded awareness and integrated being to a politics of interdependence, to social care following a logic of spiritually grounded social activism, that is, of spiritual activism, as she named it.[26]

"Now let us shift . . . the path of conocimiento . . . inner work, public acts," published in 2002, a year before her death, in *This Bridge Called Home*, co-edited with AnaLouise Keating, Anzaldúa mapped out seven stages of the continual, serpentine-like process of shedding old forms of consciousness and being and growing into new ones. She had already written (in one of the *Interviews/Entrevistas*) that growth of consciousness was terribly hard, but that it was harder not to change, harder not to write as her path of self-awareness. The concept of the borderlands as culturally in-between gave rise at the level of consciousness to states of *nepantla*. A product of the crossing of culturally different and opposing worldviews and ethos, nepantla names the cultural in-betweenness of people not fully colonized, for example. She arrived in her later work at the concept of the spiritually centered social activist—the *nepantlera*. The nepantlera is the activist who though not outside of contradictions and still lapsing into old binaries, works to shift thinking and action through acts of finding common ground even with the historically constructed enemy or the oppressor, such that she herself is also no longer mainly interpellated as victim of dominant cultural social orders.

## Anzaldúa (superscript 2): Anzaldúa to the Second Power

After four decades of engagement with Anzaldúa's earliest work, in *This Bridge Called My Back: Writings by Radical Women of Color* (1981) and *Borderlands/La Frontera: The New Mestiza* (1987), her influence has spread throughout the arts and in academia beyond the humanities to the social sciences. *Borderlands/La Frontera* has inspired a growing number of international interlocutors. Numerous new anniversary editions of *Borderlands* and the publication of new posthumous work circulate the evolution of Anzaldúa's thought and the development of concepts introduced in her earlier work such as spiritual activism, nepantla, and the Coatlicue State. An international conference meeting every year and a half dedicated to Anzaldúan thought and its attendant publication of selected conference proceedings stimulates multiple generations of scholars to continue engaging with her growing oeuvre. With all of this, the importance and the multiplicative power of her thought is beyond dispute.

Particularly in response to *Borderlands/La Frontera: The New Mestiza* (1987), scholars all over the world continue to find the complexity of Anzaldúa's thinking around "borders," premised on her analysis of the various and imbricated forms of injustice, oppression, and marginalization at the geopolitical US-Mexico borderlands highly relevant. And others have found her observation of the parallel and equally real experiences of psychological, sexual, and social "borderlands" created by the legacies of patriarchal, heteronormative, and racialized colonialism or "coloniality" important to thinking about the normative and that which is marginalized as abnormal.[27] Hemispheric thinkers of the Americas, and of Europe, in disciplines ranging from philosophy, sociology, religion, art, and gender and sexuality studies have been able to better understand domination between nations, genders, and sexualities, and to recognize the legitimacy of the ontologies and epistemologies of different cultures through Anzaldúa's investigation of the in-between realities that the lens of a borderlands as a non-binary space illuminate.[28] Anzaldúa's concept of borders has brought into visibility psychological, social, and cultural spaces, as well as gender and queer sexualities produced by dominant cultures, as places or experiences where little that is worthy happens. She argues to the contrary that precisely because borderlands experiences are in-between, ambiguous, ambivalent, and "other" than normative, they can reveal the lie of dominant cultural logic, mythology, and power dynamics and how to survive and, indeed, shift beyond them. But perhaps most importantly, borderlands or border spaces *are inhabited by* and thus *show* us other ways of being. Anzaldúa's introduction of the idea of queer genders and sexuality as ambiguous, shifting, ever-transiting and transforming border "land" identities and spaces of experience has midwifed powerful Latinx queer and trans thought.[29] Likewise, her understanding of identity as non-binary, non-essentialist, and as multiple and in transformation, further developing US women of color theories of double, triple, multiple, and simultaneous oppressions, has also been productively and widely engaged.[30] Anzaldúa's "path of the red and the black inks" and her aesthetic of hybridity in allowing herself a Spanglished multi-genre experimental text have also stimulated productive and creative reflections. As to her theorization of a spiritual borderlands, Anzaldúa lamented its neglect, which I have addressed elsewhere.[31] Keating (2000), Lara (2005), Medina (2011), Delgadillo (2011), Pérez (1998, 2007), and Conner (2015) were early thinkers who paid attention to the centrality of the spiritual in Anzaldúan thought, and presented their work well before they published it. Since then, many more recent and fruitful engagements include Garcia Lopez (2019), Tirres (2019), and Hey-Colón (2023).

In Alarcón (1990), Sandoval (2000), Lugones (2003, 2015), Pérez (1993, 1998, 2007), and Ortega (2016), Anzaldúa's contributions to a theory of knowledge, of self, and of being are given careful critical attention. What I hope to have contributed to now in this essay is to further engage Anzaldúa's logic with respect to creativity in general and the necessity of psychic integration, in the psychological, and more specifically, Jungian sense, but aimed at the possibilities of realized being under the cultural, social, economic, and political orders that create borderlands to begin with.

Finally, the future is also "the beyond" invoked in this essay's subtitle. Anzaldúa leaves a record of rebellion, like so many artists whose importance lies in their willful, self-affirming lives, even if these had elements of excess or contradiction, as much as in the objects they created. A wonderful, sister writer of Anzaldúa expressed in one of my graduate seminars the fear that Anzaldúa's work around spirituality could lead to social and political escapism. I have given this much thought because I did not know how to word my own, very different view at the time.

Anzaldúa's strategy was to agitate that we transform ourselves and in so doing, transform the social worlds we live in. Her non-binary thinking went beyond the older Left's orthodoxies and deeply took the crucial lesson that psychology offered for social transformation: that of personal transformation and healing of socially wounding normativity. She was not satisfied with blaming and critiquing the variously imbricated and multiple-sourced cultures of oppression at home, in the Chicano nation, the feminist and gay and lesbian movements, Eurocentrism, heteronormative homophobia, and so on as the core response to injustice, oppression, and marginalization. Nor was she merely critical of these earlier liberatory movements, satisfied with declaring that we are now postfeminist, post-race, post-gender, and post-queer in our identity politics. She strove to enact what she theorized: a politics of "third" spaces, and hence of "borderlands," the "queer," "new mestiza" or hybrid practice beyond binarism in her thought and in the form of her writing. She not only rebelled, "*repeló*," bolted against the –isms of the day; she also rebelled against being shaped by others' thoughts, choosing to mold her life by her own hands, as she put it, to be her own work of art.

Anzaldúa's search for truth amidst the legitimate and delegitimized fields of knowledge, those of the margins in every sense, are poorly understood when dismissed as lightweight, new age, appropriative, and so on. Her thoughts were profoundly social and political, but she was after a different ideology, a post Eurocentric, patriarchal, heteronormative Leftism, and to that end, she searched global archives for what I have called "eros ideologies" (2019), political ideologies centered in harmonious relationality between life forms understood as interdependent because made of the selfsame spirit and matter. Her goal was simultaneously her own healing and well-being, the creation of a better social world, and respectful care of animals and the planet. She described life on the planet as "interdependent," and her life as a contribution to a more respectful, socially just world and responsibly cared for planet, and she credited traditional Native American cultures, including those of her ancestral Mesoamerican, as holders of worldviews centering responsible co-existence between all life forms.

The myths of the various dominating cultures are what Anzaldúa thought had to be rewritten through new narratives and that our actual lived-in bodies, once more properly tended and listened to, and our psychological lives, once further reintegrated, and that our growing awareness and consciousness as human beings would allow us to begin glimpsing, creating, living, and storytelling about other possible, better ways to be human and to live together on this planet.

Yet, for all the appreciation I have voiced here and elsewhere for Anzaldúa's work, my greatest homage is to urge us to move beyond Anzaldúa, to not become Anzaldúans. Anzaldúa's work calls us to become aware of how we are torn between what our societies and cultures banish and repress, in order that we may resolve these binary repressions into states of greater individual and societal wholeness. With Jung's, her work calls us to move beyond her path to our own mysteries, discoveries, changing truths, shifting subjectivities, gifts, and powers. Her work was a painstaking account of self-discovery and growth of consciousness against dehumanization and victimization. She rendered her psychological, spiritual, cultural, and creative journey as a philosophical, politically consequential journey, that of the growth of consciousness and of integration of mind, body, and spirit. Her writing therefore functions as medicine, as *curandera* work, to assist in the reader's own journey of personal integration and personal integrity. She worked beyond the binary and judgmental belief that identity and work should be immutably perfect, finished, and free of contradiction. Instead, her vibrant thought embraces life and creative work as a cycle of constant transformation.

# Notes

1. An earlier draft of this essay was presented as a keynote lecture at the University of California, Santa Cruz's fiftieth anniversary celebration, "The Feminist Architecture of Gloria Anzaldúa: New Translations, Crossings, and Pedagogies in Anzaldúan Thought," April 10–11, 2015, and as a keynote address delivered for me by Mariana Ortega, at the Latina Feminist Roundtable, Department of Philosophy, John Carroll University, Cleveland, Ohio, May 1, 2015. Parts of this essay also appear in my book *Eros Ideologies: Writings on Art, Writing, and the Spiritual* (Duke University Press, 2019, ch. 13, "Undead Darwinism and the Fault Lines of Neocolonialism in Latina/o Art Worlds," 112–25).
2. I have written extensively about the s/Spirit(s) and ideas of interdependence in *Chicana Art* (2007) and *Eros Ideologies* (2019).
3. *Reader*: 125, 138 "to make face is to have face—dignity and self-respect." On the analysis of multiple forms of oppression by Martinez and Nieto Gomez, see Alma García, ed., *Chicana Feminist Thought: The Basic Historical Writings*. New York: Routledge, 1997.
4. Pérez, "Spirit Glyphs"; Pérez, *Chicana Art*; Anzaldúa, *Borderlands/La Frontera*, 95, n. 6.
5. *Interviews/Entrevistas*: 286; *Reader*: 121, 122, 108: "What happens in the imagination is not fiction."
6. See historian of psychology Sonu Shamdasani, *Jung and the Making of Modern Psychology. The Dream of a Science* (Cambridge University Press 2003) for Jung's place in the history of psychology and Jungian psychologist Murray Stein, *Jung on Evil*, (Princeton University Press 1996) for selections from Jung's oeuvre on the "shadow" and the larger problem of evil.
7. Although the observation had been long made, and Jung himself wrote about his decision to not pursue art professionally, the posthumous publication of *The Red Book* (2009) finally brought together the full set of paintings that had been partially reproduced throughout the years and by which he had sought to represent intrapsychic forces in his own psyche as part of his own mental health but also his research into the nature of the psyche. Drawing one's own intrapsychic energies as "forces" and anthropomorphizing these as expressions of one's "anima" or "animus" became an important tool for Jung himself and for Jungian therapists and their patients.
8. Sources are numerous, including Jung 1953, 1965, 1989.

9. See Murray Stein with respect to Jung's understanding of the irruption of Naziism (*Op. cit.* 1996: 12–13).
10. Meetings and conversations with African and Native American (Hopi) elders, or medicine men, led Jung to see modern European culture's Eurocentrism on the one hand, and on the other, its projection of the primitive onto the cultures of other peoples. I must note here that this made his continued usage of the language of the "primitive" and the "civilized" or "the modern" throughout his career quite unfortunate, as it unwittingly reinforced discourses about the supposed inferiority of non-European peoples, although he also wrote of the "primitive" in all people as that which was closest to the natural, less damagingly socialized self.
11. In this, she went beyond Frantz Fanon's identification of the internalization of racism in colonial subjects, in a process Foucault would later describe as the new, modern regime of state social order through internalized mechanisms of discipline and punishment in the modern subject/ed.
12. *Interviews/Entrevistas*: 45.
13. *Interviews/Entrevistas*: 52; 77–80.
14. See Ysidro Ramon Macias, *The Domingo Martinez Paredez Reader* (self-published, 2017).
15. *Interviews/Entrevistas*: 115–117. Regarding "patlache," *Reader*: 163.
16. Gloria E. Anzaldúa, *Borderlands/La Frontera: The New Mestiza* (San Francisco: Spinsters/ Aunt Lute, 1987), 21–22.
17. Anzaldúa, *Borderlands/La Frontera*, 22.
18. See *Reader* for greater elaboration: "Aspects of identity . . . in actuality they are all constantly in a shifting dialogue, relationship . . . all the multiple aspects of identity. . . ." (167). Also see Mariana Ortega for a discussion of María Lugones's notion of the multiple in Anzaldúa's 1987 work and elaboration of Ortega's own understanding of the "multiplicitous self" in Anzaldúa (*In Between: Latina Feminist Phenomenology, Multiplicity, and the Self*, SUNY 2016).
19. Irene Lara, "Daughter of Coatlicue: An Interview with Gloria Anzaldúa," in *Entre mundos/Among Worlds: New Perspectives on Gloria Anzaldúa*, ed. AnaLouise Keating (New York: Palgrave Macmillan, 2005), 48.
20. Lara, "Daughter of Coatlicue," 48.
21. Anzaldúa, *Borderlands/La Frontera*, 5.
22. I mention "anti-Hispanism" in relation to the anti-Spanish "Black Legend" that Anglo Protestant "manifest destiny" logic recirculated to justify provocation of war with

Mexico in 1846 and incorporation of the Southwest and West after 1848. The rationale was not just against Mexicans as "half-breeds," but against the Catholic Spanish. The Spanish and their descendants were "lazy," wasteful, feminine, and hence didn't deserve to settle the territories coveted by the thirteen colonies in their westward expansion.

23. See Norma Alarcón, "In the Tracks of 'the' Native Woman" *Cultural Studies* 4, no. 3 (1990): 248–56. August 22, 2006, https://www.tandfonline.com/doi/abs/10.1080/09502389000490201. Anzaldúa's autobiographical accounts in *Borderlands/La Frontera*, taken as a whole, claim Indigenous ancestry against the Mexican dominant cultural shaming of both Indigenous people and Indigenous ancestry. Guillermo Bonfil Batalla wrote against this repression of the recognition of the widespread Indigenous nature of Mexican lived culture, particularly that outside of large cities. In *México Profundo. Una civilización negada* (1987), he argued that despite the claims of the Europeanized and US-centric elite and middle classes in Mexico, the vast majority of Mexicans are mestizos and this *mestizaje* is actually and regardless of westernized clothing, language, and even indoctrination to the contrary, profoundly Indigenous. Continual inhabitation for more than 20,000 years on this continent are not erased by 500 years of invasion, he argued. Responding to critiques of Anzaldúa's claims to Indigeneity, see Randy P. Conner, "Santa Nepantla: A Borderlands Sutra Plenary Speech," in *El Mundo Zurdo: Selected Works from the Meetings of The Society for the Study of Gloria Anzaldúa 2007 & 2009*, ed. Norma E. Cantú, Christina L. Gutierrez, Norma Alarcón, and Rita E. Urquijo-Ruiz (San Francisco: Aunt Lute Books, 2010, 177–202. María Lugones considered the complexities of the occluded or "robbed" histories of the Indigenous ancestries of mestizas in "Mestizaje and the Communal," one of the keynotes at the University of California, Santa Cruz's 50th anniversary celebration, "The Feminist Architecture of Gloria Anzaldúa: New Translations, Crossings and Pedagogies in Anzaldúan Thought," April 10–11, 2015.

24. Pérez, "*El desorden*, Nationalism, and Chicana/o Aesthetics" (in Caplan et al., *Between Woman and Nation. Transnational Feminisms and the State*, Duke University Press, 1999); *Chicana Art: The Politics of Spiritual and Aesthetic Altarities*, Duke University Press 2007; *Eros Ideologies. Writings on Art, Spirituality, and the Decolonial*, Duke University Press 2019.

25. I use authentic in the psychological sense, what is for us to the degree that is possible behaviors more natural to us over those learned to gain approval and avoid disapproval and punishment. The psychological process of healing the individual who has been taught like a Pavlov dog to not pursue her own instincts, desires,

impulses, i.e., to the degree these can be called our own and natural to our unique being, is also called the journey to the authentic, towards integrity as more or less successful integration of a self that is continuously growing, changing, and readjusting sense of self and ways to live.

26. In *Eros Ideologies* (2019), I further psychic integration in the work of Jung, psychiatrist Claudio Naranjo, and feminist psychologist Clarissa Pinkola Estés, and also think further about the idea of interdependence of all life forms.

27. See Quijano for his idea of the "coloniality of power": since the invasion of the Americas, all of its development in every aspect is imbricated in the logic and effects of colonialism (2000). Hence, for example, as philosopher Enrique Dussel argued, even European modernity cannot be accurately thought of without considering how it is made possible by European imperialism and its empire transformation on multiple levels (2000).

28. Walter Mignolo, *Local Histories/Global Designs: Coloniality, Subaltern Knowledges, Border Thinking* (Princeton, NJ: Princeton University Press, 2000); Mignolo, *The Darker Side of Western Modernity: Global Futures, Decolonial Options* (Duke University Press, 2011); P. J. DiPietro, *Sideways Selves: The Decolonial Politics of Transing Matter across the Américas* (University of Texas Press, forthcoming 2024); Javier García Fernández, *Pensar Jondo. Crítica del Eurocentrismo, Descolonizacíon y Cultura* (Córdoba, España: Editorial Almuzara, S.I., 2024; Anca Parvulescu and Manuela Boatca, *Creolizing the Modern. Transylvania across Empires* (Ithaca, NY: Cornell University Press, 2022).

29. María Lugones, *Pilgrimages/Peregrinajes: Theorizing Coalition Against Multiple Oppressions* (Lanham, MD: Rowman & Littlefield Publishers, 2003); Mariana Ortega, *In-Between: Latina Feminist Phenomenology, Multiplicity, and the Self* (Albany: State University Press, 2016); DiPietro, *Sideways Selves.*

30. The term "simultaneity of oppressions" is introduced in the "Combahee River Collective Statement" (1977). It is of a piece with Chicana and other US Latina feminist thought dating to the early 1970s, which argued in complex fashion that as women of color, Chicanas experienced "triple" and quadruple oppression by race, sex, and class. Intellectuals such as Elizabeth "Betita" Martinez and Anna Nieto Gomez further argued that imperialism and colonialism were a fourth form in which Chicanas were oppressed. Nieto Gomez and Martinez further observed that "sex" for both men and women was reconstrued as a result of the racialized colonial reorganization of society in which the darker Indigenous women and their mestiza daughters were inferiorized in comparison to Spanish European women. As Betita later remarked,

what she and some of the more prominent Chicana feminists failed to take in to account as heterosexual women, was oppression by sexuality, an analysis that Anzaldúa, of that same generation famously inserted in her rather late publication, *Borderland/La Frontera: The New Mestiza*, originally published in 1987.

31. Pérez, *Chicana Art*.

# References

Alarcón, Norma. "In the Tracks of 'the' Native Woman." *Cultural Studies* Vol. 4, 1990, Issue 3, 248–56. Published online August 22, 2006, https://www.tandfonline.com/doi/abs/10.1080/09502389000490201.

Anzaldúa, Gloria E. *Borderlands/La Frontera: The New Mestiza*. San Francisco: Spinsters/Aunt Lute, 1987.

Anzaldúa, Gloria E. *Interviews/Entrevistas by Gloria E. Anzaldúa*, edited by AnaLouise Keating. New York and London: Routledge Press, 2000.

Anzaldúa, Gloria E. *Light in the Dark/Luz en lo oscuro: Rewriting Identity, Spirituality, Reality*, edited by AnaLouise Keating. Durham, NC: Duke University Press, 2015.

Bonfil Batalla, Guillermo. *México Profundo: Reclaiming a Civilization*. Translated by Philip A. Dennis. Austin: University of Texas Press, 1996 (1987).

Combahee River Collective. "A Black Feminist Statement." In *This Bridge Called My Back: Writings by Radical Women of Color*, 2nd ed., edited by Cherríe Moraga and Gloria Anzaldúa. New York: Kitchen Table: Women of Color Press 1983 (1977).

Conner, Randy P. "Santa Nepantla: A Borderlands Sutra Plenary Speech." In *El Mundo Zurdo: Selected Works from the Meetings of The Society for the Study of Gloria Anzaldúa 2007 & 2009*, edited by Norma E. Cantú et al. (San Francisco: Aunt Lute Books, 2010, 177–202.)

Delgadillo, Theresa. *Spiritual Mestizaje: Religion, Race, and Nation in Contemporary Chicana Narrative*. Durham: Duke University Press, 2011.

DiPietro, P. J. *Sideways Selves: The Decolonial Politics of Transing Matter across the Américas*. University of Texas Press, forthcoming 2024.

Dussel, Enrique. "Europe, Modernity, and Eurocentrism." *Nepantla: Views from the South* 1, no. 3 (2000): 465–78.

García Fernández, Javier. *Pensar Jondo: Crítica del Eurocentrismo, Descolonizacíon y Cultura*. Córdoba, España: Editorial Almuzara, S.I., 2024.

Garcia Lopez, Christina. *Calling the Soul Back: Embodied Spirituality in Chicanx Narrative*. Tucson, AZ: University of Arizona Press, 2019.

Hey-Colón, Rebeca L. *Channeling Knowledges: Water and Afro-Diasporic Spirits in Latinx and Caribbean Worlds*. University of Texas Press, 2023.

Jung, Carl G. *Memories, Dreams, and Reflections*. Rev. ed. Recorded and edited by Aniela Jaffé. Translated by Richard and Clara Winston. New York: Random House, 1989 (1961).

Jung, Carl G. *Modern Man in Search of a Soul*. Translated by W. S. Dell and Cary Fe. Baynes. New York: Harcourt, Brace & World, 1965 (1933).

Jung, Carl G. *Psychological Reflections: Selections*, edited by Jolande Jacobi. New York: Bollingen Foundation, 1953 (1945).

Keating, AnaLouise. "Risking the Personal: An Introduction." In *Interviews/Entrevistas by Gloria E. Anzaldúa*, edited by AnaLouise Keating. New York and London: Routledge Press, 2000, 1–15.

Keating, AnaLouise, ed. *The Gloria Anzaldúa Reader*. Durham, NC: Duke University Press, 2009.

Keating, AnaLouise. *Women Reading Women Writing: Self-Invention in Paula Gunn Allen, Gloria Anzaldúa, and Audre Lorde*. Temple University Press, 1996.

Lara, Irene. "Bruja Positionalities: Toward a Chicana/Latina Spiritual Activism." *Chicana/Latina Studies* 4.2 (Spring 2005): 10–45.

Lara, Irene. "Daughter of Coatlicue: An Interview with Gloria Anzaldúa." In *Entre mundos/Among Worlds: New Perspectives on Gloria Anzaldúa*, edited by AnaLouise Keating. New York: Palgrave Macmillan, 2005.

Lugones, María. "Mestizaje and the Communal," one of the keynotes at the University of California, Santa Cruz's fiftieth anniversary celebration, "The Feminist Architecture of Gloria Anzaldúa: New Translations, Crossings and Pedagogies in Anzaldúan Thought," April 10–11, 2015.

Lugones, María. *Pilgrimages/Peregrinajes: Theorizing Coalition Against Multiple Oppressions*. Lanham, MD: Rowman & Littlefield Publishers, 2003.

Macias, Ysidro Ramon, editor and translator. *The Domingo Martinez Paredez Reader*. Self-published, on demand, 2017.

Martinez, Elizabeth "Betita." "La Chicana." In *Chicana Feminist Thought: The Basic Historical Writings*, edited by Alma García. New York: Routledge, 1997 (1972).

Martinez, Elizabeth "Betita." "Viva La Chicana and All Brave Women of La Causa." In *Chicana Feminist Thought: The Basic Historical Writings*, edited Alma García. New York: Routledge, 1997 (1971).

Medina, Lara. "Nepantla Spirituality: An Emancipative Vision for Inclusion." In *Wading Through Many Voices: Toward a Theology of Public Conversation*, edited by Harold J. Recinos. Rowman & Littlefield, 2011.

Mignolo, Walter. *Local Histories/Global Designs: Coloniality, Subaltern Knowledges, Border Thinking*. Princeton, NJ: Princeton University Press, 2000.

Mignolo, Walter. *The Darker Side of Western Modernity: Global Futures, Decolonial Options*. Duke University Press, 2011.

Nieto-Gómez, Anna. "La Chicana—A Legacy of Suffering and Self Denial." In *Chicana Feminist Thought: The Basic Historical Writings*, edited by Alma García. New York: Routledge, 1997 (1975), 48–50.

Nieto-Gómez, Anna. "La Femenista." In *Chicana Feminist Thought: The Basic Historical Writings*, edited by Alma García. New York: Routledge, 1997 (1974).

Nieto-Gómez, Anna. "Sexism in the Movimiento." In *Chicana Feminist Thought: The Basic Historical Writings*, edited by Alma García. New York: Routledge, 1997 (1976).

Nieto-Gómez, Anna. "Chicana Feminism." In *Chicana Feminist Thought: The Basic Historical Writings*, edited by Alma García. New York: Routledge, 1997 (1976).

Ortega, Mariana. *In-Between: Latina Feminist Phenomenology, Multiplicity, and the Self*. Albany: State University Press, 2016.

Parvulescu, Anca and Manuela Boatca. *Creolizing the Modern: Transylvannia Across Empires*. Ithaca, NY: Cornell University Press, 2022.

Pérez, Laura E. *Chicana Art: The Politics of Spiritual and Aesthetic Altarities*. Duke University Press 2007.

Pérez, Laura E. "*El desorden*, Nationalism, and Chicana/o Aesthetics." In Karen Caplan et al., *Between Woman and Nation: Transnational Feminisms and the State*. Duke University Press, 1999.

Pérez, Laura E. *Eros Ideologies: Writings on Art, Spirituality, and the Decolonial*. Duke University Press, 2019.

Pérez, Laura E. "Negotiating New American Philosophies: Anzaldúa's Borderlands/La Frontera." Paper presented at Philosophy, Interpretation, Culture, Mind annual conference, Binghamton University, Binghamton, New York, April 1993.

Pérez, Laura E. "Spirit Glyphs: Reimagining Art and Artist in the Work of Chicana *Tlamatinime*," *Modern Fiction Studies* 44, no. 1 (Spring 1998).

Quijano, Aníbal. "Coloniality of Power, Eurocentrism, and Latin America." *Nepantla: Views from the South* 1, no. 3 (2000): 533–80.

Schaeffer, Felicity Amaya. "Spirit Matters." *Signs: Journal of Women in Culture and Society*, 43, no. 4 (Summer 2018): 1005–1029.

Shamdasani, Sonu. *Jung and the Making of Modern Psychology: The Dream of a Science.* Cambridge University Press, 2003.

Stein, Murray. *Jung on Evil*. Princeton University Press, 1996.

Tirres, Christopher D. "Spiritual Activism and Praxis: Gloria Anzaldúa's Mature Spirituality." *The Pluralist*, 14, no. 1 (2019): 119–140.

PART IV

*Complicating Institutional Religion*

## Chapter 10

# Liberation Theology and Its Limits in the Peruvian Andes

*MATTHEW CASEY-PARISEAULT*

In early July 1974, the Instituto de Pastoral Andina held a four-day retreat at a Catholic Church-owned farm in Yucay, fifty kilometers north of the city of Cusco. One hundred and twenty-two Andean catechists—trained lay spiritual leaders—had gathered there for the week to participate in workshops and hear talks from visiting priests. The keynote speaker was Father Gustavo Gutiérrez, who had risen to international fame three years earlier with the publication of his book *A Theology of Liberation*.[1] The theme at the core of this gathering, one of several held throughout the year, was the role of the Catholic Church in Peruvian society. The catechists were outspoken in their critiques. These *campesinos* (Indigenous farmers) noted that they had been working toward social and economic change for years, but the church had not been fully supportive of the bottom-up model of liberation theology that they promoted. They accused even reform-minded priests and nuns of offering merely rhetorical support to the liberation of the poor, while in practice backing the agents of their oppression, namely large landowners and mining companies in the region.[2] Their critical stance was a key factor that made liberation theology into a transformative movement in the Peruvian Andes during the early 1970s.

The Southern Andes of Peru, or the Sur-Andino, was one of Latin America's most important regions of rural support and contribution to liberation theology during the 1970s, a movement in many places defined by the lay leadership of the urban middle class and student activists. As the Peruvian case shows us, liberation theology could also thrive in rural Indigenous communities, incorporating the voices of a wide range of people the movement claimed to serve.[3] Andean liberation theology, like other manifestations of the movement throughout Latin America and the world, drew heavily on leftist concepts of solidarity, consciousness raising, and popular participation. These ideologies were not new to Andean communities in the 1970s, as agricultural and textile unions in the area had been involved with the

Communist party and the labor movement on and off since the 1930s.[4] But these ideas enjoyed their widest popular support after Catholic leaders began espousing them openly in the wake of the Second Vatican Council and its regional corollary, the 1968 Conference of Latin American Bishops meeting in Medellín, Colombia. The rise of a left-leaning nationalist government, the Revolutionary Government of the Armed Forces under General Juan Velasco Alvarado (1968–1975), further inspired Indigenous Catholic activists both to support—and later, critique—the movement in light of its promise to revolutionize life for Andean peasants. In turn, because of the region's status as an "underdeveloped" hinterland from the perspective of institutional seats of power in Lima, the Southern Andean region drew heightened attention from both the government and the post-Vatican II international Catholic Church.

Liberation theology in Peru's Southern Andean region was a peculiar blend of formerly disparate elements. As Catalina Romero and others have shown, intellectual and political diversity within the progressive post-Vatican II church opened up new and often competing visions for social reform via religious activism.[5] Liberation meant different things to different sectors of society in the Peruvian Andes. As in many other places, the small groups that made up the whole represented a variety of contingencies. On the clerical side, there were idealistic priests like the Canadian Carmelite Alban Quinn, who regularly cited Marx and called for radical changes to the church hierarchy. Religious sisters from Europe and North America worked closely with Andean women on projects that included feminist reading groups and education campaigns valorizing household workers. Like the priests, the sisters learned Quechua and Aymara, the dominant Indigenous languages in the region. Laypeople joined the movement in a wide array of communities, animated by causes that ranged from the socially conservative Christian Families Movement to a progressive, state-funded literacy campaign. The engine of liberation theology in the region was a veritable army of lay catechists who administered sacraments in rural villages when the priest could not visit, and who cared for the spiritual and material needs of their peers in equal measure. These various Catholic actors shared ideas at regular meetings, on rotating travel circuits, and in the Catholic press, all of which served as points of cohesion for a new pastoral method: an Andean theology of liberation.

Together, Catholic activists built a complex politico-religious project that, if only for a few years, threatened to upend the reigning social order in Peru's Southern Andes. The emergence of the base communities of liberation theology during the early 1970s reset the possibilities of Catholic political itineraries, turning the region's church into "one of the channels through which the people could express their concerns, their most pressing needs, and real interests."[6] The priests and lay leaders of these communities put forth proposals for radical change in society and within the church.

This essay uses pamphlets, newsletters, and internal documents from the Catholic Church to explore the actors and factors that made the rural Southern Andes of Peru a key locus of liberation theology between 1968 and 1975. Section one seeks to understand how two major events in 1968, the Conference of Latin American Bishops meeting at Medellín, Colombia, and the successful military coup that brought the reformist Juan Velasco Alvarado to the Peruvian presidency, made major impacts on the rural Southern Andes and why both church and state would go on to expend significant resources and energy to mobilize the region. Section two highlights the institutional shifts that brought reform-minded missionaries and religious from North America and Europe to the Sur-Andino in the years after the Second Vatican Council. The third section brings to the forefront the Indigenous Catholic activists who founded base communities and other local organizations to assert their voices amidst the reforms unfolding in both the Peruvian state and the Catholic Church.

## The Era of 1968 in the Sur-Andino

Peru was one of the Latin American nations whose government stood fully in favor of the progressive changes coming out of the 1968 Conference of Latin American Bishops in Medellín, Colombia. The brief democratic socialist regime of Salvador Allende in Chile (1970–1973) and the early years of the Sandinista revolutionary government in Nicaragua (1979) would later create similar propitious conditions for progressive Catholicism. In Peru, conditions were favorable for liberation theology to thrive from its very early stages. A progressive regime, under General Juan Velasco Alvarado, came to power just a month after the closing of the Medellín meeting. A general who served as Velasco's minister of mining put it this way: "It is not a coincidence that the church's thinking . . . in total harmony with the original Gospel message, should manifest itself in Medellín the very year of the Peruvian revolution."[7]

The Sur-Andino is a high-altitude region dominated by dramatic, hard-to-traverse landscapes and a generally cold and windy climate. During the mid- to late twentieth century, the local economy consisted of subsistence agriculture supplemented by some men's migratory participation in mining and coffee farming. A general lack of access to the resources and to the full rights of citizenship marked life for most residents. The region of Sicuani, to the south of the city of Cusco, for example, was home to just four medical doctors for a population of over 200,000.[8] According to one count, around half of the men in Sicuani—and even less of the women—were literate.[9] In one town with a population of 800, 70 children received primary school education, and only 5 went on to secondary school.[10] The local diet was rooted in the region's products that were the least marketable, which consisting mostly of barley, dried potatoes, and lima beans. Meat, fruit, and green vegetables produced elsewhere were often too expensive, or never made it to local markets.[11] Further compounding these regional economic issues, outmigration from peasant communities to regional cities and to Lima was accelerated during this period.

Land ownership and the wage economy in the region were profoundly unequal, with observers applying concepts like "colonial feudalism" to the living conditions for Andean peasants.[12] In 1969, a Peruvian social scientist surveyed 500 peasants in rural Cusco. Fifty-two percent of them agreed with the statement that "the Indians were born to serve and obey the *misti*," (the Quechua term for Spanish-speaking mestizos). Yet the hope and will for change was evident in the 91 percent of respondents who believed that through education, all people could become equal. By 1972, the economically active population receiving salaries was 42 percent nationwide, but in the Southern Andean regions of Ayacucho and Apurímac, it was 17 percent and 13 percent, respectively.[13]

Indigenous communities did not stay silent in the face of these dehumanizing conditions. Long before the birth of liberation theology and the reforms of the Velasco government, a variety of activist movements drew on a tradition of Indigenous rebellion and resistance to make the Southern Andean region a major hub of leftist organizing. Popular movements, from peasants' unions to armed guerrilla fronts, were drawn to the Sur-Andino and the people's struggles for major social and economic changes. As Nelson Manrique put it, the "great mobilization of the Cusco peasantry attracted the attention of the small insurrectional groups on the left."[14] The National Liberation Army (ELN) and the Revolutionary Left Movement (MIR), two guerrilla organizations with backing from Revolutionary Cuba, aimed to make Cusco and the Southern Andean region their base of support in these years. Both movements were defeated by the Peruvian military in skirmishes in the Sur-Andino in 1965.

The government, in turn, aimed to coopt the popular uprisings in the Sur-Andino with their own reforms. This was especially the case after the Trotskyist Hugo Blanco of the Departmental Federation of Workers in Cusco (FDTC) led a series of successful land takeovers in the northern provinces of the department of Cusco. In 1963, the newly elected President Fernando Belaúnde Terry issued an agrarian reform bill, which was intended to undermine support for Blanco and other popular left movements in the Southern Andes. But this targeted Southern Andean agrarian reform was underwhelming, never even reaching implementation in most cases. Within a few years, Belaunde's tepid reformism had lost the support of Congress and the military.

A bloodless coup on October 3, 1968, brought General Juan Velasco Alvarado to power as the leader of the Revolutionary Government of the Armed Forces, a left-leaning nationalist regime that would also focus much of its attention on the Andean south. A development-oriented modernizing project quickly unfolded, including the nationalization of the oil industry. In 1969, the regime issued an ambitious agrarian reform bill that aimed to redistribute privately owned estates to the campesinos who worked them. Symbolically, the regime sought to upend anti-Indigenous racism, romanticizing Indigeneity with bold media campaigns and slogans. The government made Quechua an official language alongside Spanish and prohibited the use of the term "indio" in favor of the class-based term *campesino*, or peasant. For many in the Southern Andes, Velasco's reforms seemed like the long-awaited solutions to the region's deep-rooted socioeconomic problems.

Just one month before the Velasco coup, the Conference of Latin American Bishops had met in Medellín, Colombia, to set the agenda for how to apply the reforms of Vatican II to the Latin American reality. The bishops were heavily influenced by intellectual trends that were popular in the region, including dependency theory, which argued that Latin America held a subordinate role in global geopolitics because of its position as a provider of raw materials. The influence of Paulo Friere's pedagogy of the oppressed is clear in the Medellín documents as well, with their emphasis on raising the consciousness of the poor so that they could contribute to their own liberation from earthly suffering. Lima's Archbishop Juan Landázuri Ricketts served as vice-president of the 1968 meeting, with Gustavo Gutiérrez as his assistant. Under Landázuri's leadership, the Peruvian Church enthusiastically aligned itself with modernizing projects circulating throughout the Catholic world. In this atmosphere of hope and commitment, the Peruvian bishops were willing to overlook the military's autocratic rise to power and opted to support the bold reforms of the Velasco government.

When Velasco issued the sweeping agrarian reform bill in 1969, the bishops argued that the regime had "engaged profoundly in the urgent process of changing the structures of the country."[15] Archbishop Landázuri stated further that "the Church sees, in the recently decreed Agrarian Reform Law, a valiant instrument of justice," calling a means for achieving "true national liberation."[16] This honeymoon period would last several more years, with church and state functioning in relative cohesion, all with the aim of upending deeply rooted social and economic inequalities that plagued regions like the Sur-Andino.

Velasco's logic ran parallel to Medellín's preferential option for the poor. "And if it is true that this Government is for all Peruvians," the General reflected in a 1969 speech, "it is no less true that it should and must be, above all, a government for the neediest."[17] During its first few years, the military government created a favorable atmosphere for the spread of progressive Catholic teachings. Indeed, as historian Jeffrey Klaiber put it, "the Peruvian military had virtually appropriated the social doctrines of the church to justify their reforms ideologically."[18] In the Southern Andean region especially, institutional reforms in the federal government and the church hierarchy created propitious conditions for liberation theology to flourish.

## (Re)Organizing for Liberation

One of the major changes in the Vatican II-era Catholic Church was a refocused, global missionary project that aimed to both convert and socially uplift some of the world's most neglected communities. In Latin America, where the overwhelming majority of people were Catholic, this meant missions to work with urban poor and peasant communities that the bishops at Medellín had placed at the center of their reforms. In Peru, Archbishop Landázuri coordinated with Pope Paul VI to bring thousands of priests and nuns from Europe and North America to work as missionaries in the cities and impoverished regions. The Southern Andean region would receive hundreds of these missionaries from a variety of religious orders. These priests and sisters from Europe and Anglo North America worked closely with the church hierarchy and laypeople in the southern departments of Cusco, Puno, Ayacucho, and Arequipa to establish a network of interrelated organizations that would convert the church of the Andean south into an innovative nexus of liberation theology. In the words of the Canadian missionary Albano Quinn, the new church movement was to be "authentically local, with its own customs, expressions, and celebrations of faith; with its own ministers."[19] This meant not only an emphasis on missionaries learning Indigenous languages and cultures, a practice long central to Catholic missionary work in the Americas and elsewhere, but it also entailed a new emphasis on uplifting local lay leadership to direct the course of religious and social change in their own communities. While the influx of foreign missionaries was a catalyst, these faith leaders arrived with the explicit purpose of helping start a social and religious groundswell of change that would become locally sustainable and require little outside intervention. For a time, this collaborative effort was a resounding success.

In addition to Indigenous communities' recent history of grassroots organizing, a drastic shortage of priests and rapid population growth throughout the first half of the twentieth century inspired shifts that would prepare the southern Peruvian Andes for revival. During this period, Peru's population was on pace to double every twenty-three years, while at the same time, the number of seminarians training for the priesthood was declining sharply. Just a generation earlier, between 1950 and 1954, 186 ordinations were made in Peru. That number fell to fifty-eight in the four-year span between 1970 and 1974.[20] Things were even worse in Cusco, where only five new priests were ordained between 1962 and 1975. By the mid-1970s, an astonishing 81 percent of the Catholic religious personnel in Peru (including nuns, monks, deacons, and priests) were foreign born. These missionaries came primarily from Anglo North America and Europe. While some remained in Peru for years, even decades, others were on shorter assignments. The main emphasis for the mission in the Sur-Andino was to address the priest shortage by training lay leaders called catechists to serve as spiritual and social leaders in their communities.

In the Andean context, a catechist is "a Christian campesino who earns a living as a farmer, and as a Christian they voluntarily commit themselves to the service of evangelization and the promotion of their brothers and sisters."[21] Beyond the mere teaching of church doctrine, they envisioned their role as equal parts religious and social; their self-proclaimed duty was to "raise the awareness of the priests and the hierarchy for a commitment of life and work for the peasants."[22] The catechist network was in many ways like a parallel structure placed alongside the preexisting organizing schema of the rural Andean church. A Maryknoll sister working in the region said, "Sometimes the catechists substitute for the priests and are mini-clerics."[23] Progressive church leaders, both Peruvian and foreign, built a network of ecclesial organizations that would foment the rise of this new cadre of trained Indigenous Catholic activists.

The Andean Pastoral Institute (Instituto de Pastoral Andina, IPA) was the most influential of these organizations. In 1969, Archbishop Ricardo Durand Flórez of Cusco and a group of bishops and other church leaders founded the Andean Pastoral Institute with support from German and US mission agencies. Durand, who came from a mestizo family in Lima, remembers having come to the idea for the institute back in 1966 while reflecting on the question: "What do I know about the Quechua soul?"[24] The IPA became the publishing house for two major academic magazines under the guidance of the Spanish Jesuit and anthropologist Manuel Marzal.[25] The organization's charter set out plans to elaborate "lines of pastoral action for evangelization that respect and encourage the cultural values of Aymara and Quechua peasants in the southern Andean region of Peru."[26] The IPA would go on to train thousands of catechists. The Andean Pastoral Institute was inspired by the Second Vatican Council's commitment to uplifting Indigenous forms of Catholicism. That it quickly evolved into a more politically oriented leftist organization helps us understand the potency of progressive religious activism in the Southern Andean region. The successes and failures of liberation theology in the southern Peruvian Andes depended on missionaries' and priests' ability to get out of their own way and allow local communities to carry out their own "prophetic mission" for spiritual and social revival.[27]

Another key missionary organization was the Regional Institute of Catechesis and Evangelization (Instituto Regional de Catequesis y Evangelización Regional, IRCEA), which served as something of a clearing house for the concerns of local communities. IRCEA was run by lay and religious leaders, called assessors, and was oriented toward training and working with local lay representatives from each community throughout the Sur-Andino. These local representatives were to collect the concerns of their base communities and report them back at IRCEA meetings so that the assessors could set the organizing agenda for the coming months. These regional missionary institutions carried out what they viewed as consciousness-raising initiatives with a multi-pronged, multimedia approach.

Beyond their more popularly focused projects, IRCEA and other organizations like the Bartolomé de las Casas Center for Rural Andean Studies (founded by Gustavo Gutiérrez) worked closely with educated rural leaders who they believed were well positioned to implement change in their own communities. One five-day symposium IRCEA and the las Casa Center hosted for medical practitioners and their assistants addressed the topic of "Public Health in the Peasant Society and Cultures of the Sur-Andino."[28] IRCEA also held regular week-long training courses (*cursillos*) throughout the Sur-Andino. These were a sort of traveling symposium series with a common agenda that was updated each year. In 1974, their standing agenda was 1) agrarian legislation, 2) Andean rural history, and 3) reading the Bible. Between eight and fifteen laypeople attended each session, with as many as forty religious helping guide the events. In regions that the organizers targeted as needing growth, IRCEA paid for the lodging, food, and transportation for the lay participants on the condition that each catechist bring with them a leader from their community who was not currently serving as a pastoral agent. These leaders were to have "real responsibilities" in their communities and were to be literate Spanish-speakers.[29]

Print media was a primary means by which lay and religious leaders built and maintained community during these years. Publications ranged from the academic monthly magazine with readership well beyond the Sur-Andino, *Allpanchis Phuturinka* (which in Quechua means "Our land will bear fruit"), to the more functional, regionally oriented *Pastoral Andina*, and local bulletins like Siucani's *Boletín Informativo*. In these media, published mostly in Spanish with occasional material in Quechua and Aymara, pastoral agents expressed their theological commitments (always steeped in references to the reforms of Vatican II and Medellín), provided local updates from their base communities, and learned of the trainings and symposia that organizations like IPA and IRCEA were holding throughout the year. These publications served to maintain an emerging, organic community of religious revival that extended beyond the periodic meetings and the pastoral circuits they traveled by car, truck and bus across the challenging landscapes of the Sur-Andino. Religious print media linked laypeople, nuns, priests, and even high-ranking bishops. For a time, the leaders of this movement constituted Peru's vanguard of both liberation theology and of the reforms of the Velasco revolution.

In line with the church and state reform movements of the day, the Andean pastoral model saw economic and religious liberation as two parts of the same process. A Quechua-speaking Bolivian priest, Toribio Porco Ticona, wrote to his Peruvian counterparts about the state of the Andean peasant. "Externally, the oppression begins in the form of economic domination." The campesino "is almost always the object of cheating and fraud. Religion itself tends to contribute to the oppression: religious practices and even preaching serve to present a false idea of God, a terrible, punishing God who is friend to the oppressor. All that one can do for this God is placate his rage with rituals." Proponents of liberation theology in the Andes sought to upend this system by seeking more opportunities for lay leadership, promoting greater access to healthcare, and working for women's rights. The social and economic problems of the region, in the eyes of Catholic activists, could be solved "by raising the consciousness of those who should be liberated."[30] In the early 1970s, this method achieved momentary success.

## Andean Pastoral

In the midst the bold reforms coming down from both the church and state, an eighteen-year-old Quechua *campesino* named Leoncio Castillo was drawing up his own revolutionary plans in the small town of Azángaro in the department of Puno. Like many who became catechists, Leoncio was also a rural union leader, and using his labor-organizing skills, he gathered a small group of like-minded followers into a base community affiliated with IRCEA. "We want to help in the creation of a theology of the Altiplano," (the high plains), he proclaimed.[31] Throughout the Andean south, *campesino* communities met the revolutionary reforms of the era by drawing on the experiences of ongoing peasant liberation movements in the region and the growing realization that Catholic communities could serve as powerful centers for social and political mobilization. Liberation theology in this region developed in direct dialogue and, for a time, in collaboration with the Velasco regime and local traditions of resistance. As Carlos Iván Degregori wrote in his work on the emergence of radical peasant activism in the Southern Andes, this was a time and place of real opportunity, and heavy historical contingency.[32] Throughout the region there was an emerging alignment of visions between the Velasco regime, progressive missionaries, and peasant leaders. This moment brought out a great potential for radical cultural and social revolution, and in many villages, a Catholic spiritual revival.

Most Sur-Andino Catholic activists trained to be pastoral agents with IRCEA before founding their own local communities. Base communities in the Andes were often run by married couples who gathered one or two times per week in the evenings, after the workday. They would study their day-to-day problems in light of the Gospel and generally end the night with food, games, and singing. Bible study was important for a variety of reasons, not least of which was to provide a theological basis for the group's actions that the "traditional Christians" could understand and accept.[33] By 1974, lay-led movements were explicitly referring to their work as "liberation theology."[34] This was meant to be the work of a revivalist vanguard, as local communities developed radical projects that became models for other iterations of liberation theology elsewhere over the coming decade.

In many cases, women were at the forefront. Catholic women in Sicuani worked closely with a group of Carmelite sisters to ensure that they received the same training and leadership opportunities as the men in the community. They reported that the men, including their own husbands, had barred them from attending the training sessions run by the Instituto de Pastoral Andina.[35] Their plight, they noted, went far beyond mistreatment from the community's men. "Just like man exploits woman, there are people who exploit all *campesinos*, both men and women." They identified these exploiters as government officials, local landowners, and even some priests and nuns. "It is in their interest that women continue to be exploited, so that the peasant class has less power.... So just as we must demand our rights from our spouses, together, we *campesinos* must demand and defend our rights against those who abuse us."[36] By the mid-1970s, initiatives to commit to local and female leadership had paid off. In 1975, the prelature of Sicuani counted fifteen people in official leadership positions. Seven of these were women, twelve were Indigenous, and two were foreign missionaries.[37]

Between 1970 and 1974, the proponents of this Andean pastoral model often aligned themselves with the reformist Velasco government. Leoncio's community in Puno, for example, worked regularly with local government officials. "We saw that it was necessary for us to study the laws of the current revolutionary government, so as to support them," recalled Leoncio. He spoke of the Velasco administration as "a revolution that all of us Peruvians are called to support and assist." "We have to raise consciousness," he continued. "We can't wait for a government functionary to do everything."[38] Patricia Gootee, a US-born nun of the Medical Mission Sisters, worked closely with the Velasco government to run the Ministry of Health's program in Arequipa, which trained local health promoters in the region's rural villages. She even took on the sole responsibility of training the health promoters when the funding and support stopped coming from Lima in 1973.[39] Sister Patricia was, in many ways, representative of the nuns and priests that moved from North America and Europe to do mission in Latin America. She had been motivated and radicalized by the bishops' meeting at Medellín in 1968 with its vigorous denunciation of the living standards of Latin America's poor majority.

But just as the Andean pastoral movement was gaining momentum and coherence, the course of national politics began to shift, and by 1974 even the most committed supporters of the Velasco regime were starting to develop a more skeptical, ambiguous stance. One group of catechists in Cusco complained that the government had failed to fulfill its lofty promises, arguing that it "favors capital more than the people."[40] When the catechists of Sicuani gathered for a five-day training workshop in September 1974, one of the main themes discussed was the Velasco regime's agrarian reform, which, five years since its inception, had become mired in bureaucratic processes and local level political maneuvering.[41] Likewise, the leaders of IRCEA argued that the only change they saw after the agrarian reform was that their old masters had been replaced by new ones.[42]

Priests and missionaries in the region began to speak more loudly about their discontent with the Velasco government. Father Víctor Ramos's reaction to the military government's expropriation of several major newspapers in 1974 exemplified the changing perspectives on the regime within the progressive church. While Ramos, a Salesian priest from the Andean city of Huancayo, agreed that the oligarchy had too long controlled important media outlets like the country's leading daily, *El Comercio*, he also feared that the newspapers would become propaganda outlets for the government instead of true representations of the will of the poor and Indigenous masses.[43] In a homily at the Cathedral in Cusco on June 24, 1975, the newly named Archbishop of Cusco, Luis Vallejos declared the Agrarian Reform of 1969 a failure, arguing that the "the land that was expropriated from the local political bosses (*gamonales*) is in no case considered to be the property of the *campesinos* and the communities."[44] That same year, the Carmelite sisters in the parish of Santo Tomás in Cusco called for a clearer separation between church and state. They wanted to promote the work of the base communities instead of working as bureaucrats (recording baptism and other vital records used by the state), training religion teachers, and teaching religion in public schools.[45] Instead of drawing inspiration from the alignment between church and state ideals, as many church leaders had done just a few years earlier, progressive leaders now lamented that the state and the church "use a similar rhetoric," and that "there is competition and confusion" between the two models.[46]

As the fervor of the 1968-era waned, the limits of liberation theology grew more evident. In one attempt to understand the recent setbacks, Sister Gloria Coll pointed out the challenges foreign missionaries faced while trying to see things from an Andean perspective. "I think that it is impossible that, from my culture, from my point of view, I could give a true idea of the life of a *campesina* woman. Although I have tried to share their lives.... I have not been able to lose my European and urban mentality and immerse myself in theirs. The hierarchy of values of the two are completely distinct. And who dare declare that theirs is the right one? ... I, for one, am skeptical of my points of view."[47] Other religious leaders were explicitly concerned that lay control had gone too far. An Aymara priest named Domingo Llanque made the case that while Andean Catholics should be allowed to organize themselves, priests needed to provide strict oversight to keep them from diverging from Catholic doctrine.[48]

If the era of 1968 created propitious circumstances for the emergence of liberation theology in the Andes, the political and religious situation of the mid-1970s did just the opposite. After a year of declining health, General Velasco died in 1975 and was replaced by a much more conservative regime under General Francisco Morales Bermúdez. This regime, which fashioned itself as the "second phase" of Peru's military revolution, took a hard line against what it perceived to be the Marxist Catholic movement in the Southern Andes. Archbishop Vallejos of Cusco, who had been referred to by his admirers as the "Monsignor of the Poor," came to be labeled a Communist by his enemies during the Morales Bermúdez years. Church-state relations under Morales Bermúdez were characterized by what Jeffrey Klaiber called "a superficial cordiality that barely hid the real tensions that existed underneath."[49] Alongside growing skepticism of some conservative priests and nuns, Peru's political shifts spelled an end of the golden years of liberation theology in the Sur-Andino.

By the time the "peculiar revolution" of the Velasco military regime was replaced by a more conservative successor, Andean liberation theology had done much to expose the concerns and raise the consciousness of Catholics in the region. Yet throughout the 1970s and 1980s, the problems that local Catholic activists set out to solve in the post-Vatican II era were still just as pressing. Lack of capital and low wages, abuses from corrupt local officials, and rapid depopulation via migration to the cities plagued Andean communities. At the 1975 regional Episcopal Assembly of the Sur-Andino, the central question remained: How can the institutional church in the region make the campesinos feel heard and how can power be granted to the base communities to take on their own path for revival and reform?

The church in the Sur-Andino would continue pushing toward the most radical realization of the call to become a church of the poor, but institutional changes in the Peruvian government and at the Vatican forced Andean liberation theology to the margins. In the last half of the 1970s, base communities and the organizations with which they worked faced accusations of subversion and were derided as Communists. Pope John Paul II's ascent to power in 1978 was marked by a turn away from the more combative, Marxist-oriented strands of liberation theology and toward the promotion of a "theology of reconciliation" and renewed, less politicized evangelization efforts.

Then, on May 17, 1980, the date of the first presidential elections since the beginning of the military government in 1968, the Southern Andean region was changed forever with a seemingly insignificant act of political protest. A group of masked *campesinos* burned ballot boxes in the rural town of Chuschi to the south of the city of Ayacucho. Cells of the Maoist faction of the Peruvian Communist Party, which called itself *Sendero Luminoso* (the Shining Path), soon gained influence throughout the Southern Andean region and a bloody civil war raged between repressive civilian governments and the terrorist-guerrilla group for the next decade and a half. The rebellion and the government's heavy-handed response claimed the lives of nearly 70,000 people, half of whom were Indigenous Andean peasants. During the years of violence, ecclesial base communities and organizations promoting liberation theology posed a direct threat to Shining Path leadership, who were ruthless with individuals and groups that refused to join the armed struggle.[50] By the time Shining Path declared its war on the government, base communities were well established in many Southern Andean communities, having been a presence in the region for nearly a decade. For these reasons, attacks like the 1989 bombing of a rural education center run by liberationist priests in Puno were all too common.[51] From the perspective of the guerrillas, liberation theology was a competing, nonviolent message of emancipation that obstructed the path of the revolution. As the violence subsided, and as the Vatican steered the church in new directions, the movement for liberation never regained the local prominence of those early years in the Sur-Andino.

Liberation theology thrived for a brief historical moment in the Sur-Andino of the early 1970s. At the institutional level, the movement counted on support from the Catholic hierarchy and benefited from its shared ideological affinities with the reformist national government, but those factors alone do not explain the success of those years. In this perhaps unexpected time and place, the movement came to incorporate the voices of the people it claimed to serve. Men and women from villages throughout the south founded and joined liberationist organizations, seeing their role as equal parts religious and social. They ministered to local Catholic community while at the same time "[raising] the awareness of the priests and the hierarchy for a commitment to life and work with the peasants."[52] These Andean Catholics worked alongside priests and sisters to build an organic movement—part revival, part social revolution—that envisioned and worked toward liberation from an oppressive, centuries-old social order.

# Notes

1. First published as: Gustavo Gutiérrez, *Teología de la liberación, perspectivas* (Lima, Peru: Centro de Estudios y Publicaciones, 1971).
2. "El encuentro de Yucay," *Pastoral Andina* 3, (1974): 5–30. Biblioteca Nacional del Perú, Sala de Hemeroteca Nacional.
3. Two recent pieces focusing on rural Andean manifestations of liberation theology are Rolando Iberico Ruiz, "The Andean Pastoral Institute (IPS) and the Others: Social Science, Pastoral and Liberation Theology in the Peruvian Highlands" and Christian Büschges "The Anthropological Pastor: Liberation Theology and the Social Representation of Andean Rural Communities (1950s–1980s). Both are chapters in Christian Büschge, Andrea Müller, and Noah Oehri, eds., *Liberation Theology and the Others: Contextualizing Catholic Activism in 20th Cenutry Latin America* (Lanham, MD: Lexington Books, 2001).
4. José Luis Rénique, *Incendiar la pradera: Un ensayo sobre la revolución en el Perú* (Lima, Peru: La siniestra, 2015).
5. Catalina Romero, ed., *La diversidad religiosa en el Perú: Miradas múltiples* (Lima, Peru: Centro de Estudios y Publicaciones, 2016).
6. "Editorial" *Prelatura de Sicuani: Boletín Informativo* no. 21 (July 1976): 3. Biblioteca Nacional del Perú, Sala de Hemeroteca Nacional.
7. Jorge Fernández Maldonado, 1973. Cited in Klaiber, *The Catholic Church in Peru* (Washington, D.C.: The Catholic University of America Press, 1992), 283.
8. Mons. Albano Quinn, "Año santo... Reconciliación?," *Prelatura de Sicuani: Boletín Informativo* no. 19 (December, 1975): 4. Biblioteca Nacional del Perú, Sala de Hemeroteca Nacional.
9. Hna. Beatriz Torres, "Convivencia en una comunidad Quechua," *Prelatura de Sicuani: Boletín Informativo* no. 19 (December 1975): 16. Biblioteca Nacional del Perú, Sala de Hemeroteca Nacional.
10. Torres, "Convivencia," 16.
11. Torres, "Convivencia," 16.
12. The Peruvian Conference of Bishops used this term to refer to the social and economic state of the countryside and peasantry in their 1969 declaration on the Velasco regime's Agrarian Reform.
13. Carlos Iván Degregori, *El surgimiento de Sendero Luminoso: Ayacucho, 1969–1979* (Lima, Peru: Instituto de Estudios Peruanos), 32.
14. Nelson Manrique, *¡Usted Fue Aprista! Bases Para Una Historia Crítica Del APRA* (Lima, Peru: Pontifícia Universidad Católica del Perú), 280.

15. *Declaración del episcopado del Perú sobre la ley de reforma agraria, Documenta* 2 (1969), 65. Biblioteca Nacional del Perú, Sala de Hemeroteca Nacional.
16. *Arzobispado de Lima, comunicado official, Documenta* 2 (1969), 45. Biblioteca Nacional del Perú, Sala de Hemeroteca Nacional.
17. Juan Velasco Alvarado, "Message to the Nation on the Agrarian Reform of the Republic of Peru (Lima, June 24, 1969)," trans. Leonore Velfort in *International Journal of Politics* 1 no. 2–3 (1971): 207.
18. Jeffrey Klaiber, *The Catholic Church*, 283.
19. Mons. Albano Quinn Wilson, "Centro de Formación de I.P.A.," *Prelatura de Sicuani: Boletín Informativo*, no. 17 (April–May 1975): 22. Biblioteca Nacional del Perú, Sala de Hemeroteca Nacional.
20. Mons. Mario Gálvez Tío, "La comunidad eclesial y pastoral de las vocaciones sacerdotales," *Pastoral Andina* 7 (March 1975): 4. Biblioteca Nacional del Perú, Sala de Hemeroteca Nacional.
21. "Informe del Consejo de Dirección del IRCEA," *Pastoral Andina* 3 (1974):36, 34–39. Biblioteca Nacional del Perú, Sala de Hemeroteca Nacional.
22. Dionisio Huayhua and Domingo Llanque, "Informe de los delegados del sur-andino en la sesión mundial de la FIMARC. Yaundé, 28 de juli0–6 de agosto de 1974," *Pastoral Andina* (1974): 28, 27–29. Biblioteca Nacional del Perú, Sala de Hemeroteca Nacional.
23. Hna. Juana Connell, M.M., "Cuarta semana pastoral en la Prelatura de Juli, Chucuito 18–22 de Noviembre 1974," *Pastoral Andina* 7 (1974): 10–16, 12. Biblioteca Nacional del Perú, Sala de Hemeroteca Nacional.
24. Ricardo Durand, S.J. "Algunas anotaciones sobre el sínodo de obispos," *Pastoral Andina* 6 (1974): 29. Biblioteca Nacional del Perú, Sala de Hemeroteca Nacional.
25. Marzal would go on to become the founder of the discipline of religious studies in the Peruvian university system. His ethnographic work on Indigenous Catholicism, the growth of evangelical Protestantism, and religiosity throughout Latin America were the first of its kind in the Peruvian academy. He founded the Departamento de Ciencias Religiosas at the Universidad Nacional Mayor de San Marcos in Lima and mentored several generations of scholars of religion.
26. Fr. Juan Hugues, "O.P. Presentación, Allpanchis Phuturinqa," *Revista del Instituto de Pastoral Andina* 1.
27. "Tercera Asamblea Episcopal Regional," *Prelatura de Sicuani: Boletín Informativo* no. 16 (November–December 1974): 18. Biblioteca Nacional del Perú, Sala de Hemeroteca Nacional.

28. "Encuentro sobre salud," *Pastoral Andina* 10 (July–August 1975). Biblioteca Nacional del Perú, Sala de Hemeroteca Nacional.
29. "Programa del IRCEA para 1975: Cursos para animadores cristianos campesinos," *Pastoral Andina* 8, no. 33. Biblioteca Nacional del Perú, Sala de Hemeroteca Nacional.
30. *Pastoral Andina* 3, 29.
31. Leoncio Castillo, "Experiencias: Los campesinos buscan su liberación," *Pastoral Andina* 6, (1974): 20–27. Biblioteca Nacional del Perú, Sala de Hemeroteca Nacional.
32. Carlos Iván Degregori, *El estudio del otro: cambios en los análisis sobre etnicidad en el Perú*, 303–32. In Julio Cotler, ed. *Perú 1964–1994: Economía, sociedad y política* (Lima, peru: Instituto de Estudios Peruanos, 1994).
33. Castillo, *Experiencias*, 26.
34. "Cuarta semana pastoral en la Prelatura de Juli," *Pastoral Andina* 7, 10. Biblioteca Nacional del Perú, Sala de Hemeroteca Nacional.
35. "Voz de un grupo de mujeres campesinas," *Pastoral Andina* 3 (1974): 24–26. Biblioteca Nacional del Perú, Sala de Hemeroteca Nacional.
36. "Voz de un grupo de mujeres campesinas," 24.
37. "Oficiales de la prelatura para el año de 1975, Prelatura de Sicuani," *Boletín Informativo* no. 17 (April-May, 1975): 33. Biblioteca Nacional del Perú, Sala de Hemeroteca Nacional.
38. Castillo, "Experiencias," 26.
39. "El equpo pastoral del vicariato episcopal de Caylloma en 1973, Allpanchis Phuturinqa," *Revista del Instituto de Pastoral Andina* (April 1974): 39. Biblioteca Nacional del Perú, Sala de Hemeroteca Nacional.
40. *Pastoral Andina* 3 (1974): 27
41. "Micronoticias, Prelatura de Sicuani," *Boletín Informativo*, no.15 (September-October 1974): 50. Biblioteca Nacional del Perú, Sala de Hemeroteca Nacional.
42. "Informe del consejo de dirección del IRCEA," *Pastoral Andina* 3 (1974): 35. Biblioteca Nacional del Perú, Sala de Hemeroteca Nacional.
43. Víctor R. Nomberto, http://blog.pucp.edu.pe/blog/victornomberto/2012/11/23/padre-victor-ramos-guija/.
44. "Del Arzobispo del Cusco," *Pastoral Andina* 11 (September 1975): 2. Biblioteca Nacional del Perú, Sala de Hemeroteca Nacional.
45. "Parroquiales Dispachos," *Prelatura de Sicuani: Boletín Informativo*, no.17 (April–May 1975): 21. Biblioteca Nacional del Perú, Sala de Hemeroteca Nacional. In response to ideas such as these, which emanated from the Second Vatican

Council, the Peruvian state and the Catholic church were officially separated in the Constitution of 1979.
46. *Pastoral Andina* 3, (1974): 29. Biblioteca Nacional del Perú, Sala de Hemeroteca Nacional.
47. Sister Gloria Coll, *Pastoral Andina* 3, (1974). Biblioteca Nacional del Perú, Sala de Hemeroteca Nacional.
48. Hna Juana Connell, "Cuarta semana pastoral," 14.
49. Klaiber, *The Catholic Church*, 300.
50. For an excellent study of the internal workings of Sendero Luminoso, see Carlos Iván Degregori, *How Difficult it is to be God: Shining Path's Politics of War in Peru, 1980–1990* (Madison, WI: University of Wisconsin Press, 2012.)
51. Jeffrey Klaiber, "Iglesia, religión y Sendero Luminoso." *Ius et Veritas*, no. 25 (2002): 390–393.
52. Huayhua and Llanque, "Informe de los delegados del sur-andino," 28.

## References

Büschge, Christian, Andrea Müller, and Noah Oehri, ed., *Liberation Theology and the Others: Contextualizing Catholic Activism in 20th Cenutry Latin America.* Lanham, MD: Lexington Books, 2001.

Degregori, Carlos Iván. *El estudio del otro: cambios en los análisis sobre etnicidad en el Perú*, 303–32. In *Perú 1964–1994: Economía, sociedad y política*, edited by Julio Cotler. Lima, Peru: Instituto de Estudios Peruanos, 1994.

Degregori, Carlos Iván. *El surgimiento de Sendero Luminoso: Ayacucho, 1969–1979.* Lima, Peru: Instituto de Estudios Peruanos, 32.

Degregori, Carlos Iván. *How Difficult It Is to Be God: Shining Path's Politics of War in Peru, 1980–1990.* Madison, WI: University of Wisconsin Press, 2012.

Gutiérrez, Gustavo, *Teología de la liberación, perspectivas.* Lima, Peru: Centro de Estudios y Publicaciones, 1971.

Klaiber, Jeffrey. *The Catholic Church in Peru.* Washington, D.C.: The Catholic University of America Press, 1992.

Klaiber, Jeffrey. "Iglesia, religión y Sendero Luminoso." *Ius et Veritas*, no. 25 (2002): 390–93.

Manrique, Nelson. ¡*Usted Fue Aprista! Bases para una historia crítica del APRA.* Lima, Peru: Pontifícia Universidad Católica del Perú.

Rénique, José Luis. *Incendiar la pradera: Un ensayo sobre la revolución en el Perú.* Lima, Peru: La Siniestra ensayos, 2015.

Romero, Catalina, ed., *La diversidad religiosa en el Perú: Miradas multiples.* Lima, Peru: Centro de Estudios y Publicaciones, 2016.

CHAPTER 11

# The *Madres de Plaza de Mayo* in a Chapel of Mendoza

A Church that is Victimizer and Victim, Catholic and Subversive

*ERNESTO FIOCCHETTO*

On March 24, 1976, before 1:00 a.m., the Argentine Armed Forces detained President Elizabeth Martínez de Perón, setting into motion the military dictatorship that lasted until 1983. During that period, also known as the Argentine Dirty War, thousands of criminal acts of state violence were perpetrated against civil society. Many of the victims were young men and women who, after being detained or abducted, became *desaparecidos*. In Argentina, the words "*desaparecer*" (to disappear) and "*desaparecidos*" (the disappeared) are used as euphemisms for the people assassinated by the state during the dictatorship. In many cases, the victims were confined in concentration camps, tortured and executed, or thrown alive into the ocean from military airplanes. A group of mothers started searching for their desaparecidos daughters and sons in the iconic Plaza de Mayo, located in Buenos Aires. They became known as the *Madres de Plaza de Mayo*. Soon, many women throughout the country joined the group, since they were facing the same situation. Mendoza, the country's most important province in the west, was not an exception.

The role of the Catholic Church in Argentina's Dirty War has been broadly addressed in newspapers, TV shows, blogs, political discussions, and academia. The topic is highly popular in the "café conversations" typical among Argentineans. Among the many scholars who have produced historical and sociological works about this period, those who addressed the relationships between church and state show a collaborative relationship between the Catholic Church and the dictatorship.[1] These narratives that shaped the Argentine historical memory of the Dirty War are generally based on opposing binaries, such as victimizers versus victims, Catholic versus subversives, hierarchy versus people, and ruling men versus vulnerable women.

This dichotomy obscures the agency and perspectives of many individuals and oversimplifies the role of both the Church and women. To illustrate this argument, I examine the first meetings of the Madres de Plaza de Mayo in the Chapel of Our Lady of Castelmonte in Godoy Cruz, Mendoza, based on the experience of Maria Dominguez, the current head of Madres de Plaza de Mayo in the province. Maria's story helps to show that the monolithic interpretation of the Church's role during the Dirty War is an oversimplification. The presence of Maria Dominguez and the Madres in an urban chapel of Mendoza created tensions that mirrored the different responses within Catholicism to state terror. Men and women, ruling religious authorities and vulnerable believers, victimizers and victims, and Catholics and subversives are all entangled in her narrative.

My theoretical understanding of religion in this essay is based on the sociological contribution of Danièle Hervieu-Léger, a leading French scholar in the sociology of religion who has been very influential in Latin America. She argues that religion is a way of believing rooted in an authoritative tradition. As Hervieu-Léger sees it, religion is a particular form of meaning construction that unites the believer with others (from the past, present, and future) based on shared tradition—a kind of chain that is an authorized collective memory. Religion is, thus, a "chain of memory."[2]

Moreover, Hervieu-Léger adds that, in contemporary Western societies, legitimization of belief is moving from religious authorities, guarantors of the truth of belief, to individuals themselves, who are responsible for the authenticity of their own spiritual approach.[3] Thus, within Christianity, for example, no single traditional authority legitimizes in an a priori way the religious memories that individuals later accept. Rather, to legitimize their religious beliefs and actions, individuals draw on different "chains of memory," different authoritative traditions that coexist within Christianity. As this essay shows, such "chains of memory" compete with each other to hegemonize their own perspectives as the legitimizing "true memory." Thus, continuing with the example, Christianity becomes a field defined by the struggle between religious memories that appeal to different authoritative traditions to legitimize themselves. Put simply, the Catholic Church in Argentina cannot be understood as a monolithic structure. Instead, for instance, conservative and progressive factions coexist within it, drawing on opposing "chains of memory" to legitimize themselves, their beliefs, and their actions.

The chapter first offers a political and ecclesiastical context of the Dirty War. Second, it narrates the beginnings of Madres de Plaza de Mayo's struggle in Buenos Aires and Mendoza. Third, an in-depth analysis of Maria Dominguez's narrative discloses the contrasting roles of four actors—the Archbishop, a priest, and two contrasting groups of women—around the presence of the Madres in the Chapel of Our Lady of Castelmonte. The last section offers perspectives on the Dirty War in Argentina and the Church's role during that period.

## Political and Ecclesiastical Context

Between 1974 and 1975, Argentina experienced an escalation in politically motivated violence owing to two expressions of Peronism. On the one hand, military forces embodied Peronism's most conservative and fascist wing. On the other hand, left-wing movements largely aligned with Peronism were growing throughout the nation. The left-wing movements became, for conservative Peronism, the enemy to be destroyed to ensure national security. The most well-known group among such leftist movements was Montoneros. As a political-military organization born within Peronism, Montoneros arose in the early 1970s to resist the military dictatorship that was initiated with the military coup d'état known as the Argentine Revolution (1966–1973). The group believed Peronism would make possible the national socialist revolution they envisioned. Peron did return after almost twenty years of exile with the controversial 1973 elections, but to the disappointment of the left-wing Peronists, he took an increasingly right-wing stance.

At that time, the Catholic Church in Latin America was experiencing irreconcilable internal tensions because of differing interpretations of the Second Vatican Council (1962–1965) and its reception within all the layers of the Church. The divergent understandings of what the Council implied for the Church had a tremendous impact on the shape of Latin American Catholicism. Conservative and progressive factions within the Church sought legitimacy through different authoritative traditions. These traditions grounded the construction of diverse and opposing religious "chains of memory" between these factions. The Church was divided by this struggle to determine the legitimate religious memory that would rule Catholicism in Latin America.

While not overly simplifying the analysis, it can be said that two distinct groups of legitimizing memories were at odds within the Argentine religious field at that time. On the one hand, under the umbrella of the theology of liberation, the interpretation of the Second Vatican Council, as conceived by the 1968 Medellín Documents that resulted from the Second Episcopal Conference of Latin American

Bishops, grounded the religious experience of numerous groups in Argentina. This perspective entailed several basic principles, namely "God's preferential option for the poor," the historical human liberation as anticipation of final salvation, a sharp denunciation of capitalism as a structural sin, and the recourse to Marxism as a social-analytical tool. Therefore, religious, social, and political values were highly connected via praxis, and consequently, that was a time of exceptional youth lay activism. Despite being a secular movement, Montoneros were among those groups that claimed this legitimizing religious memory. The movement structured its ideology with a mixture of the Peronist doctrine, elements of the revolutionary Latin American Marxism, and strong Catholic influences, especially of the Movement of Priests for the Third World—an immediate antecedent of the theology of liberation—and its Argentinean branch, the theology of the people.

On the other hand, the right-wing response of Argentine Catholicism to the secularizing advance of liberalism and socialism since the 1920s involved the rejection of modernity, the organicist conception of society, and the supremacy of religious over secular values. In the 1960s, this integralist Catholic Nationalism also sought to integrate the social, political, religious, public, and private spheres and to advance over society and the state. This legitimizing tradition framed the reception of the Second Vatican Council and the 1968 Medellin Documents as a a challenge to the authoritative religious memory of a Catholic country by mixing atheist-communism with the sacred Catholic doctrine. Thus, the most conservative sectors of the Church supported and blessed the anti-communist struggle. This right-wing Catholic tradition sought conciliation with authoritarian and violent regimes based on a dogmatic, elitist conception and a privileged relationship with the Armed Forces. Within this framework, Catholicism was imbricated in national identity, and the defense of the nation implied the defense of Catholicism, and vice versa.[4]

These two divergent authoritative traditions reflected opposing "chains of memory."[5] The Argentine bishops had raised great expectations of unity with Peron's return to the government in 1973. However, mirroring the division within Peronism and entangled with it, diverse sectors of the Church hoped that the new political situation would create optimum conditions for their particular ecclesiastical perspectives. Each sector embodied and included Peronism in their legitimation narratives: some believed that Peron would lead the country toward Christian Socialism, while others saw Peronism as a genuine secular representation of Catholic Nationalism.

The escalation of politically motivated violence between 1974 and 1976 exacerbated the split within Argentine Catholicism to the point of paroxysm. The church reflected the tensions between secular left-wing and right-wing Peronism. However, Perón's stance on such conflicting perspectives was largely unknown to both sides. Peron himself clarified the situation on Labor Day, May 1, 1974, when he "excommunicated" the Peronist Youth and Montoneros from his movement, together with the revolutionary wing. After that day, progressive sectors, both in the Church and in society, were especially vulnerable. Due to Peron's rejection, the Catholic left-wing gradually lost power within the political arena and, consequently, within conservative and powerful ecclesiastical structures as well.

When Juan Domingo Peron died on July 1, 1974, his wife and vice-president, Maria Estela Martínez de Peron, succeeded him. She rapidly lost political power in a deteriorating political and social climate. This power vacuum resulted in the increasing participation of military officials that had belonged to Peron's inner circle. Soon, they took control of the state apparatus and militarized the governance of the country.

Montoneros and other leftist groups isolated themselves, started to operate clandestinely, and perpetrated a diverse range of politico-military actions to maintain their bases. They led guerrilla and insurgency groups and conducted terrorist attacks on civilians. In response, presidential decree 261—signed in February 1975—ordered the Army to neutralize through annihilation the actions of the subversive elements within the society. The Argentine Anticommunist Alliance—Triple A—was responsible for implementing the "annihilation decrees." The Triple A was an extreme-rightist para-police terrorist organization created by sectors of Peronism, unionism, the Federal Police, and the Armed Forces. They assassinated artists, intellectuals, politicians, students, unionists, and thousands of civilians.[6]

The increasing political violence was the justification for overthrowing the democratic government. It was March 24, 1976, when the military forces detained President Martínez de Peron before 1:00 a.m. General Jorge Rafael Videla, Admiral Emilio Eduardo Massera, and Brigadier Orlando Ramón Agosti formed the military junta. The military coup pretended to respond to the needs of Argentine society and, at the same time, embodied the United States' interests: a "Process of National Reorganization" was necessary to control a chaotic state and exterminate the guerrillas. With the coup, the Dirty War began in the country as part of Operation Condor, a United States–backed campaign involving intelligence to eradicate communist influence and ideas from Latin America.[7] That military dictatorship was the bloodiest state terrorism and repression Argentine people ever experienced.

## The Catholic Church during the Dirty War

The question about the role of the Catholic Church in Argentina's Dirty War is widely discussed in the country. Most of the meaningful historical and sociological works on such issues show a collaborative relationship between the Catholic Church and the dictatorship through the construction of "true memories" based on opposing binaries, such as victims versus victimizers, Catholic versus subversives, hierarchy versus people, and ruling men versus vulnerable women.[8] Thus, for many authors, the institutional Church is considered complicit in the military government's actions and, therefore, the victimizer. For instance, Horacio Verbitsky, a recognized authority on the history of the Church in Argentina, argues that "the church hierarchy was willing to cooperate with the military power and rejected the horizontal intrusion of the lower levels. The most notable members of the Episcopate explicitly adhere to the government."[9]

In these perspectives, the opposing binaries are clear: on the one hand, the Catholic hierarchy, constituted exclusively by ruling men, cooperates with the *de facto* government and is consequently among the victimizers or perpetrators of violence. On the other hand, the lower levels of the Church that the hierarchy rejected and the military persecuted, including the *Madres* themselves, are the victims because they were considered subversives. Narratives that construct these opposing categories can erase the agency of some actors or conceptualize that action as part of the binary. Thus, those laypersons collaborating with the regime become victimizers through things like their membership in a high-conservative class or allegiance to Catholic Nationalism. Such a dichotomy excludes those bishops who are not counted among "the most notable members of the Episcopate" from the "institutional church." Hence, the construction of legitimizing "true memories" of the bishops labeled as subversives who were persecuted and assassinated are configured from the perspective of the victims and, therefore, are somehow excluded from the "institutional church." Either they are Catholic bishops, ruling men belonging to the victimizer hierarchy, or they are subversives, religious men, and, thus, vulnerable victims. The oversimplification of the opposing binaries hides other histories.

The responses to the country's situation by the top layer of the Catholic Church were contradictory. Part of the Episcopate explicitly supported the Armed Forces and their "crusade" to defend the nation from atheist communism. Other bishops, such as Eduardo Pironio and Alberto Devoto, were persecuted and threatened for their perspectives close to the 1968 Medellin Documents, and Enrique Angelelli, whom Pope Francis declared a martyr for the faith in 2018 and beatified in 2019, was assassinated for his commitment to the poor.[10] A third group ignored the situation and remained silent in the face of the atrocities. The official stance of the church hierarchy prioritized maintaining the appearance of unity within the episcopal ranks. This resulted in an official silence that was very close to complicity with the violence of the armed forces. In fact, unlike other Latin American bishops, the Argentine Bishops' Conference failed to create a framework that protected victims or documented alleged abuses.[11] Even though some of the members of the Episcopate, as individuals, confronted state terror in their sermons and other public pronouncements, the official response of the Church, as a whole, was silence.

The contradictions within the Church hierarchy existed within the larger church body. Some bishops, priests, religious sisters and brothers, and laypeople collaborated with the military regime, elaborated blacklists, and were complicit in assassinations, disappearances, and other crimes. Other members of these ecclesiastical layers welcomed the episcopal silence and remained quiet out of fear or ignorance. And yet other bishops, priests, religious sisters and brothers, and laypeople risked their lives by opposing the violence, and many of them were persecuted, tortured, disappeared, and assassinated. The story of the *Madres de Plaza de Mayo* illustrates these contradictions, even when their official story depicts the Church as complicit in the military government.[12]

## The Madres of the Desaparecidos

The state terror perpetrated by the dictatorial government took thousands of lives. In their plan to end guerrilla activity, the Junta mainly targeted unionists, students, and anyone involved in activist groups. However, they soon broadened their aggressions to the general population by arbitrarily defining the categories of "illegal," "left-wing," "subversive," and "terrorist": "To Videla, a terrorist was not defined as someone who threw grenades, but anyone who opposed 'western, Christian values.'"[13] The Military Junta imposed a plan to eliminate popular participation in political issues. Communiqué number nineteen, issued on the first day of the Argentina Coup, reads as follows:

> People are advised that the Junta of General Commanders has decided that any person who by any means broadcasts, disseminates, or propagates communiqués or images from illicit associations or individuals or groups notoriously devoted to subversive or terrorist activities shall be punished by indefinite imprisonment.[14]

State violence became an increasingly "normal" political practice. As a result, thousands of Argentine citizens were included in the lists of suspected terrorists and were taken into custody. Most of them were abducted and became desaparecidos. The number of victims started to increase. Most of them were young men and women. Thus began the Madres' struggle.

In the hope that the power structure of the Church would help them, a group of Madres met in the Military Vicarship to request an interview with bishop Emilio Grasselli, the military chaplain. Azucena Villaflor de Vicenti was there, and she claimed: "Individually, we'll get nothing. Why don't we all go to the Plaza de Mayo? When Videla sees that we are many women, he will have to receive us."[15] That same day, April 30, 1977, fourteen mothers started the collective action. It was a Saturday, and the square was empty. They decided to meet again the following Friday. New mothers joined during the first meetings, and after three or four weeks, they were more than three hundred.

In the third meeting, they decided to gather on Thursdays from 3:30 to 4:00 p.m. rather than on Fridays because this was a time in which the Plaza de Mayo was generally crowded, and the group needed more visibility. The *Madres* stood next to the May Pyramid, the oldest national monument in the city of Buenos Aires. The police officers who guarded the square told them to walk in rows of two because groups of three or more individuals were forbidden in the street. Thus, the Thursday marches were born. They agreed to wear a white headscarf to recognize one another and make themselves visible. In the beginning, the scarf was made with the fabric of the diapers that were common in those times. Such headscarves were a powerful symbol of their disappeared sons and daughters and, ultimately, the sign of the *Madres* worldwide. They still continue to walk in rows of two with their white headscarf every single Thursday in Plaza de Mayo.

In addition to the Thursday marches, many of the Madres met in other places to plan strategies and public announcements. Some Madres found refuge in Catholic churches. Such was the case of Azucena Villaflor De Vincenti, Esther Ballestrino de Careaga, and Maria Ponce de Bianco, the first *Madres desaparecidas*. They took part in a group that met in the Church of the Holy Cross in the neighborhood of San Cristobal, situated in the capital city. Between December 8 and 10, they were abducted along with nine other members of the religious group, which included two French nuns.

## The Madres and Tensions in a Mendoza Chapel: Maria Dominguez's Narrative

The divide within the ecclesiastical body is evident throughout the early stages of the Madres de Plaza de Mayo in Mendoza, a province situated at the foot of the Andes, whose capital is the most important city of the Argentine west. The different narratives I found about the organization's early history in the province all refer to the same place: the Chapel of Our Lady of Castelmonte in Godoy Cruz, one of the most populated cities in the urban area of Mendoza. Among many other testimonies, the judicial decision of the third trial for crimes against humanity in Mendoza reads:

> This committee [of the Madres] worked toward the case of their family members, and they met in the Church of Castelmonte, where the family Camín arrived due to the disappearance of Armando Camín's brother and nephew.[16]

To engage a personal experience of this early moment in the organization's presence in the region, I interviewed Maria Dominguez. Maria is the current head of the Madres in the province and embodies the Madres' struggle from their first moments. She represents the living testimony of a story and a search that has shaped the memory of Argentina. Her gaze reveals the pain of the frustrated hopes of finding her son more than three decades after the military took him away. Her words reveal the strength of a woman who, through her pain and sorrow, has understood that the struggle goes beyond her own son because it involves the collective memory of a country and, therefore, its future.

During the interview, Maria recounted how her son Walter Dominguez, aged twenty-two, and his six-months-pregnant wife, Gladys Castro, aged twenty-four, were abducted from their home on the night of December 9, 1977. Her narrative is heartrending. That night, Maria's life changed forever. The following Monday, the parents of the two young desaparecidos presented a Habeas Corpus that proved to be utterly useless. At that moment, the search began. Maria started alone because she "thought [she] was the only one who was facing this problem." She traveled to Buenos Aires because she found a "little paper under the door of [her] house" that advised her to do so. As soon as she arrived, she started a search that led her to many places in Buenos Aires.

> Someone told me about the Church Stella Maris, which belonged to the Navy. There, Mons. Grasselli received me. When I asked him about my daughter-in-law and the baby, he told me that I shouldn't worry because they treated pregnant women right. And it was the same everywhere: in the bishoprics, the embassies, the prisons.... I went to every single place they told me I should go. And nothing.

In Mendoza, the Church mirrored the ecclesiastical conflict at a national level. Tensions appeared both in the hierarchies and at the bases. When they initiated their search, the *Madres* conceived of the Church as a possible source of help. Such expectations, however, were most often frustrated. The other religions, according to Maria, did nothing. "The only Church from which we expected something was the Catholic. The others, no. Nobody even approached us."

Many months passed after the night when Walter was abducted and disappeared. After the first frustrating attempts to find information about her son in Buenos Aires, back in Mendoza, Maria Dominguez was contacted by other women who were in the same situation and wanted to join forces to search for their desaparecidos daughters and sons. The place for the meetings was an issue in itself because as soon as they started to search for their sons and daughters, they started to be persecuted. Maria narrated these first steps of the Madres in Mendoza as follows:

> We arrived in Castelmonte thanks to two Madres: Elsa de Becerra, who was our president, and Clelia Daziano. Clelia belonged to a group of women, I mean, a space for single mothers.... Both of them were related to the Church because they belonged to the Catholic Action. Clelia was a very committed religious militant until her last moments. She helped a lot.

> She obtained a place at the Church of Castelmonte because the priest was French. Truly, I don't remember his name. They obtained the place through him because the Church of Castelmonte had a big room at the end. We met there every Saturday. All the mothers went there; the mothers of the detained-disappeared and the mothers of those declared imprisoned by the National Executive Power. We didn't have a place to meet because, before that, we had been meeting in Urquiza Street, in a very small room that belonged to the Argentine League for Human Rights. But one day, these sirs [the military] entered and put explosives inside, and then, they denounced the League as if the explosives were the League's. . . .
>
> Thus, we didn't have a place to meet, so Clelia obtained that place. We went there every Saturday afternoon. We were around sixty or seventy people there. Soon, the Ladies of Catholic Action learned who we were. And it seems that they complained and asked the priest why he allowed us to be there if we were the "terrorists' mothers." And he asked us for the place back. And thus, again, we didn't have a place where to meet.
>
> But the priest was very good to us. We had a very good relationship with him. He asked us for the place back because of these other women.

When I asked her if she remembered the name or information of any of those women, Maria answered:

> No. Because we didn't see them. We were there on Saturdays, and maybe they came to the afternoon mass. We never saw them. But we learned what had happened through the priest. They had complained to him, and he . . . you can imagine . . . he was not going to stand against those women.

These events occurred between 1980 and 1982. Maria does not remember the exact dates because "we didn't register anything. We never thought we would have to struggle for the rest of our lives." The issue of where to meet was solved in 1982 when, during a gathering for human rights in Peru, they obtained a place that they used for many years. However, by that time, "We had obtained the *Plaza*. . . . We met at the *Plaza* every Thursday and continue doing so up to the present day." The Plaza that María refers to is Plaza San Martin, located in Mendoza downtown. There, every Thursday at 11 a.m., many women wearing white scarves over their heads still march in rows of two, reminding us all of a history that is alive in the memory of a people.

## The Actors around the Meetings in Castelmonte: Beyond Dichotomies

Maria's narrative about those first meetings in the Chapel of Our Lady of Castelmonte shows how the Madres' presence in that religious place created tensions that reflect diverse Catholic responses during the Argentine Dirty War. It is worth noting that the name of the priest of Castelmonte did not appear either in the interview I conducted with Maria or in many other Madres' documents and interviews. It is as if there remains a pact of silence to protect those who were willing to put their own lives in danger to help the Madres.

In those times, the Chapel of Our Lady of Castelmonte belonged to the Parish of Our Lady of Carrodilla and was served by the Oblates of Mary Immaculate.[17] Based on my research in the Historical Archive of the Archdiocese of Mendoza, Fr. Pablo Chabanon is the "French Priest" whom Maria Dominguez refers to in her narrative. The priests of his congregation that were in Mendoza at the time of my research indicated that Fr. Pablo died in 2001. He spent the last years of his life with mental issues. According to the little data about Fr. Pablo in the archive, he was a beloved and significant person in his community. Maria Dominguez also has a positive memory of him. In another interview, she said: "The Pastor there was French, and he risked himself for us and the cause. It was very complicated for him."[18] The reasons for the complications Maria mentions are twofold and are related to the actors that play different roles in relation to the meetings in Castelmonte.

On the one hand, the complications came "from above." The intransigence of Mons. Maresma regarding the Madres is significant. Like many of his episcopal colleagues, he rejected any help or support for the Madres. Maria judges the bishop's half-hearted response, apathy, and silence as "complicity":

> There was much complicity. There was much complicity between trade unionists, professors who elaborated blacklists at the

universities, and people in the Church as well. The ecclesiastical hierarchy has been complicit in the military dictatorship. Here, once we started to meet, the first thing we did was go to the archbishopric. And what did Mons. Maresma tell us?: "Don't waste gunpowder in *chimangos*."[19] That was his answer.

On the other hand, the complications came "from below." A group of "Ladies of Catholic Action" complained that the priest was concealing the "terrorists' mothers." That group of women was another actor who played a crucial role in this story. Part of the laity/faithful also opposed the Madres' struggle and their actions within the Church. Unfortunately, no record of the Ladies of Catholic Action or its members exists.[20] The names of those women might have been lost forever since, as Maria's narrative attests, they were older than the Madres and have surely passed away. However, their position against the Madres is still highly significant.

Maria's interview shows the tensions and contradictions between the four actors in her narrative, including Archbishop Olimpo Maresma, the priest Pablo Chabanon, the Ladies of Catholic Action, and Elsa de Becerra, Clelia Dazaino, and other Madres who met in the chapel. These actors' roles in the early stages of the Madres de Plaza de Mayo in Mendoza cannot be conflated into opposing binaries. Victims and victimizers, Catholics and subversives, hierarchy and people, ruling men and vulnerable women are all entangled in her narrative.

Within the hierarchical structure of the Church, the positions of the two ruling men, namely the archbishop and the priest, are manifestly in opposition. While the priest opened the chapel doors to the Madres and suffered the complaints of the Ladies of Catholic Action, the bishop refused to help and dismissed the Madres. While a group of women was vulnerable before Mons. Maresma, the other group of laywomen was powerful enough to pressure Fr. Chabanon to throw the "terrorists' mothers" out of the chapel. The situation cannot be explained in terms of the difference in status between the archbishop and the priest. Indeed, in other dioceses, the situation within the hierarchy was precisely the other way around. For instance, in La Rioja, a province located north of Mendoza, Bishop Angelelli advocated an "option for the poor," in which the Church actively struggled for freedom and justice based on the liberation theology and the perspectives set forth by the Second Vatican Council and the documents from the 1968 Bishop's Conference in Medellín, considered by many to be the *magna carta* of liberation theology.[21] While he was manifestly critical of the military government that jeopardized personal freedoms and perpetrated violent crimes, many priests in his diocese opposed his position and collaborated with the dictatorship. In that case, the story of conspiracies between some priests, conservative sectors of Catholicism, and the political-military power resulted in the assassination of Bishop Angelelli.

The juxtaposed roles of women in the narrative are highly significant. According to Maria Dominguez, both the "ladies" of the chapel and some of the Madres took part in the same Catholic institution, namely the Catholic Action. However, these two groups of women embodied different perspectives regarding religion and the sociopolitical situation of the country. On the one hand, the Madres Elsa de Bacerra and Clelia Dazaino "were related to the Church because they belonged to the Catholic Action. Clelia was a very committed religious militant until her last moments." Clelia embodied the new model of a woman rooted in the legitimizing religious memory constructed by the Specialized Catholic Action following the Belgian and French theological perspectives.[22]

Such a model left the traditional female roles as defined by conservative Catholicism: the woman as a biologically different being who is spiritually superior, and therefore, religious, and whose role implies domesticity linked to marriage, motherhood, and production of lineage. Instead, the Specialized Catholic Action proposed a female ideal that involved social and political participation, equality of rights, access to university and science, and a different way of living the religious experience based on the conciliar ideal of commitment to the world. Indeed, Celia was socially and politically committed before she started the search for her disappeared son, Hugo Enrique Fornies. Within the Church, she helped in "a space for single mothers." The negative connotations of the stigma of unwed motherhood among the Church's conservative sectors contrast Celia's religious values and pastoral action.

On the other hand, the "Ladies of Catholic Action" embodied the opposite traditional model. Following Italian and Spanish theological perspectives, the General Catholic Action had arrived in Argentina during the thirties and had strengthened during the forties and fifties. They formed the Christian Democracy and championed Catholic Nationalism. They preached a model of a woman that was centered on motherhood and home. Even when they took part in the same Catholic initiative as Clelia and Elsa, namely, Catholic Action, these "Ladies" conceived of politics as a no-female space, because the space for women was home. Maria remembered that these women said that the Madres "should have cared for their children so that they would not have suffered what they suffered." The conception of the Church as the religious place for women, who are the spiritual and religious element of the home, led them to reject any political action within the religious institution. A group of "terrorist mothers," who had not observed their Catholic duties and, consequently, were in such a situation, could not be readily accepted in a healthy Catholic community.

The four actors made visible in Maria Dominguez's interview challenged the narratives that analyze the role of Catholicism during the Dirty War based on opposing binaries. The split and contradictions throughout all the layers of the Catholic Church show that binary simplifications hide the agency and perspectives of many individuals. Beyond such ecclesiastical split and contradictions, diverse theologies, views of the role of women within church and society, political stances, and understandings of Church and nation were at stake. Differing religious memories compete for legitimacy, complicating the categories of men, women, hierarchy, laypeople, Catholics, subversives, victims, and victimizers in in the process. They show the complexity of different Catholicisms within Catholicism.

Maria has never found her disappeared son, but she continues her search together with hundreds of Madres. At the end of August 2016, a thirty-seven-year-old woman confirmed through genetic testing that she was Walter Dominguez and Gladys Castro's daughter. She was born in captivity and became the 117th recovered grandchild. After thirty-eight years of her son's abduction, Maria Dominguez met her granddaughter for the first time.

The history of the Madres de Plaza de Mayo is long and complex. The interview with Maria illustrates how the Madres' presence in the Chapel of Our Lady of Castelmonte created tensions at different levels and, thus, disclosed the different catholicisms that produced diverse responses within Catholicism during one of the bloodiest periods of Argentine history. The actors that play different and contrasting roles in this story show the complexity of the Catholic Church. A conservative bishop refused to help and support the Madres. A priest risked himself so that they would have a place to meet. A group of "Ladies of Catholic Action" succeeded in driving the Madres out of the chapel when they confronted the priest by suggesting that he was hiding the "terrorists' mothers." Two Madres, committed religious militants until their last moments, searched tirelessly for their desaparecidos.

Maria Dominguez's interview shows that it is inadequate to analyze history from the perspective of opposing binaries, and that Argentine Catholicism is not a monolithic structure without contradictions. Such an oversimplification hides the complexity of the Argentine society and Church, manifested in the construction of diverse and contrasting religious memories that compete for legitimacy. The experience and words of Maria Dominguez challenge such narratives and show a broad spectrum of perspectives at all layers of the Church, whose split and contradictions go beyond any simplification. Maria shows a Church comprised of men and women who could be ruling religious authorities or vulnerable believers. Her story depicts a Church that is, at the same time, victimizer and victim, Catholic and subversive.

## Notes

1. Emilio Fermín Mignone, "Iglesia y dictadura: La experiencia argentina." *Nueva Sociedad*, no. 82 (1986): 121–28; Horacio Verbitsky, *La mano izquierda de dios: La última dictadura, 1976–1983* (Buenos Aires: Ed. Sudamericana vol. 4, Historia Política de La Iglesia Católica, 2010).
2. Danièle Hervieu-Léger, *Religion as a Chain of Memory* (New Brunswick, NJ: Rutgers University Press, 2000), 82.
3. Hervieu-Léger, "In Search of Certainties: The Paradoxes of Religiosity in Societies of High Modernity," *The Hedgehog Review* 8, no. 1–2 (March 22, 2006): 61–62.
4. Mignone, *Iglesia y Dictadura*, 127–29; Mario I. Aguilar, *Pope Francis: His Life and Thought*, 1st ed. (The Lutterworth Press, 2014), 62–65.
5. Virginia Dominella discusses how the vocation for the political intervention of such different factions of Catholicism had a common matrix: integral Catholicism. She argues that this particular structuring of the Argentine religious field helps to understand why Argentine Catholics rarely developed autonomous political forces. On the contrary, they developed positive affinities with diverse political options, as in the case of Peronism. See: Virginia Dominella, *Catolicismo y política en Argentina en los años '60 y '70: Apuntes sobre las implicancias políticas del aggiornamento eclesial y la opción por el peronismo* (VII Jornadas de Sociología de la UNLP, (La Plata, Provincia de Buenos Aires, Argentina: Memoria Académica, 2012), 22.
6. Marguerite Guzman Bouvard, *Revolutionizing Motherhood: The Mothers of the Plaza De Mayo, Latin American Silhouettes* (Wilmington, Del: Scholarly Resources Inc, 1994), 19–23; Aguilar, *Pope Francis*, 65–6.
7. David Sheinin, *Argentina and the United States: An Alliance Contained, The United States and the Americas* (Athens: University of Georgia Press, 2006).
8. Mignone, *Iglesia y Dictadura*; Bouvard, *Revolutionizing Motherhood*; Verbitsky, *La Mano Izquierda De Dios*.
9. Verbitsky, *La Mano Izquierda De Dios*, vol. 4, loc. 64.

10. Ernesto Fiocchetto, "Eduardo Pironio: Un Hombre Fiel a su Hora," in *Obispos de la Patria Grande: Pastores, Profetas y Mártires*, ed. Ana María Bidegaín (Bogotá, D.C., Colombia: Consejo Episcopal Latinoamericano CELAM, 2018), 71–102; Cynthia Folquer, "A Orillas del Tapocó: Alberto Devoto, Obispo de Goya (Corrientes, Argentina)," in *Obispos de la Patria Grande: Pastores, Profetas y Mártires*, ed. Ana María Bidegaín (Bogotá, D.C., Colombia: Consejo Episcopal Latinoamericano CELAM, 2018), 207–37; Fortunato Mallimaci, "Monseñor Angelelli, Catolicismo Intransigente y Opción por y con el Mundo de los Pobres," in *Obispos de la Patria Grande: Pastores, Profetas y Mártires*, ed. Ana María Bidegaín (Bogotá, D.C., Colombia: Consejo Episcopal Latinoamericano CELAM, 2018), 341–73.
11. Gustavo Morello, *The Catholic Church and Argentina's Dirty War* (Oxford: Oxford University Press, 2019), loc. 215.
12. Asociación Madres de Plaza de Mayo, "La historia de las Madres, Madres de Plaza de Mayo," accessed September 2, 2022, https://madres.org/index.php/la-historia-de-las-madres/.
13. Asociación Madres de Plaza de Mayo, "Argentina's History and The Dirty War," (Madres de Plaza de Mayo, October 1, 2012).
14. Junta de Comandantes and en Jefe de las Fuerzas Armadas, *Comunicado N° 19* (March 24, 1976) https://www.educ.ar/recursos/129056/comunicado-n-19-de-la-junta-de-comandantes-en-jefe-de-las-fu/download/inline. (The author's translation)
15. Azucena Villaflor de Vicenti, *Diario de Mar de Ajó* (July 13, 2005) http://www.diariomardeajo.com.ar/AzucenaVillaflor.htm. (The author's translation)
16. Tribunal Oral en lo Criminal Federal N° 1 de Mendoza, Fundamentos del Fallo del Tercer Juicio por Crímenes contra la Humanidad en Mendoza, Sr. Juez de Cámara Dr. Juan Antonio González Macías (Tribunal Oral en lo Criminal Federal N° 1 de Mendoza 2013). (The author's translation)
17. Consequently, Archbishop Mons. Olimpo Maresma was responsible for the appointment of the Pastor of the Parish, but the appointment of the priests who would work in each chapel was made according to the internal rules of the Oblates. Therefore, there is no official decree in the Historical Archive of the Archdiocese of Mendoza with the appointment of the priest in question.

  Two unofficial documents elaborated by members of the community disclose the name of the priest. The archive conserves a "History of the Chapel of Our Lady of Castelmonte." It is only three pages long and was written in a very familiar language. It is not signed or dated, but the data show that it was produced no before 1992. The document reads: "In 1967 our Fr. Pablo arrived and is still with us. . . . We can see that this community, which was very small in the beginning, slowly grew and became a large community. Thus, we can appreciate the work of our oblate Fr. Pablo, who, after arriving in a little chapel, now finds himself within a true community of Christian believers.

    The document does not mention the family name of the priest who is tenderly called by the anonymous writer "our Fr. Pablo" and "our Oblate Fr. Pablo." In a letter written by the community in 1999 to Mons. Arancibia, they asked the bishop to consider the possibility of creating the Parish of Our Lady of Catelmonte. The letter reads, "We feel urged due to the community necessity of spiritual, moral, and personal care through the pastoral work of a priest. For 33 years, we received the testimony of the true vocation of Fr. Pablo Chabanon. . . ."

18. Trade Union of Educational Workers. *Madres: lucha, verdad, esperanza y justicia* (November 20, 2010), http://www.sute.com.ar/Noticias.asp?id=412 (author's translation).
19. The chimangos are a type of hawk that is completely useless because their feathers or meat are not good for consumption. Therefore, the popular saying "Don't waste gunpowder in chimangos" means that a person should not waste energy, time, or money on something or someone that is not important.
20. In the Archdiocesan Historical Archive, there are no traces of this small group of women from the chapel. Besides, the Church of Our Lady of Castelmonte has not an archive that goes beyond the mandatory files of episcopal decrees and documents.
21. Renata Keller, "The Martyrdom of Monseñor Angelelli," *Journal of Religion and Society* 12 (2010: 23).
22. Ana María Bidegaín, "El cristianismo y el cambio socio político de las mujeres latinoamericanas," *Sociedad y Religión* XXIV, no. 42, (October 2014): 160–93.

# References

Aguilar, Mario I. *Pope Francis: His Life and Thought.* 1st ed. The Lutterworth Press, 2014. https://doi.org/10.2307/j.ctt1cgdz3p.

Bidegaín, Ana María. "El cristianismo y el cambio socio político de las mujeres latinoamericanas." *Sociedad y Religión* XXIV, no. 42 (October 2014): 160–93.

Bouvard, Marguerite Guzman. *Revolutionizing Motherhood: The Mothers of the Plaza De Mayo.* Latin American Silhouettes. Wilmington, DE: Scholarly Resources Inc, 1994.

Dominella, Virginia. "Catolicismo y política en Argentina en los años '60 y '70: Apuntes sobre las implicancias políticas del aggiornamento eclesial y la opción por el peronismo," 22. La Plata, Provincia de Buenos Aires, Argentina: Memoria Académica, 2012. https://www.memoria.fahce.unlp.edu.ar/trab_eventos/ev.1840/ev.1840.pdf.

Fiocchetto, Ernesto. "Eduardo Pironio: Un hombre fiel a su hora." In *Obispos de la Patria Grande: Pastores, Profetas y Mártires*, edited by Ana María Bidegaín, 71–102. Bogotá, D.C., Colombia: Consejo Episcopal Latinoamericano CELAM, 2018.

Folquer, Cynthia. "A orillas del Tapocó: Alberto Devoto, Obispo de Goya (Corrientes, Argentina)." In *Obispos de la Patria Grande: Pastores, Profetas y Mártires*, edited by Ana María Bidegaín, 207–37. Bogotá, D.C., Colombia: Consejo Episcopal Latinoamericano CELAM, 2018.

Hervieu-Léger, Danièle. "In Search of Certainties: The Paradoxes of Religiosity in Societies of High Modernity." *The Hedgehog Review* 8, no. 1–2 (March 22, 2006): 59–69.

Hervieu-Léger, Danièle. *Religion as a Chain of Memory*. New Brunswick, NJ: Rutgers University Press, 2000.

Keller, Renata. "The Martyrdom of Monseñor Angelelli." *Journal of Religion and Society* 12 (2010): 21.

Mallimaci, Fortunato. "Monseñor Angelelli, Catolicismo Intransigente y Opción por y con el Mundo de los Pobres." In *Obispos de la Patria Grande: Pastores, Profetas y Mártires*, edited by Ana María Bidegaín, 341–73. Bogotá, D.C., Colombia: Consejo Episcopal Latinoamericano CELAM, 2018.

Mignone, Emilio Fermín. "Iglesia y dictadura: La experiencia argentina." *Nueva Sociedad*, no. 82 (1986): 121–28.

Morello, Gustavo. *The Catholic Church and Argentina's Dirty War*. Oxford: Oxford University Press, 2019.

Sheinin, David. *Argentina and the United States: An Alliance Contained*. The United States and the Americas. Athens: University of Georgia Press, 2006.

Verbitsky, Horacio. *La mano izquierda de dios: La última dictadura, 1976–1983*. Vol. 4. Historia Política de La Iglesia Católica. Buenos Aires: Ed. Sudamericana, 2010.

CHAPTER 12

# From Gang Leaders to Church Leaders

Masculine Ideals among Peruvian Criminals Converting to Pentecostalism

*VÉRONIQUE LECAROS*

In Peru, criminals leaving gangs for Pentecostal churches tend to be attracted to churches that are conservative and demanding. Pentecostal pastors work to rehabilitate ex-gang members through born-again-type conversions, which stress a radical change of life through strict obedience to their rules.[1] Ex-criminals who become church leaders capitalize on their past by presenting spectacular testimonies of conversions. While these testimonies prove attractive to their former incarcerated peers, they raise many questions about their underlying Pauline-type model of conversion. Existing scholarship is not able to explain why many convicts, after giving strong testimonies, leave churches and return to gangs.

In what follows, I explore why convicted criminals in Peru are so attracted to Pentecostal churches. I argue that, beyond certain spiritual, social and/or material advantages that conversion affords, convicted criminals who convert in prison relate easily to Pentecostal churches because of a deep connection between their previous gang ethos and their new church ethos. A similar worldview, with several related facets discussed below, enables relatively easy transitions from criminal gangs to church communities. Core ideals are no doubt redefined through conversion but are nevertheless often based on similar parameters, including social hierarchies, a certain deference to authority (divine and human), and a masculine ideal of machismo. Though gang leaders turn from the power of guns to the power of God, as church leaders, they continue to rule their community and family, proving once again to be a respected and, to a certain extent, untouchable and privileged human being. Beyond the obvious transformation involved in a religious conversion in jail, there remains a core of strongly rooted beliefs and patterns of behaviors.

This essay will first examine the living conditions in jail and the role played by churches. Then it will turn to the structures of authority in church communities, representations of masculinity, and conceptions of God's power, examining how they parallel ideologies and hierarchical structures of gang life.

This chapter is based on a 2019–2020 research project (made possible by a Jack Shand Research Grant) on the Piura jail in northern Peru. I interviewed local authorities (the director and people in charge of security), psychologists, lawyers and twelve prisoners (among them, five church members and seven not involved in Pentecostal churches). Participant observation in religious services, both Catholic and Evangelical, enabled me to hold casual conversations that often proved more revealing than formal interviews. Outside of the jail, I also interviewed pastors, leaders and ex-inmates, as well as six female family members of prisoners and ex-prisoners. Taken together, I interviewed a total of thirty people. For the purpose of this chapter, I also make use of previous research done in Limenian jails and on conversion of Catholics to Pentecostal churches.[2]

## Surviving in Jail

Located in the suburbs of Piura, a medium size city in northern Peru, E. P. Piura (Establecimiento Penitenciario Piura, or "Piura Penitentiary Institute") was built in 1995 for 1370 inmates and, as of 2020, holds 4,000 men. The overcrowding and collapsing infrastructure of E. P. Piura is typical for Latin American jails, where inmates endure very harsh conditions. Thirty people are often living in cells designed for eight people.

The official and formal aims of prisons are to prevent the development of criminality by deterrence and to pave the way for the social reintegration of delinquents.[3] Although Peru's Instituto Nacional Penitenciario (or "INPE")—the national administrative institution in charge of the country's many prisons—maintains that reintegration is the objective of imprisonment, the available resources fall short of the official purpose.[4] No educational classes or degrees are offered in Peruvian prisons. Although participation in workshops and psychological sessions are taken into account for reduced sentences, such resources are only available in a very limited way. Only 25 percent of inmates are able to participate in workshops, and, to do so, they generally have to bribe prison authorities. Four part-time psychologists attend four thousand inmates.

While safe reintegration is an official goal of the INPE, for most people in Peru, prisons are simply a way of reducing crime by expelling criminals from society.

Indeed, the choice of language used by the E. P. Piura director reflects this sentiment well. The director describes the prison as a "human dumping ground."[5]

As most interviewees attest, corruption is rampant in the prison. Inmates see it every day. However, corruption also happens in more intricate and subtle ways that may not be readily apparent to those in jail. There also exist complex relations between government officials, INPE staff, inmates, and the criminal world. To illustrate this more intricate level of corruption, the political scientist Francisco Durand has developed a theory that divides Peruvian society into three levels that cohabit and work together: the "formal," the "informal," and the "illegal."[6] In jail, contrary to official discourses and objectives, informal and illegal patterns dominate. Inmates described exactions perpetrated by INPE officials in an environment where the law of the strongest prevails.

Apart from its official objective, the jail is, in fact, run by unofficial rules that enable prisoners to survive and INPE staff to raise some extra income. Prisoners face a number of financial obligations. Among them, they have to pay for a mattress, compensate for paltry food portions, and assume family financial obligations. Additionally, INPE staff ask for "tips" from inmates whenever possible. Faced with financial pressures, and to compensate for their many deprivations, prisoners have developed an informal economy, such as found in shanty towns, from which most of them originate.[7] While formal education is not part of their upbringing, they have learned how to survive in adverse situations. Andrew Johnson describes Rio's prisons as "favelas behind bars"; the same can be said about E. P. Piura and E. P. Lurigancho, another prison located on the outskirts of Lima.[8]

Illegal mechanisms, as understood by Durand, are also at work in jail. As in many other Latin American countries,[9] huge quantities of drugs enter the premises, likely with INPE complicity. Several interviewees mentioned the wide availability of drugs in jail, and the E. P. Piura director suggests that 85 percent of inmates consume drugs and that drugs sedate them. To a certain extent, illegal drug use helps to create more submissive inmates.

Cellphones and some weapons also enter the premises, probably through similar channels. They are used to plan felonies from inside jail.[10] Cellphones keep the boundaries between the jail and the external world porous, so much so that conflicts in jail may involve settling scores both inside and outside of the jail.

Durand's tripartite theory of the formal, the informal, and the illegal underscores how behaviors at all three levels are interwoven, contributing to a status quo that violates human rights and forces inmates to survive in harsh conditions. It is an entangled system with ramifications in the external criminal world.

Both in Peru and in Latin America more broadly, prisons are considered "universities of crime."[11] In fact, 25 percent of Peruvian inmates boast more than one stay in prison.[12] To survive in such surroundings, one has to assimilate criminal habits and behaviors. Like most prison systems, the Peruvian one, in Michel Foucault's words, "fails apparently without missing its aim"; that is, it helps "recruit high level delinquents."[13]

In this threatening surrounding, an isolated inmate is in danger. Inmates thus form close-knit bands that are ruled, in a hierarchical and authoritarian way, by powerful, charismatic, and often ruthless leaders. As Byron Johnson has argued, the formation of gangs as a means of protection from penitentiary staff and violent inmates is part of prison culture worldwide.[14] In their studies of Argentinian and Mexican jails, Algranti and Velvet Romero add that leaders are constantly challenged by associates who contest their authority.[15] Gangs also often provide much needed income for struggling inmates.

## Churches in the Jail Inferno

In this context of vulnerability and necessity, churches play an important role as independent and officially recognized entities. Churches are often perceived as corruption-free and, as such, are respected institutions.[16] Either through formal conventions such as the one signed between INPE and the Catholic Church or through more informal relationships, as is the case with other denominations, most religious institutions develop pastoral activities within prisons.

The Catholic Church organizes sporadic celebrations of the Mass in E. P. Piura. Catholic pastoral programs in jail mainly rely on volunteers.[17] In E. P. Piura, lay volunteers (mostly well-intentioned women, over sixty years old) visit prisoners twice a week. Some nuns give workshops and motivational talks but not on a regular basis. These pastoral programs depend entirely on the initiative, availability, and capacity of nuns and volunteers. Because of the lack of coordination, these programs tend to be fragmented. Although Catholic outreach efforts do bring solace to some distressed prisoners, the overall effectiveness of these programs is limited.[18]

Pentecostal outreach efforts, however, are much more widespread and focused in their intentions. They aim to save inmates through born-again type conversions, which involve the adoption of a very strict disciplines and habits. From the prisoners' point of view, conversion points to an utterly radical change: no drugs, no alcohol, no robbery, sex only within marriage, money only earned through jobs, and so on.

In E. P. Piura, two churches have developed programs and are actively present: the *Movimiento Misionero Mundial* (The Worldwide Missionary Movement, or MMM) and *Iglesia de Dios de la Profecia* (The Church of God of Prophecy, or IDP). The MMM members are less numerous (with around thirty to forty people). I shall mainly focus on the IDP, an omnipresent church in E. P. Piura.

The IDP (which claims over 30,000 members nationwide) has a very active jail ministry, especially in northern Peru. Pastor William Mainsa, an ex-convict, is in charge of the jail ministry. Within the prison itself, IDP boasts 300 members, 150 disciples, and 50 "listeners," or men with some interest. The IDP has formed a "local church" inside jail. A Colombian inmate, Oscar Caicedo, convicted of drug-trafficking and sentenced to seventeen years in prison, is an ordained pastor. As he mentioned to me with pride, his name is included in the church's official list in the US "state of Carolina" (he did not specify it this North or South Carolina). Besides Caicedo, two leaders from each unit are responsible for the IDP activities.

By strictly organizing prisoners' space and time, IDP creates an invisible barrier to protect its members from the temptation of drugs, idleness, and easy money that pervades the premises. IDP also strives to give new orientation to its members and create hope for successfully reshaped lives.[19]

Within each unit's patio, a special space has been allotted for religious services. Members have painted these spaces afresh, decorating them with Bible verses. A special emphasis is given to the IDP Church's "ladder of spiritual evolution," which encourages adherents to progress from listener to pastor. Services are held every morning. During the day, church members are expected to work and study the Bible. At night, members regroup inside cells in order to "speak about God and the Bible." Interviewees have repeatedly mentioned the essential role played by the community in helping them to withstand, without aggressively reacting to the insults, rebuffs, and sarcastic remarks of their fellow inmates. The sectarian stance of the community is reinforced by visible signs of belonging. The dress code includes clean clothes, shoes, pants, and shirts. Members are also asked to carry their Bible everywhere.[20]

The IDP offers a visible, viable, and desirable alternative to criminality. Pastors and leaders in charge of the pastoral project are ex-inmates. They provide credible models of the changes one may undergo through conversion. They speak the language of prisoners and understand their challenges. Moreover, members may succeed in being promoted in the church structure, from a listener without commitment to a member, then a leader, and, eventually, a pastor. The IDP gives its members access to religious formation. Consequently, most inmates who were interviewed consider their stay in jail as a time of formation designed by God to prepare them for missionary labor and for their personal salvation.

In these supportive and yet severe surroundings, inmates have an opportunity to develop a valuable and rewarding identity.[21] By assuming the born-again perspective, church members build a new story about themselves.[22] Because Pentecostals enjoy a reputation of honesty, ex-inmates become credible and may look for reintegration in the society. Their church membership becomes a sort of certificate of good conduct.

By reading their conversion along those lines, church members, as well as scholars researching the topic, focus on the radical transformation it implies. However, while changes are obvious and should not be minimized, we must also consider the continuities that these outward changes can hide. This is especially important for understanding the fragile and potentially dangerous features of such conversion.

## Church Communities: Gangs among Others?

Beyond the spectacular transformation already analyzed, we must also attend to the core beliefs and patterns of behavior that remain unchanged as one transitions from gang leader to Church leader.

Inside the jail, the IDP community functions in ways that are similar to how gangs operate in the prison. In both cases, close-knit groups are formed under the leadership of a "strong man."[23] The leader must be familiar with the jail rules and unofficial ways of transgressing them. He must also create alliances with the INPE and other groups inside and outside of prison. Unlike other "strong men," religious leaders benefit from the official recognition of the IDP Church, a highly respected external institution, which confirms them as legitimate and authoritative leaders.

In E. P. Piura, Pastor Caicedo represents a clear example of a respected leader. Apart from having a physically strong appearance and enjoying the prestige of the pastoral ordination from a US-based church, he has successfully formed clientelist bonds with INPE and has established a profitable makeshift cafeteria. Moreover, Pastor Caicedo has displayed his authority by thwarting attacks against himself and his belongings. In this surrounding, the prestige related with religion does not fully exonerate the community leader from challenges to one's authority. The legitimacy of pastors is based not only on church recognition, but also on their capacity to demonstrate bravery and charisma as leaders.

Although most scholars have not directly discussed the possible similarities between gangs and church communities inside jails, scholars do discuss the way church communities are used by inmates as an alternative group to protect themselves against violent exploitations from fellow inmates. Along those lines, specialists contest the genuineness of many conversions in jail.[24] If inmates can use church communities as an alternative to a gang, then it logically follows that there are similarities between both types of groups, even though they may not be readily apparent. From this perspective, Algranti's comments on the conversion of criminal "strong men" into religious members/leaders is revealing.[25] Even if they have to make sacrifices in terms of lifestyle, the transition comes naturally because of the similar structure involved in both types of groups. As criminal strong men, they have to prove their bravery and leadership. They tend to be admired and envied and, thus, have to withstand constant challenges from competitors. Conversion, in this perspective, appears as a form of secure retirement, capitalizing on previous exceptional deeds.

In many criminal gangs, commitment and obedience are obtained by threat and violence.[26] In Peru—and in Piura, in particular—methods are not typically brutal but compliance to the orders is still the rule. Beyond obvious differences, the styles of leadership among gangs and churches share this emphasis on obedience. The church community functions in a hierarchical and authoritarian way. In E. P. Lurigancho, in the cell converted to a small temple of the IDP Church, a posted panel explicitly states ten rules that the members have to follow. Apart from requiring compliance with the dress code and attendance at church activities, the Church Decalogue mentions the commandment of obedience twice: "Comply with the orders given by the authorities enforced by God; ask for permission for everything." If a member fails to comply, he is excluded from the community. To reintegrate, he has to sleep on the floor by the community dorm for a week. In E. P. Piura, the same holds true.

Most followers hope for a promotion and dream of becoming a leader. The criteria for becoming a leader are not clearly specified, but the obedience and faithfulness of the candidate, as well as his personal charisma, are key. Ultimately, these characteristics help to maintain community cohesion and reinforce existing hierarchies in the prison.

Once released from prison, the gap between being a leader involved in jail pastoral programs and being a full-fledged pastor in well-established churches is not easy to bridge. Because of the stigma attached to their past, many ex-convicts often encounter subtle limitations that prevent them from reaching their aim outside of jail. Some of them end up in charge of a temple in a kind of outpost position, such as a violent suburb or a more rural area. Others try to build their own individual church. They start by inviting family, neighbors, and friends to their house or to an improvised temple, hoping that their followers will eventually grow in number. In the Pentecostal and neo-Pentecostal movement, independent churches are proliferating in Latin America. In Peru, such churches are opening opportunities for leaders who are, in the Weberian sense, "charismatic" and who have no formal theological training.

Certainly, there are obvious differences between criminal gangs and Christian communities. Most interviewees have referred to the "peace" they have found in religious services, in particular, or in religious communities, in general. However, what remains similar are the rules related to blind obedience and some of the general goals. While ex-inmates may change habits (drug consumption, among others), they keep others, particularly those related to the dynamics of human relationships.

## Masculinity: Domination of Another Sort?

As Andrew Johnson makes clear, conceptions of masculinity are often rampant in prison culture. Johnson writes that "masculinity plays an important part of prison subculture in both the gang-controlled cells and the Pentecostal cells."[27] In both arenas, masculinity is a central topic.[28]

Many scholars have addressed this topic in the context of Latin America,[29] and Elizabeth Brusco's work on machismo has been especially influential.[30] Brusco identifies two conflicting valences of the concept. In gangs, an exceptionally strong version of machismo prevails, one that is characterized by "aggression, violence, pride, self-indulgence and an individualistic orientation in the public sphere." In contrast, Pentecostal conversion implies a reshaping of masculine ideals toward "peace seeking, humility, self-restraint, and a collective orientation and identity within the Church and the home."

Brusco tends to contrast the two, often suggesting an overhaul of masculine ideals. However, a closer scrutiny reveals that appearances hide a deeper form of underlying continuity. Accordingly, Norma Fuller's work on masculinity is more suited to this particular case. Fuller contrasts two types of masculinities:

"perverse" masculinity, which may be assimilated to the gang ideals of manhood, and "virtuous" masculinity, which would be closer to the Pentecostal ideals.[31] For Fuller, the perverse version that enhances physical forces and sexuality, as well as transgression, corresponds to the archetypes of the warrior or the macho. Meanwhile, the virtuous version would be closer to the patriarch who cares for his family and for his dependents.[32] In making the transformation across these two types, ideals are inverted, yet, most crucially, the worldview is not deeply shaken. Although they may do it in a different way and not with the same people, men still dominate (or hope to do so).[33] In both, men are also expected to express bravery through transgression, whether in the form of violent individual acts, or in the form of religious sacrifice for the sake of one's family. In both cases, men define themselves in contrast to what is perceived as women's weakness and emotional fragility. This logic also serves to shun homosexuals for their perceived "feminine" qualities.[34]

At the surface level, conspicuous signs of individual change can often elide questions of masculinity and deeper forms of transformation. After all, converted inmates participate in highly emotional Pentecostal services where they express feelings and shed tears, an attitude usually associated with women. However, this should not be interpreted as a sign of an entirely new "alternative" masculinity.

Instead, my hypothesis here is that masculinist ideals are reoriented but not fundamentally redefined. Among other places, this is seen in the fact that church members call each other "man of God" ("varón de Dios"). Two words in Spanish translate as man: "hombre," which can also signal a human being in general, and "varón," which refers specifically to a male. By using "varón", the gender is stressed.

The qualities related to bravery and heroism are strongly associated with masculinity.[35] Within this framework, the harsh discipline required from church members is not a deterrent. On the contrary—it represents a valiant challenge to prove one's bravery. Masculine force is corroborated not by muscles or guns, but rather, by self-dominion. Pastor Caicedo relates with pride that when his wife was sick, he stayed kneeling for two and a half hours, begging to God for her health. As he recounts, "The guards and his fellow-inmates were astonished." Such displays of spiritual discipline replace other violent acts of bravado, allowing convicted criminals to prove their virility in other ways. In short, to be respected, a Pentecostal must prove his resilience through prayers, fasting, and abstinence from drugs and sex.

These "new" forms of conversion continue to maintain a strong masculinist tinge, which often tends to debase women. In Peru, and in Latin America more generally, some of the worst insults are related to the domination that husbands fail to extend over their wives.[36] On one hand, churches can help mitigate and, in the words of Elizabeth Brusco, help "tame" men who are carelessly and destructively macho. Within church frameworks, men are transformed into breadwinners, responsible for the well-being of their entire family. A major objective of the IDP Church, for example, is the "restoration of families," which implies a reassessment and reinforcement of family bonds. Under the church's canopy, men are encouraged to support family members. On the other hand, however, the "taming" mentioned by Brusco is largely limited to the domestic sphere. Most husbands, in accordance with the church's teaching, keep tight control of their wives. Pedro, an ex-convict, describes the relationship with his wife this way: "Where I go, she is with me so as not to sin, drug me or [allow me to] go with [other] women, because she knows how men are. . . . She takes great care of me and of the house. She [makes sure I go] to church so as not to relapse." While it is true that Pedro's wife serves as an important influence on him, it should be equally clear that Pedro continues to dominate her. He controls her money and public life, and he does not allow her to interact with other men.

This patriarchal stance is characteristic of most Pentecostal and neo-Pentecostal Latin American churches, particularly those associated with jails. As scholars widely recognize, many passages of the Bible are often interpreted literally to justify and buttress an unequal perspective on gender relations.[37] Pastors in Peru tend to stick to literalist readings of the Bible. Indeed, the North American evangelical perspective on masculinity and femininity, with its special emphasis on "submissive wives," has helped to buttress Latin American gender biases. Outside of jails, the IDP, following its North American foundations, offers courses on "Virility at its Best" ("Hombría al maximo"), which celebrates submissive wives. Their syllabus follows the North American program.

## Subservient Subjects Under the Power of an Almighty God

In the jails that I visited, "converted" inmates rely heavily on an image of God as an almighty Being who guarantees order in the world by judging people's actions.[38] Many interviewees refer to their delinquent and drug-addicted past in terms of "sin," "disobedience," and "fragility." In contrast, as converts they feel "shielded" by God's "strength." They describe God as a "savior," a "liberator," and an operator of "miracles." Most respondents speak of moments of theophany in dreams and visions. The omnipotent and omnipresent power of God is mentioned repeatedly, as if nothing could be done successfully without the help of God. As Da Costa and colleagues explain in their study of Uruguayan prisons, this appeal to miraculous interventions is prevalent among believers and church members in prison.[39]

This perception of an all-knowing benevolent God involved in all of the minute challenges of one's daily life is shared by most Peruvians and Latin Americans, albeit with some differences across contexts.[40] When analyzing interviews of Latin American respondents living in poverty, Gustavo Morello notes the persistent reference to a good and powerful God. "The contemporary image of God is that of a superhuman power with a human face. The emphasis is in the proximity. God is a reachable entity."[41] This conception of God is shared by Catholics and Pentecostals alike, and it raises several vexing questions: How do converted inmates interpret God's role in their past? Could one become estranged from God's shield? Does God punish?

Interviewees never use the word punishment; instead, they prefer to think of their imprisonment (and sufferings) as an ordeal designed to lead them to a change of life. Felipe, an ex-convict, who still participates in church life, mentions a common saying in E. P. Piura and Peruvian jails in general: "When the Lord wants to enter into your life, He has three ways: death, hospital or jail." His fellow inmates would add: "You were lucky, you had the mild way because death is irreversible, and diseases may leave you crippled." Though God's methods may be severe, God is still perceived as loving and caring, because God's ultimate purpose remains salvation.

However, salvation is not always guaranteed. If a conversion and a change of life do not happen, the consequences may be dire. God is conceived of as behaving as an omnipotent, and at times frightening, judge who keeps count of our actions. As a Peruvian saying states, "God takes time but never forgets."[42] Evangelists' proselytism often includes both direct and veiled threats of hell and suffering, language that inmates can easily comprehend. Several Catholic volunteers use the same method. As one volunteer bluntly puts it, "To force a reaction, I tell them that if they do not come back to God, they are going to roast in hell." As a result, many convicts describe their inner self as a battleground between devil's temptations and God's power, hoping that God will finally give them the strength to defeat the devil.

Curiously, many church members do not spontaneously express remorse for damage caused to others. There may be several motives for this attitude. Some scholars observe that most criminals kill in self-defense in gang wars. Byron Johnson also explains that convicts tend to justify themselves through external reasons related to the global lack of justice; they portray themselves as victims of an unfair and oppressive society.[43] However, another motive related to this worldview usually comes out in individuals' interviews: the sentiment that "we are paying" for what we have done. Following this line of thought, prisoners accept the harsh conditions they experience in prison as a logical consequence of their actions in keeping with predominant societal norms and perspectives. Even though God (through the church) brings hope of redemption, justice remains retributive. According to another popular Peruvian saying, "In this life, everything has to be paid"; ill actions are paid for by suffering. In this manner, convicts perceive that their stay in jail will definitively erase their debt to both society and their victims.

These representations of church leaders, masculinity, and God are not entirely separable. Rather, they form a coherent whole that helps to make sense of suffering, gives meaning to life, and offers an orientation for action. This coherent whole may be understood as a "social imaginary," which Gustavo Morello defines as a "collective mental tool that combines ideas, representations, beliefs, and practices instituted by a given social group in order to figure out the way in which that group understands itself, its location and interactions with the world."[44] In the context of Peruvian prisons, the image of an authoritarian God who uses violent means to reestablish order helps to justify pastors' own severe leadership style and husbands' stiff control of their wives.

In many respects, most interviewees envision God in light of the traits of an ideal church leader who protects his subjects and provides them with goods. Both God and church leaders impose rule and do not hesitate to cast out disobedient people. Furthermore, church leaders often identify God with patriarchal attitudes, owing to their literal readings of the Bible.[45] This said, feminist theologians rightly point out that such patriarchal conception do not do full justice to the text. Many biblical passages, especially those dealing with God's mercy, tend in fact to associate God with a feminine figure, especially a mother tenderly taking care of her baby, namely Israel. The word mercy in Hebrew, *rahamim*, also means womb. And yet, Pentecostal pastors tend not to focus on God's mercy; on the contrary, their favorite way to refer to God is as God of Hosts (i.e., "God of Armies"), who destroys his enemies without pity. In this light, God is the epitome of a certain virility characterized by strength, bravery, and determination.[46] This image of God helps to justify the authoritarian and, at times, harsh actions of church leaders.

# Conclusion

In Piura, the transition from convicts and drug addicts to dedicated Pentecostals represents a spectacular life transformation. But the social imaginary of these men—especially core beliefs related to God, justice, and masculinity—remains largely, if not fundamentally, unchanged. In both contexts, power is exerted in an authoritarian way and is justified by a conception of God as an omnipotent and masculine Being in charge of reestablishing order by keeping count of all our deeds.

Considering the many deficiencies of penitentiary institutions, Pentecostal churches are, without a doubt, performing a highly valuable task in helping to bring hundreds of convicts out of delinquency. However, the permanence of an authoritarian "social imaginary" may help explain why conversions are often so fragile and why the guidance of Pentecostal churches does not always serve as a viable bulwark against violence and crime. Among the respondents in this study, most narrate how they have oscillated for years between religion and delinquency. Authoritarian social imaginaries facilitate the transit both ways.

A different pathway has yet to be tried in Peru: one based on God's mercy and corresponding practices of restorative justice. Such an approach would likely contribute to more lasting forms of conversion through the development of empathy for others.[47] In the long run, this perspective would need to entail a fundamental rethinking of the purpose and organization of incarceration. Should prison be a human dumping ground that stresses retributive justice, or should it be approached a pathway toward reintegration and restoration? The latter would only be feasible through concrete changes in the social imaginary of Peruvian culture. As the ongoing conversation about the reintroduction of the death penalty in the country shows, the public does not yet seem prepared to give new opportunities to criminals. Some Peruvian groups, most of them associated with Jesuit spiritual centers or with historically Protestant churches, work along the lines of restorative justice, but they represent a tiny minority and lack influence on a more widespread social level.

## Notes

1. Helena Hansen, *Addicted to Christ. Remaking Men in Puerto Rican Pentecostal Drug Ministries* (Berkeley: University of California Press, 2018); Kevin O'Neill, *Secure the Soul. Christian Piety and Gang Prevention in Guatemala* (Berkeley: University of California Press, 2015); Edward Orozco, *God's Gangs, Barrio Ministry, Masculinity and Gang Recovery* (New York: New York University Press, 2014); Robert Brenneman, *Homies Hermanos, God and gangs in Central America* (Oxford: Oxford University Press, 2011).
2. Véronique Lecaros, *Fe cristiana y secularización en el Perú de hoy* (Lima: Prensas Universitarias, Universidad Antonio Ruiz de Montoya, 2018); Véronique Lecaros, "Conversion as a safe-way out of crime in Peru," In *Lived Religion, Conversion and Recovery*, ed. Srdjan Sremac and Ines Jindra (New York: Springer Publishing, 2020), 187–213.
3. Marcelo Bergman, *More Money, More Crime; Prosperity and Rising Crime in Latin America* (Oxford: Oxford University Press, 2018), 279.
4. Lucia Nuñovero, "Las razones y los sentimientos del encierro: consideraciones político económicas acerca del aumento de las poblaciones penitenciarias en el Perú," in *Pensar las cárceles de América Latina*, ed. Chloé Constant (Lima: IEP, IFEA, PUCP, 2016), 232.
5. See Jonathan Rosen and Martin Brienen, *Prisons in the Americas in the Twenty-First Century: A Human Dumping Ground* (New York: Lexington Books, 2015).
6. Francisco Durand, *El Perú fracturado, formalidad, informalidad y economía delictiva* (Lima: Fondo editorial del Congreso del Perú, 2007), 43; Francisco Durand, "El que puede puede: dinámicas informales e ilegales en los espacios rurales," in *El problema agrario en debate/ Sepia XVI*, ed. Francisco Durand, Jaime Urrutia and Carmen Yon, (Lima: Sepia, 2016), 21–86.
7. Lecaros, *Fe cristiana y secularización*, 164; Lecaros, "Conversion as a safe-way"; Chloé Constant, "Delincuencia y justicia en el Perú urbano: desigualdades frente al riesgo de encierro carcelario," in *Pensar las cárceles de América Latina*, ed. Chloé Constant (Lima: IEP, IFEA, PUCP, 2016), 251–74; Bergman, *More Money, More Crime*.
8. Andrew Johnson, *If I Give My Soul, Faith Behind Bars in Rio de Janeiro* (Oxford: Oxford University Press, 2017), 59.
9. Marín et al., "Adicciones, Disciplinamiento y pentecostalismo carcelario en Chile: reflexiones para iniciar un debate," *Sociedad y Religión* 27, no. 48 (2016).
10. Bergman, *More Money, More Crime*.

11. José Luis Pérez Guadalupe, *Faites y atorrantes, una etnografía del penal de Lurigancho* (Lima: Centro de Investigaciones Teológicas, 1994), 137; Lecaros, "Conversion as a Safe-Way"; Bergman, *More Money, More Crime*, 299.
12. Instituto Nacional Penitenciario (INPE), https://www.gob.pe/instituto-nacional-penitenciario, accessed 3/25/2020.
13. Michel Foucault, *Surveiller et punir, naissance de la prison* (Paris: Gallimard, 1975), 281–307.
14. Byron Johnson, *More God, Less Crime* (Conshohocken: Templeton Press, 2011), 125.
15. Joaquin Algranti, "The Making of an Evangelical Prison: Study on Neo-Pentecostalism and its Leadership Processes in the Argentine Penitentiary System," *Social Compass*, 65, no. 5, (2018); Velvet Romero, "De mamás, chequeras y borregas: la construcción de jerarquías a partir de masculinidades dominantes, cómplices y subordinadas," in *Pensar las cárceles de América Latina*, ed. Chloé Constant, (Lima: IEP, IFEA, PUCP, 2016).
16. Lecaros, *Fe cristiana y secularización*, 92.
17. Nestor Da Costa et al., *Fe entre rejas* (Montevideo: Fundación entre todos, 2013).
18. In other jails (E. P. Lurigancho: program ANDA, among others) and in some violent districts (El Agustino in Lima: father Chiqui, among others), some Catholic initiatives are noteworthy and have yielded some good results of transformation and reintegration. However, there are few of them and most of them are limited in scope.
19. Lecaros, "Conversion as a Safe-Way."
20. Johnson, *If I Give my Soul*, 100.
21. Axel Honneth, *The Struggle for Recognition, The Moral Grammar of Social Conflict* (Cambridge: Polity, 1995); Véronique Lecaros, *La conversión al evangelismo* (Lima: Prensas Universitarias PUCP, 2016); Lecaros, *Fe cristiana y secularización*, 164; Lecaros, "Conversion as a Safe-Way."
22. Nancy Ammerman, *Sacred Stories, Spiritual Tribes* (Oxford: Oxford University Press, 2014); Danièle Hervieu-Léger, *Le pèlerin et le converti, la religion en mouvement* (Paris: Flammarion, 1999); Lecaros, *Fe cristiana y secularización*; Lecaros, "Conversion as a Safe-Way,"
23. Algranti, "The Making of an Evangelical Prison."
24. Algranti, "The making of an evangelical prison,"; Irene Becci, "European Research on Religious Diversity as a Factor in the Rehabilitation of Prisoners: An Introduction," in *Religious Diversity in the European Prisons*, ed. Irene Becci and Olivier Roy (Switzerland: Springer International Publishing, 2015).
25. Algranti, "The Making of an Evangelical Prison."

26. Bergman, *More Money, More Crime.*
27. Andrew Johnson, *If I Give My Soul*, 109.
28. José Luis Pérez Guadalupe, *La construcción social de la realidad carcelaria* (Lima: Fondo Editorial Pontificia Universidad Católica del Perú, 2000); Johnson, *More God, Less Crime*, 125; Edward Orozco, *God's Gangs.*
29. Orozco, *God's Gangs*, 113; Hansen, *Addicted to Christ*, 92; Johnson, *If I Give My Soul*, 111.
30. Elizabeth Brusco, *The Reformation of Machismo: Evangelical Conversion and Gender in Colombia* (Austin: University of Texas Press, 1995).
31. Norma Fuller, "Masculinidad desafiada," in *Difícil ser hombre, nuevas masculinidades latinoamericanas*, ed. Norma Fuller (Lima: PUCP, 2018).
32. Norma Fuller, "Repensando el machismo latinoamericano," in *Masculinities and Social Change* 1, no. 2 (2012): 128.
33. Pierre Bourdieu, *La domination masculine* (Paris: Seuil, 1998); Fuller, "Repensando el machismo," Norma Fuller, "La conversación entre amigos y la constitución de la identidad masculina entre varones urbanos del Perú," in *Deconstruyendo la masculinidad, cultura, genero e identidad*, ed. Joan Sanfélix, Javier Martínez, and Anastasia Téllez (Valencia: Tirant Humanidades, 2019).
34. Homosexuality remains one of the major stigmas. Timoteo, a pastor ex-convict and ex-transvestite converted in jail, considers himself a "living testimony" of God's power. Speaking about his "sinful" ("pecaminosa") life, he cites indifferently homosexuality, drug addiction, and drug dealing, all of them sins of similar magnitude for him. While he gives a special emphasis to his "previous homosexuality," he also mentions with pride that he has procreated five children with his wife.
35. Fuller, *Repensando el machismo.*
36. Some examples of insults include calling a man "saco largo" (long jacket, i.e., a jacket similar to a dress) or saying that "his wife wears the pants."
37. Wilda Gafney, *Womanist Midrash* (Louisville: Westmister, John Knox Press, 2017).
38. Véronique Lecaros, "¿Dios castigador, Dios juez o Dios amado?, Imágenes de Dios en medios católicos y pentecostales peruanos," *Horizonte, Belo Horizonte* 15, no. 46, (2017).
39. Da Costa et al, *Fe entre rejas.*
40. Véronique Lecaros, "Les oxymores religieux latino-américains, Étude sur l'enchantement et les processus de sécularisation au Pérou," *Social Compass* 55, no. 3 (2020).
41. Gustavo Morello, "Latin America's Contemporary Religious Imaginary," 100.

42. Lecaros, "Dios castigador, Dios juez o Dios amado?"
43. Johnson, *More God, Less Crime*, 129.
44. Morello, "Latin America's Contemporary Religious Imaginary," 89.
45. Alice Dermience, "Théologie de la Femme et théologie féministe," *Revue Théologique de Louvain* 31, (2000); Elizabeth Johnson, *She Who Is* (New York: The Crossroad Publishing Company, 2002).
46. Lecaros, *La conversión al evangelismo*; Lecaros, "Dios castigador, Dios juez o Dios amado?"
47. Johnson, *More God, Less Crime*.

## References

Ammerman, Nancy. *Sacred Stories, Spiritual Tribes: Finding Religion in Everyday Life*. Oxford: Oxford University Press, 2014.

Algranti, Joaquin, and Rodolfo Brardinelli. "Contra el principio de excepcionalidad. Reflexiones sobre las creencias en condiciones de encierro." *Sociedad y religión* 27, no. 48 (2017): 176–90.

Algranti, Joaquin. "The Making of an Evangelical Prison: Study on Neo-Pentecostalism and its Leadership Processes in the Argentine Penitentiary System." *Social Compass* 65, no. 5 (2018): 549–65.

Becci, Irene. "European Research on Religious Diversity as a Factor in the Rehabilitation of Prisoners: An Introduction." In *Religious Diversity in the European Prisons*, edited by Irene Becci and Olivier Roy, 1–11. Switzerland: Springer International Publishing, 2015.

Bergman, Marcelo. *More Money, More Crime: Prosperity and Rising Crime in Latin America*. Oxford: Oxford University Press, 2018.

Bourdieu, Pierre. *La domination masculine*. Paris: Seuil, 1998.

Brenneman, Robert. *Homies Hermanos: God and Gangs in Central America*. Oxford: Oxford University Press, 2011.

Brusco, Elizabeth. *The Reformation of Machismo: Evangelical Conversion and Gender in Colombia*. Austin: University of Texas Press, 1995.

Constant, Chloé. "Delincuencia y justicia en el Perú urbano: desigualdades frente al riesgo de encierro carcelario." In *Pensar las cárceles de América Latina*, edited by Chloé Constant, 251–74. Lima: IEP, IFEA, PUCP. 2016.

Dermience, Alice. "Théologie de la Femme et théologie féministe." *Revue Théologique de Louvain* 31 (2000): 492–523.
Da Costa, Nestor, Fernando Ordoñez, and José Techera. *Fe entre rejas*. Montevideo: Fundación entre todos, 2013.
Durand, Francisco. *El Perú fracturado, formalidad, informalidad y economía delictiva*. Lima: Fondo editorial del Congreso del Perú, 2007.
Durand Francisco. "El que puede puede: dinámicas informales e ilegales en los espacios rurales." In *El problema agrario en debate/ Sepia XVI*, edited by Francisco Durand, Jaime Urrutia and Carmen Yon, 21–86. Lima: Sepia. 2016.
Foucault, Michel. *Surveiller et punir, naissance de la prison*. Paris: Gallimard, 1975.
Fuller, Norma. "Repensando el machismo latinoamericano." *Masculinities and Social Change* 1 no. 2 (2012):114–33.
Fuller, Norma. "Masculinidad desafiada." In *Difícil ser hombre, nuevas masculinidades latinoamericanas*, edited by Norma Fuller. Lima: PUCP. 2018.
Fuller, Norma. "La conversación entre amigos y la constitución de la identidad masculina entre varones urbanos del Perú." In *Deconstruyendo la masculinidad, cultura, genero e identidad*, edited by Joan Sanfélix, Javier Martínez and Anastasia Téllez, 51–68. Valencia: Tirant Humanidades, 2019.
Gafney, Wilda. *Womanist Midrash*. Louisville: Westminster, John Knox Press, 2017.
Hansen, Helena. *Addicted to Christ: Remaking Men in Puerto Rican Pentecostal Drug Ministries*. Berkeley: University of California Press, 2018.
Hervieu-Léger, Danièle. *Le pèlerin et le converti, la religion en mouvement*. Paris: Flammarion, 1999.
Honneth, Axel. *The Struggle for Recognition: The Moral Grammar of Social Conflict*. Cambridge: Polity, 1995.
Iglesia de Dios de La Profecia, https://iglesiadediosprofecia.org/historia/, accessed March 25, 2020.
Instituto Nacional Penitenciario (INPE), https://www.gob.pe/instituto-nacional-penitenciario, accessed 3/25/2020.
Johnson, Andrew. *If I Give My Soul: Faith Behind Bars in Rio de Janeiro*. Oxford: Oxford University Press, 2017.
Johnson, Byron. *More God, Less Crime*. Conshohocken: Templeton Press, 2011.
Johnson, Elizabeth. *She Who Is*. New York: Crossroad, 2002.
Lecaros, Véronique. *La conversión al evangelismo*. Lima: Prensas Universitarias PUCP, 2016.

Lecaros, Véronique. "Dios castigador, Dios juez o Dios amado?: Imágenes de Dios en medios católicos y pentecostales peruanos." *Horizonte, Belo Horizonte* 15 no. 46 (2017): 557–605.

Lecaros, Véronique. *Fe cristiana y secularización en el Perú de hoy.* Lima: Prensas Universitarias, Universidad Antonio Ruiz de Montoya, 2018.

Lecaros, Véronique. "Conversion as a safe-way out of crime in Peru." In *Lived Religion, Conversion and Recovery,* edited by Srdjan Sremac and Ines Jindra, 187–213. New York: Springer Publishing, 2020.

Lecaros, Véronique. "Les oxymores religieux latino-américains. Étude sur l'enchantement et les processus de sécularisation au Pérou." *Social Compass* 67, no. 3 (2020): 304–16.

Marín, Nelson, and Luis Bahamondes. "Adicciones, disciplinamiento y pentecostalismo carcelario en Chile: reflexiones para iniciar un debate." *Sociedad y religión* 27, no. 48 (2017): 214–36.

Morello, Gustavo. "Latin America's Contemporary Religious Imaginary," *Social Imaginaries* 4, no. 2 (2018): 87–106.

Nuñovero, Lucia. "Las razones y los sentimientos del encierro: consideraciones político económicas acerca del aumento de las poblaciones penitenciarias en el Perú." In *Pensar las cárceles de América Latina,* edited by Chloé Constant, 231–250. Lima: IEP, IFEA, PUCP, 2016.

Orozco, Edward. *God's Gangs: Barrio Ministry, Masculinity and Gang Recovery.* New York: New York University Press, 2014.

O'Neill, Kevin. *Secure the Soul: Christian Piety and Gang Prevention in Guatemala.* Berkeley: University of California Press. 2015.

Pérez Guadalupe, José Luis. *Faites y atorrantes, una etnografía del penal de Lurigancho.* Lima: Centro de Investigaciones Teológicas, 1994.

Pérez Guadalupe, José Luis. *La construcción social de la realidad carcelaria.* Lima: Fondo Editorial Pontificia Universidad Católica del Perú, 2000.

Romero, Velvet. "De mamás, chequeras y borregas: la construcción de jerarquías a partir de masculinidades dominantes, cómplices y subordinadas." In *Pensar las cárceles de América Latina,* edited by Chloé Constant, 311–28. Lima: IEP, IFEA, PUCP, 2016.

Rosen, Jonathan and Martin Brienen, editors. *Prisons in the Americas in the Twenty-first Century: A Human Dumping Ground.* New York: Lexington Books, 2015.

PART V

*Spiritual Invasions and Contagions*

CHAPTER 13

# Immunity, Vaccines, and Other Holy Things

PAUL RAMÍREZ

We are made up of organisms, surrounded by them, dependent on them for food and shelter. They make us sick, as the "biological allies" of the Europeans settlers did to millions of Native Americans, with runny pustules, flayed skin, disfiguring scars, and blindness often leading to death. But they can also make us well. We humans are made and remade by nonhuman things.[1]

In the eighteenth century, the possibility that society might "harness a virus" and use it to provide immunity against smallpox generated waves of excitement throughout the Américas.[2] The virus was cowpox, a bovine variant of human smallpox, and there were frantic searches for sources of it on cattle ranches everywhere. Trained physicians joined priests, royal officials, unlicensed healers, and parents to propagate the vaccine fluid in cities, towns, and pueblos. It was a watershed moment in the history of medicine, noteworthy in the sheer numbers of vaccinated children and distances traversed by medical teams. However difficult to quantify, people experienced the "weight of the state" through public health measures in unprecedented ways in this moment.[3]

And yet successes in technological and epidemiological terms can obscure the enormous confusion that surrounded the practice, one that emerged at the nexus of the organic and inorganic, the human and nonhuman, the natural and manmade. In cities, skeptics of immunization's safety and efficacy entered the public sphere, where doubts were amplified in *boleros* and rhymed verse. Parents everywhere worried about the risks to their children of domesticating nature by making them sick. Rural inhabitants frequently immunized in the absence of trained physicians, yielding contradictory views about just who possessed the skills to practice. Emphasizing these anxieties—and reviewing the various answers that contemporaries offered—affords an opportunity to see the colonial state, in the words of cultural anthropologist Clifford Geertz, "against the background of the sort of society in which it is embedded—the confusion that surrounds it, the confusion it confronts ... [and] causes [and] responds to."[4]

This chapter traces the adoption of inoculation and vaccination—part of a longer history of attempts to manage epidemic disease in the Américas—with a focus on the highly stratified, paternalistic society of colonial Mexico, then known as New Spain. The method is to center cultural productions that sought to provide answers to questions about immunization and stabilize its many possible meanings. Promoters who needed to persuade, reassure, and even awe diverse communities of laypeople enlisted a variety of *things*, such as candles, garments, glass slides, ships, sacred buildings, pastoral letters, and other genres of writing, alongside organic virus matter, to do this work. In a climate of uncertainty around reform and technological change, advocates used these things to coax skeptical audiences to adopt an unfamiliar or unknown procedure, in a dynamic process that redefined the vaccine itself. Physicians became masters of persuasion alongside others with minimal training. The resulting plans, instruction manuals, and sermons were not mainly intellectual exercises in patriotic pride, nor were they technical manuals aimed at a restricted elite.[5] They were pragmatic, prescriptive works intended to produce immediate effects and responses among diverse social groups. The approach taken here is therefore less top-down or bottom-up than sideways, approaching by way of the routines and genres and media that defined the technology, initiated dialogues, stirred debate, and in other ways conditioned the world of state-sponsored immunization.

The confusion generated by this alchemical world has bewildered many scholars ever since. Take for instance the reception of Guatemala's renowned professor of medicine, the creole José de Flores, who during outbreaks of smallpox in Guatemala championed inoculation, or variolation, a dangerous form of immunization whereby live smallpox was extracted from pustules on the bodies of the sick and injected under the skin of nonimmune persons.[6] By 1803, with news circulating throughout the Atlantic world about the experiments of an English physician named Edward Jenner with pus from a *vaca*, the Crown was eager to adapt the *vacuna*, as the bovine material was called, and enlisted Flores to advise. Flores conceived a plan in which two swift *barcos* departing from the southern port of Cádiz would transport children and infected cows, forming a chain of nonimmune humans to propagate the life-saving fluid on the long crossing. Noting that the Native chiefs of North America had already acquired cowpox from Thomas Jefferson, Flores stressed the Spanish king's obligation to do the same to protect his Indian subjects.[7]

At the center of Flores's proposal were Catholic churches, whose spaces and ceremonies enshrined the vaccine in the Américas. In head towns, the most expert physicians would learn the operation and form instructions "adapted to the nature and care of the Indians." In pueblos and missions without Spanish or *ladino* physicians, priests and missionaries were to vaccinate and introduce the practice at the parish level by merging vaccination with Catholic liturgy and sacramental practice. Four to six months after baptism, the parish priest would persuade godparents to return to the church for a vaccination ceremony featuring an altar boy with lit candle, the priest in full liturgical garb, and blessings and prayers for the child's health. A reserve of vacuna lymph was to be preserved in glass slides in a box in the sacristy with the holy oils, while medical practitioners, where available, would operate in the consecrated space of the church.[8] For Flores, these ceremonial considerations were how appropriate gravity and reverence would be conferred on the novel invention. Thus consecrated, vaccine might provoke the appropriate feelings and responses in humans.

In the end, despite having invoked his prior experience and "knowledge of the país" in proposing to make Jennerian vaccination available to American populations, Flores's plan was not adopted, as some have suggested it was.[9] Nor did these campaigns represent the moment when medical science and religion began to diverge, as others have argued about the following Royal Vaccination Expedition.[10] If projects to improve the human condition frequently discarded "situated," "locally superior" knowledge of the kind possessed by Flores, in the matter of immunity, residents would need to make up the difference once the organic material and vaccinating teams arrived in their towns and villages.[11] Recognizing that this process was contested and ongoing allows us to appreciate the ordinary people who handled the vaccine and made it viable before and after the vaccination expedition. For them, the power inherent in things—religious, biological, and medical—was a matter for discernment, and not so easily dismissed.

The appeals to emotion and sensibility espoused by the Guatemalan José Flores were not so indispensable to medical campaigns everywhere in the Américas. In Cuba, for example, as plantations expanded following the demise of Haitian sugar, enslaved men and women were given little choice in the matter. They were forced to submit to vaccination upon their arrival in the island's ports, and thus Jennerian vaccine fused with a broader effort to bolster the profitability of slavery, in a centralized, coercive practice that effectively ensured a continuous supply of bodies to propagate the virus.[12] Elsewhere, a captive population for vaccine's transmission was far less certain. Those who advocated for the procedure appealed to royal concern for agriculture, industry, labor, profit, and imperial rivalries, targeting audiences of ministers, *philosophes*, and kings.[13] For their part, laypeople were left with many more questions than answers.

The court physician Esteban Morel, a graduate of the prestigious University of Montpellier, authored one of the few works that appealed directly to their concerns. In 1778 he arrived in Mexico City, the capital of New Spain, from the sugar island of Guadeloupe, where he had certified surgeons and apothecaries, inspected medications in pharmacies, and overseen inoculations among the island's enslaved workers and plantation owners. Of more than 8,000 operations, he claimed to have witnessed only four or five deaths.[14] Given the dangers inherent in infecting human beings with a live human virus, it may well be that more of the enslaved perished from complications, unknown to Morel. We must imagine the unsanitary conditions of the quarantine houses in which they were contained to prevent the spread of smallpox and may never know how they received the strange surgeons who made the incisions. In the words of a physician in Belém, Brazil, who inoculated thirty-three enslaved Africans in the same year, the subjects were fearful, but "they had no choice but to obey."[15]

In Mexico City, with its complex social hierarchies, institutions, and corporations, power and persuasion worked in different ways. To begin, Morel had to convince its elite population of creoles that inoculation was a worthy and safe practice. Shortly after his arrival, with an outbreak of smallpox imminent, the city's councilmen placed Morel in charge of a ward in the convent hospital of San Hipólito, where he applied his extraordinary expertise.[16] The city advertised inoculation for individuals aged three and up under the expert care of Dr. Morel, who inoculated six Indian and eight European children in their homes, or in a makeshift clinic of beds in his own. But residents began spreading rumors of botched operations, which soon complicated the campaign.[17]

Morel composed his "Treatise on the Utility of Inoculation" in part to assuage fears and publicize the success of his method. Not only does the treatise document the first known inoculation trials in Mexico City, in attending to the fears, expectations, and sensibilities of parents, it also stands as evidence of the kinds of arguments a man of science employed to persuade laypeople of the benefits of a medical innovation. His contemporaries would have considered him an expert, an empiricist, and the epitome of enlightened rationalism—things he clearly valued. Yet Morel also leaned on religion, illuminating ideas about his adopted home. The result was an eclectic, artfully executed work of persuasion that simultaneously insisted on the value of evidence, situated inoculation in a fully rendered providential framework, and calculated its benefits within an imaginative depiction of destruction, combining experience and emotion in what one historian has called the "sentimental empiricism" of the age.[18]

Morel employed a two-pronged strategy in seeking to connect with lay publics, above all parents.[19] The first was to characterize smallpox as an ailment that threatened everyone. In a prefatory letter, Morel addressed the city's councilmen, thanking them for their support and commenting on the Christian piety and acts of charity and spiritual aid he had witnessed in the city. Morel reminded them that the convent hospital and its beds lay empty, while potential trial subjects succumbed to natural smallpox daily. He insisted that the effects of smallpox were too terrible to describe, then described them in horrific detail anyway: the man covered in pustules, whose facial deformities exceeded those of the leper; the pained mother who no longer recognized her disfigured child; a man of learning who had lost his sense of judgment and rationality. Everyone was a potential victim, but all might use their capacity for self-preservation to remove themselves and their children from harm.[20]

Second, Morel highlighted properties of inoculation that were most likely to sway his audience, arguing that inoculation was popular, well-known, and God-given. Morel insisted that among *gente distinguida* of European states, "It has already become, if I may put it this way, fashionable [*de moda*]."[21] Morel cited the tender, loving care of mothers in Tuscany, who were reported by experts to inoculate their sleeping children while hidden from husbands and fathers. Why did women take charge? Because men relied too much on rational judgment (*juicio*) rather than feelings (*sentidos*) and therefore did not see its benefits. To show that inoculation belonged in the Américas just as much as Europe, Morel dwelt on the climate and topography of Mexico City. In a time when healers considered climate a key factor in the health of the body, his medical experiments aimed to show inoculation's local safety and efficacy—he deemed the city as healthy as any in which inoculation had already been practiced.[22]

In making some of these arguments, the treatise appropriated the template of Morel's famous compatriot, Charles Marie de la Condamine, whose *Essay on Smallpox Inoculation* (*Mémoire sur l'inoculation de la petite vérole*) was published in France in 1754. Less familiar in the Spanish-speaking world (it was translated into Castilian but denied license for publication owing to its controversial subject), the *Mémoire* featured a set of hypothetical objections. Could someone contract smallpox twice? Could inoculation transmit other diseases? Did the introduction of an illness for the purpose of protection contradict divine will? La Condamine's responses rebutted each doubt. For instance, if inoculation was against God's will, then all therapies used to prevent or treat disease should be considered offensive.[23]

Morel likewise sought to render an unfamiliar "remedy" in terms familiar to his audience. In Morel's version, objections and concerns were placed into the mouth of a loving father (*padre tierno*) who fears turning a child over for inoculation. This hypothetical parent notes that since the devastating outbreak of 1737, only three epidemics had struck New Spain, and that many individuals reached the end of life without contracting smallpox. Why risk inoculation? Morel's response is that the introduction of free trade had linked Europe and the Americas in unprecedented ways, and more commerce meant more epidemics.[24] Morel repeatedly deferred to theological arguments to validate and explain inoculation's virtues. When the father raises the possibility of contracting an illness from inoculation and losing a child, Morel cites God's will, admitting the limits of human science and asking the reader to have faith. In the absence of a sure antidote, inoculation was the only remedy "sent by the Omnipotent" to protect against an illness that "alone kills a seventh of those killed by all sicknesses combined."[25] To an objection that immunization contradicted God's plan, Morel responds that God had given medicine to humankind. If medicine contradicted God's will, parents did so daily with the many bleedings, purges, mercury treatments, and "other innumerable remedies" popularly used. Properly acknowledged as a divine gift, to refuse it would be an offense to God.[26] In fact, like bleeding, purgatives, emetics, and *vejigatorios* (irritants used to raise blisters), the aim and mechanism of inoculation was the same, "to evacuate the cause of some sickness, or at least part of it, through the veins."[27]

This final observations derived from the fact that Morel, like his peers, followed a medical practice founded on an early modern understanding of disease transmission, in which air-bound materials exhaled from the human body propagated deadly contagion. In this framework, inoculation worked because it caused humors in the body to be "spent" and well-disposed to infection.[28] These beliefs about illness and the body allowed Morel to draw points of coincidence between his practical knowledge and that of the public he sought to convince. Morel thought that the bare facts—fourteen successful inoculations "in the time of an epidemic that has carried away at least 20 percent (from what I can ascertain) of the infected"—should suffice for adoption, but he knew the matter would not end there.[29] He therefore made careful use of knowledge in common to introduce a therapy he considered superior, including but not limited to knowledge about the authorizing power of religion.[30]

The significance of this strategy comes into relief when we consider that Morel was not especially devout. Years later, he was among dozens of French residents arrested and jailed by the Inquisition in an atmosphere of paranoia about the French Revolution.[31] By then he had been denounced for nearly every offense imaginable against Catholic religion, including interest in Voltaire, Rousseau, and Montesquieu. During a procession for Our Lady of Remedios, on May 14, 1789, he had reportedly said that residents brought out sacred images for rain in seasons when it was likely to rain anyway. Skeptical of the devotional practices he witnessed, Morel was also reported to have said, on multiple occasions, that although one followed another philosophy, one might live safely under the watch of the Inquisition by conforming in exteriors to the country's religion.[32]

This is what Morel's unpublished treatise had achieved, insofar as it deliberately appropriated providential authority to lend legitimacy to inoculation. As relations between Morel and the city council soured, the authorities declined to publish the treatise and instead opted for an instruction penned by one of the city's own physicians that targeted the atmospheric conditions of disease.[33] Not until smallpox arrived from Chiapas and Guatemala at the end of 1795 did popular protest compel the government to overturn its quarantine mandate and finally endorse inoculation.[34] Morel did not live to see the moment. Arrested by the Inquisition, he was found covered in blood in his cell from a self-inflicted wound, by which time he must have despaired of his strategy of adhering to religion's "externals." He submitted reluctantly to last rites, dryly uttering "si" when asked whether he was a Catholic and believed in God and the Holy Trinity, and thus died months before a new epidemic forced New Spain's government to revisit the practice he had so energetically supported.[35]

Infectious disease has tangible effects on human populations. It can offer an impulse to reform, even if not all sectors of society are yet prepared for change. Morel's unpublished treatise contained a prescient warning to this effect, that the immediacy of a disease epidemic ("a time of ruin") provided short-lived urgency to the work of persuasion and gave immunization a chance. "If one does not open his eyes in such horrific times, who will, once the epidemic subsides?"[36] In other words, the spread of a pathogen not only made available the organic material that rendered inoculation possible but also facilitated mechanisms of rule and reform that were scarcely conceivable otherwise.

No less than physicians, Catholic clergy were central to these transformations. Against those who predicted that baroque funerary rites, public pageantry, and the

Catholic hierarchy would cede ground to the rule of hospitals, medical professionals, and royal officials, priests and Catholic ceremony continued to orient both urban and rural life in Mexico.[37] As representatives of the royal and ecclesiastical spheres, priests were not only expert pastors, adept at imparting understanding of things both secular and sacred. They were also skilled healers. A striking example of their proficiency comes from studies of the Cesarean operation, a surgical technique to save the lives—and souls—of unborn fetuses after the mother's death. In regions where surgeons, doctors, and midwives were in short supply, the Cesarean became the purview of priests. With the operation placed in their hands, Enlightenment goals of population growth were fulfilled, as the historian Adam Warren has noted, but cast in theological, evangelical, and civilizing terms as a battle for the hearts and souls of Indigenous Andeans.[38]

We find evidence of this technical and symbolic force in the sermon and the closely related pastoral letter, genres that crossed domains of expertise and offered a distinctive discursive space for inoculation and vaccination.[39] In the Américas, the sermon had multiple goals, authors, and settings. It offered instructive commentary on the birth of a royal heir, the meaning of absolutist rule, the dangers of the French Revolution, and the moral risks of fashion and alcohol consumption, to cite just some topics. In striving to make better Christians and vassals of listeners, the modern sermon acquired an importance that "overflowed the religious or ecclesiastical spheres."[40] During emergencies, it provided lessons on Christian charity and exhorted parishioners to action. On September 27, 1785, a time of fevers and famine in Mexico, a sermon delivered in honor of Cosme and Damian—patron saints of medicine—enjoined listeners to emulate Christ's healing and to practice charity toward one's neighbor, "so that, though not professors of medicine, we may assist the suffering sick as we are able," and thereby warrant mercy.[41]

This rhetorical tradition contains surprising histories of edification and debate as populations were urged to turn to preventive medicine. In the summer of 1798, following the practice of thousands of inoculations in Durango, Guanajuato, and Monterrey, Durango's bishop delivered a sermon in which he marveled that so many among the lowest classes (*la plebe*), ordinarily so hesitant to emulate their social betters, had hurried to inoculate their children. He drew on biblical references as he sought to standardize the practice for newborns, urging congregants to give thanks and shun the ingratitude of the Israelites after the Red Sea parted and manna fell from the skies. To help with practical understanding, the prelate offered further metaphors. Though inoculation might well seem like introducing a serious illness into an otherwise healthy body, it was instead as if doing battle with an enemy who was disarmed, not yet grown, and still in baby blankets (*mantillas*). Alternatively, it was like cutting weeds (*las maleas*) in agriculture before they had a chance to mature and sprout.[42] Recent medical developments were thus infused with theological, biblical, and agricultural significance.

Around this time, Mexico's archbishop circulated copies of a medical pamphlet with instructions for inoculation to the roughly 200 parishes in the archbishopric. Priests were ordered to copy the text into parish books, so that they might instruct themselves and "exhort and persuade" parishioners to practice. Authored by medical officials in Mexico City, the brief pamphlet treated technical matters in lay terms, including the preparation of children for inoculation, the use of a lancet to inject smallpox superficially into the hollow between fingers, and the care and recovery of the inoculated child, who was to be kept from scratching and made to drink refreshing beverages.[43] Both the pamphlet's format and its route through a network of rural parishes served to make the technology accessible to rural parishioners living hundreds of miles away. We can begin to imagine how recognizably medical works acquired new life in ecclesiastical spaces, where oral transmission and instruction were more commonplace than literate digestion of pamphlets and more erudite forms of print.

This ecclesiastical structure channeled information about vaccine as well. By the end of 1803, a version of the plan laid out by Dr. Flores was becoming reality with the help of local officials, priests, and parents. In November, the Royal Vaccination Expedition set sail from the northwestern port of Coruña to transport cowpox vaccine to Spanish subjects in the Américas under the direction of the Spaniard Francisco Xavier de Balmis, an acknowledged authority on vaccination.[44] Over several years, sub-expeditions traversed thousands of miles in a feat that has been characterized as the first global public health campaign.[45] How would parishioners be prepared for this vast and potentially disruptive endeavor? In the south of Mexico, the bishop of Oaxaca, Antonio de Bergosa y Jordán, issued a pastoral letter (*carta apostólica*, or *edicto*) to parishioners and clergy in the diocese of Oaxaca in which he announced that the king had sponsored an expedition "at great cost and expense to his royal treasury" and was "eager to protect you from the contagious illness of smallpox." Explaining that vaccination was the result of providential observations made in Gloucester on milkmaids by the "wise physician Jenner," the bishop exhorted parishioners directly. "Do not allow a sudden plague of smallpox to snatch your children and grandchildren from your arms for the tomb, covering your hearts and poor *chozas* [huts] in mourning, but instead vaccinate them in a timely fashion, which would be the same as liberating them from smallpox, and death." For their part, priests were reminded that they were not only physicians of the soul but of the body as well.[46] To further assist in institutionalizing the practice, the letter offered forty days' indulgence (remission of sins) to those who willingly submitted to or toiled for vaccination.

In the process, the pastoral letter—a genre dedicated to the instruction of parish priests and the moral reform of parishioners—was recast by the vaccine. A traditional ecclesiastical missive, the *carta*'s distinctive opening included familiar references to parishioners—"you all" (*vosotros*) and "my beloved children"—along with invocations of an omniscient God and benevolent king. Also typical was its moralizing discourse on duty, salvation, charity, and obedience. Simultaneously, the letter adopted the conventions of a medical guide, with detailed instructions for vaccination.[47] For instance, parishioners learned that, unlike inoculation, vaccination required no preparation, might be practiced at all ages and seasons, and was not transmissible through the air. The operation was accomplished by injecting the lymph superficially by means of a needle on the inside of the arm. This was done so easily that "fathers, mothers, or *chichiguas* [wet nurses, from the Nahuatl, *chichihua*] can do it without fear, and with the same felicity and good effect, because in fact it is an operation more proper to women owing to the greater softness of their hands." The procedure was so "safe, easy, and inexpensive," the bishop elaborated, that 200,000 vaccinations had been performed the previous year without a single case of human smallpox.[48] In these ways—references to patients' bodies and international authorities, detailed descriptions of the procedure and its physical effects, and recourse to the authorizing force of statistics, unbiased observation, and experiments—the pastoral letter came to resemble medical writings of the day. Both genres were steeped in personal, exhortatory language aimed to move and instruct an audience, and both were disposed to highlight the ceremonial action and divine etiologies that gave persuasive heft to new things.

For some royal authorities, the *carta* was also cause for concern. Bergosa y Jordán had offered to make vaccine widely available, not only to mothers and wet nurses but also to male clergy. In his missive, the bishop announced that he had acquired many iron instruments (*punzones*) on the recommendation of physicians, which he would distribute to all parish and assistant priests who requested one, and to others who might make use of one.[49] But regulations on vaccine issued for Oaxaca appeared to prohibit practice by unauthorized persons, as the bishop soon realized. By offering subjects in his diocese broad permission to vaccinate and the tools to do so, the bishop had envisioned an approach at odds with what the Expedition's director, Francisco Xavier de Balmis, was at the time attempting on the ground.

In Mexico, Balmis made three noteworthy adjustments in consultation with local officials.[50] The first was to place vaccine under the care of central vaccination committees (*juntas*) rather than the governors (*corregidores*) indicated for Spain, considering the challenges to following royal orders at such a great distance from metropolitan authority.[51] Second, administrators were to operate in municipal buildings rather than the hospitals designated by royal order. Balmis had spent years in New Spain's most prestigious hospitals, where he studied the anti-syphilitic properties of Mexican agave (or maguey) and begonias.[52] Nevertheless, he acknowledged that hospitals, instead of reassuring parents about the care of their children, implanted fears by associating the procedure with sickness—a common and widespread refrain.[53] And third, regulations aimed to restrict practice to trained vaccinators selected by officials. Although "the practice of vaccination may be so simple and easy that mothers will eventually execute it by themselves," only professors of medicine and surgery were to have access to vaccine lymph.[54] The restrictive clause barring unauthorized persons from practice was found even in the tropical port of Acapulco, a region chronically short on medical practitioners.[55]

In allowing for broader lay and clerical participation, the bishop drew on years of experience in his diocese, where a shortage of practitioners necessitated such concessions.[56] Officials of the king's executive arm acknowledged this experience but divided on the matter of vaccine's accessibility. One official remarked that Bergosa y Jordán's "reglas" conformed so closely with what had been written on vaccine that "the bishop appears to have formed an extract of the best authors, [but] simpler and accommodated to the limited knowledge of the practitioners and *curanderos* usually found in the interior pueblos of his diocese." Nevertheless, it seemed prudent to restrict vaccination to professors and other experts who might instruct and distinguish between viable and spurious operations, with clergy focused on public preaching.[57] A second minister viewed the procedure as so simple that it ought to be "popularized [*vulgarizarle*]" as much as possible. He agreed that the regulations should be followed but recommended that bishops, the viceroy, and officers make the practice "popular y común" right away, especially in rural villages with few practitioners, and eventually everywhere with the help of a simple guide, "so that even mothers can execute it, as is done in many parts." Separate orders went out to this effect.[58]

Little has been made of the *carta* or the disruption it caused in Spain, perhaps because regalist bishops like Bergosa y Jordán have been imagined as reflexive followers of royal prerogatives and dismissed as predictable and thus uninteresting.[59] But vaccine's arrival remade a familiar genre, the pastoral letter, whose generic conventions conjured a public health campaign in strikingly imaginative, pragmatic, and detailed ways. Outpacing royal policy, the bishop moved to incorporate vaccine into the symbolic, soteriological, and hierarchical realms of the Church. That same year, Guatemala's *protomédico* José Flores issued his proposal for an expedition, which presumed that the parish church and its sacred spaces accorded with the obligations of the monarch to protect his subjects from infectious disease. Flores had pointed out how well enlightened rulers knew that they needed to enlist religious ceremony when they introduced new customs, "to manage skillfully the religious impulse."[60] This perspective echoed the writings of state ministers of state on the ideal role for the Church in public life.[61] In their ways, all drew imaginatively on their knowledge of how things worked, and of the force such things might have on laypeople who were vulnerable to infectious disease.

We have glimpsed some of the people who reflected on immunization's properties, who in their own ways produced knowledge about an artifact that traversed boundaries. With extensive experience as a military and civilian doctor, Esteban Morel's treatise on inoculation abounded in extra-medical references and arguments that exceeded his medical practice and training. Likewise, the Guatemalan physician José Flores, looking over the vast landscape of Spanish America, expressed a vision for an expedition in which medical matter, technique, and practitioners were enshrined in the sacred spaces and rituals of the Church. Oaxaca's bishop used the authority of the pastoral letter to do the same, drawing on structures and personnel to transmit the vaccine from one child to the next. All were convinced by the power that inhered in sacred things, and all sought to use this power to persuade European and Amerindian subjects.

To put things differently, these examples suggest some of the ways that inoculation and vaccine were epistemic objects, known in different ways through linguistic and textual practices. At the same time, inoculation and vaccination were ontological objects, made up of skin cells, blood, and human carriers, whose use and efficacy depended on human hands, ships, carriages, lancets, children's arms, cows, and even exposure to tropical climates. Contemporaries knew that biological matter deteriorated over time and space, and with it the efficacy of the vaccine, which is why they preferred to use human bodies as incubators. Together these properties provide a clearer picture of the process by which technological artifacts acquire the applications and efficacy that are so often taken for granted.

By way of conclusion, we can consider two cases that further illustrate the role played by Mexico's populations in effecting these adaptations. People in colonial Mexico engaged directly with vaccine not only through speech and other discursive practices, but also through embodied, multi-channel spectacles of tribute, reverence, and celebration.[62] In Olinalá, in modern Guerrero state, Indian officials of the *cabecera* (head town) planned a festival in anticipation of the arrival of the vaccination expedition in October 1806, to which they invited leaders of surrounding pueblos to enjoy fireworks and ethnic *danzas*. In this they observed regulations that prescribed public demonstrations of gratitude, so that Indian subjects might understand the benefits of vaccine and hand over their children.[63] But things did not go according to plan. When the team arrived early, the leaders who assembled to greet and transport the vaccine to their communities had to improvise. They offered up other gifts—of *aguardiente*, cheese, and cookies—along with half a peso for the children who, injected with fluid, would carry the virus in their diminutive bodies for future use.[64] Months later, when Olinalá's plaza was enclosed for bullfights, villagers expressed confusion about whether these festivities were in thanksgiving for vaccine or, as the priest insisted, in honor of the Virgin of Guadalupe, as was tradition.[65] As a result of these multimedia celebrations, new and unexpected meanings, connections, and associations emerged, apparently including the Virgin of Guadalupe. In these campaigns, immunity required an assemblage of local, biological, edible, sensorial, and sacred goods and objects.

With processions and chords of the Te Deum erupting across Mexico, populations everywhere encountered viscerally the material manifestation of immunization. In the town of Santa María Izucar, in Puebla, as in so many instances, officials sponsored festivities with bullfights, fireworks, flowers, music, Indigenous dances, masses of thanksgiving, and a reception for the expedition featuring a Spanish and *mulato* boy in procession. On nearby Raboso Hacienda, a group of young Black workers, seeing that the estate owner intended to wait for authorization before proceeding to vaccinate them, reportedly took things into their own hands. They acquired cowpox and, with the barbed branches of a local acacia tree called "Huichache" made the incisions and vaccinated one another. The authorities offered this as proof of the effectiveness of the ceremonies they had sponsored, which had inspired even the most stolid individuals to comply.[66]

There are other ways of looking at colonial subjects who practiced without permission. Rather than see it as the outcome of official intentions and designs, we can imagine that efficacy resided in the acacia branches, and with the people who knew how to use them.[67] It may be that the tree offered another solution to the problem of immunization, calling to mind the way that inoculation had worked in the past, and calling forth the knowledge possessed by workers of African descent. It is a reminder that vaccination was not only an imperial project, nor was it merely a European medical intervention. It was also known and adapted in the actions of colonized and enslaved people.[68]

Although vaccine arrived from Spain, long before ship set sail, residents of its colonies were contributing the common sense, logistical aptitude, and ritual meanings that went missing from the simplified state program. Adjustments made during the journey were foretold in decades of debate on the topic that confirmed that hospitals were frightful places, that the perceived safety, accessibility, and ease of the procedure would be key in vaccine's acceptance, and that a circumscribed arena for practitioners was untenable in rural areas. Unpublished writings, oriented by the requirements of medical practice, ecclesiastical rituals, and the expectations of colonial audiences, prefigured these outcomes, with a confusion of indexical, stylistic, and thematic elements that pointed to the transition happening in the world beyond.[69] Along with the timely intervention of Raboso's estate workers and village leaders in Olinalá,, these productions are evidence of a liminal moment of transition, doubt, and possibility, a time when novel medical practices spawned mixed genres and even priests, wet nurses, and manual laborers might be vaccinators.

Though vacuna came from Spain, it truly was made in the Américas.

## Notes

1. Bruno Latour has offered some of the most influential formulations of this view. See also the useful overview of "vital materialism" in Jane Bennett, *Vibrant Matter: A Political Ecology of Things* (Durham: Duke University Press, 2010). Portions of this chapter appear in slightly different form in Paul Ramírez, *Enlightened Immunity: Mexico's Experiments with Disease Prevention in the Age of Reason* (Palo Alto: Stanford University Press, 2018), chapter 4. The author is grateful to the Latin American History Working Group at the University of Notre Dame for comments on a previous version.

2. The phrase is from the writer Eula Biss. "Vaccination is a kind of domestication of a wild thing," she observes, "in that it involves our ability to harness a virus and break it like a horse." Eula Biss, *On Immunity: An Inoculation* (Minneapolis, MI: Graywolf Press, 2014), 41.
3. Alan Knight, "The Weight of the State in Modern Mexico," in *Studies in the Formation of the Nation State in Latin America*, ed. James Dunkerley (London: Institute of Latin American Studies, University of London, 2002), 214–20, stresses that a state's interactions with society are what determines its legitimacy and ability to reproduce.
4. Clifford Geertz, "What Is a State If It Is Not a Sovereign? Reflections on Politics in Complicated Places," *Current Anthropology* 45, no. 5 (December 2004): 580.
5. The types of productions fruitfully analyzed in Jorge Cañizares-Esguerra, *Nature, Empire, and Nation: Explorations of the History of Science in the Iberian World* (Stanford: Stanford University Press, 2006).
6. Archivo General de Indias (hereafter AGI) Indiferente 1558a, Madrid, February 28, 1803, Proposal submitted by Doctor Joseph Flores, 327r and 329r-330r.
7. AGI, 330r-v. Flores was an exemplary figure in an era of minute observation and practical, original inventions in science, medical training, and health care. Born in 1751 in Ciudad Real, Chiapas, Flores graduated from the University of San Carlos de Borromeo, and showed an interest in immunization as early as 1778, when he presented for a teaching post in medicine at the University of Guatemala with a treatise on the advantages of inoculation and the need to establish it in Guatemala. Eventually he served as *primer protomédico* of Guatemala's Protomedicato, whose formal constitution he oversaw on June 21, 1793, until his departure, in 1796, to inspect the medical facilities and techniques of Cuba, the United States, Germany, Holland, France, Italy, and Spain. Martha Eugenia Rodríguez, "El doctor José Felipe Flores, primer Protomédico de Guatemala," *Boletín Mexicano de Historia y Filosofía de la Medicina* 13 (1990): 111–23; José Aznar López, *El Doctor don José de Flores: una vida al servicio de la ciencia* (Guatemala: Editorial Universitaria, 1960); and Carlos Martínez Duran, *Las ciencias médicas en Guatemala*, 3rd ed. (Guatemala: Editorial Universitaria, 1964).
8. Flores, 331v–332r.
9. It has been tempting to find in the proposal evidence of the influence of American creole expertise in the development of an ensuing global vaccinating campaign. But as forcefully and creatively as Flores made his case, his proposal was discarded in favor of a streamlined program that utilized a single ship and dispensed with

live cows. Whereas Flores had placed the medical procedure in churches, the royal plan expunged all references to liturgical practice and vaccinating priests. The order announcing the expedition specified only that the procedure be performed using the more reliable arm-to-arm method in "both Américas" and the Philippines, "observing the anomalies of diversity of climate and castes." (AGI Indiferente 1558a, Palacio Real, July 31, 1803, Royal Decree, 399–400) A printed circular indicated vaccination in capitals, where physicians and others might be instructed in the practice, and invoked the charitable dimensions of *religión*, directing prelates to help introduce vaccine by exhorting priests and missionaries to aid the expedition, with "the influence that ministers of the Church regularly have over public opinion" (AGI Indiferente 1558a, San Ildefonso, September 3, 1803, 465f). But the rituals described with such care in Flores's plan, including storage of vaccine in the sacristy and the capacity of the clergy to vaccinate, go unremarked in official documents, despite the physician's insistence that these were integral to success. Martha Few, "Circulating Smallpox Knowledge: Guatemalan Doctors, Maya Indians, and Designing Spain's Smallpox Vaccination Expedition, 1780–1806," *British Journal for the History of Science* 43, no. 4 (2010): 519–37, takes Flores's proposal as evidence of the physician's influence on the official program.

10. For historian Susana Ramírez Martín, who has published several studies on the Royal Vaccination Expedition, the clergy in epidemics were in charge primarily of the ideological content of an increasingly scientific problem, but they were not immunization's practitioners or facilitators. According to this view, the religious component "entrará en conflicto con la visión científica que se va imponiendo en el pensamiento médico." Susana Ramírez Martín, *La mayor hazaña médica de la colonia: La Real Expedición Filantrópica de la Vacuna en la Real Audiencia de Quito* (Quito: ABYA-YALA, 1999), 68–72 and 174–81.

11. James Scott, *Seeing Like a State: How Certain Schemes to Improve the Human Condition Have Failed* (New Haven: Yale University Press, 1998), 51–2.

12. On vaccination rates and the broader expansion of Cuba's sugar economy, see Adrián López Denis, "Inmunidades imaginadas en la Era de las Revoluciones," in Gilberto Hochman et al., *Patologías de la patria: Enfermedades, enfermos y nación en América Latina* (Buenos Aires: Lugar Editorial S.A., 2012), 29–57, esp. 44–45.

13. For the Spanish debates, see Timoteo O'Scanlan, *Ensayo apologético de la inoculación, o demostración de lo importante que es al particular, y al Estado* (Madrid: Imprenta Real, 1792), Pilar León Sanz and Dolores Barettino Coloma, *Vicente Ferrer*

*Gorraiz Beaumont y Montesa (1718-1792), un polemista navarro de la Ilustración* (Pamplona: Fondo de Publicaciones del Gobierno de Navarra, 2007), and José Amar, *Instrucción curativa de las viruelas, dispuesta para los facultativos y acomodada para todos* (Madrid, 1774). In the Peninsula, the decision to frame the issue in starkly utilitarian terms responded to Spain's well-publicized clashes with imperial rivals over access to trade and mineral wealth in its American colonies. For the economic, scientific, and imperial dimensions of natural history collecting, Paula de Vos, "Natural History and the Pursuit of Empire in Eighteenth-Century Spain," *Eighteenth-Century Studies* 40, no. 2 (2007): 209-39.

14. Esteban Enrique Morel, "Disertación sobre la utilidad de la inoculación, escrita de encargo de la nob.ma Ciudad de Mexico," Archivo Histórico del Distrito Federal (AHDF) 3678, exp. 2, 15v, 24r, and Schifter Aceves, *Medicina, minería e inquisición*, 37.
15. Cited in Elise Mitchell, "On Slavery, Medicine, Speculation, and the Archive," *Historical Studies in the Natural Studies* 53:1 (2023): 82-85. Following Saidiya Hartman, Sasha Turner, and Ada Ferrer, among others, Mitchell argues for further speculation and imagination when writing about the historical experience of inoculation among enslaved people.
16. He was one of several hundred French men and women living there under the Francophile Bourbon monarchy of Spain. Jacques Houdaille, "Frenchmen and Francophiles in New Spain from 1760 to 1810," *The Americas* 13:1 (April 1957): 1-29, here 4-7.
17. Morel, "Disertación," AHDF 3678, exp. 2, 58r-v.
18. Jessica Riskin, *Science in the Age of Sensibility: The Sentimental Empiricists of the French Enlightenment* (Chicago: The University of Chicago Press, 2002).
19. The author shifts from second to third person to write about the city's medical professionals and officials, as when he pleads with *facultativos* not to let themselves be swayed by "invenciones maliciosas" and implies that some had contributed to the spread of rumor. Morel, "Disertación," AHDF 3678, exp. 2, 62v.
20. Morel, "Disertación," AHDF 3678, exp. 2, 4r-9r.
21. Morel, "Disertación," AHDF 3678, exp. 2, 15v, 24r.
22. Morel, "Disertación," AHDF 3678, exp. 2, 11r-12r, 15v-18v.
23. Charles Marie de la Condamine, *Mémoire sur l'inoculation de la petite vérole* (Paris: Chez Durand, 1754), 31-59.
24. Morel, "Disertación," AHDF 3678, exp. 2, 26r-27r.
25. Morel, "Disertación," AHDF 3678, exp. 2, 40r-v, 41v.

26. Morel, "Disertación," AHDF 3678, exp. 2, 52v–53v. This argument is reminiscent of Cotton Mather's, writing in Boston in 1721, when he asked rhetorically whether man did not make himself sick with artificial purges in order to avoid death by a deadlier, natural variety. This man "will give Thanks to GOD for teaching him, how to make himself sick, in a way that will save his Life." Cotton Mather, *Sentiments on the Small Pox Inoculated*, reprinted in Increase Mather, *Several Reasons Proving that Inoculation or Transplanting the Small Pox, Is a Lawful Practice, and That It Has Been Blessed by God for the Saving of Many a Life* (Cleveland: 1921 [Boston: 1721]), 76f.
27. Morel, "Disertación," AHDF 3678, exp. 2, 41v–42v. "You consent on every occasion to bloodlettings and purges for your children; you solicit them! It is fashionable, you say . . . in the day, inoculation is fashionable as well."
28. Morel, "Disertación," AHDF 3678, exp. 2, 16v, 20v–21r, 24v, 46v–47v.
29. Morel did eventually get around to numbers, in an appendix, where he carefully documented the *hechos* of the trials. Here he ranged over the bodies and faces of the six indigenous and eight European children to demonstrate success "even in the Indians." Morel, "Disertación," AHDF 3678, exp. 2, 59v–61 and 62v–63r.
30. Thus, inoculation was "that singular medicine that appears more like a Divine inspiration than a human invention." Morel, "Disertación," AHDF 3678, exp. 2, 10v. Or it was "religious zeal" (*el celo de la Religión*) that inspired parents to take responsibility for the health children, and *nuestra sagrada Religión* that opened eyes to "other less sensible, and truer goods." (Ibidem, 13r)
31. Houdaille, "Frenchmen and Francophiles in New Spain from 1760 to 1810," 14–15.
32. Transcriptions of Inquisition testimonies in Schifter Aceves, *Medicina, minería e inquisición*, 51–54.
33. José Ignacio Bartolache, *Instrucción que puede servir para que se cure a los enfermos de las viruelas epidémicas*, discussed in Donald B. Cooper, *Epidemic Disease in Mexico City, 1761–1813* (Austin: University of Texas Press, 1965), 63–69.
34. Ramírez, *Enlightened Immunity*, ch. 3.
35. Schifter Aceves, *Medicina, minería e inquisición*, 62.
36. Morel, "Disertación," AHDF 3678, exp. 2, 45v.
37. Mexico City's upwardly mobile *sensatos* are discussed in Pamela Voekel, *Alone before God: The Religious Origins of Modernity in Mexico* (Durham: Duke University Press, 2002).
38. Adam Warren, "An Operation for Evangelization: Friar Francisco González Laguna, the Cesarean Section, and Fetal Baptism in Late Colonial Peru," *Bulletin of the History of Medicine* 83:4 (winter 2009): 647–75, here 650. See also José G. Rigau-Pérez,

"Surgery at the Service of Theology: Postmortem Cesarean Sections in Puerto Rico and the Royal Cedula of 1804," *Hispanic American Historical Review* 75, no. 3 (August 1995): 377–404.

39. A survey of twenty-four works printed on immunization in Mexico between 1777 and 1840 confirms the impression that these dialogs about immunization's efficacy involved individuals with little or no formal medical training, with nearly half authored by ecclesiastics and administrative bodies, as opposed to military or civilian physicians and public health personnel. See Susana María Ramírez Martín, "Fuentes bibliográficas para el estudio de la inoculación y la vacunación en la Nueva España," in *El impacto demográfico de la viruela en México de la época colonial al siglo XX*, vol. 1, ed. Chantal Cramaussel et al. (Zamora, Michoacán: El Colegio de Michoacán, 2010). It is an imperfect accounting, with two works that only marginally treat immunization and one unpublished piece, and other unpublished works omitted.

40. Carlos Herrejón Peredo, *Del sermon al discurso cívico: México, 1760–1834* (Zamora, Michoacán: El Colegio de Michoacán; El Colegio de Mèxico, 2003), 367 and 374–75.

41. Andrés Mariano de Quintana, *Sermón de S. Cosme y S. Damián, patronos de la Iglesia y Real Hospital de Enfermos de la Ciudad de Antequera Valle de Oaxaca* (Mexico City: Felipe de Zúñiga y Ontiveros, 1786), cited in Herrejón Peredo, *Del sermón al discurso cívico*, 104–6.

42. Joseph Esquivel Navarrete, *Sermón eucarístico por la felicidad que logró la ciudad de Durango en la epidemia de viruelas del año de mil setecientos noventa y ocho* (Mexico City: Imprenta Madrileña de Joseph Fernández Jáuregui, 1799).

43. *Método claro, sencillo y fácil que para practicar la Inoculación de viruelas presenta al Público el Real Tribunal del Protomedicato de esta N.E. por Superior orden del Exmo. Señor Marqués de Branciforte* (México, 1797), in AGN Bienes Nacionales 873 exp. 195, and Tacubaya, October 6, 1797, "Señores Curas propios, Interinos, Coadjutores, Vicarios de pie fixo, y R.R. P.P. Ministros...," signed Alonso Arzobispo de Mexico, in ibidem.

44. The court's legal counsel, recommending that Flores take charge of the expedition, added Balmis as another possibility, noting his translation of Moreau de la Sarthe's history of vaccination ("el tratado mas completo sobre la vacuna"), multiple trips to New Spain, and lengthy residence in Mexico City. As a result of these, "he knows that *país*." AGI Indiferente 1558a, Madrid, March 17, 1803, 321–3. For an early variation that involved the physician Lorenzo Vergés accompanying the

new viceroy to Nueva Granada to deliver cowpox, which similarly would have saved the Crown funds, see Frías Núñez, *Enfermedad y sociedad en la crisis colonial del antiguo régimen*, 189.

45. Catherine Mark and José G. Rigau-Pérez, "The World's First Immunization Campaign: The Spanish Smallpox Vaccine Expedition," 1803–1813," *Bulletin of the History of Medicine* 83:1 (Spring 2009).

46. AGI Indiferente 1558a, Villa de Etla, December 7, 1804, Nos el Doctor Don Antonio Bergosa, 820r-v. Five sent through the bishopric were copied into parish books, their relevant passages presumably read aloud to parishioners. See, e.g., Archivo Histórico de la Arquidiócesis de Oaxaca, Sección Gobierno, Serie Parroquias, 1800–1813, "Libro Tercero de las Cordilleras que vienen a San Francisco Caxonos," 6–9.

47. Apparently adapted from Pedro Hernández, ed. and trans., *Orígen y descubrimiento de la vaccina* (Madrid: Oficina de don Benito García, y Compañía, 1801), in which the author stressed the accessibility of the practice, the importance of a simple style directed at parents, and the use of an *aguja* (needle) instead of a lancet.

48. AGI Indiferente 1558a, Villa de Etla, December 7, 1804, Nos el Doctor Don Antonio Bergosa, 818r.

49. AGI Indiferente 1558a, 821r.

50. The regulations established for Caracas served as a model for other capitals. See Smith, *The "Real Expedición Marítima de la Vacuna,"* 21–2, and Ramírez Martín, *La salud del Imperio*, 196 and 186–88.

51. AGI Indiferente 1558a, Madrid, February 12, 1807, Balmis to Marques Caballero, 1414v. The *juntas de vacuna* were collaborations between civil and ecclesiastic members, along with private citizens of means.

52. Michael Smith, *The "Real Expedición Marítima de la Vacuna,"* 16–17, Ramírez Martín, *La salud del Imperio*, 90–91, 94–6, and Fernández del Castillo, *Los viajes de don Francisco Xavier de Balmis*, 32–5, 89–96, 134–5.

53. AGI Indiferente 1558a, Madrid, February 12, 1807, Balmis to Marques Caballero, 1413r–v, 1414v–1415r; AGI Indiferente 1558a, Reglamento de S.M. para perpetuar en Indias la Vacuna, no place, no date (submitted to crown February 12, 1807), 1422–1427, article 5. See also Sherburne Cook, "Francisco Xavier Balmis and the Introduction of Vaccination in Latin America," *Bulletin of the History of Medicine* 12:6 (1942): 70–101. Public vaccinations were to be carried out either in *casas consistoriales* or the bishop's palace, both centrally located and away from hospitals. For evidence that these modifications were made elsewhere, e.g., AGI Indiferente 1558a, Durango, November 15, 1804, Bernardo Bonavia to

José Antonio Cavallero, 778–9r. The governor reported that he had composed a *reglamento* for *provincias internas* and made a change suggested by Balmis that a building other than a hospital be designated for vaccination.
54. AGI Indiferente 1558a, Reglamento de S.M. para perpetuar en Indias la Vacuna, article 15. Balmis dedicated his translation of Jacque-Louis Moreau de la Sarthe's *Traité historique et pratique de la vaccine*—copies of which were distributed during the expedition—to mothers. As is clear from subsequent correspondence, he did not intend for laywomen to pick up the lancet, only to bring their children to be vaccinated in a show of maternal love.
55. AGI Indiferente 1558a, Acapulco, February 5, 1805, Reglamento para propagar, y perpetuar la presiosa Vacuna en este Puerto de Acapulco, 982–985v, article 17.
56. This impulse also went against broader trends in the professionalization of medicine. See Luz María Hernández Sáenz, *Learning to Heal: The Medical Profession in Colonial Mexico, 1767–1831* (New York: Peter Lang, 1997), on attempts by medical professionals to restrict medical practice in this period.
57. AGI Indiferente 1558a, no place, no date ("Nota" following summary of bishop's letter of December 11), 810v–811v, emphasis added. There was uncertainty about whether the governor of Oaxaca had the authority to impose such limitations, when it was recalled that a royal decree had ordered the creation of *reglamentos* tailored to each place in consultation with Balmis. As a result: "En algunos [países] se advierte la prohibición de que nadie vacune por ahora, si no los Facultativos aprobados por las juntas Provinciales para evitar falsas vacunas; y esto es lo que habrá sucedido en Oaxaca." AGI Indiferente 1558a, no place, no date (written on a slip of paper folded over the file, at top: "S.E. desea saver si el Govierno de Oaxaca tubo facultades para este bando"), 813.
58. AGI Indiferente 1558a, no place, May 25, 1805, 811v–812v. For the corresponding *borrador* of the decree sent to the bishop, AGI Indiferente 1558a, Madrid, July 12, 1805, Crown to Obispo de Antequera de Oaxaca. For the order to the viceroy, AGI Indiferente 1558a, Madrid, June 12, 1805, Crown to Viceroy of New Spain, 835r–v.
59. Susana Ramírez Martín, making use of the same documentation, excerpts the edict in her study on the Expedition in a section on the attitudes of the clergy toward vaccination but seems not to know what to make of the bishop's peculiar proposals. For Ramírez Martín, the clergy in epidemics were in charge primarily of the ideological content of an increasingly scientific problem, and not immunization's practitioners or facilitators. According to this view, the religious component "entrará en conflicto con la visión científica que se va imponiendo en el pensamiento médico" at century's end. *La mayor hazaña médica*, 68–72 and 174–81.

60. AGI Indiferente 1558a, Madrid, February 28, 1803, Proposal submitted by Doctor Joseph Flores, 331r–v.
61. Gabriel Paquette, *Enlightenment, Governance, and Reform in Spain and Its Empire, 1759–1808* (New York: Palgrave Macmillan, 2008), 74. On the Church and religious ideology influencing royal legitimacy and state rule, William B. Taylor, *Magistrates of the Sacred: Priests and Parishioners in Late Colonial Mexico* (Stanford: Stanford University Press, 1996), 6.
62. On rumors as social facts, see Ramírez, *Enlightened Immunity*, 227–38.
63. *Estatutos, que la Real Junta Central Filantrópica General de la Vacunación Pública de San Carlos de la Ciudad de Puebla, ha dictado para el establecimiento y gobierno de las foráneas que han de erigirse en toda la Diócesis y Provincia* (Puebla, Mexico: D. Pedro de la Rosa, 1805), article 27.
64. Archivo General Municipal de Puebla (AGMP) 72, leg. 856, Villa de Tlapa, February 10, 1807, 109–10, declarations of several Indian *repúblicas* in an investigation into whether the Spanish official (*teniente*) of the district had demanded any monetary contributions for *vacuna* from pueblos.
65. AGMP 72, leg. 856, Certification of Don Carlos Mayor, Olinalan, February 13, 1807, 119r: "en el proximam[en]te pasado Enero, los vecinos de este Pueblo cercaron con barreras la plaza, para jugar toros, no para celebrar la vacuna, aunque asi lo entendió el vulgo; sino para solemnizar la funcion de N[uestr]a S[eñor]a de Guadalupe, sin ser nuevo por haverse acostumbrado todos los años. . . ."
66. AGMP Expedientes 198 leg. 2278, Izucar, April 30, 1806, Junta Central General Filantrópica de Vacunación Pública, 349v–350r.
67. The natural wonder-working crosses of colonial Mexico included one in Tamazula, Jalisco, discovered in the roots of a *huizache* plant. See William B. Taylor, "Placing the Cross in Colonial Mexico," *The Americas* 69:2 (October 2012): 145–78, here 160.
68. The forthcoming book projects of historians Elise Mitchell and Farren Yero stand to fundamentally reorient our understanding of the contributions of enslaved and free people of African descent.
69. On "ambivalent genres," "blended genres," "boundary works," and historical change in emergent discourse, William F. Hanks, "Discourse Genres in a Theory of Practice," *American Ethnologist* 14:4 (1987): 64–88, and "Language and Discourse in Colonial Yucatán [1996]," in *Intertexts* (New York: Rowman & Littlefield Publishers, 2000), 271–311. On the transformation of patriotic sermons into mixed or secularized civic discourse in Mexico's insurgency years, see Herrejón Peredo, *Del sermón al discurso cívico*, 340–42, 356–57, and Part III *passim*.

# References

Aceves, Schifter. *Medicina, minería e inquisición en la Nueva España: Esteban Morel, 1744–1795.* Mexico City: UAM Xochimilco, 2002.

Amar, José. *Instrucción curativa de las viruelas, dispuesta para los facultativos y acomodada para todos.* Madrid, 1774.

Aznar López, José. *El Doctor don José de Flores: una vida al servicio de la ciencia.* Guatemala: Editorial Universitaria, 1960.

Bennett, Jane. *Vibrant Matter: A Political Ecology of Things.* Durham: Duke University Press, 2010.

Biss, Eula. *On Immunity: An Inoculation.* Minneapolis, MI: Graywolf Press, 2014.

Cañizares-Esguerra, Jorge. *Nature, Empire, and Nation: Explorations of the History of Science in the Iberian World.* Stanford: Stanford University Press, 2006.

Cook, Sherburne. "Francisco Xavier Balmis and the Introduction of Vaccination in Latin America." *Bulletin of the History of Medicine* 12, no. 2 (1942): 70–101.

Cooper, Donald B. *Epidemic Disease in Mexico City, 1761–1813.* Austin: University of Texas Press, 1965.

de la Condamine, Charles Marie. *Mémoire sur l'inoculation de la petite vérole.* Paris: Chez Durand, 1754.

de Quintana, Andrés Mariano. *Sermón de S. Cosme y S. Damián, patronos de la Iglesia y Real Hospital de Enfermos de la Ciudad de Antequera Valle de Oaxaca.* Mexico City: Felipe de Zúñiga y Ontiveros, 1786.

de Vos, Paula. "Natural History and the Pursuit of Empire in Eighteenth-Century Spain." *Eighteenth-Century Studies* 40, no. 2 (2007): 209–39.

Esquivel Navarrete, Joseph. *Sermón eucarístico por la felicidad que logró la ciudad de Durango en la epidemia de viruelas del año de mil setecientos noventa y ocho.* Mexico City: Imprenta Madrileña de Joseph Fernández Jáuregui, 1799.

Few, Martha. "Circulating Smallpox Knowledge: Guatemalan Doctors, Maya Indians, and Designing Spain's Smallpox Vaccination Expedition, 1780–1806," *British Journal for the History of Science* 43:4 (December 2010): 519–37.

Frías Núñez, Marcelo. *Enfermedad y sociedad en la crisis colonial del antiguo régimen.* Madrid: Consejo Superior de Investigaciones Científicas, 1992.

Geertz, Clifford. "What Is a State If It Is Not a Sovereign? Reflections on Politics in Complicated Places." *Current Anthropology* 45, no. 5 (2004): 577–93.

Hanks, William F. "Discourse Genres in a Theory of Practice." *American Ethnologist* 14, no. 4 (1987): 64–88.

Hanks, William F. *Intertexts*. New York: Rowman & Littlefield Publishers, 2000.
Hernández, Pedro, ed. and trans. *Orígen y descubrimiento de la vaccina*. Madrid: Oficina de don Benito García y Compañía, 1801.
Hernández Sáenz, Luz Maria. *Learning to Heal: The Medical Profession in Colonial Mexico, 1767–1831*. New York: Peter Lang, 1997.
Herrejón Peredo, Carlos. *Del sermon al discurso cívico: México, 1760–1834*. Zamora, Michoacán: El Colegio de Michoacán; El Colegio de Mèxico, 2003.
Houdaille, Jacques. "Frenchmen and Francophiles in New Spain from 1760 to 1810." *The Americas* 13, no. 1 (1957): 1–29.
Knight, Alan. "The Weight of the State in Modern Mexico." In *Studies in the Formation of the Nation State in Latin America*, edited by James Dunkerley. London: Institute of Latin American Studies, University of London, 2002, 214–20.
León Sanz, Pilar, and Dolores Barettino Coloma. *Vicente Ferrer Gorraiz Beaumont y Montesa (1718–1792), un polemista navarro de la Ilustración*. Pamplona: Fondo de Publicaciones del Gobierno de Navarra, 2007.
López Denis, Adrián. "Inmunidades imaginadas en la Era de las Revoluciones," in Gilberto Hochman et al., *Patologías de la patria: Enfermedades, enfermos y nación en América Latina*. Buenos Aires: Lugar Editorial S.A., 2012, 29–57.
Mark, Catherine and José G. Rigau-Pérez. "The World's First Immunization Campaign: The Spanish Smallpox Vaccine Expedition, 1803–1813." *Bulletin of the History of Medicine* 83, no. 1 (2009): 63–94.
Martínez Duran, Carlos. *Las ciencias médicas en Guatemala*. 3rd ed. Guatemala: Editorial Universitaria, 1964.
Mather, Cotton. *Sentiments on the Small Pox Inoculated*, reprinted in Increase Mather, *Several Reasons Proving that Inoculation or Transplanting the Small Pox, Is a Lawful Practice, and That It Has Been Blessed by God for the Saving of Many a Life*. Cleveland: 1921. Originally published in 1721 in Boston.
*Método claro, sencillo y fácil que para practicar la Inoculación de viruelas presenta al Público el Real Tribunal del Protomedicato de esta N[ueva] E[españa] por Superior orden del Exmo. Señor Marqués de Branciforte*. Mexico City: 1797.
Mitchell, Elise. "On Slavery, Medicine, Speculation, and the Archive." *Historical Studies in the Natural Studies* 53, no. 1 (2023): 82–5.
O'Scanlan, Timoteo. *Ensayo apologético de la inoculación, o demostración de lo importante que es al particular, y al Estado*. Madrid: Imprenta Real, 1792.
Paquette, Gabriel. *Enlightenment, Governance, and Reform in Spain and Its Empire, 1759–1808*. New York: Palgrave Macmillan, 2008.

Ramírez Martín, Susana María. "Fuentes bibliográficas para el estudio de la inoculación y la vacunación en la Nueva España." In *El impacto demográfico de la viruela en México de la época colonial al siglo XX*, vol. 1, ed. Chantal Cramaussel et al. Zamora, Michoacán: El Colegio de Michoacán, 2010.

Ramírez Martín, Susana María. *La mayor hazaña médica de la colonia: La Real Expedición Filantrópica de la Vacuna en la Real Audiencia de Quito*. Quito: ABYA-YALA, 1999.

Ramírez Martín, Susana María. *La salud del Imperio: La Real Expedición Filantrópica de la Vacuna*. Ediciones Doce Calles, 2002.

Ramírez, Paul. *Enlightened Immunity: Mexico's Experiments with Disease Prevention in the Age of Reason*. Palo Alto: Stanford University Press, 2018.

Rigau-Pérez, José G. "Surgery at the Service of Theology: Postmortem Cesarean Sections in Puerto Rico and the Royal Cedula of 1804." *Hispanic American Historical Review* 75, no. 3 (1995): 377–404.

Riskin, Jessica. *Science in the Age of Sensibility: The Sentimental Empiricists of the French Enlightenment*. Chicago: The University of Chicago Press, 2002.

Scott, James. *Seeing Like a State: How Certain Schemes to Improve the Human Condition Have Failed*. New Haven: Yale University Press, 1998, 51–52.

Smith, Michael. *The "Real Expedición Marítima de la Vacuna" in New Spain and Guatemala*. Philadelphia: The American Philosophical Society, 1974.

Taylor, William B. *Magistrates of the Sacred: Priests and Parishioners in Late Colonial Mexico*. Stanford: Stanford University Press, 1996.

Taylor, William B. "Placing the Cross in Colonial Mexico." *The Americas* 69:2 (October 2012): 145–78.

Voekel, Pamela. *Alone before God: The Religious Origins of Modernity in Mexico*. Durham: Duke University Press, 2002.

Warren, Adam. "An Operation for Evangelization: Friar Francisco González Laguna, the Cesarean Section, and Fetal Baptism in Late Colonial Peru," *Bulletin of the History of Medicine* 83:4 (winter 2009): 647–75.

CHAPTER 14

# Contagious Women and Spiritual Status in Colonial Latin America
A Theoretical Proposal

JESSICA L. DELGADO

Writing in the seventeenth century, Franciscan Friar Agustín de Vetancurt celebrated the memory of a woman of African descent who lived in the Mexican convent of Santa Clara in the early years of its existence.[1] Remembered for her piety and prophetic and healing abilities, Sor Leonor de los Angeles had arrived at the convent involuntarily. Her father had "given" her to the convent—by his own account, dedicating his young daughter's life to God after she was saved from drowning.

Like most colonial convents, Santa Clara required that its novices possess racial purity, (*limpieza de sangre*) legitimate birth, and a dowry. However, there were other ways to enter and live in convents. Most convents housed large numbers of slaves and servants, and many also included women who took less formal religious vows and wore a white veil, rather than the black habit that full-status nuns wore. These "lesser" cloistered women were known as lay sisters, or "nuns of the white veil." In place of entering with a dowry, many performed menial labor, and, in most cases, their vows were not permanently binding. However, some of these lesser lay sisters did, in fact, commit to a lifetime of labor in return for quasi-religious status. They were known as *donadas*, or "given" women, either because they themselves "gave" their lives to the convent, or because they were "given" to the convents by their parents. Such was the case with Sor Leonor de los Angeles, a woman of African descent.

While it was common for convents to own or employ women of African descent as slaves and servants, non-white women were rare even among the population of donadas and other women of the lower-tiered religious vows. Whatever Leonor's father's intentions may have been in sending her to Santa Clara, the most likely outcome would have been for the nuns to ignore any pious aspirations Leonor may have had and to treat her as an ordinary servant or an enslaved woman.

Leonor, however, forged an entirely different path. By all accounts, her piety was extraordinary, and her persistent devotion eventually captured the attention of her fellow residents. Nuns, lay sisters, and servants alike regularly sought out her counsel and healing abilities. Near the end of her life, the convent gave Leonor a black habit, signaling her status as a fully professed nun, which was something almost unheard of at the time for a woman of African descent. What is more, her prominence grew further with her death, as many perceived her to be a saint. Prominent townspeople attended her funeral; the convent's vicar tried to remove a finger from her body to preserve it as a relic, but it bled as if she were still alive; and twenty years after her death, when the nuns sought to transport Leonor's bones to their convent's new location, her remains exuded a sweet smell. These were all signs of sanctity common to hagiographic accounts of holy women and men but were almost never attributed to people of African descent in colonial Latin America.

No doubt, the story of Sor Leonor de los Angeles is an incredible one. Yet, we must ask: What, exactly, makes it so incredible? The answer rests largely on one's interpretive framework, which leads us to ask further: What features of the story are highlighted, and what categories of analysis are used to explain them? Writing in the seventeenth century, Vetancurt interpreted Leonor as an inspirational individual who, by the grace of God, overcame the "natural" limitations of her racial status. Like others in his day, Vetancurt did not understand race as a socially constructed category, but rather as a "natural" fact. As such, Vetancurt interpreted Leonor in saintly terms, emphasizing her virtuous qualities as an exceptional individual.

In what follows, I offer a more intersectional interpretation of Sor Leonor de los Angeles that underscores how religion operated as a category of power and difference in the seventeenth century. In particular, I am interested in how women's "spiritual status" complicated racial and class hierarchies. As I will argue, spiritual status was gained through a public recognition of sexual virtue (or the absence of sexual scandal) and a public recognition of proper piety (or the absence of religious error). These two elements were intimately related, since ideas of religious piety and error themselves were saturated with gendered ideas about proper sexual behavior. A woman's engagement with the sacraments of confession and communion, her connections to religious cloisters, organizations, and clergymen, and her general pious disposition were always interpreted in light of her reputation for sexual virtue. If a woman's sexual reputation was in doubt, her piety was suspect. And perceptions of both piety and sexual virtue were shaped by a woman's perceived racial and economic status. All told, spiritual status, race, and class were co-constituted in gender-specific ways, and social hierarchies of "religion" were entangled with hierarchies of race and class. Together, these social forces shaped women's status, power, and life circumstances.

## Theoretical Stakes

Historians of colonial Latin America have long theorized about coloniality's role in histories of race, gender, and inequality. However, many terms and definitions central to these discussions developed in relation to geographies and historical circumstances that were significantly different from those of the particular and peculiar workings of power in the early modern Iberian colonies of the Americas. Increasingly, historians of this time and place are recognizing that we need to "do" our own theory and come up with our own categories and frameworks—not only to make sense of the historical contexts we study, but to ensure that collective theorizing about the origins of global inequality in the service of combating it includes the crucial role of Spanish and Portuguese colonialism.

One of the most significant ways that colonial Latin Americanists can contribute to and nuance decolonial analysis is through an intersectional understanding of "religion." The historically specific ways that religious beliefs, practices, and institutions shaped subjectivity and power dynamics should lead us to see religion not as merely a *subject* or *object* of historical analysis, but as a *category* of it. "Religion" was not a separate sphere of life or experience in colonial Latin America, nor the early modern Mediterranean world in general. Rather, the systems, practices, and values we now identify as "religious" were entirely imbricated in politics, economics, and culture and were fundamental to the development of social hierarchies.[2] "Religion" was therefore productive of power and difference in ways that were co-constitutive with historically specific forms of race, class, and gender. We need better language for understanding these imbrications and for describing the role of "religion" within social hierarchies and power relations.[3] In this essay, I am proposing the term "spiritual status" as one example—not as a phrase used by historical actors, but as an analytical category of analysis to help us understand a specific historical dynamic.

The story of Sor Leonor is an exceptional case, but not for the same reasons Agustín Vetancurt thought it was. Whereas Vetancurt framed Sor Leonor's exceptionalism in terms of a "natural" difficulty for someone of her racial caste to rise to such spiritual heights, I am interested in the ways in which her story and others like it invite us to think about how the gendered workings of spiritual status complicated and reinforced other forms of socially constructed power. Vetancurt framed Leonor's racial caste as an obstacle that God overcame to provide an example of exceptional piety to people of more privileged social backgrounds. But convent records and legal petitions reveal that other mixed-race women with the ability to de-emphasize their racial background could sometimes gain entrance into prestigious cloisters by presenting themselves as *españolas*.[4]

Money, family connections, and other aspects of social status could change public and legal perceptions of racial status in colonial Latin America. Scribes and judges sometimes described poor Spaniards as *mestizos* or *mulatos*, while wealthy individuals whose birth records identified them as mestizos and mulatos might appear in similar documents classified as the *casta*[5] category *español*. And in some cases, people publicly perceived as *españoles* of pure, old Christian descent (*Cristiano viejo*), but whose genealogies told a different story, might make this "fiction" official by petitioning for and purchasing certificates of limpieza de sangre from the king, thereby redacting any taint of Jewish, Muslim, Indigenous, or African blood from their legal records.[6] In my work on women's participation in the construction of colonial Catholic culture, I have found that a public reputation for virtue and piety could impact women's social status in similarly intersectional ways.[7]

I offer the term "spiritual status" as a way of naming the gendered social power related to public piety and sexual reputation. Spiritual status—like other forms of social status—could sometimes change public perception of racial identity and economic status, thereby affecting women's experience of colonial social hierarchies. When we approach the study of religion as a lens for doing historical analysis rather than merely as a subject of it, what I am calling "spiritual status" emerges as a ubiquitous and distinct form of power and difference shaping women's privilege and prestige (or lack thereof) in colonial Latin America.

## Understanding Spiritual Status for Women

Religious authorities and lay people alike understood sin and scandal as capable of spreading in invisible ways, but with material consequences. I have found the metaphor of contagion—both positive and negative—along with the language of spiritual sickness and health to be useful here. Priests described themselves as spiritual "doctors" and the sacraments they administered as "medicine" and "cures." Clerics and laypeople alike described the troubled, suffering souls of parishioners in need of the sacrament of confession as spiritually ill. *Espcrúpolo* was the term they used to capture this painful experience. However, in this historical and spiritual context, it implied more than just "scruples" or a troubled conscience. People talked about escrúpulo as spreading beyond the boundaries of the individual "self." Escrúpulo posed a host of dangers to both individuals and society because of the absence of divine grace it caused. Because God could not be in the presence of sin, a person suffering escrúpulo became a weak spot in the spiritual collective. If left unresolved, suffering individuals became more vulnerable to the devil's temptations. And if these individuals succumbed to sin, people witnessing this sin could themselves "*formó escrupulo*"—or enter into a state of escrúpulo—through the experience of being "scandalized" (*escandalizado*) by this witnessing. A person thus troubled by seeing or hearing about someone else's sin was also then tainted and thus experienced God's absence. Escrúpulo—whether caused by one's own sin or that of another—required the intervention and healing of the sacrament of confession.[8]

Women occupied a paradoxical position in relation to these widespread beliefs about how individual behavior and experience impacted collective spiritual health. On the one hand, their supposed spiritual and physical weakness and greater emotionality made them more vulnerable to sin and escrúpulo, making them dangerous vectors of *negative* spiritual contagion. On the other hand, the same conceptual framework also positioned virtuous women as capable of inoculating others from the spread of sin, scandal, and escrúpulo. In fact, when exceptionally virtuous women were concentrated into cloistered communities of prayer and ritual devotion, they were capable of sanctifying surrounding neighborhoods, communities, and towns—in other words, they became capable of *positive* spiritual contagion.[9]

Within this context, preoccupation with women's spiritual status was ubiquitous. Religious and political authorities—and to a great degree, ordinary folk too—believed that individual women had the power to bring significant harm to the spiritual well-being of their communities. Inquisitors even expressed concern that this harm had the power to negatively impact the strength of Spain's political hold in the "New World." Conversely, religious authorities considered the special power of exceptionally virtuous women to sanctify their surroundings to be an essential part of conversion, regulation of religious practices, and of the spiritual economy in general, from the earliest post-conquest moments to the end of the colonial era.[10]

Cloistering practices were key to activating women's positive spiritual contagion and protecting society from negative spiritual contagion. In addition to allowing for ecclesiastical oversight, cloisters protected women's virtue and allowed them to devote their energies to prayer and devotion. Communities of cloistered religious women held a mystique that male monastics did not possess. Convents and cloisters were among the first institutions built, and founders' petitions described them as central to the conquest and conversion of Native Americans and the establishment of Spanish power. And throughout the colonial era, towns and communities vied for permission to build convents and went to great lengths to achieve the financial means to support them.

Not all women had equally damaging or redemptive potential, however. Racialized theologies of gender difference constructed a hierarchy of danger linking femininity, spiritual capacity, poverty, and notions of "blood"—or inheritable traits. Ecclesiastical authorities and laypeople presumed a correlation between poverty and sin that positioned "unprotected" women as particularly dangerous. Unprotected women, or *mujeres desamparadas*, were those women who lived outside patriarchal authority—be it a husband or other male relative economically powerful enough to keep them secluded at home, or the ecclesiastical authority of a religious cloister. Women of Indigenous or African descent, or those with "new Christian" blood (Jewish or Muslim ancestry) were theoretically barred from religious institutions. Women of African and Indigenous descent often occupied lower economic and social positions, as well, which required them to work for a living and move about in public, making seclusion virtually impossible.

These realities helped construct a socioeconomic, racial, and religious hierarchy, which—combined with notions of gendered spiritual contagion—positioned women in very different places. Women recognized as "Old Christian" (Cristiana Vieja) and of Spanish descent (española) required vigilant protection to keep their sanctifying virtue intact. This was especially true in relation to those racially "pure" women (those recognized as having limpieza de sangre) who were without economically strong fathers or husbands. Here the risk that these women would "lose" their virtue and becoming threats to the social order was of paramount concern. Church leaders, colonial authorities, and ordinary people combined their efforts and financial resources to build institutions and raise funds to protect the virtue of this category of women. On the other side of the spectrum, the same racial, social, and economic hierarchy and these same understandings of sin and virtue positioned women of New Christian, (Cristiana Vieja), African, or Indigenous descent—along with women of Spanish descent who worked for a living, had children outside of marriage, or engaged in other kinds of deviant behavior—as social threats in need of containment.

Sexual behavior and reputation were central to this gendered social hierarchy. Ecclesiastical authorities judged the sincerity of women's religiosity and their capacity for genuine and orthodox piety by their sexual circumstances and public reputation for gendered virtue. Ecclesiastical authorities generally believed that God would not choose unmarried women known to have had sexual relations—be they consensual or not—to experience certain kinds of spiritual experiences and that such women were more vulnerable to religious error. Religious and civil authorities alike also presumed that women without strong patriarchs to protect, defend, and control them; women of mixed, Indigenous, and African descent; as well as women living in poverty were all less capable of maintaining sexual purity than women of Old Christian, Spanish descent who lived under the authority of wealthy Spanish husbands, fathers, or other male relatives.

On the other hand, socially, economically, and racially disadvantaged women who somehow managed to cultivate a strong reputation for sexual chastity and religious piety could use this reputation to their advantage. Poor women and "*huerfanas*,"[11] (girls and women without fathers) known for their sexual and spiritual purity sometimes garnered the attention of lay religious organizations or church authorities to become beneficiaries of pious foundations that provided dowries for marriage or entry into cloisters. Such women had the power to elevate not only their own spiritual status but also that of their entire community. In other words, while it was more difficult for poor women and those of mixed or non-Spanish ancestry to achieve a high level of spiritual status, it was possible. And when it happened, religious authorities and pious society understood this achievement as a sign of both God's grace and the power of colonial religious institutions, organizations, and authorities to "save" women—and in turn to save society from the danger of female contagion.

## Spiritual Contagion

Before turning to a more detailed discussion of some of the ways spiritual status worked with racial and economic status, it is important to examine more deeply women's complicated relationship to spiritual contagion. In the early modern Iberian world, the dominant ontological and theological view of humanity and the cosmos figured human beings as divided into binary parts at war with one another. Individual persons all had a spiritual nature that longed for intimacy with

God and a physical nature with desires that created distance from God. However, as in the rest of the early modern Catholic world, people often wrote and spoke of the suffering, perils, joys, and longings of the spiritual nature through a rhetoric of physicality that seemed to collapse this distinction between body and spirit. Certain very material practices, like the investing of saints' physical remains with sacred power in the form of relics, further complicated the supposed opposition of spirit and physicality. Sacramental teachings claimed that to be affective, confession must be accompanied by "*dolor verdadero*"—dolor (pain) being a word that implied a literal somatic experience of sorrow—a physically inflected emotionality—rather than merely an intellectual understanding of one's wrongs. For most of the colonial era, baroque styles of devotion, images, and architecture celebrated an emotional and physical experience of God over intellectual understandings of the Divine. In other words, the war between body and spirit was not a clear dualism, in which the goal was always to separate from bodily experience, but rather a paradoxical division in which the body was both the site of the devil's temptation and God's grace. The well-being of the soul was experienced *within* the body, and the two were intimately tied.

In this ongoing, inevitable, and inevitably destructive battle, spiritual failings were discursively figured through disease metaphors. Being in a state of sin was described as a sickness that required the "medicine" and "healing" of penitence, in which confessors became spiritual doctors. But spiritual sickness was not only an individual experience. Like physical diseases, spiritual illness was contagious. Like a rotten apple spreading its decay throughout the whole barrel, the presence of infected individuals could weaken an entire community in its defenses against sin and disorder.

Priests and parishioners spoke and wrote about sin, scandal, and shame as contagious forces. Concretely, sin led to scandal, (escándalo), which in turn led to a painful experience of shame or troubled conscience (escrúpulo). Escándalo was an emotional trauma resulting from witnessing or learning about a sinful act, word, or thought. Escrúpulo was a longer-term and more consequential emotional and spiritual state of being. It was an indefinite state of guilt and shame one entered into after committing a sin or being scandalized by someone else doing so. While escándalo could be temporary, escrúpulo, like sin itself, necessitated the formal healing of the sacrament of confession. When sin or scandal caused one to formó (form) or entró en (enter into) escrúpulo, the resulting spiritual contamination and danger was the same as if one had sinned because in either case, God could not be in the presence of sin.[12] Like someone guilty of sin, an individual suffering escrúpulo could not take communion, risked more time in purgatory, and was more vulnerable than usual to additional spiritual disorder while they were separated from God's grace. Only confession could rectify this danger, and the time before one received the cure of confession was known as being *en hora mala*—literally, in a bad time.

Within this theological framework, priests and ecclesiastical judges treated private sin as less of a concern than publicly known sin. Truly private sin only endangered the soul of the sinner, whereas public sin affected and infected others.[13] Scandal, by its nature, was a communal affair. And escrúpulo, like the emotional burden of a secret or gossip, tended to demand relief through speech. Priests sought to meet this need through confession, which also alleviated the eschatological consequences of sin and escrúpulo. However, the limited number of priests in many locations meant that "gossip" networks—and what I have named elsewhere "informal confessions"—tended to spread news of sinful behavior before formal confession could halt the damanging effects of escándalo and escrúpulo.[14] According to these ideas, a community of individuals embroiled in these emotional and spiritual experiences was a community whose defenses were weakened against demonic forces of temptation and disorder.[15] And women, imagined to be the most vulnerable community members, were therefore also the most contagious. As such, they caused the greatest anxiety within this epistemological framework.[16]

## Blood, Poverty, and *Recogimiento*

This relationship between the contagion of sin and scandal and female weakness parallel notions of contagion that were part of early modern racial discourse and practice—notably, the idea of limpieza de sangre. Maria Elena Martínez has traced changes in the ways limpieza de sangre operated between the Iberian Peninsula of the fifteenth and sixteenth century, and the seventeenth and early eighteenth-century Mexico. In the Iberian Peninsula, "New Christians" were people with Jewish or Muslim ancestry and did not possess limpieza de sangre. In the Americas, the concepts of old and new Christian, and thus limpieza de sangre expanded to include Africans and Native Americans. By the late eighteenth century, the primacy of the categories of old/new Christian within the notion of limpieza de sangre eventually gave way to a more codified system of racial and cultural difference known as the *systema de castas*. However, one thing that remained consistent throughout this evolution was the idea that virtue, spiritual strength and weakness, and tendencies toward morality, immorality, piety, and religious error were passed through bloodlines.[17]

The mechanism by which this happened was literally through the blood, which in the medieval science of humors, became semen in the hot, dry body of men and breastmilk in the damp, cool bodies of women. Not only was it thought that these substances carried behavior and cultural traits, which included religious sensibilities and practices, but in the sixteenth century Iberian world, the primary distinction between groups of people and the quality of their blood was related to what we would call religion—namely genealogies of Judaism and Islam versus "old Christian" ancestry.

This religio-racial discourse was also gendered, and arguably became even more so in the colonial context. Spanish women's blood was supposedly weaker, more permeable, and more easily tainted than Spanish men's, which made it important to control the sexual activity of "pure" blooded, old Christian españolas to prevent miscegenation, in spite of the fact that men of Spanish descent openly fathered a great many children with women of non-Spanish descent. However, in spite of, or perhaps because of, widespread mestizaje or "racial" mixing in the colonies, Indigenous and African women were nonetheless depicted as dangerously contaminating agents. The danger they posed was not only through the public example of religious error, to which they were supposedly prone, but also through their roles as nursemaids to racially "pure" españoles, through which they might literally pass their tainted "blood" to Spanish offspring.

The notion of genealogically transmitted vice and virtue was mapped onto cultural and racial identity—whether in the form of Jewish, Muslim, African, or Indigenous ancestry—but was also applied to people of Spanish descent found guilty of heresy, or who were the products of extramarital sexuality. Having a clean bloodline (limpieza de sangre), coming from an old Christian family, and having a genealogy free from the stain of religious error or illegitimate birth translated to concrete, material privileges. They were requirements for many professional and religious posts. Convents and other cloisters required them for entrance. Judges evaluated witness credibility and even shaped verdicts based on these factors. While not identical, these requirements were often related; the prevalence of concubinage and sexual violence in the conquest era led to a strong association between racial mixing and illegitimacy. And along with the stain of illegitimacy, the blood of mestizos and mulatos was thought to carry a tendency toward religious error and sexual promiscuity.

Class was also significant but complex. Economic resources mattered, but particular professions, geographies, and family lineages also formed part of what made up what we might think of as "class." Depicted in the historically specific meanings of words like *educación, cultura, vecindad, gente de razón*, various elements of social and economic class made up part of someone's *calidad*, which was an umbrella term describing not only social and economic class, but also racial categories, religious behavior, professional and other corporate identities, gender, and other aspects of social position and status. However, the relationship between economic status and virtue contained contradictory impulses in colonial Latin America. The tradition of monastic poverty and a celebration in general of the "virtuous poor" were both strong. In the late eighteenth century, the institutionalization of poverty—discouraging the giving of alms and charity in preference for the construction of poorhouses—changed the look of the "virtuous poor," but the symbolic spiritual power of eschewing material goods remained a part of the pious imaginary. Nonetheless, ecclesiastical authorities and pious society worried over the contagious effects of poverty. People without fixed employment were seen as aimless, shiftless, and amoral, and certain professions seemed further from virtue than others. And all of these qualities were imagined within a genealogical framework that centered "blood," and in which women were of particular concern.

Religious and civil colonial authorities recognized that poverty amplified the dangers that women's "natural" vulnerability posed to colonial society. Unwed pregnancy, prostitution, and other kinds of publicly visible sexual disorder, even if it was the result of sexual exploitation and violence, spread spiritual and social damage. Church institutions, religious organizations, and pious institutions treated women's physical and economic vulnerability as an important social problem; "*mujeres desamparadas*," or unprotected women—namely those who lacked economic resources and strong male supervision—required vigilant protection and control. By the early seventeenth century, an extensive institutional infrastructure emerged to protect society from the dangers of poor and "unprotected" women. Cofradias, bishops, prominent individuals, and widespread popular donation created and supported a host of cloistering institutions and practices known collectively as *recogimiento*. The founding documents of institutions and funds designed to protect poor, unprotected explicitly named the spiritual danger these vulnerable women posed to society if they lost their virtue.[18]

There was a larger economic context behind these efforts, as well. As employment opportunities became scarcer in Spain throughout the seventeenth century, an influx of poorer and less educated Spaniards began arriving in the Spanish Americas. Colonial authorities and elite Spaniards expressed anxiety that the growing number of Spaniards in the lower economic and social classes challenged the proper racial hierarchy necessary for maintaining colonial rule. The intricate *systema de castas*, or casta system that developed in the eighteenth century—which included an explosion of largely fictional racial categories, laws attempting to strengthen social distinctions, and elite artistic and discursive production imaginatively depicting and ordering people into these "casta" categories—had its origins in these fears. What many elite voices referred to negatively as the "*imperio mixto*" or the "mixed empire" included not only the increasing number of people of mixed Spanish, Indigenous, and African descent, but also people who did not fit properly into colonial hierarchies like poor Spaniards and unprotected women of Spanish descent.

Fears about this imperio mixto were at once economic, racial, and religious, and were highly gendered. Religious ignorance, lax piety, and questionable virtue went hand in hand with poverty and vagrancy from this elite perspective. Religious authorities in the eighteenth century increasingly policed "false" female mystics and women of Spanish descent seeking out healing and magical services from Indigenous women. They conjectured that the growing number of people of apparently pure Spanish descent in the "plebian" classes was in fact evidence of the hidden presence of non-Spanish blood resulting from improper protection of Spanish women.[19] In this context, the lay brotherhoods, wealthy pious donors, and clergymen who founded and supported recogimientos were particularly focused on women of Spanish descent.[20]

The flip side of the ideal that women were dangerous vectors of negative spiritual contagion was the idea that female virtue could also spread, and in doing so, inoculate their communities. Founding and regulating documents of voluntary female cloisters expressed the idea that properly cloistered virtuous women could sanctify their communities. In inventories and annual visits, bishops and cofradia officers kept track of the residents leaving for marriage, professing as nuns, and those choosing to stay indefinitely. Though securing a proper marriage was one of the stated goals of placing young women in these institutions, the annual visit records especially celebrated those who remained permanently cloistered. Colonial authorities frequently praised the efforts of these voluntary recogimientos, calling them "jewels" of their cities and towns that honored and pleased both God and King. These practices of cloister had the dual effect of containing female sin and fostering the spread of sanctifying female virtue.[21]

However, as these "jewels" became increasingly exclusive, the concern to protect poor women of Spanish descent and the focus on the sanctifying power of properly cloistered virtuous women ironically led to even more widespread fears about the dangers posed by racially "impure" women. In the sixteenth century, there existed two kinds of voluntary institutions: those for "virtuous and poor" *doncellas* (maidens or virgins) and those for repentant women—former prostitutes, adulteresses, or other women of ill repute. Known popularly as "Magdalena houses," after Mary Magdalen, the latter institutions were popular sources for pious donation in the early colonial period. But as they grew in wealth, many of them gained prestige as well. Originally these cloisters housed both nuns and repentant women, so that the former could educate the latter, and they housed both españolas and women of mixed race. But as their collective spiritual status raised, they increasingly resembled recogimientos for poor and virtuous women. Some of these eventually petitioned to become *beaterios*, (cloisters for laywomen taking religious vows similar to nuns). Some benefited from wealthy parents paying to place their children for educational purposes. And some took in increasing numbers of virtuous but poor españolas, shifting the balance away from both repentant and racially mixed women. By the end of the seventeenth century, most of the institutions for "repentant" women had implemented entrance requirements that excluded the kinds of women they were originally intended to support.[22]

## Claiming Spiritual Status

Women could most reliably cultivate a public reputation for virtue and piety through cloistered living, as either a housebound wife or resident of an institutional shelter, and publicly recognized piety through sacraments and other church sanctioned devotional practices. Both of these avenues were far more accessible to elite women. Convents required dowries and limpieza de sangre to enter. Lay cloisters meant to house virtuous poor women grew increasingly racially exclusive over time. Poor women living outside of cloisters, even if married, generally had to work outside of the home. Frequent access to sacraments and personal relationships with clergymen were more available in urban areas and among elite society. And ecclesiastical authorities' racialized ideas of spiritual capacity led them to interpret the religious practices Indigenous and African women differently than that of españolas, even when they were known for their seemingly orthodox piety.

Recogimiento, in addition to referring to institutions of cloister, was an ubiquitous term describing the ideal qualities of a virtuous women. A woman who possessed recogimiento was known to be pious, modest, obedient, and literally living in seclusion in either a home or cloister. Elite definitions of recogimiento defined a properly *recogida* woman as someone who remained indoors most of the time, was modestly covered when outside, and did not speak to men outside of their own family. For women who worked in markets and taverns or traveled between homes as domestic servants, this idealized form of recogimiento was unattainable. Thus, from an elite perspective, women whose economic and social circumstances required them to work outside of their homes—no matter how faithfully they participated in church sanctioned spiritual practices—were already morally suspect.

In spite of these obstacles, women excluded from these avenues of virtuous and pious reputation still sought out informal, community-recognized forms of spiritual status. For instance, in their testimonies before ecclesiastical judges, many non-white, poor, and unmarried women forcefully made claims to spiritual status by defining recogimiento differently than did elite women. Poor women of Indigenous, African, and mixed descent frequently used the term "*muy recogida*" to describe themselves in court testimonies and petitions. Women who worked in public spaces and even those who had given birth outside of wedlock claimed to be recogida, defining recogimiento as sexual respectability—even if they could no longer claim to be virgins, wear modest dress, and demonstrate subdued, obedient behavior—even if they could not afford to be utterly dependent on men for their livelihood.[23]

In ecclesiastical court petitions and complaints, women of lower social status challenged the loss of spiritual status by turning the notional of female contagion on its head own. Using the language of escándalo and escrúpulo, women argued that judges had an obligation to protect society from the scandal caused by their own loss of virtue by punishing men who had sexually violated, abandoned, or abused them. These wronged women reminded judges that the men who had harmed them personally had also forced them publicly into a position that was against God's laws and could scandalize everyone around them, thus threatening collective spiritual health. But even while describing themselves as potential sources of scandal, they sought to retain spiritual status, by calling themselves "recogida" and demanding that the judges help them return to their previous state of virtue. In other words, they laid claim to a level of spiritual status in a way that not only warranted respect and protection, but if honored, could also halt negative spiritual contagion and potentially spread virtue.

In addition to redefining the concept of recogimiento to lay claim to spiritual status outside of cloistered living, poor, non-white women also sometimes sought out informal access to cloistering institutions. Some women left domestic service work to commit themselves to working in convents. Like Leonor de los Angeles, whose story opened this essay, some of these women became donadas—"donating" their labor in perpetuity and wearing the white veiled habit of a lay sister. Other women known as *niñas*, no matter how old they were, lived as dependents of individual nuns. While many of these women arrived as young girls, some chose to accompany female relatives at an older age. Even enslaved women living in convents, who arguably had little agency in relation to being cloistered or not, laid claim to the quality of recogimiento in their testimonies before ecclesiastical judges and cited their residence as evidence of their piety.

Like poor women who worked outside of the home, convent laywomen redefined recogimiento and claimed spiritual status in counter cultural ways. The purity and integrity of cloistered nuns' spiritual status was made possible by the fact that the large population of laywomen living in and working for the convent were explicitly not cloistered. By performing menial labor, running errands and delivering messages outside of the convent, and providing comfort and company, these lay residents allowed nuns to focus on prayer and other religious practices, receive news of the outside world, and develop quasi-familial relationships that sustained them. And yet enslaved women, servants, and "niñas" claimed virtue in the form of recogimiento based on their proximity to cloisters, increased access to sacraments, and reputations free from scandal.

## Conclusion

For women in colonial Latin America, spiritual status was determined through public reputation for virtue and piety, but was discursively and materially linked to poverty and race and shaped by notions of spiritual contagion. Racially "impure" women were morally suspect, and poor, "unprotected" women of Spanish descent could easily become threats to collective spiritual health. Virtuous women, if properly protected and cloistered, could redeem their communities. The interlocking forces of race, gender, class, and spiritual status set up teleological options that controlled and protected white women and made it difficult for most non-white women and many poor women to achieve recognition for virtue and piety.

Legitimacy, orthodoxy, and virtue were all coded for race: racial mixture was associated with illegitimate birth, improper Christianization, and sexual immorality; Indigenous people were understood as permanent neophytes, incapable of either understanding and practicing correct religion or living up to the stringencies of Christian morality; and people of African descent carried the taint of sexual excess, slavery and servitude, as well as the "old world" legacy of Islam. At the same time, poor women of both Spanish and non-Spanish descent were more likely to be cohabitating in consensual domestic and sexual relationships outside of marriage, even with children, and by necessity they often performed labor that put them in the category of "public women."

In other words, religion as a category of social power and difference worked intersectionally with race, class, and gender to maintain colonial hierarchies. High levels of spiritual status were difficult for non-white and non-elite women to achieve, but not entirely out of reach. Such women *could* achieve public recognition for their piety, if they could manage to protect their public reputation for virtue, in spite of all the obstacles in the way of doing so. Poor women of Indigenous, African, and mixed racial descent claimed spiritual status in both discursive and material ways. By redefining recogimiento, using ideas of contagion to argue for protection, and through informal relationships with institutional cloisters, non-elite women sought to mitigate their place in racial, economic, and social hierarchies through claims to virtue and piety. When they were able to do this, spiritual status became social capital that could partially mitigate the other categories of non-privilege they inhabited. Tied to gendered ideas of spiritual contagion, women who were otherwise seen as posing a threat to collective spiritual health could raise their spiritual status by publicly reducing the danger they posed or by joining the ranks of the exceptionally virtuous women who spread positive spiritual contagion, thereby sanctifying their communities, as was the case with Leonor de los Angeles.

The ideas I have proposed here suggest a reframing of our understanding of religion so that it becomes a category not only of belief and practice, but also of power and social difference. By naming "spiritual status" as a discrete, gendered category of colonial power, I hope to continue the important work of María Elena Martinez and others who have traced the antecedents of our modern categories of race, class, gender, and sexuality. In this chapter, I have offered some initial observations based on my research on laywomen's piety and engagement with the church, but I hope other scholars will take up the notion of spiritual status and think through other questions as well. These include: how spiritual status might operate for men; how it shaped women's economic possibilities; how it may have factored into domestic life; and in a more detailed way, how it shaped and social networks of particular communities. Scholars of early modern Spanish colonialism have learned from and contributed to theoretical discussions of power developed with other historical contexts in mind. However, one of the primary goals of this chapter has been to forge historically specific theoretical tools—like "spiritual status"—that help to show how "religion" produces social relations and subjectivities that are intrinsically gendered.

## Notes

1. Augustín de Vetancurt, *Teatro mexicano: Descripción breve de los sucesos ejemplares, históricos y religiosos del Nuevo Mundo de las Indias. Crónica de la Provincia Del Santo Evangelio De México. Menologio franciscano de los varones más señalados, que con sus vidas ejemplares, perfección religiosa, ciencia, predicación evangélica en su vida, ilustraron la Provincia del Santo Evangelio de México.* 1. Ed. facsimilared. Biblioteca Porrúa, 45 (México: Editorial Porrúa, 1971).
2. I would argue that they still are, albeit in a less visible way. However, the entanglement was so thorough in the early modern world that the modern distinction between religion and not-religion would have been nonsensical to people living at the time.
3. For an overview of these discussions, see: Jessica L. Delgado and Kelsey C. Moss, "Religion and Race in the Early Modern Iberian Atlantic," *The Oxford Handbook of Religion and Race in American History*, ed. Kathryn Gin Lum and Paul Harvey (Oxford University Press, 2018).
4. Español and Española were casta categories that designated men and women of Spanish descent, but often born in the colonies. "*Peninsular*" was the term used to designate someone born in Spain. Español could refer to both people of Spanish descent born in the colonies and peninsulares, but the former operated more like what we might think of as a genealogical ethnic or racial category, whereas the latter was a designation of "national" origin, culture, and education. For clarity, I will use the Spanish term español/a when referring to the casta category, rather than "Spaniard."
5. Casta, generally translated as caste, refers to the *systema de castas* (caste system) that developed by the eighteenth century in Latin America. It was a complex racial categorization system that named and hierarchically ordered offspring of different "casta" groups into more than forty categories. At this level, it was primarily

symbolic, represented in art known as the casta paintings. However, there were legal codes attempting to regulating dress, employment, and behavior of various kinds by casta category, and identifying casta category was a part of most official documentation, from birth, baptism, marriage and death records to all legal testimonies, petitions, and contracts. Though some categories were rarely used outside of the casta paintings, the most common ones had been a ubiquitous part of colonial life and identity from the early sixteenth century on. These included español/a, indio/a, negro/a, mestizo/a, mulato/a, castizo, and morisco.

6. Ann Twinam, *Purchasing Whiteness: Pardos, Mulattos, and the Quest for Social Mobility in the Spanish Indies* (Stanford: Stanford University Press, 2015); María Elena Martínez, *Genealogical Fictions: Limpieza De Sangre, Religion, and Gender in Colonial Mexico* (Stanford, CA: Stanford University Press, 2008); See also Ann Twinam, *Public Lives, Private Secrets: Gender, Honor, Sexuality, and Illegitimacy in Colonial Spanish America* (Stanford, CA: Stanford University Press, 1999) for the history of purchasing similar certificates of "legitimate" birth by those seeking to erase the stain of illegitimacy for themselves or their children resulting from out-of-wedlock birth.

7. Jessica L. Delgado, *Laywomen and the Making of Colonial Catholicism in New Spain, 1630–1790* (Cambridge: Cambridge University Press, 2018).

8. Escándalo and escrúpulo translates to scandal and scruples respectively, but their usage in this historical and religious context implies more than is contained by these English words. Delgado, "Sin Temor de Dios: Women and Ecclesiastical Justice in Eighteenth-Century Toluca," *Colonial Latin American Review* 18, no. 1 (April 2009): 99.

9. Delgado, "Sin Temor de Dios"; Kathryn Burns, *Colonial Habits: Convents and the Spiritual Economy of Cuzco, Peru* (Durham, NC: Duke University Press, 1999); Delgado, *Laywomen*.

10. Burns, *Colonial Habits*. Asunción Lavrín, *Brides of Christ: Conventual Life in Colonial Mexico* (Stanford, CA: Stanford University Press, 2008).

11. Huerfanas literally means "orphans," but in colonial documentation of women seeking shelter in recogimientos, it often meant fatherless. In fact, mothers frequently were the ones petitioning for entrance for their "huerfana" daughters and sited the fathers' deaths as justification.

12. Confessors, penitents, and people presenting testimony before ecclesiastical courts spoke of escrupulo in this way: *entró en escrúpulo*, or *formó escrúpulo*.

13. This does not mean that confessors did put a great deal of time and ink into detailing the proper regulation of private sin. This is what Serge Gruzinski and Jorge Klor de

Alva argue led to a greater individualization of self in the subjectivities of Native Americans in the sixteenth century. While this observation is important, it should not distract us from the continued concern with collective spiritual wellbeing on the part of Spanish American confessors and a continued corporate identity at play alongside the individualizing tendencies of confession.

14. Delgado, *Laywomen*, ch. 3.
15. Particularly articulate examples of these beliefs can be found in the testimonies of women speaking as witnesses before the Inquisition, describing how they felt compelled to tell their confessor about someone else's crime after having the experience of "escrúpulo," and of confessors defending their female penitents for having waited to report something until they experienced escrúpulo, arguing that they did not know they had an obligation to do so until their conscience told them through the suffering of escrúpulo.
16. That women were seen as a weak link in the battle against the forces of Satan is a notion visible in trials against women for witchcraft, false visions, and other religious crimes. Solange Alberro, "Herejes, brujas, y beatas: mujeres ante el tribunal del Santo Oficio de la Inquisición en la Nueva España," in *Presencia y transparencia: la mujer en la historia de México*, ed. Carmon Ramos Escandón (Mexico: El Colegio de México, 1987), 79–94; Giles, *Women in the Inqusition*; Nora Jaffary, *False Mystics: Deviant Orthodoxy in Colonial Mexico* (Lincoln: University of Nebraska Press, 2004); Martha Few, *Women Who Live Evil Lives: Gender, Religion, and the Politics of Power in Colonial Guatemala* (Austin: University of Texas Press, 2002); Laura Lewis, *Hall of Mirrors: Power, Witchcraft, and Caste in Colonial Mexico* (Durham: Duke University Press, 2003).
17. Though writing about two very different historical contexts, both Kelsey Moss's notion of "spiritual racialization," as well as Judith Weisenfeld's term "religio-racial" are both very helpful theoretical frameworks for understanding the process Martínez traces. Kelsey Moss, "On Earth as it is in Heaven: Spiritual Racialization and the Atlantic World Economy of Salvation in the Colonial Americas." 2018, Princeton University. Judith Weisenfeld, *New World a Coming: Black Religion and Racial Identity during the Great Migration* (New York: NYU Press, 2017). Judith Weisenfeld, "The House We Live In: Religio-Racial Theories and the Study of Religion," *Journal of the American Academy of Religion*, 88, no. 2 (June 2020): 440–59.
18. Delgado, *Laywomen*, ch. 4.
19. This is a central theme in the story of María Gonzales, about which I'm writing my in current book, *The Beata of the Black Habit: Gender, Race, and Religious Authority in Late Eighteenth Century Mexico*.

20. Delgado, *Laywomen*, chs. 4 and 5.
21. Delgado, *Laywomen*, ch. 5.
22. Delgado, *Laywomen*, ch. 4; Muriel, Josefina. *Los Recogimientos De Mujeres: Respuesta a Una Problemática Social Novohispana*. Universidad Nacional Autónoma De México, Instituto De Investigaciones Históricas, 24 (México: Universidad Nacional Autónoma de México, Instituto de Investigaciones Históricas, 1974).
23. Nancy van Duesen traces the contested elite and non-elite definitions of *recogimiento* in Peru, in her important study of the complex concept, practice, and institutions referred to by the word *recogimiento*. Nancy E. Van Deusen, *Between the Sacred and the Worldly: The Institutional and Cultural Practice of Recogimiento in Colonial Lima* (Stanford, CA: Stanford University Press, 2001).

## References

Burns, Kathryn. *Colonial Habits: Convents and the Spiritual Economy of Cuzco, Peru*. Durham, NC: Duke University Press, 1999.

Delgado, "Sin Temor de Dios: Women and Ecclesiastical Justice in Eighteenth-Century Toluca," *Colonial Latin American Review* 18, no. 1 (April 2009).

Delgado, Jessica L. *Laywomen and the Making of Colonial Catholicism in New Spain, 1630–1790*. Cambridge: Cambridge University Press, 2018.

Few, Martha. *Women Who Live Evil Lives: Gender, Religion, and the Politics of Power in Colonial Guatemala*. Austin: University of Texas Press, 2002.

Giles, Mary. *Women in the Inquisition: Spain and the New World*. Baltimore: Johns Hopkins University Press, 1999.

Lavrín, Asunción. *Brides of Christ: Conventual Life in Colonial Mexico*. Stanford, CA: Stanford University Press, 2008.

Lewis, Laura. *Hall of Mirrors: Power, Witchcraft, and Caste in Colonial Mexico*. Durham: Duke University Press, 2003.

Martínez, María Elena. *Genealogical Fictions: Limpieza De Sangre, Religion, and Gender in Colonial Mexico*. Stanford, CA: Stanford University Press, 2008.

Moss, Kelsey. "On Earth as it is in Heaven: Spiritual Racialization and the Atlantic World Economy of Salvation in the Colonial Americas." PhD Diss., Princeton University, 2019.

Moss, Kelsey, and Jessica Delgado. "Religion and Race in the Early Modern Iberian Atlantic." In *The Oxford Handbook of Religion and Race in American History*, edited by Kathryn Gin Lum and Paul Harvey. Oxford University Press, 2018.

Muriel, Josefina. *Los recogimientos de mujeres : respuesta a una problemática social novohispana.* México: Universidad Nacional Autónoma de México, Instituto de Investigaciones Históricas, 1974.

Nora Jaffary, *False Mystics: Deviant Orthodoxy in Colonial Mexico.* Lincoln: University of Nebraska Press, 2004.

Solange Alberro, "Herejes, brujas, y beatas: mujeres ante el tribunal del Santo Oficio de la Inquisición en la Nueva España." In *Presencia y transparencia: la mujer en la historia de México,* edited by Carmon Ramos Escandón. Mexico: El Colegio de México, 1987, 79–94.

Twinam, Ann. *Public Lives, Private Secrets: Gender, Honor, Sexuality, and Illegitimacy in Colonial Spanish America.* Stanford, CA: Stanford University Press, 1999.

Twinam, Ann. *Purchasing Whiteness: Pardos, Mulattos, and the Quest for Social Mobility in the Spanish Indies.* Stanford: Stanford University Press, 2015.

Van Deusen, Nancy E. *Between the Sacred and the Worldly: The Institutional and Cultural Practice of Recogimiento in Colonial Lima.* Stanford, CA: Stanford, 2013.

Vetancurt, Augustín de, *Teatro mexicano: Descripción breve de los sucesos ejemplares, históricos y religiosos del Nuevo Mundo de las Indias. Crónica de la Provincia Del Santo Evangelio De México. Menologio franciscano de los varones más señalados, que con sus vidas ejemplares, perfección religiosa, ciencia, predicación evangélica en su vida, ilustraron la Provincia del Santo Evangelio de México.* 1. Ed. facsimilared. Biblioteca Porrúa, 45. (México: Editorial Porrúa, 1971).

Weisenfeld, Judith. *New World a Coming: Black Religion and Racial Identity during the Great Migration.* New York: NYU Press, 2017.

Weisenfeld, Judith. "The House We Live In: Religio-Racial Theories and the Study of Religion," *Journal of the American Academy of Religion,* 88, no. 2 (June 2020): 440–59.

CHAPTER 15

# Spectral Comrades and Comandantes

## Latinx Hauntology and the Day of the Dead in Orange County, California

*DAISY VARGAS AND JENNIFER SCHEPER HUGHES*

> For our spectral comrade,
> Luis León,
> in memoriam.

> "I am a future ghost. I am getting ready for my haunting."
> —EVE TUCK AND C. REE, "A GLOSSARY OF HAUNTING"

> "What seems almost impossible is to speak always of the specter, to speak to the specter, to speak with it, therefore especially to make or let a spirit speak."
> —JACQUES DERRIDA, SPECTERS OF MARX

Day of the Dead festivals entered the public religious landscape of California a half-century ago, in the early 1970s, and have now "come of age." The US improvisation of the traditional Mexican Catholic religious observance has entered the mainstream, proliferating in urban centers across the Mexican diaspora, becoming the most immediately recognizable Latinx holiday.[1] Typical of this fast growing American holiday, temporary altars to the deceased line city streets, attendees dress in skeletal "Catrina" costumes, vendors sell culturally themed merchandise as musicians serenade, and long lines of hungry festival-goers of all races and ethnicities wind through crowds to food stands selling steaming tacos. A small but significant scholarly literature from various fields has emerged to analyze and interpret the US iteration of Día de los Muertos, probing its political, healing, artistic, commercial, and identity-forming potencies.[2]

We contend that more still needs to be understood about the diverse US articulations and meanings of the Day of the Dead within the field of religious studies. In Santa Ana, California, a supermajority Mexican city in the heart of Orange County, local activist altar builders have fought hard to create and preserve their unique observance, *Noche de Altares* (Night of Altars), for more than two decades. The stakes are high for the organizers: for them, Noche de Altares represents nothing less than a struggle for the soul of Santa Ana. At the heart of this struggle is the integrity and sustainability of working-class Latino cultures, economies, and community against gentrification, displacement, and erasure. *Santaneros* (as they call themselves) labor to preserve their celebration's political and spiritual purpose. Simultaneously deeply somber and ebullient, Noche de Altares seamlessly integrates community-led ritual labor and social justice activism in a way that is particularly Latin American (and entirely Santanero) in its ethos.

What we offer here emerges from a sustained ethnographic study that interprets how Noche de Altares is both embedded in the specificity of its community context and connected to local webs of experience and meaning.[3] In exploring how Noche is part of the ritual and spiritual fabric of the Santa Ana community but in a de-ecclesial mode (a term we introduce and define below), we seek to contribute to the emerging body of ethnographic scholarship on Latinx religion.[4] Our exploration began ten years ago with a collaborative humanities study conducted by an interdisciplinary team of faculty researchers, graduate and undergraduate students, and a filmmaker.[5] Together, we completed dozens of open-ended interviews with organizers and participants, and logged more than a thousand hours of participant observation.[6] Our most intensive period of research was between 2013 and 2015—though we have returned to it periodically up until the present, including attending Noche in 2023. We have also directed and produced a documentary film that is in the final stages of post-production.[7]

Of central importance for this study is Santaneros' perception of the real presence of ghosts and spirits.[8] The souls of the dead are summoned to the celebration with meals laid out on altars, copal incense, ritual dance and music, and the ceremonial Catrina procession that lends Noche its particular solemnity. These summoned spirits make themselves known in the wind that gently rustles the *papel picado* (perforated paper) adorning the altars—though sometimes more dramatically, by disrupting preparations and knocking items off altars. Nor are the ghosts of Santa Ana confined to the annual Day of the Dead celebration. The ghosts and spirits that are invited often linger on the streets even after they are meant to return to the afterworld. Sometimes they accompany Santaneros year-round, as reminders of loss, tragedy, and the search for home. In discussing our analysis, we have settled on the term *Latinx hauntology* to account for the participation of spirits central to both the Noche de Altares celebration and the transgressive political power of the commemoration. The ghosts invoked in Santa Ana are spectral comrades whose haunting of downtown city streets furthers the political struggle for human rights, community sovereignty, and social justice.

Our approach in adopting the vocabulary of hauntology is Derridean in nature. With *Spectres of Marx* (published in 1993 in French and the following year in English), Jacques Derrida inspired a multidisciplinary line of inquiry in which specters and ghosts serve as lenses to theorize the politics of exclusion and of visibility and invisibility—especially (for US scholars) with respect to race, class, and gender.[9] For almost two decades, the radical theorist made an annual sojourn from Paris to the University of California, Irvine, where he taught a class until his death in 2004. From his Orange County post, scarcely ten miles from Santa Ana, Derrida explored revenant Marxism—Marxism's survival even after the supposed triumph of liberal capitalism and the "end of history" pronounced by Francis Fukuyama.

However, what we strive for here is not so much a Derridian interpretation of the ghosts of Santa Ana, but rather a Santanero haunting of Derrida. We position Derrida within his Orange County ethnographic context—in particular the very segregationist race and class politics in which Noche de Altares intervenes. In keeping with this cultural and social milieu, Derrida seems to have remained removed from the borderland realities of Santa Ana. His reflections are not grounded in or responsive to the material conditions of Orange County, where he sometimes lived. To be clear, Santaneros do not need Derrida to theorize what is already an inherently Marxist and theoretical—and specifically theopolitical—rite, as we discuss here. Thus, we follow the activist altar builders of Santa Ana in their annual celebration.

Drawing on what we learned in Santa Ana, we define Latinx hauntology as (1) a way of understanding space and place that is related to the borderlands gothic; (2) spectral: centered on the real presence, power, and agency of spirits; (3) de-ecclesial: resisting secularization but distancing itself from formal religious institutions and church structures, centering instead Indigenous Mesoamerican lines of descent; and (4) Marxist, explicit in its critique of capitalist structures of power, and manifesting the deep ties between religious practice and social justice in Latin America. Through community observances and effort, revenant, rebel spirits of the Mexican borderlands may yet haunt.

## Facing the Twin Threats of Commercialization and Secularization

At their origin, US Day of the Dead celebrations were expressions of the Chicano movement, asserting politically radical critiques of the violent and deadly consequences of US immigration and economic and foreign policy—critiques relayed via politically themed altars. Regina Marchi offered the first comprehensive book-length study of Day of the Dead festivals in the United States, describing how early celebrations organized by the Mexican Museum in San Francisco included altars protesting the Latin American death worlds wrought by Ronald Reagan's foreign policy. A 2001 Day of the Dead celebration in Holt, Texas, was held in a potter's field where unnamed migrants were buried. Protestors used the celebration to demand that the anonymous dead be identified through DNA testing.[10] Most Day of the Dead commemorations began like these—as grassroots observances with a social justice and activist ethos. However, over the last two decades, Day of the Dead celebrations have mostly succumbed to a seemingly inevitable drive toward commercialization, homogenization, and secularization that has facilitated the entrance of the cultural ritual into the mainstream. Largely sanitized of political, religious, and otherwise transgressive content, they have been absorbed within the framework of neoliberal multiculturalism.

In California, this process of absorption and secularization has been facilitated by the incorporation of Day of the Dead into the public school curriculum. It is true that teachers have used this curriculum in powerful ways, to lift up Latinx students and incorporate Chicano history and culture into instruction. At the same time, the inclusion of religious cultural practices has created a new set of problems. In the name of multiculturalism, Latinx and non-Latinx school children alike now rehearse part of the Mexican Catholic liturgical year: in classrooms across the state, students commemorate All Saints/All Souls, Las Posadas, and Three Kings.[11] These lessons trespass on church-state boundaries in grounding ritual practice and belief: students build and decorate altars to deceased family members, cut *papel picado*, light candles, and reflect on human mortality and the nature of souls and spirits. The ambiguity of instruction led to a legal complaint in 2003 (*Bricker v. Petaluma City Schools*). Finding for the defendant, California's courts ruled the teaching of Day of the Dead "cultural" rather than "religious" instruction.[12] With respect to the incorporation of Chicano Studies into the California curriculum, we note the recent successful challenge to California's Ethnic Studies requirement on the basis of separation of church and state.[13] In effect, Day of the Dead has been secularized by legal ruling. Notably, these decidedly religious observances could not be taught in public schools across the border in Mexico, prohibited under its version of revolutionary nationalist secularism. Finally, the Pixar film *Coco* (2017), beloved by many, also served to transform the Day of the Dead into an accessible, sentimentalized holiday, one nearly devoid of meaningful political or religious challenge to mainstream, Anglo-Protestant America.

Countering these trends, local Day of the Dead celebrations still have the potential to cohere communities and challenge structural violence, a capacity discovered in ongoing resistance to the twinned processes of commercialization and secularization and, importantly, in the invocation of spirits. Through tremendous community effort over twenty years, Noche de Altares activists have successfully resisted both commercialization and secularization—preserving community autonomy and integrity and maintaining the political and spiritual independence of their unique, innovated street ritual. The example of Noche de Altares illuminates the persistent power of Day of the Dead celebrations to unsettle politically, culturally, and religiously. Where other observances have succumbed, Noche has successfully resisted. At its height during the time of our initial study, the Noche de Altares festival was the largest community-sponsored Day of the Dead celebration in Southern California. With almost 200 individual altars and as many as 40,000 visitors, Noche sprawled out over several city blocks in Santa Ana's working-class, Mexican, thriving downtown city center.

For Santaneros the counterpoint to and antithesis of their celebration is Los Angeles' Hollywood Forever Cemetery Day of the Dead festival. With upwards of 60,000 attendees (in 2016), four stages, and massive corporate sponsorship (Disney and AT&T have had altars), Hollywood Forever has displaced smaller and more meaningful community celebrations, like the one organized by Self Help Graphics in Boyle Heights and the Festival de la Gente near 6th Street.[14] Many Noche de Altares activists regard Hollywood Forever with a sort of horror—as a garishly secularized, unholy bastardization and as a threat.

## Contested Space, Gentrification, and the Mexican Borderlands Gothic

*Noche* began in 2002 under the impetus of one of Santa Ana's most important community organizations, El Centro Cultural de México, founded by Mexican anthropologist Socorro Sarmiento. The celebration reached new heights, in scale and the numbers of attendees, largely due to the labor and organizational prowess of Rudy Cordova and his then-wife, Jackie. At the time, they owned and operated

Café Calacas, an organizational center of operations for the festival. The committee of organizers are human rights activists and political visionaries who distinguish Noche de Altares from other Day of the Dead festivals by their staunch refusal to accept corporate, city, or state sponsorship, even at the risk of the sustainability and viability of the celebration itself.[15] The ongoing threat of gentrification and redevelopment in the historically immigrant downtown lends the religious festival its particularly pointed political edge.

Through the invention, reinvention, and innovation of traditional Mexican religious practices, community members and activists articulate their spiritual and political claim to Santa Ana. Most significantly in this regard, beginning around 2012, the growing ritual celebration took over Calle Cuatro (Fourth Street), with Santa Ana's contested downtown struggling to resist gentrification. In the haunting of spirits through the altars and its uniquely innovated Catrina procession, discussed at more length below, Noche de Altares is a religio-political battle for geographical and spiritual territory: one in which ghosts and spirits are deployed as spectral comrades whose haunting makes spatial claims to the city center.

The long history of borderlands racism, displacement, and segregation is repeated in contemporary gentrification and urban redevelopment projects in Santa Ana—as throughout Southern California. More specifically, the political and economic violence imposed by city and state actors on the Mexican and Mexican American community evokes the nineteenth-century dispossession wrought by the Treaty of Guadalupe Hidalgo. Here we bring to bear the idea of the borderlands gothic to reflect on the spatial politics articulated in the Noche commemoration. During Noche de Altares, the presence of the spectral affirms the importance of geographic and political location; Santaneros and their spectral comrades recall the legacies of occupation and displacement that haunt the present. Though the concept of the borderlands gothic is still emerging, in its original British formulation the gothic is defined in part in relation to supernatural haunting and threats of violence and death.[16] We also draw from the aesthetic and literary conventions of the gothic and, by extension, the postcolonial gothic to locate Santa Ana as a location "inevitably haunted by the colonial past."[17] Like the postcolonial gothic, the borderlands gothic centers the colonial (and postcolonial) subject and positions the dominant racial and racist order as the horrific; racial capitalism and the apparatus of state is named responsible for terror and violence. Literary theorist Jesse Alemán explores the idea of the gothic in relation to Mexico's history of conquest and subsequent relation to the United States, describing it as "what is repressed, what is hidden, unspoken, deliberately forgotten."[18] The gothic speaks to the threat of the supernatural—its capacity to haunt and trouble us in the present.[19]

Santa Ana is, in fact, a borderland, not only by virtue of its history and proximity to the US-Mexico border, but also as a sociocultural and economic space where, as Gloria Anzaldúa puts it, the "third world grates against the first and bleeds."[20] Today, almost 80 percent of the city is Latino, with almost 60 percent of all residents low or very low income and almost half born outside of the United States. The city has the nation's highest concentration of Spanish speakers and the highest population density per housing unit; it also has the highest rates of domestic violence in the state.[21] Ten years ago, the Rockefeller Foundation ranked Santa Ana first in its national Urban Hardship Index, making it worse off than Detroit, Michigan, or Newark, New Jersey. In his 2013 interview with us, Benjamin Vasquez, an organizer and public school teacher, elaborates,

> There are still businesspeople who want to get rid of the Mexican side [of Santa Ana] and erase it. They want to get rid of poor people.... In America we always see poverty as something you look down upon ... but how do you live with dignity, or have a policy that allows people in poverty to live with dignity? They are still attacking where poor people live.... Being able to celebrate Día de los Muertos is not so much taking back the city but claiming a piece of ownership of the city.

Santa Ana's celebration of Noche de Altares stands as a spectral and gothic disruption: an uncanny, unhomely reminder that "collapses the otherwise clear distinctions between native and foreigner, domestic and international, and America and América."[22]

Imagined as a borderlands gothic city, Santa Ana remembers and recollects the long history of settler-colonialism and Western imperialism, framing the city's race to displace and erase the Mexican population. Mexico itself "rests at the center" of Orange County, and non-Mexican residents continuously confront the foreign "other" embedded at the center of the US neoliberal fantasy.[23] To put the matter in more Derridean language, one could say that Orange County is inhabited in its inside—that is, haunted by a foreign guest.[24] In *American Gothic*, James Crow similarly affirms that the Gothic has given voice to suppressed groups, and has provided an approach to taboo subjects.... The study of the Gothic offers a forum for discussing some of the key issues of American society, including gender and the nation's continuing drama of race.... As a literature of borderlands, the Gothic is naturally suited to a country that has seen the frontier (a shifting geographical, cultural, linguistic, and racial boundary) as its defining characteristic.[25]

Orange County may seem at first to be a strange backdrop for this annual cultural celebration, this Mexican American, religio-political ritual. In mediated representations, Orange County continues to be the generative birthplace of a particularly Californian version of a late capitalist luxury class. From the 1960s, "the OC's" hyperplanned, post-suburban sprawl drew a distinct class of white settlers from across the United States. In search of affluence, these fortune seekers came to construct and inhabit a world defined and demarcated by "McMansions" and evangelical Christian megachurches. From Crystal Cathedral to Saddleback Church to Trinity Broadcasting Network, the OC was also the birthplace of a distinctive California version of conservative, evangelical Christianity. But the landscape against which these fantasies play out is also occupied Mexican territory: lands that were ceded by Mexico to the United States in the Treaty of Guadalupe Hidalgo in 1848 remain contested territories. Reflecting on the impossibility—the seeming irreconcilability—of a thriving, surviving Latino community in the context of OC racism and wealth, journalist, OC historian, and Santanero Gustavo Arellano explained the following to us in 2013:

> Santa Ana is one of the most interesting cities because here you really have the future of the United States. It is a city that is overwhelmingly Latino and that is also facing a lot of gentrification issues. People have a sense of pride about themselves, especially knowing that they live in one of the most corrupt, disgusting places in the country: Orange County. At Noche de Altares you get fifty thousand people every year seeing this amazing, new, Orange County, or rather an Orange County that has always been here but is only now coming out and is now unafraid: exalting in what it is.

For the last fifty years, Santa Ana's vibrant working-class downtown has served as a Mexican immigrant commercial and cultural center. It was also the strategic location of Noche de Altares at the height of the festival. Calle Cuatro appeals to recently arrived migrants eager for a connection to the cultural homeland. According to Arellano, the city's downtown shopping district's division by racial lines can be traced back to 1916.[26] Fourth Street, east of Main Street, was considered the Mexican side, while the west side was considered whites only. Since the 1960s, the Fourth Street shopping district of Santa Ana, "La Cuatro," has been predominantly Latinx, evidenced by the predominance of successful businesses catering to Mexican shoppers, including *quinceañera* shops, money-wiring kiosks, restaurants selling regional cuisine, *botánicas*, street vendors, and immigration law firms.

In the late 1980s, the city of Santa Ana began implementation of a large-scale revitalization effort in the downtown area. A series of redevelopment plans sought to mitigate or altogether erase the strong Mexican character of Calle Cuatro by prioritizing single-family homes, implementing noise-control regulations, and imposing limitations on street vendor activity and the use of foreign-language (Spanish) signage. Such zoning changes function as a direct attack on Latinx shoppers and business owners. Although the planning commission was attentive to historic and cultural preservation, it ignored a half-century of Latinx history, conjuring instead a more remote past, referring "largely to history preceding World War II—before the transition of Santa Ana to a largely Spanish-speaking, immigrant, and working-class city."[27]

Since 2007, Santa Ana has been amid a new redevelopment plan focused on drawing urban-style "hipsters" from Los Angeles.[28] Deployed via misguided city redevelopment policies as part of a racist and classicist gentrification project, these hipsters threaten the identity of Calle Cuatro as a thriving, working-class, Latinx commercial district. In conversation, one of the founding organizers of Noche de Altares, Gabe Cordova—event artist and brother of Rudy Cordova—describes how the conflict between activists and redevelopment plans comes to play in the annual celebration on Calle Cuatro:

> Fourth Street is an interesting place; it is the mecca of Hispanic culture in Santa Ana. Some people have called it Little Mexico. It is shop after shop and business after business that are here to serve the Hispanic community. This is where they are buying the things they need for *Quinceañeras*, First Communions, and

> *Noche de Altares*. The fact that we are having this event here in this location helps to solidify the idea of having a place in Santa Ana that we can call our own.... I can't describe what it is like to have over a hundred altars and 45,000 people in the same spot. All of that going on in Santa Ana, in the mecca of Hispanic culture, where there has been a big struggle with hipsters and gentrification. It becomes that much more important for us as a society to celebrate *Noche de Altares* here on *Calle Cuatro*.

Most importantly, through religio-political ritual performance Noche de Altares refuses the erasure of Mexican culture and people from the landscape of Orange County. In an interview with our team, Gustavo Arellano elaborates:

> Orange County has always hated Mexicans. Santa Ana, the city, has always hated Mexicans. By doing this event, it's a big "fuck you" to all those people who say there's no culture in Orange County. To all these people who don't want Mexican culture to happen. It is one of the biggest events of its kind in the nation and we can't believe that it's happening in Orange County.

Santa Ana's celebration is also unique in emphasizing the cultural specificity of altar building: El Centro works hard to feature distinct styles of altars from each of the thirty-two Mexican states. In their impressive totality, they represent a clear irruption, the mapping of Mexican geographies onto Orange County.

At times, wealthier newcomers have come into conflict with the Noche de Altares celebration, submitting noise and nuisance complaints for what has traditionally been a subdued and somber celebration; for example, no alcohol is sold. Santaneros recall one year when disgruntled newcomer residents demanded that event organizers shoulder the costs of putting them up in hotels and boarding their pets for the evening. Redevelopment plans have consistently failed to address the concerns of the local Latino/a community.[29] A critical investigation of Santa Ana's 2007 Renaissance Specific Plan for development of the downtown area concluded that the plan "overwhelmingly erases the existing barrios and La Calle Cuatro from its 150 pages.... It also fails to mention barrio history with urban planning issues."[30] The threat of gentrification and violent displacement continues in the present. In 2022 the city began a massive infrastructure project to construct a commuter rail

FIGURE 16. Folklórico dancer. Courtesy of G. Bernard Gordillo.

line right down Calle Cuatro, and they did so without community consultation. The new train makes it all but impossible for Calle Cuatro to serve as a ritual or ceremonial space, and today the commemoration has retreated to a nearby park, where it bears its silent witness.

Noche de Altares responds to these social, historical, and political realities; it is here that activist organizers seek to intercede. Gabe explains, "Santa Ana is everything to all of us.... Everybody who lives here feels that Santa Ana is their home. The fact that we are having this event here in this location helps to solidify the idea of having a place in Santa Ana that we can call our own."[31] Some Noche organizers have sometimes understood their labors as a "*Reconquista*"—a sort of counter-conquest, a reclaiming of territory for disenfranchised Latinx immigrant communities. For Chicano Studies scholars Lara Medina and Gilbert Cadena, Day of the Dead celebrations are about "claiming public space to honor these 'others'... an ultimate act of resistance against cultural domination."[32] For Jacques Derrida, the condition of displaced or stateless immigrants such as those that are the majority in Santa Ana constitute one of the ten plagues of the New World Order. In *Specters of Marx* he decries the "massive exclusion of homeless citizens from any participation in the democratic life of States, the expulsion or deportation of so many exiles, stateless persons, and immigrants from a so-called national territory."[33] For us, these are Latinx hauntologies resonant with the borderlands gothic, in which unsettled ghosts do the political work of haunting against the backdrop of the US-Mexican borderlands, a place of disruption and possibility, hybridity and transgression.

## Latinx Spectrality: The Real Presence of Spirits at the Altars of Santa Ana

Noche de Altares is but one event in the ritual fabric and rhythm of the community. It conceals and contains longer processes of preparation, organization, and ritual labor. Participants plant marigolds months (often years) in advance of the ritual celebration, file for city permits and permissions, rehearse musical performances, and delegate roles and responsibilities for the day of the event. But it is also integral to and integrated into a larger religio-cultural apparatus extending beyond La Calle Cuatro. The spectral spills onto the streets of the city and into a larger Southern California borderlands gothic landscape; in fundraiser Catrina fashion shows and in neo-indigenist Little Day of the Dead celebrations deep in the mountains of the Los Angeles Forest, participants engage and acknowledge the co-presence and agency of spirits.

Deeply, almost prophetically attuned to the material conditions of Santaneros is José Cruz Gonzalez's play *The Long Road Today/El Largo Camino de Hoy*, which centers on Santanero mourning and healing following the fictional hit-and-run death of a young deaf boy. Performed at Civic Center Plaza in September 2014, one block away from Calle Cuatro, the play is divided into four different scenes with four different characters; performed out of sequence and simultaneously, it blurs temporality and order. The audience follows both living and spectral characters. In one scene a neighbor explains, "Ghosts live [in SanTana].... There are ghosts everywhere." Referencing the most well-known spectral figure of Mexican folklore, La Llorona, the same character reveals, "You won't see her in la Irvine or Costa Mesa. She haunts her own *gente* in SanTana." Two months later, the spirits arrived and announced their presence at Santa Ana's Noche de Altares celebration by causing disruption and unrest. On the eve of the event, as volunteers finalized their preparations on Calle Cuatro (less than three miles away), three thirteen-year-old girls from Santa Ana were struck and killed by a hit-and-run driver while trick-or-treating. The deaths of twins Lexi and Lexandra Pérez and their friend Andrea Gonzalez shocked and devastated the community; it added an additional somber valence to the ritual festival. Their deaths underscored the structural racism, economic disparity, and lack of social services experienced by many Latinx Santaneros.

The next morning, as volunteers and organizers on La Calle Cuatro placed the finishing touches on their altars, and as the Mesoamerican *danzantes* prepared for the opening ceremony, a rustling was heard. *Papel picado*, the colorful, delicate tissue paper banners strung on the altars, fluttered as gusts of wind violently disrupted the time-consuming preparations. For an entire hour, the famous Santa Ana winds knocked offerings from altars, broke candles, and frustrated food vendors, as organizers pleaded for calm.

We joined cofounder and organizer of Noche de Altares—Rudy Cordova and his then-wife, Jackie—in their Santa Ana living room. Sitting hand in hand with his wife, Cordova explained to us, "Those winds are the spirits now, coming into our world, and they've found us—they've found our altars, they've found their families."[34] Organizers frequently remind us of the Indigenous resonance of their commemoration, and that wind, in Nahuatl, is associated with voice, spirit, and breath. "The source of voice is spirit," writes anthropologist Maria Cristina Gonzales; "to tell a story, one must use the wind, must harness this force." Likewise, for participants and organizers of Noche de Altares, wind is an animating and emanating force: wind marks Santa Ana as another locus of enunciation, a location of epistemic and spiritual knowledge.

During Noche de Altares, the spirits haunt the streets of Santa Ana. Summoned to altars through deep ritual praxis, the presence of spirits marks Noche as a spectral event and irruption: defying the boundary between the here and the hereafter, the dead and the living. Santaneros' insistence on the real presence of the spectral also affirms the importance of geographic and political location discussed in the previous section: Santaneros and their spectral comrades recall the legacies of occupation and displacement that haunt the present, resisting the violent realities of racial capitalism's efforts at erasure. Essential to Latinx spectrality is the horizontal, "congregational" (from Jane Bennett) nature of the agency of spirits. Following subaltern historian Dipesh Chakrabarty, we recognize that taking seriously the agency of the subaltern also requires taking seriously the agency of the divine: for the subaltern, so often the actions of God and the spirits are coeval with the human.[35]

In asserting real presence, in insisting that their ghosts are real, Santaneros offer their greatest resistance to the secularization impulse evident in so many other

Day of the Dead celebrations. Gustavo Arellano explains, "For the people who are building altars and participating in the event, it is real to them. They sincerely think that by putting up the offerings and the pictures of the lost ones that they will return, and they will be able to spend time with them." Jackie Cordova, an Anglo woman of Mormon upbringing, started coming to the celebration when she married Rudy. She eventually became a force behind the success of Noche de Altares. Sharing her personal experience of the presence of spirits, she reflected:

> I think we know that our spirits are talking to us.... That's why we love the whole holiday, because it's an awesome reminder of those people who are guiding you. Life is so busy these days that you don't hear the whispers in your ears, you have so many distractions. I ask the spirits to speak loudly so that I can hear them. I think those spirits guided us through the organization of the event. They wanted a place to go, and I just think there has to be someone else behind you pulling strings.

Scholar of lived religion Robert A. Orsi writes of the need for scholars to be responsive to the presence of spirits, deities, and other non-corporeal entities: "The problem is that we have no idea what to make of the bonds between humans and the spirits really present to them within the limits of our critical theories.... [Indeed,] presence requires a history of its own, and experiences and practices of presence suggest the lineaments of that history."[36] The Noche de Altares celebration illuminates and reckons with the complexity of these bonds. For example, Gabe drew on his memory of a visit to Mexico as a young adult:

> Going to Mexico and seeing how it is celebrated is eye-opening. ... The more indigenous people were, the more they believed. Emotions were real: people crying and laughing because they believed these souls were coming back. They believed it was real and was doing something. This is the understanding that people pass on [in Santa Ana at Noche de Altares]: that the indigenous people believe that people come back. That is what this holiday is about: it is about spending one more night with people who have passed on. This is the concept of *el convivio*.

Encapsulating the idea of real presence in a Latinx context is Gabe's use of the Spanish word *convivio*. The verb *convivir* translates as "to live together, to cohabitate, or coexist." In religious contexts it has an added valence of fellowship. From anthropologist C. Jill Grady, we understand that the spectral is also an agentive category—not manifestations born simply out of melancholia or loss, but as extensions of community.[37] For us the impulse and ethos of convivio is definitive for Latinx hauntology.

The Latinx hauntology of Santaneros and El Centro Cultural is a complex, autonomous, and organic praxis informed and grounded in Latin American political movements and non-Western spiritual practices. We leverage the Derridean hauntological uncomfortably, and only insofar as it helps provide us with an existing theoretical language to grapple with the "real presence" of the ghosts of Santa Ana. Of his invention of the word *hauntology*, Derrida writes, "We will take this category to be irreducible, and first of all to everything it makes possible: ontology, theology, positive or negative onto-theology."[38] Avery Gordon's influential elaboration of hauntology similarly responds to "modern forms of dispossession, exploitation, representation, and their concrete impacts on the people most affected by them and on our shared conditions of living."[39] Reflecting, for example, on Toni Morrison's titular character *Beloved*, Gordon describes *haunting* as

> an animated state in which a repressed or unresolved social violence is making itself known.... The whole essence of a ghost is that it has *real presence* and demands its due, your attention. Haunting and the appearance of specters or ghosts is one way ... we are notified that what's been concealed is very much alive and present.[40]

Though we acknowledge the primacy and influence of Derrida's theory in academe, his hauntological is a starting point for us to explore how the agency of spirits and the agency of disenfranchised communities align. It is a prelude to extricating Santanero spectral and political engagement from discourses of legitimacy rooted in abstract European Marxism while also recognizing the resonances between the two. Noche de Altares is an already fundamentally theo-political exercise running parallel to Derrida's Marxist critiques and part of the same ethnographic and geographic context of the borderlands gothic.

The activist organizers and altar builders of Noche de Altares tend with care and attention to both the arrival of spirits and their departure at the close. In Santa

Ana, the practice of altar building and *ofrenda* (offering) to summon the spirits of the dead not only marks the presence of ancestors but also serves to contest the limits of citizenship, counter erasure, and articulate messages for those who cannot speak, both literally and figuratively. For Santaneros, the articulation of grievance moves in synchrony with the act of grieving. As we describe, Noche de Altares one can encounter family altars for deceased grandparents or for a beloved teacher, but alongside these are altars with more explicitly political and critical themes. Among the altars along Fourth Street are those that remember disappearances. One is for the local women who were victims of domestic violence and whose murderers remain free and at large. Another memorializes and mourns (summons the spirits of) the abduction and murder of forty-three Mexican *normalista* students from the Ayotzinapa Rural Teachers' College in Iguala, Guerrero, Mexico, in September of 2014. The clear involvement of the Mexican state in their disappearance led to local and international protest. The Ayotzinapa memorial altar is an important example that illustrates the political dimension of the Noche celebration. Noche altars sometimes also display a critical stance against state-sanctioned violence and the shortcomings of governmental policies within the United States: most years there is at least one altar with an FTP (Fuck the Police) message. During Noche de Altares, the streets of downtown Santa Ana are simultaneously sacralized and politicized: cultural expressions and spiritual practices are at once political demonstrations.

As gentrification and economic redevelopment threaten Mexican immigrant space and histories of Santa Ana, activists and local community members summon ghosts and spirits to claim their place in the city center, contesting governmental policies through ritual performance. Through Noche de Altares, Santa Ana becomes un *mundo al reves*, a world turned inside out.

Ben explains that the spirits begin to arrive even as preparations begin early in the morning:

> We take great pride in trying to keep this event honest to itself for the spirits. We do it for the spirits. Every altar is important. As people start to put up the altars and as people are putting up the candles you have a sense that the spirits are coming to visit. We try to keep it as close to what's honest ... for the spirits. When people are setting everything up and bringing out the flowers and candles you have a sense that the spirits are coming to visit you. And you welcome the spirits.

Dora, a Santa Ana resident and volunteer at El Centro, similarly lingers on the presence of spirits at Noche de Altares. Of all the organizers, Dora hews most closely to the Mexican cultural ideal celebration that she brings with her from her pueblo of origin in the state of Morelos. The Indigenous community of Ocotepec proudly boasts one of the most traditional and expansive celebrations in all of Mexico. For Dora, the Santa Ana celebration is not just cultural but also intensely spiritual. In her garden of *cempaxuchitl*, the traditional marigolds that beckon the ancestors to their Día de los Muertos altars with their strong scent, Dora recounted to us the traditions of her childhood.

"What do you feel when the dead arrive?" we asked. Dora paused to gauge our intentions, sitting in silence for a moment. Then, with a deep breath she began, "I am going to tell you a story. You don't have to believe it, but I'm going to tell you anyway. Okay?" In the foggy twilight between wake and sleep, the spirits appear to Dora. They ask for favors, seeking to relieve their families from the anguish of mourning. Dora delivers messages, telling parents not to cry for their lost ones, and to keep their memories alive. It is something that happens suddenly, Dora explains. There is no choice in the matter. When they want to, the spirits manifest themselves to her: "I feel their presence. It is *un don*, a gift that I have. This is why I have always enjoyed celebrating Day of the Dead. When the air, when the wind comes, it is the spirits. The spirits enter through the *papel picado*, and I feel them when they arrive. *Siento pesado*, I feel them heavy on my body, a knot in my throat, a sudden and intense fatigue."[41]

## The Catrina Procession: Conjuring the Spirits of the Disappeared: The Saints, Spirits, and Sorrows of Santa Ana

At the heart of Santa Ana's unique observance is a two-hour solemn religious rite: a procession by La Catrina, Mexico's iconic skeleton woman. Unique to Santa Ana, the sunset ritual is for many altar builders and participants the central act of the celebration. Processing with her entourage down streets made redolent of *copal* by Azteca *concheros*, and with the intonation of *son jarocho* reverberating its sonic blessing, at each altar La Catrina pauses and lights a single candle. In silence she summons the spirits. It is at the precise moment when the first altar candle catches flame that the spirits are said to be fully present. Noche can thus be understood as hauntological in the sense in that community members' invocation, "conjuration"[42] of the spirits of the dead in ritual performance, calls attention to the historical and material conditions of Mexican communities in Santa Ana while also foreshadowing a justice that is yet to come.

The woman who created and has assumed the role of La Catrina is a powerful and unsettling presence, herself a sort of ghost. (Here we have not revealed her identity, which we understand to be her preference.) From the time she dons her costume and skeleton-face makeup, she enters an altered state: speaking not a word she offers mute witness. *Santaneros* recall the time one of the altar candles lit her hair on fire. But even then, the Catrina did not depart her prayerful trance, neither moving nor speaking as members of her entourage quietly extinguished the flames.

The Catrina absorbs the grief of hundreds unto herself. Reflecting on her role, the woman who has created and assumes the part of Catrina explains,

> She represents Mexicans' ability to welcome death, to see it as comfort, to regard it with honor and respect.... But what I really want them to feel is that I want to be a sponge, a vessel, to take all their negative energy, everything that makes them sad about death, the fact that they miss their family members, and I want to take that away and leave them just with good memories. I want the rest of the night to be a celebration, to honor those who have died. That is what we can do during this event: keep their memories alive and they become a legacy.

The La Catrina procession, in its Santa Ana iteration, shares more in common with La Llorona of Mexican folklore than she does with Santa Muerte—the grim reaper of *narcocultura* fact and fiction, with whom she is often confused by outsiders.[43] Indeed, Santa Muerte is explicitly excluded from Noche de Altares observances. In his book-length consideration, Luis León writes of La Llorona's capacity to narrative borderlands religion: "Religious poetics does not ignore but confronts the reality and drama of suffering and orders, narrates, and ultimately resolves it."[44] Santa Ana's La Catrina shares a similar gendered potency.

La Catrina's annual ritual appearance is a moment of enunciation and annunciation, a singular, originary rite through which spiritual and epistemic knowledge are generated.[45] Over the last decades other celebrations have adopted the Catrina

FIGURE 17. Participant as La Catrina. Courtesy of G. Bernard Gordillo.

procession from Santa Ana, but they are at best duplications, or simulacra: for none haunts as she does in Santa Ana.

There is more than one iteration of the Ayotzinapa altar at Noche worthy of mention, and more than one woman who does the work of collective mourning. Also beginning in 2014, college professor Lisa Alvarez transformed her body into an altar, donning a black thrift store dress that she has adorned with photographs and newspaper clippings of the forty-three murdered students. Alvarez embodies maternal grief and anger as she walks the streets of La Calle Cuatro. Silent but for the red-paper rustling of her ankle-length dress, Alvarez only gestures with her painted red palm. Her gray hair and rebozo are reminiscent of the wailing woman La Llorona, whose specter wanders in eternal search for her murdered children. Alvarez reflects on the power of her body as altar "to make a powerful witness in a public space."[46]

Through these gendered, spectral figures, Noche de Altares is an invitation; it is a ceremonial invocation to temporal transgressions between life and death, and time and space. Through engagement with cultural practices rooted in pre-Hispanic traditions, Chicanx participants cross temporal boundaries to connect with the ancestral; it is a recalling and a reckoning with the past and futures-to-come. Justice (in the Derridean sense) also transcends time and is also bound to the spectral. At Noche de Altares, justice—as *revenant* (the spectral in perpetual return) and *arrivant* (the spectral that is always arriving)—is always in process.

Latinx hauntology also refers to the capacity of spirits to haunt and trouble us in the present and has deep roots in Mexican religious culture. Chicana/o/x scholars of religion, including Gloria Anzaldúa, Lara Medina, and Laura Pérez, serve as important resources for theorizing alternative spatial and temporal models. In *Borderlands/La Frontera*, Gloria Anzaldúa locates mourning as a central component of radical Chicana epistemology. In her interpretation, the epistemic violence of colonialism against the Indigenous peoples of Mexico created splits and dichotomies between spirit and body and "disrupted the equality and balance between female and male."[47] Thus, "female rites of mourning were rites of defiance protesting . . . cultural changes . . . their demotion to a lesser status, their denigration. Like Llorona, the Indian woman's only means of protest is wailing."[48] Healing this rupture, at the heart of Anzaldúa's borderlands spirituality, includes the bridging of the spirit-body divide and the material effects of spirits and the spectral. Instead, Chicana/o/x spirituality rejects the "false split between political activism and spirituality which can limit social change."[49]

We extend Derrida's hauntological theory into this Chicanx epistemological framework into our research with Santaneros. Engagement with the spectral "is not escapist metaphysics, but an ethical force that binds [individuals] to concrete reality."[50] This Latinx hauntological approach to the study of religion bridges the metaphorical with the material, drawing from the work of Chicana/o/x scholars to transcend and exceed the boundaries that often divide our academic methodologies. And as always, Santa Ana's engagement with spirits and haunting points to the historical and material conditions of immigrant Mexican communities.

## Latinx Hauntology as De-ecclesial Praxis

Jonathan Calvillo's 2020 book, *Saints of Santa Ana: Faith and Ethnicity in a Mexican Majority City*, correctly positions the city at the center of the religious landscape of the United States.[51] Calvillo, a sociologist of religion, describes Santa Ana as a city of churches, drawing a richly textured portrait of the distinct identities of first-generation Mexican Catholics and Evangelical Christians. Adding to his observations of religious complexity and diversity, we introduce Noche de

Altares as a third spiritual space in Santa Ana.[52] Noche de Altares is spiritual, even religious, we argue: part of its struggle is to resist secularization—which goes hand in hand with its struggle against gentrification. It is also fundamentally de-ecclesial, we argue. We introduce the term *de-ecclesial* to indicate a particular form of decolonial religious resistance through which colonized communities shed the oppressive, hierarchical, and institutional religious structures that are the inheritance from global, imperial, ecclesial trajectories. We feel that this designation is more accurate than "nones" (the more passive term typically applied to non-affiliated Latinx subjects). That is, although Day of the Dead/ *Día de los Muertos* in Mexico clearly has historical roots in the Roman Catholic liturgical calendar (from All Saints/All Souls), Santaneros make explicit that their celebration is definitely *not* Catholic in origin or affiliation. (As a case in point, organizers recall only one instance in which a Catholic priest attended the event.) Rather, they explain, Noche descends from Mesoamerican Indigenous traditions. Santaneros are also clear that the celebration—including especially the deeply spiritual, even numinous, Catrina procession—is their own, unique innovation. Yet, their process of de-ecclesialization is not the same as secularization. Rather, they practice a de-institutionalized rite, disaffiliated but still richly inhabited by spirits and characterized by power, memory, community, ritual labor, and a richly imagined future, alternative, justly constructed world.

Chicanx celebrations of Day of the Dead like Noche incorporate traditional elements of Mesoamerican culture as an expression of cultural continuity and retrieval. Under the leadership of their spiritual teacher, Cuezalin Rios, a group of Aztec *danzantes* practicing Mesoamerican Macehualo religion blesses the downtown and its altars with thick clouds of *copal* incense. For Cuezalin, Day of the Dead is a Mesoamerican Indigenous ritual best understood as cathartic spiritual ceremony, not street festival.

The hauntological ethos of Noche de Altares therefore also finds parallel and resource in Mesoamerican cosmologies that similarly privilege the agency and presence of the dead.[53] The Aztec offering of Cuezalin's danzantes embodies the concept of Nahui Ollin, the four cardinal directions and their movements.[54] Cuezalin expresses an ambivalence to souls and spirits that simultaneously affirms the presence of the dead among us on a continuous plane:

> It may be surprising [to outsiders] but in classical Nahuatl we don't have a word for spirit; we don't have a concept of spirit. We also

don't have a word for god.... [Instead] everything is divine. There is no separation between spirits.... For us there is no afterlife: there is only one line of life. If you are dead, there is only one line, and it is not separate [from the living]. For religious purposes, we don't utilize this idea of "spirit." The place beyond death is translated as "the place in which somehow one lives." This does not mean that one becomes a ghost or spirit; it means that after you are gone, if you leave something behind like a painting, or a temple, or children, or students, then somehow you are living. And this is reflected in poetry: I am your fingernails, I am your hair, I am the color of your skin, I am your blood.

Cuezalin rejects Western dichotomies of body and soul; he refuses to separate being into divine and human forces, the material from the spiritual world, or body from soul. The ceremonial rites of Noche de Altares exemplify this horizontality and reflect an understanding of life inclusive of spirits: all life—both human and spirit beings—possess agency. For one night, Noche de Altares, downtown Santa Ana moves from periphery to center. For one night, it is axis mundi, where the shared temporal and existential plane of humans and spirits is manifest.

## Zapatista Religion in Orange County: Marx Comes again to Orange County

Essential to Latinx hauntology as we understand it is its explicitly critical engagement with neoliberal capitalism. As we observed, the activist-organizers of Noche are often explicitly theoretical and sometimes explicitly Marxist in their work. Through the Zapatista activism of El Centro Cultural and its organization of Noche de Altares, the specter of Marxism haunts Orange County.[55] In the Noche celebration, the hidden and suppressed realities of structural violence and borderlands sorrow and suffering spill out onto city streets. That is to say, Santa Ana is not just a city of churches; it is also a city with an activist history and with a leftist, socialist ethos that permeates the religious evocations of Noche de Altares. Noche de Altares is, in the words of Gustavo Arellano, a religious celebration done "Zapatista style"—a reference to the revolutionary Indigenous-rights movement in Chiapas, Mexico, that we discuss at more length below. While participants and organizers must work within the parameters of local government policy and procedures to ensure Noche de Altares takes place, activists vocalize their distrust and apprehension, pointing to police brutality against local Mexican youth, the incarceration of undocumented migrants, and the violence of California's carceral cultures.

As a religio-political ritual, the local, communitarian processes by which Noche de Altares is organized offers an alternative political imaginary, one that draws on Latin American liberationist strands while it contests the neoliberal status quo with its empty appeals to multiculturalism. El Centro Cultural de México, the animating force behind the Noche celebration, was founded in 1994 by Socorro Sarmiento. Sarmiento emigrated to Santa Ana with her family and was looking to build a sense of community and safety for undocumented Mexican mothers. The year of El Centro's founding also marked the year that the Ejército Zapatista de Liberación Nacional (EZLN), a leftist, Indigenous movement in Chiapas, Mexico, declared war against the Mexican state. The EZLN effectively articulated their radical anti-neoliberal stance via a series of global communiqués, and the Zapatistas quickly became a transnational movement.[56] We also note the influence of Liberation Theology and the Christian Base Community movement on the birth and evolution of the Zapatistas. They were fostered, in part, by the work of the radical "red" bishop of Chiapas, Don Samuel Ruíz, who was known for his work supporting human rights for Indigenous people and for sponsoring the diocese's famous Indigenous deacons' program.

This liberationist strand of Latin American religion has clearly found its way into the Noche celebration via Zapatismo.[57] The EZLN's radical, Marxist-inflected ideology and its autonomous and de-centered organizational structure inspired the founding of several community centers in the Los Angeles area, El Centro Cultural among them.[58] Zapatista subaltern politics appealed to many Latinx youth in Southern California, including artists and activists in Los Angeles and Santa Ana.[59] In 1995, Zapatista supporters from Orange County made the news for their protest against US foreign policies.[60] Along with other local Santaneros, Carolina Sarmiento, Socorro's daughter, for a time assumed the role of Center Director, helping to shape the direction of El Centro and solidifying a more radical political direction.

The influence of Zapatismo is evident in El Centro's mission, guiding principles, organizational and leadership structure, and activism. El Centro is modeled after the EZLN's participatory democratic structure known as *caracoles*.[61] Each autonomous committee (volunteers, coordinators, *frente*, community partners, transnational collaborations, and *mesa*) elects rotating leaders to be part of a central committee, who meet to consult with one another and to make larger decisions. As Ben Vasquez shared, El Centro operates along two mottos: *"El Centro es de quien lo trabaja"* (The center belongs to those who work it), and *"Cuando la cultura muere, la gente muere"* (When a culture dies, its people die). This structure of shared governance and responsibility is central to El Centro's guiding principles of community solidarity, participatory democracy, social imagination, and individual responsibility. Members of El Centro affirm the interconnectedness of global struggles for housing, economic justice, communal land ownership, and economic justice. Arellano, an active supporter and one-time board member of El Centro, writes that it "functions as a breeding ground for radicals," as its members take strong political stances against deportations, gentrification, and police surveillance.[62] In addition to organizing and preparing for Noche de Altares, a labor that takes place almost year-round, El Centro Cultural provides an alternative space in downtown Santa Ana, just one short block from Calle Cuatro. El Centro promotes cultural and artistic education to residents, and offers a curriculum of weekly music, dance, and self-defense classes. During the COVID-19 pandemic, El Centro Cultural allowed more than seventy-five homeless people to set up tents on their property. (In March 2022, they were ordered to clear the premises.)

In sum, Noche de Altares is organized following a Zapatista model of leftist activism that is both radical in its critique and utopian in its aim. While El Centro Cultural de México is a secular organization without an explicitly religious agenda or purpose, these utopian principles help define the structure and ethos of the Noche de Altares celebration. The religious, ritual, and spiritual dimension evolved organically in the diffuse, decentralized process of planning, which allowed for the leadership and influence of many community members.

## Conclusion

Through the interplay of spirit communication and altar building on La Calle Cuatro, *la cultura vive* (culture lives), *los espiritus estan presentes* (the spirits are present), and the invisible others at the margins of the nation-state are brought into close proximity—embraced as full members of the community. We remember that spirits and hauntings do not pertain solely to the realm of theory but also to the realm of human action. If ghosts such as those that occupy the streets of Orange County are rendered purely metaphorical, then they lose their disruptive potency to unsettle capitalism. We highlight and juxtapose the close geographical proximity and theoretical distance of Jacques Derrida's spectral Marxism from the material realities of the borderlands gothic. There are no ghosts in the hyperplanned suburbs of Irvine, California, except the ones we conjure to haunt and occupy Derrida's theoretical silences. The ghosts in Santa Ana, we hold, are simultaneously figurative and literal, both co-present and co-participant in political and cultural resistance against racial capitalism and neoliberalism. Noche de Altares's unique example illuminates the processes by which celebrations elsewhere have been absorbed and secularized as celebrations of corporatized multiculturalism. Where other observances have succumbed, Noche has successfully resisted.

## Notes

1. On the distinctions between the original celebration in Mexico and emerging US practices, see Regina Marchi, "Hybridity and Authenticity in US Day of the Dead Celebrations," *Journal of American Folklore* 126, no. 501 (2013): 272–301, https://doi.org/10.5406/jamerfolk.126.501.0272.
2. By far the most cited of these is now almost twenty years old: Regina M. Marchi, *Day of the Dead in the USA: The Migration and Transformation of a Cultural Phenomenon* (New Brunswick: Rutgers University Press, 2009). But see also Lara Medina's groundbreaking "Communing with the Dead: Spiritual and Cultural Healing in Chicano/a Communities" in *Religion and Healing in America*, ed. Lina L. Barnes and Susan S. Sered (Oxford: Oxford University Press, 2005), 205–15; and Stanley Brandes, *Skulls to the Living, Bread to the Dead: The Day of the Dead in Mexico and Beyond* (Hoboken, NJ: John Wiley & Sons, 2009). Most recent are Linda Levitt, "Skeletons, Marigolds, and Sugar Skulls," in *Culture, Celebrity, and the Cemetery: Hollywood Forever* (New York: Routledge, 2018) and Laura Pérez, "Fashioning Decolonial Optics: Days of the Dead: Walking Altars and Calavera Fashion Shows in Latina/o Los Angeles," in *meXicana Fashions: Politics, Self-Adornment, and Identity Construction*, ed. Aída Hurtado and Norma E. Cantú (Austin: University of Texas Press, 2021), 191–215.
3. We are currently planning a coauthored book-length study based on this research.
4. For example, many of the organizers of and participants in Noche might be identified on a survey as part of the increasing percentage of Latinx "nones"—those claiming no religious affiliation. Troubling these statistics, participants in Noche may be religiously unaffiliated, but they are nevertheless actively involved in local ritual

life. We feel the concept of "de-ecclesial" is more precise than "nones" to describe this particular form of Latinx religious identity.

5. Jennifer Scheper, James Kyung-Jin Lee, Amanda Lucia, and S. Romi Mukherjee, "Take It Outside: Practicing Religion in Public," *Boom: A Journal of California* 5, no. 4 (2015): 54–63, https://doi.org/10.1525/boom.2015.5.4.54.

6. Our multi-year research project, "Global Religious Festivals in Secular Cityscapes," was funded through the Religion in Diaspora and Public Affairs grant by the Luce Foundation and the University of California Humanities Research Institute. We are Jennifer Scheper Hughes (PI, UCR), Daisy Vargas (Doctoral PI, UCR), Amanda Lucia (Co-PI, UCR), James K. Lee (Co-PI, UCI), and Romi Mukerjee (Co-PI, Sciences-Po, Paris). Bernard Gordillo documented the festival photographically. Vargas originally identified Noche de Altares in Santa Ana as a field site and framed initial research questions.

7. *Night of Altars/Noche de Altares: Recreating Day of the Dead in California*, directed and produced by Jennifer Hughes and Daisy Vargas (with James Ault), 2016. Premier screening, Downtown Independent Theater, Los Angeles, CA, Friday, October 23, 2015. Funded by the Luce Foundation.

8. On the "realness of presence," see Robert A. Orsi, *History and Presence* (Boston: Harvard University Press, 2016).

9. Our shared campus, the University of California, Riverside, was the location of the lectures that were ultimately published in *Specters of Marx*.

10. Regina M. Marchi, *Day of the Dead in the USA: The Migration and Transformation of a Cultural Phenomenon* (New Brunswick, NJ: Rutgers University Press, 2009), 74–6. Marchi's is the first book-length study to identify the tensions between political radicalism and commercialization that characterized the celebrations.

11. This curriculum and teaching material has been in circulation since at least the 1970s, and also includes suggestions for incorporating music related to Mexican Catholicism. See John N. Hawkins, *Teacher's Resource Handbook for Latin American Studies: An Annotated Bibliography of Curriculum Materials, Preschool through Grade Twelve*, UCLA Latin American Reference Series, vol. 6 (Los Angeles: UCLA Latin American Center Publications, 1975).

12. "Bricker v. Petaluma City Schools," July 25, 2003, vLex, https://case-law.vlex.com/vid/bricker-v-petaluma-city-892379153; see Stanley Brandes's discussion of this case in Stanley Brandes, *Skulls to the Living, Bread to the Dead: The Day of the Dead in Mexico and Beyond*. (Hoboken, NH: John Wiley & Sons, 2009), 147–49.

13. The lawsuit representing Californians for Equal Rights foundation appealed to the Establishment clause against the use of In Lak'Ech taught in San Diego, citing that the poem by Luis Valdez and a chant involving Nahui Ollin was a violation of the separation of Church and State. See Californians for Equal Rights Foundation, Eric Gonzalex, Steve Houbeck, *Jose Velasquez v. State of California*, California State Board of Education, California State Department of Education (2021).
14. Ivan Fernandez, "Has Corporate Sponsorship Ruined Hollywood Forever's Day of the Dead Event?" *LA Weekly*, October 31, 2016, https://www.laweekly.com/has-corporate-sponsorship-ruined-hollywood-forevers-day-of-the-dead-event/.
15. The burden of this refusal created a rift between the organizers, leading to the separation of the event into two distinct celebrations in 2015, when one of the main organizers departed to launch a new, less political, and commercially sponsored event near the train station. Gabriel San Román, "Days of the Dead: Is Santa Ana Big Enough for Two Día De Los Muertos Street Festivals?" *OC Weekly*, October 30, 2015, https://www.ocweekly.com/days-of-the-dead-is-santa-ana-big-enough-for-two-dia-de-los-muertos-street-festivals-6577463/.
16. Carol Margaret Davison, editor, *The Gothic and Death*, International Gothic Series (Manchester: Manchester University Press, 2017), 2. British gothic literature also relied heavily on Protestant conceptions of the Roman Catholic Other. See, for instance, Horace Walpole's *The Castle of Otranto* (1764), widely considered the first Gothic novel, and Ann Radcliffe's *The Italian* (1796).
17. Also inverting and refracting Euro-centric engagement with the racial and religious Other. David Punter, *Postcolonial Imaginings: Fictions of a New World Order* (Edinburgh University Press, 2000), https://www.jstor.org/stable/10.3366/j.ctvxcrgtp, quoted in Gina Wisker, "Postcolonial Gothic," in *Teaching the Gothic*, ed. Anna Powell and Andrew Smith (London: Palgrave MacMillan, 2006), 173.
18. Charles L. Crow, *History of the Gothic: American Gothic* (Cardiff: University of Wales Press, 2009), https://www.jstor.org/stable/j.ctt9qhk57.
19. The Gothic has deep roots in Mexican literature and has made a significant return in contemporary Latinx popular culture. See Silvia Moreno-Garcia's *Mexican Gothic* (2020) and *The Daughter of Doctor Moreau* (2022).
20. Gloria Anzaldúa, *Borderlands/La Frontera: The New Mestiza Consciousness* (San Francisco: Aunt Lute Books, 1987), 25.
21. Erualdo R. Gonzales and Raul P. Lejano, "New Urbanism and the Barrio," *Environment and Planning* 41, no. 12 (2009): 2950–51, https://doi.org/10.1068/a41360.

22. Jesse Alemán, "The Other Country: Mexico, the United States, and the Gothic History of Conquest," *American Literary History* 18, no. 3 (2006): 409, muse.jhu.edu/article/202142.
23. Alemán, "The Other Country."
24. Jacques Derrida, *Specters of Marx: The State of the Debt, the Work of Mourning and the New International*, trans. Peggy Kamuf (London: Routledge, 2012), 3.
25. Crow, *History of the Gothic*, 1–2.
26. Gustavo Arellano, "The Untold Story of Santa Ana's Fiestas Patrias," *OC Weekly*, September 17, 2008, https://www.ocweekly.com/the-untold-story-of-santa-anas-fiestas-patrias-6465817/.
27. Gonzales and Lejano, "New Urbanism," 2952.
28. "Santa Ana Renaissance Specific Plan," California Environmental Quality Act, Governor's Office of Planning and Research, 2006–2010, amended 2016, https://ceqanet.opr.ca.gov/2006071100.
29. Victoria Beard and Carolina Sarmiento, "Planning, Public Participation, and Money Politics in Santa Ana (CA)," *Journal of the American Planning Association* 80, no. 2 (2014): 168–81, https://doi.org/10.1080/01944363.2014.953002.
30. González and Lejano, "New Urbanism," 2955–56.
31. All quotes are taken from ethnographic field interviews conducted on site by the authors from 2013 to 2015 unless otherwise indicated.
32. Lara Medina and Gilbert R. Cadena, "Días de los Muertos: Public Ritual, Community Renewal, and Popular Religion in the United States," in *Horizons of the Sacred: Mexican Traditions in U.S. Catholicism* (Ithaca and London: Cornell University Press, 2002), 86.
33. Derrida, *Specters of Marx*, 101.
34. Rudy Cordova, interviewed by our team, October 2013.
35. See Jennifer Scheper Hughes, *Biography of a Mexican Crucifix: Lived Religion and Local Faith from the Conquest to the Present* (Oxford: Oxford University Press, 2010), and Hughes, "The Niño Jesús Doctor," *Nova Religio: The Journal of Alternative and Emergent Religions* 16, no. 2 (November 2012): 4–28, https://doi.org/10.1525/nr.2012.16.2.4. See also Jalane Schmidt and Jennifer Hughes, "Introduction: Material Religion in Latin America" *Material Religion* 13, no. 4 (2017): 409–13, https://doi.org/10.1080/17432200.2017.1385344.
36. Robert A. Orsi, "Abundant History: Marian Apparitions as Alternative Modernity," *Historically Speaking* 9, no. 7 (September/October 2008): 14–15, https://doi.org/10.1353/hsp.2008.0033.

37. We follow the critiques of anthropologists like C. Jill Grady, who argues that the use of European theoretical frames, "to extend the dominant discourses of the dead rather than to explain [them]," contain and limit/diminish the spectral to the metaphorical. See C. Jill Grady, "Ancestors, Ethnohistorical Practice, and the Authentication of Native Place and Past," in Phantom Past, Indigenous Presence: Native Ghosts in North American Culture and History, ed. Colleen E. Boyd and Coll Thrush (Lincoln: University of Nebraska Press, 2011), 287, https://doi.org/10.2307/j.ctt1df4h07.15.
38. Derrida, *Specters of Marx*, 2012.
39. Avery F. Gordon, *Ghostly Matters: Haunting and the Sociological Imagination* (Minneapolis: University of Minnesota Press, 2008), xv. Emphasis ours.
40. Gordon, Ghostly Matters, xvi.
41. Dora Trejo, interview by RIDAGA, November 3, 2013.
42. "Conjuration signifies. . . . The magical incantation destined to evoke, or bring forth with the voice, to convoke a charm or spirit. Conjuration says in sum the appeal that causes to come forth with the voice and thus it makes come, by definition, what is not there at the present moment of the appeal. This voice does not describe [but rather] . . . its words cause something to happen." Derrida, *Specters of Marx*, 51.
43. See Daisy Vargas, "Mexican Religion on Trial: Race, Religion, and the Law in the US-Mexico Borderlands)" (PhD diss., University of California, Riverside, 2018), https://escholarship.org/uc/item/80r0v7v4. In this dissertation for deconstruction of the categories of narco-religion and narco-violence she argues that these terms are wielded and constructed within a larger context of racialized policing and surveillance.
44. Luis D. León, *La Llorona's Children: Religion, Life, and Death in the US–Mexican Borderlands* (Berkeley: University of California Press, 2004), 14, https://doi.org/10.2307/j.ctv11hprsn.
45. Walter D. Mignolo, *Local Histories/Global Designs: Coloniality, Subaltern Knowledges and Border Thinking* (Princeton: Princeton University Press, 2000), and Mignolo, "I Am Where I Think: Epistemology and the Colonial Difference," *Journal of Latin American Cultural Studies* 8, no. 2: 235–45, https://doi.org/10.1080/13569329909361962.
46. Sarah Mosqueda, "'La Maestra' at Santa Ana's Crear Studio Teaches Important Lessons," *Los Angeles Times,* October 22, 2021, https://www.latimes.com/socal/daily-pilot/entertainment/story/2021-10-22/la-maestra-at-santa-anas-crear-studio-teaches-important-lessons.
47. Anzaldúa, *Borderlands/La Frontera*, 43.

48. Anzaldúa, *Borderlands/La Frontera*, 43.
49. AnaLouise Keating, "Daughter of Coatlicue: An Interview with Gloria Anzaldúa," in *Entre Mundos/Among Worlds: New Perspectives on Gloria E. Anzaldúa*, ed. AnaLouise Keating (New York: Palgrave Macmillan, 2005), 27.
50. Michael Hames-Garcia. "How to Tell a Mestizo from an Enchirito: Colonialism and National Culture in the Borderlands," *Diacritics* 30, no. 4 (Winter 2000): 116, https://www.jstor.org/stable/1566310.
51. Jonathan E. Calvillo, *The Saints of Santa Ana: Faith and Ethnicity in a Mexican Majority City* (Oxford: Oxford University Press, 2020).
52. Indeed, a "third space," from Homi Bhabha and Edward Said.
53. Santa Ana shares its name and geography with the "Santa Anas"—the scorching winds that bluster inland from the desert, stoking fires and blowing dust over Southern California. In the popular non-Latino imagination these winds are sinister, the "devil's wind" that has the capacity to cause homicide and drive people insane. In Noche de Altares, the presence of wind that signals and accompanies the arrival of the spirits takes on a contesting meaning. See accounts of the Santa Ana winds by Christian settlers, including Kent E. St. John, "The Devil's Wind," in *Spiritual Fits of Travel: The Best of Traveler's Tales,* ed. James O'Reilly and Sean O'Reilly (Palo Alto: Traveler's Tales, 2002); John Needham, "The Devil Winds Made Me Do It: Santa Anas Are Close Enough to make Anyone's Hair Stand on End," *Los Angeles Times,* March 12, 1988, https://www.latimes.com/archives/la-xpm-1988-03-12-li-942-story.html; and Anne M. Butler, Across God's Frontiers: Catholic Sisters in the American West, 1850–1920s (Chapel Hill: University of North Carolina Press, 2015).
54. Ernesto "Tlahuitollini" Colin, *Indigenous Education through Dance and Ceremony* (New York: Palgrave Macmillan, 2014), 107.
55. Derrida, *Specters of Marx*.
56. Alex Khasnabish, *Zapatistas: Rebellion from the Grassroots to the Global* (London: Zed Books, 2010), ch. 4: "World Made of Many Worlds: The Transnational Impact of Zapatismo." See also Thomas Olesen, "Globalising the Zapatistas: From Third World Solidarity to Global Solidarity?" *Third World Quarterly* 25, no. 1 (2004): 255–67, https://doi.org/10.1080/0143659042000185435.
57. J. Charlene Floyd, "A Theology of Insurrection? Religion and Politics in Mexico," *Journal of International Affairs* 50, no. 1 (Summer 1996): 142–65, https://www.jstor.org/stable/24357408.
58. Gabriel San Romàn, "El Centro Cultural de México finally gets a home—but will OC's next generation of activists come?" *OC Weekly*, April 28, 2017,

https://www.ocweekly.com/el-centro-cultural-de-mexico-finally-gets-a-home-but-will-ocs-next-generation-of-activists-come-8065700/.
59. Martha Gonzalez, *Chican@ Artivistas: Music, Community, and Transborder Tactics in East Los Angeles* (Austin: University of Texas Press, 2020), https://doi.org/10.7560/321126. Also, on the influence of Zapatismo on California see Abigail Andrews, "How Activists 'Take Zapatismo Home': South-to-North Dynamics in Transnational Social Movements," *Latin American Perspectives* 38, no. 1 (2011):138–52, https://doi.org/10.1177/0094582X10384217.
60. Mimi Ko, "Countrywide, Zapasta Supporters Protest U.S. Actions," *Los Angeles Times*, March 29, 1995, https://www.latimes.com/archives/la-xpm-1995-03-29-me-48454-story.html.
61. "Democratic Structure," El Centro Cultural de México website, n.d., accessed April 23, 2022, http://elcentroculturaldemexico.org/democratic-structure.
62. Gustavo Arellano, "The Best Community Space Orange County 2013: El Centro Cultural de México," *OC Weekly*, October 19, 2013.

# References

Alemán, Jesse. "The Other Country: Mexico, the United States, and the Gothic History of Conquest." *American Literary History* 18, no. 3 (2006): 409. muse.jhu.edu/article/202142.

Anzaldúa, Gloria. *Borderlands/La Frontera: The New Mestiza Consciousness*. San Francisco: Aunt Lute Books, 1987.

Arellano, Gustavo. *Orange County: A Personal History*. New York: Simon and Schuster, 2008.

Arellano, Gustavo. "The Untold Story of Santa Ana's Fiestas Patrias." *OC Weekly*, September 17, 2008. Accessed October 20, 2024. https://www.ocweekly.com/the-untold-story-of-santa-anas-fiestas-patrias-6465817/.

Beard, Victoria A., and Carolina S. Sarmiento. 2014. "Planning, Public Participation, and Money Politics in Santa Ana (CA)." *Journal of the American Planning Association* 80 (2): 168–81. doi:10.1080/01944363.2014.953002

Brandes, Stanley. Skulls to the Living, Bread to the Dead: The Day of the Dead in Mexico and Beyond. Hoboken, NJ: John Wiley & Sons, 2009.

*Bricker v. Petaluma City Schools*. July 25, 2003. vLex. https://case-law.vlex.com/vid/bricker-v-petaluma-city-892379153.

Californians for Equal Rights Foundation, Eric Gonzalez, Steve Houbeck, *Jose Velasquez v. State of California*, California State Board of Education, California State Department of Education, 2021.

Crow, Charles L. *History of the Gothic: American Gothic*. Cardiff: University of Wales Press, 2009. Accessed October 20, 2024. https://www.jstor.org/stable/j.ctt9qhk57.

Davison, Carol Margaret, ed. *The Gothic and Death*. International Gothic Series. Manchester: Manchester University Press, 2017.

Derrida, Jacques. Specters of Marx: The State of the Debt, the Work of Mourning and the New International. Translated by Peggy Kamuf. London: Routledge, 2012.

Fernandez, Ivan. "Has Corporate Sponsorship Ruined Hollywood Forever's Day of the Dead Event?" *LA Weekly*, October 31, 2016. https://www.laweekly.com/has-corporate-sponsorship-ruined-hollywood-forevers-day-of-the-dead-event/.

Gonzales, Erualdo R., and Raul P. Lejano. "New Urbanism and the Barrio." *Environment and Planning* 41, no. 12 (2009): 2950–51. https://doi.org/10.1068/a41360.

Hawkins, John N. Teacher's Resource Handbook for Latin American Studies: An Annotated Bibliography of Curriculum Materials, Preschool through Grade Twelve. UCLA Latin American Reference Series, vol. 6. Los Angeles: UCLA Latin American Center Publications, 1975.

Hughes, Jennifer Scheper, James Kyung-Jin Lee, Amanda Lucia, and S. Romi Mukherjee. "Take It Outside: Practicing Religion in Public." *Boom: A Journal of California* 5, no. 4 (2015): 54–63. Accessed October 20, 2024. https://doi.org/10.1525/boom.2015.5.4.54.

Hughes, Jennifer Scheper, and Daisy Vargas, directors and producers. *Night of Altars/Noche de Altares: Recreating Day of the Dead in California*. 36 min. 2016. Premier screening, Downtown Independent Theater, Los Angeles, CA, Friday, October 23, 2015.

Levit, Linda. Culture, Celebrity, and the Cemetery: Hollywood Forever, New York: Routledge, 2018.

Marchi, Regina M. Day of the Dead in the USA: The Migration and Transformation of a Cultural Phenomenon. New Brunswick, NJ: Rutgers University Press, 2009.

Marchi, Regina. "Hybridity and Authenticity in US Day of the Dead Celebrations." *Journal of American Folklore* 126, no. 501 (2013): 272–301. https://doi.org/10.5406/jamerfolk.126.501.0272.

Medina, Lara. "Communing with the Dead: Spiritual and Cultural Healing in Chicano/a Communities." In *Religion and Healing in America*, edited by Lina L. Barnes and Susan S. Sered, 205–215. Oxford: Oxford University Press, 2005.

Punter, David. *Postcolonial Imaginings: Fictions of a New World Order*. Edinburgh: Edinburgh University Press, 2000. https://www.jstor.org/stable/10.3366/j.ctvxcrgtp.

San Román, Gabriel. "Days of the Dead: Is Santa Ana Big Enough for Two Día De Los Muertos Street Festivals?" *OC Weekly*, October 30, 2015. https://www.ocweekly.com/days-of-the-dead-is-santa-ana-big-enough-for-two-dia-de-los-muertos-street-festivals-6577463/.

"Santa Ana Renaissance Specific Plan." California Environmental Quality Act. Governor's Office of Planning and Research, 2006–2010; amended 2016. https://ceqanet.opr.ca.gov/2006071100.

Wisker, Gina. "Postcolonial Gothic." In *Teaching the Gothic*, edited by Anna Powell and Andrew Smith. London: Palgrave MacMillan, 2006.

# Contributors

**Lloyd D. Barba** is an assistant professor of religion and core faculty in Latinx and Latin American Studies at Amherst College. He is the author of *Sowing the Sacred: Mexican Pentecostal Farmworkers in California* (Oxford, 2022), co-editor of *Oneness Pentecostalism: Race, Gender and Culture* (Penn State, 2023), and editor of *Latin American and U.S. Latino Religions in North America* (Bloomsbury, 2024). He earned his PhD in American culture from the University of Michigan.

**Cristina Borges** is an Umbandist practitioner, though not a medium. She is an associate professor of ciência da religião (study of religion/s) at UNIMONTES, Montes Claros, MG, Brazil (PhD, ciência da religião, Pontifícia Universidade Católica de São Paulo). She is currently completing postdoctoral studies at the Pontifícia Universidade Católica de Minas Gerais.

**Matthew Casey-Pariseault** is a faculty member in the School of Historical, Philosophical & Religious Studies at Arizona State University. Matthew's research focuses on religion as a force for social change in modern Latin America. His current manuscript project uses internal church documents, testimonies, and missionary correspondence to follow Catholic and Protestant activists as they mobilized across the polarized political spectrum in twentieth-century Peru. Matthew's public-facing scholarship has been featured in *Salon*, *U.S. News & World Report*, and NPR's *Latino USA*.

**Tatyana Castillo-Ramos** is a PhD candidate in Religious Studies with a concentration in American Religious History at Yale University. She specializes in Latinx and Latin American religion. She has published on the Sanctuary Movement in peer-reviewed journals such as *American Religion* and *Perspectivas*. She has also published on the Virgin of Guadalupe as a resistance symbol in *Latin American and U.S. Latino Religions in North America* (Bloomsbury, 2024). Her dissertation focuses on the history of religion and immigrant rights activism on the San Diego-Tijuana border.

**Joel Morales Cruz** (PhD, Lutheran School of Theology) is the author of *The Mexican Reformation: Catholic Pluralism, Enlightenment Religion and the Iglesia de Jesús Movement in Benito Juárez's Mexico (1859–1872)* (Wipf & Stock, 2011), *The Histories of* *the Latin American Church, A Handbook* (Fortress, 2014), and several chapters and articles on Latin American Christianity and on Latinx theology. He is a member of Holy Trinity Lutheran Church in Chicago, IL. His current interests include Puerto Rican theology, the thought of Sor Juana Inés de la Cruz, the intersection between Latinx theology and popular culture, the environment, and anticolonial resistance.

**Jessica L. Delgado** is an associate professor of women's, gender, and sexuality Studies and history at the Ohio State University. Her primary areas of teaching and research are the histories of women, gender, sexuality, religion, and race in Latin America—particularly in Mexico in the sixteenth, seventeenth, and eighteenth centuries. She is the author or *Troubling Devotion: Laywomen and the Church in Colonial Mexico, 1630–1770* (Cambridge, 2018), and she is currently working on a book project called *The Beata of the Black Habit: Race, Sexuality, and Religious Authority in Late Colonial Mexico*.

**Guaraci Dos Santos** is the pai de santo of one of the oldest Afro-Brazilian terreiros in Belo Horizonte, founded in the 1930s by his adoptive mother. He leads rituals of Umbanda, Candomblé Angola, and Reinado/Congado in the house. He has a BA in psychology and an MA in ciências da religião and is a licensed clinical psychologist. He is a PhD student in ciências da religião at PUC-Minas.

**Steven Engler** is a professor of religious studies at Mount Royal University in Calgary. He researches spirit incorporation religions in Brazil, as well as theory and methodology in the study of religion(s). He is lead researcher of the joint project Ritual Polyphony in Afro-Brazilian Religions (funding from SSHRC and the American Academy of Religion).

**Alejandro Escalante** is a lecturer in social anthropology at the University of Edinburgh. As an ethnographer, he is interested in the performances of gender and race and their co-imbrications. His work draws from Black studies, Caribbean theory and philosophy, and queer theory to think about the various ways we make, re-make, and can unmake ourselves as humans. His current research project explores these themes through rituals cross-dressing during a religious feast in Puerto Rico. He is also part of the multidisciplinary research collaborative TERA Collective (Technology, Ecology, Religion, and Art) based at McGill University.

**Ernesto Fiocchetto** is an Argentinean sociologist from Universidad Nacional de Cuyo. At Florida International University, he earned a master's in religious studies and a master's in international studies. His current research revolves around the multiple intersections of gender and sexuality, religion, and international politics in forced migration contexts. His dissertation in international relations focuses on the agency of Faith Actors in the reception and integration of LGBTIQ+ Latin Americans claiming asylum in Spain and the United States

**Ann Hidalgo** is a specialist in Latin American feminist theologies. She earned a PhD in religion, ethics, and society from Claremont School of Theology. Her dissertation, *Liberating Liturgy: Voices of Latin American Theology*, uses feminist and decolonial theory to examine liturgies in the liberation theology tradition that empower marginalized communities. Ann currently teaches online for the Universidad Bíblica Latinoamericana in San José, Costa Rica, and is the acquisitions librarian for the Digital Theological Library.

**Alexandre Kaitel** is an Umbandist medium (formerly a Kardecist/Spiritist medium). He has an MA in psychology and is a licensed clinical psychologist and an instructor in the Psychology Department at PUC-Minas. He is a PhD student in ciências da religião at PUC-Minas.

**Véronique Lecaros** holds a PhD in theology from the University of Strasbourg. She is a researcher and professor in the department of theology at the Pontificia Universidad Católica del Perú (PUCP) and is currently head of the Department of Theology (2024–2027). She was a Tinker Visiting Professor at Stanford in 2019. Her expertise lies in religious phenomena in Peru with a special emphasis on the Catholic Church, religious conversion, evangelical communities, and secularization. Since 2021, she has been in charge of the Listening Commission for victims of abuses in the Archdiocese of Lima. With Ana Lourdes Suárez, she has edited *Abuse in the Latin American Church, An Evolving Crisis at the Core of Catholicism* (Routledge).

**Michelle Gonzalez Maldonado**, PhD (Michelle A. Gonzalez), is a professor of theology and religious studies at the University of Scranton. She is the author of eight books including *Afro-Cuban Theology: Religion, Race, Culture and Identity* (University Press of Florida, 2006), *A Critical Introduction to Religion in the Americas: Bridging* *the Liberation Theology and Religious Studies Divide* (NYU, 2014), and *Judaism, Christianity, and Islam: An Introduction to Monotheism,* co-authored with Aman De Sondy and William S. Green (Bloomsbury, 2020).

**Laura Elisa Pérez** is the author of *Chicana Art: The Politics of Spiritual and Aesthetic Altarities* (Duke University Press, 2007); *Eros Ideologies: Writings on Art, Spirituality, and the Decolonial* (Duke University Press, 2019); *Consuelo Jimenez Underwood: Art, Weaving, Vision* (Duke University Press, 2022), co-edited with Ann Marie Leimer; and the exhibition catalog *Amalia Mesa-Bains: Archaeology of Memory* (University of California Press and Berkeley Art Museum and Pacific Film Archive, 2023), co-edited with María Esther Fernández. She curated *Chicana Badgirls: Las Hociconas* (2009), with Delilah Montoya; *Labor+a(r)t+orio: Bay Area Latina@ Arts Now* (2011); and the traveling retrospective *Amalia Mesa-Bains: Archaeology of Memory* (2023–25), with María Esther Fernández. She is a professor in Chicanx, Latinx, and ethnic studies and chair of the Latinx Research Center at the University of California, Berkeley. She received her PhD at Harvard University and a BA/MA joint degree at the University of Chicago.

**Axel Presas**, PhD, is an assistant professor of Spanish at Eckerd College and also a Babalawo. His research includes Afro Latinx cultures, literatures, and visual arts of the Caribbean and of the Southern Cone; gender and Afro Latin/x cultures; Afro Latinx music; Afro Latin/x religions; cultural history of Afro Cuban religions, and Afro Cuban religions in the United States. He has published book chapters and articles in academic peer review journals about the influence of African culture and religions in Cuba and in the Southern Cone, particularly in Argentina, Chile, and Uruguay. Currently, he is working on a book project that examines Afro Latinx political and cultural poetics in the United States.

**Paul Ramírez** is an associate professor of history and religious studies at Northwestern University. A historian of Mexico with interests in devotional practice, health, technology, and the lives of peasants, he is the author of *Enlightened Immunity: Mexico's Experiments with Disease Prevention in the Age of Reason* (Stanford, 2018). He is writing a history of salt and spiritual geographies in Mexico, with support from the Newberry Library, the John Carter Brown Library, and the Stanford Humanities Center. At Northwestern, he has directed the interdisciplinary Science in Human Culture Program.

**Jennifer Scheper Hughes** is a professor in the Department of History at the University of California, Riverside. She is a historian of religion focusing on Latin American and Latinx religions with special consideration for the spiritual lives of Mexican and Mexican American Catholics, a subject explored in two books: *The Church of the Dead: The Epidemic of 1576 and the Birth of Christianity in the Americas* (NYU, 2021) and *Biography of a Mexican Crucifix: Lived Religion and Local Faith from the Conquest to the Present* (Oxford, 2010).

**Christopher D. Tirres** is the Michael J. Buckley Endowed Chair in the Department of Religious Studies at Santa Clara University. He is the author of *The Aesthetics and Ethics of Faith: A Dialogue between Liberationist and Pragmatic Thought* (Oxford, 2014) and *Liberating Spiritualities: Reimagining Faith in the Américas* (Fordham, 2025). He has published widely in the areas of liberation theology, US Latine theology, philosophical pragmatism, women of color feminism, and critical pedagogy.

**Dr. Cecilia Titizano** is a native of Bolivia of Quechua-Aymara descent. For many years, Dr. Titizano has worked among Quechua and Aymara communities. She is currently the director of Latina/o Theology and Ministry Leadership Network of the Jesuit School of Theology of Santa Clara University. She also teaches at NAITTS, an Indigenous Learning Community (formerly known as the North American Institute for Theological Studies). Her research areas include Indigenous philosophies and ethics, relational ontologies, and feminist decolonial thought. She currently serves in *Memoria Indígena* as an advisory board member and is part of the *Comunidad de Sabias y Teólogas Indígenas del Abya Yala (COSTIAY)*.

**Daisy Vargas** (University of Arizona) is an ethnographer and historian specializing in Catholicism in the Americas; race, ethnicity, religion and the law in the United States; Latinx religion; and material religion. Vargas has published articles and chapters on pilgrimage and embodiment, Latinx Catholicism, religion in the United States, and anti-Catholicism. She is involved in museum advisory and curatorial work. Vargas serves as current co-chair (alongside Jessica Delgado) of the Religions in the Latina/o Americas unit of the American Academy of Religion.

www.ingramcontent.com/pod-product-compliance
Lightning Source LLC
Chambersburg PA
CBHW030103170825
30846CB00001B/7